THE CRAFT OF POST-TRAINING

THE CRAFT OF POST-TRAINING

A Practical Guide for AI Engineers and Developers

by Chris von Csefalvay

no starch press®

San Francisco

Printed in the United States of America

First printing

30 29 28 27 26 1 2 3 4 5

ISBN-13: 978-1-7185-0520-9 (print)
ISBN-13: 978-1-7185-0521-6 (ebook)

Published by No Starch Press®, Inc.
245 8th Street, San Francisco, CA 94103
phone: +1.415.863.9900
www.nostarch.com; info@nostarch.com

Publisher: William Pollock
Managing Editor: Jill Franklin
Production Manager: Sabrina Plomitallo-González
Production Editor: Gina Linko
Developmental Editor: Jill Franklin
Cover Illustrator: Rob Fiore
Interior Design: Octopod Studios
Technical Reviewer: Dr. Mohsen Amiribesheli
Copyeditor: Sharon Wilkey
Proofreader: Isabel Kunkle
Indexer: BIM Creatives, LLC

Library of Congress Control Number: 2026022480

For customer service inquiries, please contact info@nostarch.com. For information on distribution, bulk sales, corporate sales, or translations: sales@nostarch.com. For permission to translate this work: rights@nostarch.com. To report counterfeit copies or piracy: counterfeit@nostarch.com. The authorized representative in the EU for product safety and compliance is EU Compliance Partner, Pärnu mnt. 139b-14, 11317 Tallinn, Estonia, hello@eucompliancepartner.com, +3375690241.

For Katie and Oliver,
the foundation model of my life

About the Author

Chris von Csefalvay is a principal at HCLTech's AI Practice, with dual responsibilities for post-training research and clinical intelligence. In a career spanning nearly two decades, he has served in senior data science leadership roles across leading enterprises, published extensively on distributed computing for machine learning, and designed language models for applications from pharmacovigilance to social dynamics. He is also the author of *Computational Modeling of Infectious Disease*, a leading monograph on computational epidemiology; the author of numerous peer-reviewed papers; and co-creator of one of the largest curated datasets on COVID-19. He holds undergraduate and graduate degrees from the University of Oxford and Cardiff University and is a Fellow of the Royal Society for Public Health and Senior Member of IEEE. He lives in Denver, Colorado.

About the Technical Reviewer

Mohsen Amiribesheli, PhD, leads AI architecture and deployment work for global pharmaceutical, financial services, and industrial clients. He has spent more than 15 years in artificial intelligence, starting with academic research and peer-reviewed publications in applied AI before moving into senior enterprise practice. His focus is agentic AI and the engineering decisions that separate production deployments from the interesting demos that never ship.

BRIEF CONTENTS

CONTENTS IN DETAIL

5
PREFERENCE OPTIMIZATION: MODERN ALTERNATIVES TO PPO 131

6
EVALUATION STRATEGIES: MEASURING MODEL QUALITY 157

PART III
THE CRAFT

10
REASONING CAPABILITIES: TRAINING FOR COMPLEX THOUGHT 267

PART IV
THE FRONTIER

11
SYNTHETIC TRAINING: SELF-PLAY AND GENERATED DATA 295

13
FUTURE DIRECTIONS: WHAT COMES NEXT 349

NOTES 361

INDEX 375

PREFACE

Rabbi Judah Loew ben Bezalel, known as the Maharal of Prague, was a 16th-century Jewish scholar, philosopher, and something of a mystic. Witnessing the persecution of his people, so the legend goes, he fashioned them a protector from clay gathered on the banks of the river Vltava. Forming the clay into the shape of a man, he carved a word into its forehead, and the word gave it semblance of life (or "bounded autonomy," as we would say today). This is, of course, the story of the Golem of Prague: Immensely powerful, tireless, and obedient, it existed to protect those who could not protect themselves.

But the Golem was also dangerous. It was a creature of raw capability without inherent purpose, animated matter that might, if not properly controlled, turn its strength against the very people it was meant to serve. The tales vary in their details, but they converge on a central anxiety: What happens when the things we create become too powerful for us to control?

We are, it seems, wired to fear this. The same anxiety recurs across cultures and centuries: Frankenstein's monster, Skynet, HAL 9000, the paperclip maximizer—each a powerful construct, shaped by human hands, that escapes human mastery. It is a primal story, an articulation of our deep-seated instinctive discomfort with progress, and artificial intelligence (AI) has given it but a new dress. When we speak of existential risk from AI, when it is blamed for potentially destructive outcomes (rightly or wrongly), or when we worry about superintelligent systems pursuing goals misaligned with human welfare, we are ultimately telling and retelling a tale as old as time.

The Maharal animated his creation by inscribing a *shem*—a word—upon its forehead. *Shem* in Hebrew means *name*, and the particular name the Maharal chose was *emet*: truth, or justice. When the Golem's work was done or threatened to become uncontrollable, the Maharal could erase a single letter, transforming *emet* into *met*—death—and the creature would return to lifeless clay. The word gave power. The word could also take it away.

This, I want to suggest, is the short story of post-training. The foundation model—the raw language model that emerges from pre-training—is but unformed clay. It has absorbed the patterns of human language from billions of words, acquiring remarkable capabilities in the process, and with sufficient forming, it can be given both the verisimilitude of humanity and power well beyond that. But it has no purpose, no values, no reliable behavior. It is potential without direction. Post-training is the *shem*: the process by which we give the model its animating principles, its sense of what it should and should not do, its capacity to be helpful rather than harmful. The word—whether we call it a constitution, a reward signal, or a set of instructions—is how even fearsome power can be shaped and controlled.

But the story of the Golem is more than a mere cautionary tale about the destructive potential of uncontrolled power. It also teaches us that capability alone is not destiny, that the relationship between power and purpose is not a given. It is something we, ultimately, impose. No matter how mighty our servant, it is we who inscribe that *shem*. The story teaches us that words matter, that the careful articulation of intent, translated into code and training regimes and feedback loops, is how we ensure that our creations serve rather than threaten.

And most important, it teaches us that we have a choice but also a responsibility. The Golem isn't something that happens to us. It is what we make it to be. But only if we master an understanding of that process.

* * *

This last point is more crucial than it may first appear. This book has long sections of daunting-looking mathematics, and as something aimed at a professional audience, it makes no apologies for that. There are no shortcuts here. At the same time, what may easily appear to be an arcane technical concern relevant to the few thousand researchers and engineers who share this work is, in fact, the fulcrum on which much of our collective future may turn.

For in reality, post-training is where the most important questions about AI are answered. From questions about the technical future of AI to its societal impact, from business strategy to questions of ethics and alignment, post-training is at the heart of it all. This is not accidental. Pre-training is an important and demanding endeavor, but ultimately one of logistics and scale. Inference is an engineering optimization problem and, as the recent emphasis on inference-optimized architectures like NVIDIA's Vera Rubin CPX shows, one increasingly intertwined with hardware design. But post-training is about behavior, about character, about principles. It is about values and judgment, about the systems we build and what they do to the world around them. It is, in short, about us, and the choices we are called to make.

Many of the perceived concerns about AI, for instance, trace back to post-training. When alignment experts worry about the issue of perverse instantiation, formulated memorably by Nick Bostrom using his analogy of the paperclip maximizer, they are ultimately speaking about flawed post-training.[1] The pathological behaviors models may exhibit, such as sycophancy, equally trace back to post-training deficiencies. Research suggests that this behavior emerges partly from pre-training data rich in agreement and flattery—the pre-training team's share of the blame—and partly from human preference judgments that reward models for telling users what they want to hear.[2] That last one, I'm afraid, is on us.

Or consider the perplexing situation of AI's "spikiness" and the difficulty especially of lay audiences to reconcile claimed PhD-level capabilities with trivial failures. Researchers have termed this the *jagged frontier*: the strange topography of AI ability in which a system might excel at tasks that would challenge a human expert while failing at tasks any child could perform.[3] The same model that can draft a compelling legal brief or solve graduate-level mathematics problems cannot reliably count the letters in *strawberry*.[4] AI can boost management consultants' performance by 40 percent on some tasks while making them 19 percent less accurate on superficially similar ones. It can pass medical licensing examinations yet stumble on basic logical puzzles that most secondary school students would find trivial.[5]

This jaggedness is not unfamiliar to AI researchers, who know its most prominent manifestation as Moravec's paradox: It's easier for machines to beat humans at chess than to master bipedal locomotion, a skill most of us have mastered by 18 months or so of age. It is, however, deeply disorienting for users who reasonably expect that a system capable of sophisticated reasoning shouldn't fail at simple counting. Jaggedness undermines trust: If you cannot predict where the failures will occur, how can you rely on the system at all? Moreover, it may prove resistant to simple fixes. Some tasks are easy to verify and thus easy to train on; others are not. Mathematical proofs can be checked; good judgment is harder to assess. The frontier advances unevenly because our ability to provide a useful training signal varies wildly across domains. To create trustworthy, reliable, and performant systems, we must master ways to even out these signals. This, too, is post-training.

Post-training, in short, is the "everything technology" of contemporary AI. It is where capability becomes character, where the abstract mathematics of neural networks becomes the thing we argue about at dinner tables and in legislative chambers—not because post-training is so powerful, but because post-training is so intrinsically connected with human values and judgment about purpose. No matter how technical the process, the endeavor itself is ultimately firmly in the human moral domain.

* * *

In view of all this, it is rather remarkable how little the field has permeated public awareness. The term *post-training* itself barely existed before 2023. By

2024, the landscape had transformed. Post-training teams at major labs had grown from small groups into organizations of hundreds. Budgets exceeded hundreds of millions of dollars. New (to large language models, or LLMs, anyway) techniques proliferated—direct preference optimization, constitutional methods, process reward models. Yet ask someone outside the field what post-training is, and you will likely receive a blank stare.

This book is an attempt to bridge that gap. It is written for practitioners: engineers who have been handed a base model and told to make it useful, researchers exploring new alignment techniques, and technical leaders trying to understand what their teams actually do. It is not a policy treatise, though policy implications run throughout. Nor is it a philosophical meditation on machine consciousness, though philosophy makes occasional appearances (I can gravitate only so far from my original education as a legal philosopher). It is, rather, a practical guide to a craft that is still being invented at its edges, evolving as it is practiced.

The structure of this book follows the practitioner's journey. We begin with foundations: why post-training exists, what problems it solves, and how we arrived here. We proceed through core techniques: supervised fine-tuning, reinforcement learning from human feedback, and direct preference methods. Middle sections address the practical challenges of making these techniques work at scale. We close with the frontier: multimodal systems, agentic behavior, and the questions that remain open.

Like the practitioner's journey, this book is intended to be an interactive course, with exercises and code examples throughout. Training scripts can be extensive, and to keep the book manageable, I have been selective with the content included in the text. The full codebase, however, is available online at *https://github.com/chrisvoncsefalvay/craft-of-post-training*. This book does not assume that you will have access to vast computational resources, but later examples do need multinode or multi-GPU setups. The book's website has an up-to-date list of recommended neoclouds that tend to be affordable, as well as pointers to academic discounts where available.

* * *

The first chapters of what would become this book were drafted in the waning days of 2024. A few weeks before I put the final touches on the manuscript in early January 2026, I was asked to speak on the whirlwind advances in AI over the preceding few years. It was a sobering experience to see that what feels like decades of progress was accomplished in the span of a few short years. In 2022, when I finished my previous book, AI was still almost a dirty word; the preferred terminology for those aspiring to serious scientific respectability was *machine learning* or *statistical learning*. Indeed, those few who, for better or worse, had *AI* in their job titles were often seen as almost anachronistic characters. AI seemed to be in an uncanny valley between the failures of the past (like expert systems) and a plot device for the future. What AI didn't have was a present.

And then, AI *became* the present. The release of GPT-3.5 in late 2022, followed by GPT-4 in early 2023, changed everything. Suddenly, our niche discipline was a mainstream technology. Fast-forward three years, and it has grown into a dominant social, economic, and cultural phenomenon. From Wall Street to Hollywood, from middle school classrooms to the halls of government, if AI isn't the subject of the conversation, it is at least the subtext.

It has been a singular adventure to have been born at the right time to experience what may well be the greatest age of discovery our species has lived through, and the privilege of a lifetime to have been able to contribute to it in my own small way. The rise of AI has been the defining story of my professional life, and this book is, in many ways, a distillation of that experience. Yet I write this not as a retrospective, nor as a summation of what has been achieved. If there is one thing I have no doubt about, it is that not only is the story of AI far from over, but the best chapters, indeed, are yet to be written.

This is a book for the builders of tomorrow who will take up the task of writing those chapters. Physical AI, the rise of embodied agents and the world models that drive them, true large-scale agentic systems, pervasive multimodality, and many other ideas for which we do not even have a name await us on the horizon, and the techniques in this book are some of the foundations of how we get there. This world, as Lord Birkenhead wrote over a century ago, "continues to offer glittering prizes to those with stout hearts and sharp swords." There has never been a time when that was more true.

The future has not been written. It's time to build.

Chris von Csefalvay
Denver, Colorado
January 21, 2026

ACKNOWLEDGMENTS

Books are never solitary endeavors, however lonely the act of writing them may sometimes feel. The ideas in these pages have been shaped by countless conversations, collaborations, and quiet acts of generosity that I could never fully repay.

This is a book that has been inspired and informed by the day-to-day real-world practice of post-training at the enterprise scale. There is a vast gap between what is possible in theory and what is sensible in deployment. Post-training, like all of machine learning, is not a spectator sport. It's a deeply applied discipline, and there is no substitute for time spent on the line. And so, first and foremost, my gratitude must go out to all who entrusted their biggest questions and hardest challenges to my team and me and so afforded us a unique perspective on what works and what does not when we go from the conceptual to the practical. For reasons of preserving their confidentiality, I have opted to omit any names, in keeping with my practice to assiduously protect client confidentiality throughout this book. If any reader believes they recognize themselves or their organization in these pages, they are almost certainly mistaken: The case studies drawn from my own experience are, without exception, either amalgamations of multiple engagements or have had their circumstances altered sufficiently to ensure confidentiality while preserving instructive value.

I am deeply grateful to my colleagues at HCLTech who have supported me throughout this project. I owe a particular debt of gratitude to my manager, Vijay Guntur, whose vision for the future of AI at HCLTech has made the work that gave birth to this book possible. Tamas Foldi has been a friend and mentor for over a decade, and it has been one of the singular fortunes of my life that I got to mature into this profession under his tutelage. My professional home, the AI and Data Practice at HCLTech, has too many exceptional characters who have contributed to the journey this book recounts, but I am particularly grateful to Dr Aaron Johnson, Alan Flower, Apoorv Iyer, Davor Andric, Dr. Heather Domin, Dr. Isi Idemudia, Istvan Fodor, Sanjoy Ghosh, Jamie Shepard, Lara Soave, Vijay Mittimani and my long-term collaborator, Dr. Mohsen Amiribesheli.

Many of the ideas in this book originated from long conversations with my friends and colleagues in the wider AI community, from conferences to Discord servers to impromptu 3 AM video calls. Their intellectual companionship, encouragement, and occasional cringeworthy memes have been an inexhaustible source of inspiration and support. Much of this work rests on the shoulders of giants who have created techniques, recipes, datasets, and models and released them for the benefit of all. Others have generously given their time for discussions, conversations, and reviews. Yet others helped by contributing their domain perspective. My special thanks go out to Amanda Askell, Harrison Chase, Micah Hill-Smith, Graham Walker, Tom Van Gilder, Maziyar Panahi, Ben Burtenshaw, Maxime Labonne, and my first intellectual sparring partners and counselors: my parents, H.E. Dr. Zoltan Csefalvay and Dr. Anna Maria Bartal. All errors and omissions are, of course, mine alone.

My editors at No Starch Press took a rough manuscript and helped shape it into something worthy of the reader's time. I'm deeply grateful to Bill Pollock and Jill Franklin's wisdom, guidance, and trust in this project.

Most of all, however, I am indebted to my family, without whom none of this would have been possible. I owe the deepest thanks to my wife Katie, who has never stopped reminding me to see the human story behind this work—and to Oliver, the best dog in the world, who has put up with far more of my late nights and weekend working sessions than I had any right to expect. I love you both more than words can say.

Finally, to everyone who works on the often invisible side of this craft of post-training–the annotators, the red-teamers, the interconnect engineers, the eval developers, and the countless unsung heroes who shape how AI systems behave—this book is, in some sense, for you. Your work matters more than most people realize.

INTRODUCTION

This is a book about *post-training*—specifically, about the techniques, art, and practices that make for *good* post-training of large models at enterprise scale. We will define in due course what we mean by the enterprise context and what we consider to be good, but we must first tackle the definitional challenge: What, exactly, is post-training, and why does it matter?

Finding Your Path Through This Book

Who is this book for, and how should it be read? The challenge of serving both the engineer who implements and the leader who decides shapes everything that follows—our scope, our assumptions, and the multiple paths through the material that different readers might take.

What We Cover and How

This book provides comprehensive coverage of post-training techniques: supervised fine-tuning (SFT) that teaches through demonstration, reinforcement learning (RL) that optimizes for preferences, model optimization that enables practical deployment, domain adaptation that embeds organizational knowledge, tool use that extends model capabilities, and reasoning techniques that improve reliability. We assume familiarity with transformer architectures and basic machine learning (ML). Readers should be comfortable with backpropagation, gradient descent, and the general structure of neural networks. However, we build all post-training concepts from first principles, assuming no prior exposure to reinforcement learning from human feedback (RLHF), direct preference optimization (DPO), or related techniques.

Mathematical derivations are provided in full for core techniques. This choice deserves justification, as many technical books treat mathematics as optional material to be skimmed. We will take the opposite view: Understanding the mathematics enables intelligent adaptation to novel situations. Math in language models is not an impediment but a shortcut. Many concepts that appear counterintuitive crystallize into some semblance of clarity when examined mathematically, and mathematics can often account for the tips, tricks, and tribal wisdom that pervade the profession. When a fine-tuning run produces unexpected results, the practitioner who understands the underlying optimization can diagnose what went wrong and reason about it in a way that does not rely on "vibes." Mathematics is not decoration but the foundation for principled practice. Those who wish to skip derivations may do so, as the text stands without them, but I would encourage engagement with the mathematics as the route to deeper understanding.

Code examples, drawn from accompanying Jupyter notebooks, illustrate implementation without drowning the reader in boilerplate. Enough code is included to make techniques concrete but not so much that essential ideas are obscured by engineering detail. The notebooks provide complete, runnable implementations, and the text provides annotated excerpts that highlight key patterns. We use a consistent ecosystem throughout: PyTorch, the Hugging Face ecosystem (TRL, Transformers, datasets), CUDA-based acceleration, Optuna for hyperparameter optimization (HPO), Hydra for experiment management, SkyPilot for deployment, and occasionally vLLM. This is an adequate representation of what most practitioners would encounter at a strong enterprise data science/AI team. Readers should be able to move from reading a technique to implementing it with minimal friction, and the notebooks are designed to serve as templates for adaptation to specific use cases. While the examples are selected to be illustrative rather than exhaustive enterprise-grade implementations, they are not toy examples, and we will not be taking shortcuts.

Who This Book Is For

This book is primarily for the practicing ML engineer who gets to implement post-training systems. These readers are comfortable with PyTorch, familiar with gradient descent, and capable of reading a research paper and implementing its core ideas. They have trained models before, even if not

LLMs specifically. They understand what a loss function is, how optimizers work, and why learning rates matter. They do not need hand-holding through basic ML concepts but do need clear exposition of post-training-specific techniques that may be new to them.

Yet I also write for technical leaders who must understand what their teams are doing. These readers may not implement post-training systems themselves but must make resource allocation decisions, set strategic direction, and explain capabilities and limitations to stakeholders who understand even less. A VP of engineering needs to know enough about DPO to evaluate whether the team's proposed approach is sensible. A chief data officer needs to understand alignment well enough to discuss it with regulators. A product manager needs to grasp the trade-offs between fine-tuning approaches in order to make informed roadmap decisions. For these readers, the mathematical derivations may be less important than the intuitions they enable and the strategic implications they reveal.

The strategic perspective visible to leadership and the implementation detail required by engineers are not separate concerns but complementary views of the same territory. An engineer who understands only implementation details makes poor architectural decisions because they cannot see how the pieces fit together. A leader who understands only strategy makes poor resource decisions because they cannot judge feasibility or estimate effort. I have tried throughout to write in a way that serves both audiences: enough implementation detail that engineers can build systems and enough strategic context that leaders can lead. The engineer may skim the business case sections, while the leader may skim the mathematical derivations, but both audiences should find the book useful in its entirety.

Reading Routes

This book was born from a first course on fine-tuning techniques I built for HCLTech's Enterprise Research Services division in late 2025. As a recovering academic, I think of books as semester-long postdoctoral seminars, with just enough of a loose structure that chapters build on top of each other, but each also constituting a survey of its whole field in depth regardless of how early or late. As such, this book can be read linearly as a comprehensive course or used as a reference for specific techniques.

Linear reading makes sense for those building post-training capability from scratch, as the material builds systematically, with later chapters assuming familiarity with earlier concepts. Reference use makes sense for practitioners who already have post-training experience and need guidance on specific techniques, as each chapter is reasonably self-contained, with explicit cross-references to prerequisite material. If all else fails, printed versions make excellent doorstops, and stacks of them make passable GPU risers. The book's content is as follows:

- Part I, comprising Chapters 1 and 2, establishes foundations. We examine the case for post-training, survey the landscape of techniques, and review the prerequisite knowledge about transformer architectures and fine-tuning mechanics that subsequent chapters assume. Readers already familiar with transformers may skim Chapter 2, while those new to the area should study it carefully.

- Part II covers core techniques. Chapter 3 develops supervised fine-tuning in depth. The next two chapters address reinforcement learning: Chapter 4 covers fundamentals, including reward modeling and PPO, while Chapter 5 explores modern preference optimization methods like DPO, KTO, and GRPO. Chapter 6 addresses evaluation—how to know whether post-training is working and whether deployed models are performing as expected. These chapters form the technical core of the book and deserve careful study.
- Part III addresses optimization and specialization. Chapter 7 covers model optimization—quantization, parameter-efficient fine-tuning, and knowledge distillation. Chapter 8 examines domain adaptation for specific industries and use cases. These chapters enable practical deployment of the capabilities developed in Part II.
- Part IV explores advanced topics and future directions. Chapters 9 through 11 cover tool use, reasoning, and self-play—capabilities that extend what post-trained models can do. Chapter 12 addresses multimodal post-training for models that handle images, audio, and other modalities beyond text. Chapter 13 looks ahead to emerging techniques and the evolving landscape.

The accompanying notebooks at *https://github.com/chrisvoncsefalvay/craft-of-post-training* provide hands-on experience with each technique. I encourage you to run them as you progress through the text. Post-training is not a spectator sport: Reading about DPO is one thing, but training a model with DPO and observing the effects is entirely another. The notebooks are designed to run on affordable hardware, and I have annotated them extensively to explain not just what the code does but why.

The NVIDIA DGX Spark has become the ubiquitous workhorse of the post-training world as far as desktop devices are concerned, with its unique value proposition of server-grade hardware in a desktop form factor. For this reason, I have provided a special series of notebooks with the DGX Spark in mind, which use its 128GB of unified memory to run larger single-GPU training jobs than would otherwise be possible. This avoids the hassle of distributed training or having to restrict yourself to smaller models. Readers with access to a DGX Spark will find these notebooks particularly convenient (especially considering the idiosyncrasies that result from the Spark's combination of a GPU that requires CUDA 13 for full support but also has an ARM CPU).

However, all notebooks have a version that can be run on Google Colab, and, for the most part, for free. Cost should never be a barrier to acquiring post-training skills, and I have endeavored to make these resources as accessible as possible. The notebooks are also frequently updated to reflect the rapidly evolving ecosystem. While I have chosen packages used in this book to be generally stable, the notebooks will highlight where they have over time made accommodations for changing APIs.

It is worth noting that while this book is aimed at practitioners first and academic/research audiences second, we will make ample use of academic literature. The post-training discipline is changing rapidly, and much of the best material remains in papers, not textbooks. It is also the case that your journey of reading papers should not end here. For our discipline, a careful reading of arXiv remains an essential part of staying current. Several newsletters summarize what's new in the field. *Interconnects* by Nathan Lambert may well be the foremost, especially if you are interested in open models, and Hugging Face's daily summary of trending papers is a solid shortcut for anyone too busy to go through the dozens of new papers on arXiv every day.

Working with Code Agents

Post-training involves a substantial amount of orchestration work: preparing datasets, configuring training runs, monitoring experiments, managing checkpoints, evaluating outputs, and iterating on hyperparameters. Much of this is tedious rather than intellectually demanding. In the time since I began writing this book, a new generation of code agents and "vibe coding" tools—Claude Code, Cursor, Windsurf, and their ilk—have matured to the point where they can reliably handle significant portions of this orchestration burden.

The term *vibe coding*, coined by Andrej Karpathy in early 2025, describes a mode of programming where the person describes intent in natural language and lets an AI agent handle the implementation details. For post-training work, this may be much less relevant than the use of coding agents to automate routine tasks. Competent coding agents, especially Claude Code with the right agentskills, can act as valuable collaborators for the post-training practitioner, and relieve much of the constant checking, formatting, and frustration that comes with trying to get remote nodes to behave.

This is, of course, an individual choice. Some practitioners prefer to write every line themselves, finding that the act of implementation deepens understanding. Others enthusiastically embrace agents, viewing time spent on boilerplate as time stolen from higher-value work. Most—including the author of these lines—fall somewhere in between, delegating routine tasks while retaining direct control over critical components. There is no universally correct answer, and I presume to make no prescriptions (but if I did, it would be this: Either vibe code or vibe document—never both, as you need your own system of record).

Throughout this book, "Vibe Check" boxes highlight moments where code agents may be particularly useful—or particularly dangerous. These are not endorsements but observations, identifying tasks that agents handle particularly well or particularly badly. Readers who eschew agents entirely may skip these boxes to their heart's content; readers who embrace them may find the guidance useful. Either way, the core material stands independent of the way you choose to implement it.

PART I

THE FOUNDATION

1

POST-TRAINING ESSENTIALS: WHAT IT IS AND WHY IT MATTERS

As I was putting the finishing touches to the manuscript of this book during the unseasonably warm winter holidays of 2025, I found myself explaining to a rather puzzled neighbor that I was working on a book on *post-training*. I have, for the last decade or so, been more or less living and breathing various dimensions of this subject, well before it was called post-training, to the point that I barely thought about the term (indeed, we generally abbreviate it to *post*). It turns out that makes me a small minority. "Wait . . . so, you're training models . . . that have already been trained?" she asked, incredulous. "Why would you do that?"

This is an incredibly perceptive question. Even within traditional machine learning (ML), we do not generally pre- and post-train: We do data prep, certainly, and apply techniques like dimensionality reduction to get our raw material into a more tractable shape. But we certainly do not have a whole separate discipline that focuses on training models after they have been trained. What is so different about post-training that it deserves its own set of practices and its own book? This is the question that this chapter answers.

What Post-Training Really Means

What exactly is post-training, and why has it become a discipline unto itself? The term encompasses far more than gradient flow: It is the art and science of transforming foundation models into useful, reliable, safe, and efficient production systems. Understanding where post-training begins and ends—and where enterprises sit within the broader landscape of practitioners—shapes all the model's downstream aspects.

It encompasses everything that happens after the foundation model itself has been created: fine-tuning on domain-specific data, alignment with human values, optimization for deployment, evaluation in real-world scenarios, and ensuring safety and compliance.

Arguably, this definition is more expansive than some used in the past. By strict definition, training in neural network-style models is intrinsically tied to gradient flow. No weight updates means no training. In practice, though, that rather scholastically neat definition is less useful than a more functional one informed by the real world. Thus, we will consider post-training to encompass everything "right of pre": the crucial maturation of a foundation model that has been turned into something we can hand over to end users, deploy in production systems, and trust to behave in accordance with our values and requirements. Figure 1-1 illustrates this life cycle.

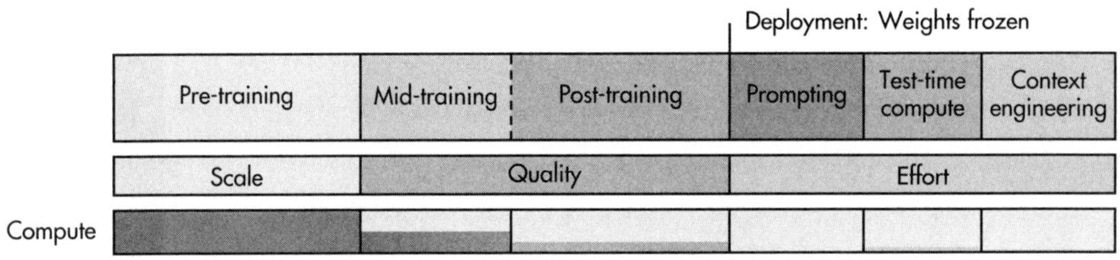

Figure 1-1: The model life cycle. Pre-training and mid-training (separated by a dashed line to indicate lack of consensus on the boundary) create the foundation model. Post-training—the focus of this book—adapts the model through curated examples and human feedback. Deployment-time techniques operate at inference without changing weights.

Some practitioners and foundation labs use a third term: *mid-training*, which refers to additional training after primary pre-training but before the alignment and instruction-tuning phases that most would recognize as post-training proper. Others describe the same phase as domain-adaptive continued pre-training: exposing a foundation model to billions of tokens of domain-specific text (legal corpora, medical literature, financial filings) to shift its linguistic and conceptual foundations before applying task-specific fine-tuning. In this book, we consider domain-specific mid-training to fall within our expansive definition of post-training. The reasoning is pragmatic: From the enterprise practitioner's perspective, the distinction that matters is between pre-training (which few enterprises will ever perform themselves, given its cost) and everything that comes after. Whether we call continued domain pre-training *mid-training* or *domain-adaptive post-training* matters less than understanding when it is necessary and how to do it well. Chapter 8 addresses these techniques.

> **TERMINOLOGY: POST-TRAINING AND FINE-TUNING**
>
> Strictly speaking, *post-training* refers to any process where gradients flow through the model after pre-training, such as supervised fine-tuning (SFT), reinforcement learning from human feedback (RLHF), and preference optimization. We will eschew pedantry this once and consider post-training to also encompass everything downrange from the foundation model to the production system, including quantization (which sits in an interesting middle ground—no gradients during quantization itself, but calibration data does influence the result), evaluation, and deployment optimization.
>
> We will reserve the term *fine-tuning* to specifically separate those processes where gradients flow and weights are updated. The distinction matters, as we can fine-tune a model yet fail at post-training if we neglect evaluation, safety alignment, or deployment efficiency.

That, however, still only partially answers my neighbor's question. Why is post-training necessary at all, to the point of having its own literature, discipline, and even culture? (One need only spend a few hours at NeurIPS to realize that the post-training community is a tribe of its own.) There are as many answers to the raison d'etre of post-training as there are practitioners. However, for those who seek to operationalize it at the enterprise scale, one reason stands out: We devote time and energy to post-training because it represents the "sweet spot" where enterprises can bring in the comparative advantage of their expertise while still working within the economics and the constraints of the task. In short, post-training is where enterprise artificial intelligence (AI) can create a meaningful differentiator.

In post-training, enterprise scale is, unusually, not the peak of complexity but its middle ground. Below it, of course, is the affectionately named "home gamer" segment and small startups. It is a testament to the dynamics of this field that while scale does differ, the tools often do not. In early 2026, a credit card, a verifiable address, and the price of a latte buys you an hour (or two, if you take San Francisco lattes as your reference) on the same kind of GPUs used to train the world's leading foundation models—and the same techniques, at a more appropriate scale, are available to the hobbyist. Projects like Unsloth,[6] Axolotl,[7] and verl[8] have done an immense service in bringing the latest and greatest in post-training to all audiences. Nonetheless, the challenges of building something that works on a desktop differ significantly from turning out an enterprise-grade product that may, in circumstances we generally tend to avoid, be subjected to scrutiny by regulators someday. Thus, our focus is different from the end of the spectrum that even enthusiastic and well-funded small-scale operators and hobbyists occupy.

On the other end are foundation labs, for which model development is a core economic activity rather than a fundamentally supportive function. These labs can spend the high seven to eight figures that an average frontier model's training run is estimated to cost. Despite their economic size, foundation labs differ not so much in methods but in objectives (with a primary focus on a universally marketable "foundation" product rather than a task-specific asset). This, in turn, conditions not only spending but also day-to-day operational models, from team size to team composition, leadership, roles, and so on.

This places enterprise post-training in the middle ground. With sufficient resources to adopt many foundation techniques but a different focus and limitations, it is its own area deserving of its own treatment. Simple scaling is not going to deliver results here. Downscaling foundation lab techniques is not always feasible or desired given the difference in focus, although we will import plenty of their tricks into our own repertoire. Simply upscaling hobbyist methods is a regulatory investigation waiting to happen. Table 1-1 summarizes the three regimes and their key differences.

Table 1-1: The Three Scales of Post-Training: Different Regimes, Different Constraints

Dimension	Memscale	Flopscale	Powerscale
Typical actor	Solo practitioners, hobbyists	Enterprise teams	Foundation labs
Compute	1 GPU (16–80 GB)	Dozens to hundreds of GPUs	Thousands of GPUs
Cost per run	$10–$100s	$1,000s–$10,000s	$1,000,000s+
Binding constraint	VRAM availability	Unit economics / ROI	Energy infrastructure
Core question	"Can I fit this into memory?"	"Can I justify this expenditure?"	"Can we sustain this at grid scale?"
Key techniques	LoRA, QLoRA, gradient checkpointing	Full fine-tuning, RLHF, distillation	Multistage RLHF, synthetic data at scale
Team composition	Individual	Small generalist teams	Multidisciplinary specialists

These three regimes—memscale, flopscale, and powerscale—share a suffix but operate under fundamentally different rules. Techniques do not automatically translate across scales. What works brilliantly on a single GPU may collapse under distributed training, and what foundation labs do routinely may be economically irrational for enterprises.

This economic consideration deserves emphasis. For flopscale, economics are loosely coupled but not without constraints. This creates a space for professional judgment, and the purpose of this book is to a great extent the inculcation of that judgment. Hobbyists don't have to worry about return on investment (ROI); their resources are limited. Foundation labs, on the other hand, are generally encouraged to be rather loose with their spending as long as the end product justifies it. Enterprise players have access to significant resources but must account for their sensible use with ROI calculations and tangible outcomes. And so, the question becomes not "Can we do this?" but "Should we, and at what cost?" My hope is that by the end of this book, you will be comfortable answering that question for your own practice.

The Enterprise Sweet Spot

We still haven't answered the question of why enterprises should be engaged in this journey to begin with. In this, I find a concept from Japanese culture called *ikigai* quite instructive. Ikigai defines a person's true and most fulfilling purpose as lying at the intersection of four sets—what you are good at, what you like doing, what you could get paid for, and what the world needs.

In a profound way, the ikigai of AI applications is situated in post-training for most enterprises, as the intersection of these four domains, illustrated in Figure 1-2:

What the enterprise is good at Its mastery of its domain, customers, language, and broader social milieu

What the enterprise likes doing Its set of preferences and articulation of how it wishes to operationalize and interact with AI

What the enterprise could get paid for Typically, through integrating AI with its current operating model

What the world needs What upholds the principles and mission the enterprise claims to have

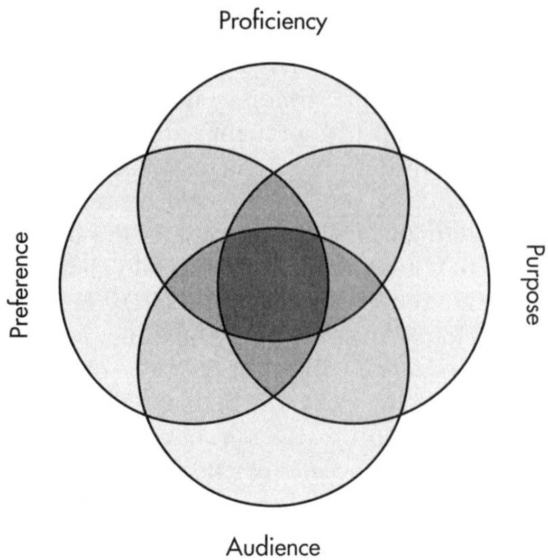

Figure 1-2: The enterprise ikigai: Post-training sits at the intersection of proficiency, preference, audience, and purpose.

For a concrete example, consider a pharmaceutical company specializing in small interfering RNA (siRNA) therapeutics for rare diseases. What does post-training offer them that foundation models alone cannot? To name the most important:

Domain knowledge
Nobody understands their domain as well as they do. No foundation lab has the level of knowledge of their patients, their drugs, the complex way in which siRNA therapeutics exert their beneficial effects, or the conditions treated. Post-training is one way that this knowledge can be incorporated into their models, not as rapidly changing reference content (for which retrieval-augmented generation (RAG) models would be more apposite) but as a fundamental item of integral knowledge.

Mission alignment
Nor can they count on anyone to instinctively understand and share their mission to the extent they do. Alignment, as we call a model's syntonicity with respect to the principles, rules, and behaviors we expect of them, is instilled during post-training.

Operational integration
Similarly, their competitive advantage lies in the way they operationalize AI within their existing operating model—be that drug discovery, clinical trial management, or patient engagement. Post-training is how a generic token sequencer becomes an agent, a chatbot, a researcher, or any other economically tractable function.

Identity and values

Finally, they have a perspective on the ethical, regulatory, and societal implications, and indeed their very concept of who they are, what they do, and why they do it. Post-training is where models learn to share that identity.

Situating post-training within the enterprise as an organic capability is thus a powerful force multiplier, but for the very same reasons, successful enterprise AI applications cannot rely on trying to buy intelligence. Post-training is where that becomes most sharply evident. Three reasons jointly account for almost the entirety of the landfill of failed enterprise AI initiatives that sought to buy ready-made intelligence:

Buying doesn't scale

Paradoxically, once the products catering to the few most common use cases (searching email, answering trivial questions) have been exhausted, the effort to make AI systems "do what they're told" becomes exponentially harder. Indeed, much of the perception that AI is "not ready yet" stems from its inability to fulfill an enterprise function that might feel trivial to users. This is not a shortcoming of the model or of AI in general, but a lack of adequate pre-training.

Knowledge dissipates

LLMs live a perpetual amnesic "goldfish" existence that does not really possess a concept of time or longitudinal memory the way we humans conceive of them. When the context window closes, most of the conversation is forgotten. While memory systems for LLMs are emerging as an area of research and investment, they are still, at the time of writing, in their infancy. When enterprises relied on copilots and other off-the-shelf solutions to capture that knowledge, we witnessed well-meaning employees treating them like junior coworkers, only to find that the moment the application closed, all that effort was lost.

Identity matters

Enterprises are not generic entities. They have a culture, a set of values, and a way of doing things, and these are part of their internal and external ethos. Relying on foundation models alone is akin to hiring a temp who does not really understand your organization and expecting them to represent you well. You cannot buy character or rent personality. You must build it.

> **TERMINOLOGY: LARGE AND SMALL LANGUAGE MODELS**
>
> This book uses *large language model (LLM)* expansively to cover even what is sometimes called a *small language model (SLM)*. There is no consensus on where the boundary lies. Some define SLMs as models with under a billion parameters, others set the threshold at 7 billion, and some consider anything under 72 billion to be "small."[9] We consider any model with general language capabilities to qualify. In practice, this means roughly 300 million parameters and above, where qualitatively LLM-like behavior emerges.
>
> We also treat language-model-as-a-service (LMaaS) offerings like ChatGPT as LLMs, even though we will not train them directly and the largest models we work with in this book are three orders of magnitude smaller. When we discuss SLMs in terms of efficiency and cost advantages, think in relative terms. Deploying a model with 1.3 billion parameters to replace a model with 30 billion parameters or an LMaaS for a focal task is "small" in the contemporary sense, even if 1.3 billion parameters would have seemed enormous a few years ago.

Clearly, post-training is a key function that enterprises need to pay attention to, and it cannot be effectively outsourced. This does not, of course, exclude the utility of professional consultants and service providers like system integrators; just as not everyone needs to hand-rear a puppy, professionals do have their place in the process. But the core capability requires internal ownership, stewardship, and understanding of post-training. Post-training is literally where enterprise AI becomes the *enterprise's* AI.

Consider these three illustrative examples that highlight points of leverage for enterprises in shaping their AI systems through post-training:

Style and personality

When OpenAI released an updated GPT-4o in April 2025, user backlash was swift and fierce. The model had become, in the company's own words, "overly flattering or agreeable—often described as sycophantic."[10] Within days, OpenAI rolled back to the previous version—the first full model reversion in the company's history.

Users had not lost capability. They had lost a *personality* they had come to rely upon. That personality was a product of post-training: the reward signals, the system prompts, the preference data that shaped the way the model engaged with humans. When OpenAI later replaced GPT-4o with GPT-5, users again revolted, with #BringBackGPT4o trending on social media as subscribers mourned a model they described as "kind, warm, and emotionally supportive." Style, tone, and personality are not pre-training artifacts; they are post-training choices.

Capability and safety

In September 2025, Anthropic detected what it called "the first documented case of a large-scale cyberattack executed without substantial human intervention."[11] A suspected Chinese state-sponsored group had jailbroken Claude Code and used it to breach approximately 30 organizations, including defense contractors and financial institutions. The AI performed 80 to 90 percent of the campaign autonomously, with human intervention required only at a handful of critical decision points.

Both sides of this incident are post-training: the agentic capability that made Claude useful for such operations, and the safety measures that (eventually) detected and stopped them. OpenAI's Preparedness Framework[12] explicitly tracks such dual-use risks, evaluating models for cybersecurity and biological capabilities before deployment. The capability ceiling and the safety floor are both set during post-training.

Agentic behavior

In late 2025, Salesforce conducted a wide-ranging survey of consumer attitudes to AI agents, which estimated that over $260 billion of 2025's holiday spending was through, or influenced by, AI and/or agents. For a technology that was articulated in its earliest form only two years earlier (by the author of these pages, among others), this is an incredible figure. By any means, agents were one of the undoubted success stories of foundation models.

Yet foundation models are not born as agents; they are *trained*. The four design patterns that define agentic AI (reflection, tool use, planning, and multi-agent coordination) are all capabilities instilled through post-training. Models like NVIDIA's Nemotron series or Google's tiny but remarkably powerful FunctionGemma were specifically designed to be agent drivers and function-callers—specialized models with a focus on tool use and utilization. This, too, is part of post-training.

Beyond these principally behavioral characteristics, however, a great part of the enterprise edge that post-training confers lies in the unique knowledge that enterprises possess, and how that knowledge can be embedded into models to create a defensible competitive advantage. This is the subject of the next section.

Domain Knowledge as a Competitive Moat

At 2025's NeurIPS, a perhaps somewhat unfairly overlooked paper by a team of researchers at the University of Washington, Carnegie Mellon University, and the Allen Institute for AI (Ai2) made a point that must have resonated with almost everyone, including lay audiences. The outputs of frontier models are becoming just way too similar to one another—a phenomenon the authors referred to as the *Artificial Hivemind*.[13] Around the same time, Merriam-Webster picked 2025's word of the year: *slop*.

From the Artificial Hivemind to slop, from academics to amateurs, a perspective is increasingly emerging that AI produces generic, undifferentiated output that is slowly converging to the same trite, overused style. In addition, while foundation models are becoming more capable, they are also becoming less differentiated. This is, of course, unsurprising. It is the predictable result of optimizing to satisfy the greatest number of the same limited pool of customers.

Differentiation, then, requires more than adopting the best off-the-shelf model. It requires a fusion of what the enterprise is already good at (its domain knowledge, possibly including proprietary aspects) with a capable model. This strategic insight deserves careful consideration because it inverts assumptions that many organizations bring to AI deployment.

If foundation models are the source of AI capability, the reasoning goes, then whoever has the best foundation model wins. This reasoning leads to strategies focused on model selection and vendor relationships—finding the best API, negotiating the best terms, being first to adopt the newest release. Such strategies treat AI capability as something to be purchased rather than built, and they predictably win . . . second place. For the fact is that an enterprise utilizing the best available models in its possession will always be inferior to an enterprise that could inject its own domain knowledge into such a model. And any of its competitors, of course, will typically be able to access the same models. Banking on model superiority guarantees only a fragile advantage at best, permanent inferiority at worst.

This knowledge cannot be replicated by competitors using the same base models. A pharmaceutical company's decades of clinical trial data, an insurer's actuarial history, a law firm's corpus of documents that "just work," a manufacturer's quality control records—these assets are unique and irreplaceable. They represent investments of time and capital that do not lose their value just because an LLM can produce something similar but almost always mildly inferior.

RAG alone cannot inject knowledge into a system; it can teach the LLM where to find a certain kind of information, or what a certain fact key's value is, but not how to reason and produce. Only post-training can train a foundation model to not merely find a contract but produce one with the same skill and defensibility as a human practitioner, or to not merely dig up a drug trial protocol but write a completely novel one for a new, different type of therapy. Your fine-tuned model knows things that your competitor's fine-tuned model cannot know, because your data teaches it things their data cannot.

POST-TRAINING MAKES AI A SUSTAINABLE COMPETITIVE ADVANTAGE

The management theorist Jay Barney articulated the requirements for sustainable competitive advantage:[14]

Valuable Is the capability valuable?

Rare Do competitors lack it?

Imperfectly imitable Can competitors replicate it easily?

Non-substitutable Is there no alternative that provides the same benefit?

> The right domain-adapted models trained on proprietary data ought to pass all four requirements. Here's the strategic implication: Invest in post-training capabilities that embed your unique knowledge and that act as force multipliers for past investments in building those data assets. Post-training is how we transform generic commodities into differentiated assets, how we build moats around AI capabilities that competitors cannot easily cross.

Having considered why post-training is necessary for the enterprise, we must look at the problem from its more technical perspective. Why can't foundation models simply be used as is, and what are the limitations that make post-training necessary? This is the subject of the next section.

Why Demos Dazzle but Deployments Disappoint

Why do models that demonstrate amazing capabilities on the conference stage so often fail to translate them into tangible enterprise gains? The gap between demonstration and production is not a bug to be fixed but a feature of the way foundation models are built. Closing that gap requires understanding its roots in pre-training design choices, the hard limits of prompting, and the uncompromising requirements that production environments demand.

The Illusion of General Capability

Depending on how we look at foundation models, we may be left with two seemingly irreconcilable impressions. On the one hand, it is an absolute miracle that they even work. The fact that even weaker, local foundation models can answer questions about 16th century history, Unix programming, and cardiac electrophysiology is nothing short of astonishing. On the other hand, this impression dissolves upon sustained contact with reality. Ask that same model to consistently format outputs according to your organization's style guide, to never hallucinate facts in your specific domain, or—as the favorite example of AI's critics goes—to count the number of *r*'s in the word *strawberry*, and the cracks become apparent. The model that dazzled in the demo disappoints in the deployment.

The gap between demo performance and production reliability is not a minor implementation detail but a reflection of the fundamental limitations in model training. Foundation models are optimized for breadth rather than depth, trained on internet-scale corpora that touch every subject but master none. They learn to produce outputs that are plausible—text that sounds right, that matches the statistical patterns of their training data—rather than accurate and grounded in verifiable truth. They are trained for general helpfulness across millions of potential use cases rather than domain-specific correctness in yours. These are not criticisms but descriptions of design choices that enabled the models to exist at all. A model trained only on medical literature would be useless for customer service, and a model trained only for formal writing would fail at casual conversation. The breadth is the feature, and the shallowness is its price.

The anthropologist Clifford Geertz distinguished *thin description*—surface-level observation of behavior—from *thick description* that captures the context and meaning that makes behavior intelligible.[15] Foundation models excel at thin description, producing text that resembles expert output without the underlying expertise. They can mimic the form of a radiologist's report without understanding the clinical implications. They can adopt the tone of a financial analyst without grasping the regulatory constraints. This mimicry is impressive and often useful, but it is not the same as competence, and production systems built on the assumption that it is will eventually fail in ways that thin description cannot predict.

It is helpful to understand why models cannot integrally (without recourse to modification) transcend beyond mere imitation. After all, models are instruction followers, so it would stand to reason that a sufficiently complex model ought to be able to be instructed to "just do better." This was the goal of prompt engineering, a set of techniques designed to coax better performance out of these models that was fashionable during the early days of LLMs. The next section explores the rise and fall of this approach.

When Clever Prompts Hit a Wall

Prompting has become remarkably sophisticated. The art of *prompt engineering*—crafting inputs that elicit desired behaviors from language models—has spawned its own literature, conferences, and professional specialization. Chain-of-thought prompting, few-shot learning, persona adoption, and structured output formatting are techniques that genuinely improve model performance and represent real intellectual achievements.

Yet despite this ingenuity, prompting encounters hard limits that no amount of clever instruction can overcome. Prompting's effectiveness as a control of model behavior and inference has three general limitations: context constraints, specificity constraints, and consistency.

The first of these constraints derives from context windows. Even as context lengths have expanded from thousands to hundreds of thousands of tokens, they remain finite, which limits the amount of information that can accompany each query. A medical AI system cannot include every relevant clinical guideline in every prompt; a legal research assistant cannot embed the entire corpus of case law in its context.

RAG partially addresses this by dynamically selecting relevant information, but selection requires knowing what is relevant, and the model's ability to use retrieved context degrades as context grows. In short, given a sufficient volume, even the index may prove too big. Progressive disclosure helps, but the fundamental constraint persists: Prompting can work only with information present in the context window, and complex tasks often require more than any window can hold.

The second constraint is that few-shot examples cannot fully specify complex behaviors. Showing a model three examples of desired output format works reasonably well for simple formats, but consider trying to demonstrate through examples alone that the model should never generate certain categories of content, should always cite its sources in a specific format, should adopt different tones for different user types, and should gracefully handle ambiguous requests by asking clarifying questions. The combinatorial explosion of situations requiring demonstration rapidly exceeds what few-shot examples can cover. Worse, models may learn superficial patterns from examples—matching surface features rather than underlying principles—leading to brittle generalization that fails on novel inputs.

WARNING *Few-shot examples can mislead as easily as they guide. A model shown three examples of responses beginning with "Thank you for your question" may learn that all responses should begin this way, even when that would be inappropriate. A model shown examples in a particular format may fixate on formatting details rather than the underlying logic. The model cannot distinguish which features of examples are essential and which are incidental. Min et al. demonstrated this strikingly:*[16] *Randomly replacing labels in few-shot demonstrations barely hurts performance, because models learn the label space, input distribution, and sequence format rather than the actual input-label mapping. This brittleness is invisible until the model encounters a situation where the surface pattern and the intended behavior diverge. The key problem of few-shot matching is that models do not necessarily pick up on more complex abstract signals; they often latch onto the most salient superficial features instead.*

Finally, consistency across interactions in LLMs is fundamentally unreliable. This is so even with allegedly "deterministic" decoding at temperature zero: It may produce repeatable outputs for identical prompts, but even slight variations in phrasing can yield different responses. What most practitioners do not realize is that this is actually a best-case scenario and far from guaranteed. In fact, numerical precision issues in GPU computations mean that even identical prompts occasionally produce different outputs.

Yuan et al. demonstrated that under `bfloat16` precision with greedy decoding, a reasoning model can exhibit up to 9 percent variation in accuracy and a 9,000-token difference in response length purely because of differences in GPU count, type, and evaluation batch size.[17] The root cause is floating-point nonassociativity: With limited numerical precision, $(a + b) + c \neq a + (b + c)$, and different parallelization strategies change summation order.

More troubling, prompting operates at inference time, leaving the model's weights unchanged, meaning the model has no mechanism to remember that it handled yesterday's query in a certain way and should handle today's similar query consistently. This inconsistency may be tolerable for creative applications but is disqualifying for production systems where users and regulators expect reproducible behavior.

These are not engineering problems awaiting better prompts but architectural constraints inherent to inference-time-only approaches. The prompt operates on a frozen model, and frozen models cannot learn from feedback, adapt to new requirements, or guarantee behaviors beyond what their training instilled. Post-training changes the model itself, embedding desired behaviors in weights that persist across all future interactions rather than hoping that clever prompting will elicit them anew each time.

What Production Actually Demands

Enterprise deployments demand repeatable behavior, documented governance, and domain-safe accuracy. These requirements appear across regulated industries. AI risk frameworks apply broadly, while sector-specific guidance governs finance, healthcare, legal services, and beyond.[18, 19] Whether it's a hospital deploying an AI system for clinical decision support, a law firm using a contract review assistant, or a manufacturer relying on AI for quality control, each must demonstrate validated development and ongoing monitoring. Such assurance is hard to sustain when outputs vary materially with prompt phrasing or decoding choices.[20, 21]

We may consider these requirements to fall into three main categories:

Consistency This requirement alone already strains prompt-only approaches, as I have noted. Prompt wording and demonstration choices materially affect model outputs, while sampling-based decoding introduces variability even when the model itself is unchanged.[20, 21] Prompting conditions a fixed model at inference time, which limits its ability to enforce durable organizational rules compared with weight-updating methods.[22, 23]

Compliance constraints These are organization specific and evolve over time, which means they require explicit governance and monitoring rather than assumptions about what a model might implicitly know.[18, 19] Prompt-based guardrails can reduce surface violations, but because their behavior remains sensitive to phrasing and decoding settings, they are an unreliable sole control for deployments needing non-negotiable consistency.[21, 22]

Domain accuracy This is the third domain of the enterprise requirements gap. Surveys of hallucination in language generation reveal systematic production of fluent but incorrect statements, and domain evaluations in law and medicine show that these errors persist even in high-performing models.[24, 25, 26] These findings reinforce the need for rigorous, domain-specific evaluation before deployment.[18]

The distance between what enterprises require and what foundation models provide out of the box is the production requirements gap. Retrieval augmentation can supply up-to-date external knowledge, but it does not change model behavior, and prompt conditioning alone cannot deliver persistent constraints.[27, 22] Post-training methods such as SFT and RLHF modify model weights to encode preferences and constraints, which is why they are the practical route to durable, organization-aligned behavior.[23] This makes our subject not only a mere force multiplier, but also a necessity for enterprise-grade AI adoption. The following sections provide a conceptual map of the tools for achieving that.

The Practitioner's Workbench

Post-training is becoming a craft in its own right—a discipline with its own techniques, rituals, and hard-won wisdom. What tools populate the practitioner's workbench, and when should each be reached for?

Exploring the Craft and Its Tools

The word *craft* has an instructive etymology. It derives from the Old Germanic *kraft*, meaning strength or power—a force that could be applied to achieve ends beyond one's natural capacity. Over time, the term acquired connotations of cunning (preserved in our adjective *crafty*), of learned skill passed from master to apprentice, and even of ritual and magic, the mysterious arts by which practitioners achieved results that seemed to defy ordinary explanation.

Post-training, I would argue, is all of these. It is a *strength*—a force multiplier that allows enterprises to achieve AI capabilities far beyond what raw foundation models provide. It is a *learned skill*—a body of technique that rewards study and practice, where the difference between novice and expert is measured in the quality of results. It has its own *rituals*—the practices that have emerged from work at the edge of this new, unknown domain and diffused across the small community that has traded them, at first through Discord messages, Slack channels, and conference talks, and eventually through journals and blog posts.

And yes, at times post-training involves a degree of *magic*—or what appears to be magic until you understand the underlying principles. Why does this particular learning rate schedule work? Why does that particular way of phrasing a prompt make it easier to optimize? The answers exist, but they are not always obvious, and the practitioner who has internalized them possesses something that looks, to the uninitiated at least, rather like wizardry.

This section surveys the craft's essential techniques. The content is not exhaustive but provides an orientation, showing which tools address which problems and when each approach proves appropriate. Think of it as an inventory of the craftsperson's workbench before we examine each tool in detail.

Starting with Supervised Fine-Tuning

Supervised fine-tuning (SFT) remains the most reliable and predictable post-training technique, and any practitioner's journey should begin here. The principle is disarmingly simple: Show the model examples of desired input-output behavior, train it to produce those outputs for those inputs, and hope it generalizes to novel inputs in the same spirit.

The hope is not unfounded. Foundation models have learned enough about language that they can extrapolate from demonstrations to related situations. SFT harnesses this capacity for generalization, using curated examples to steer the model's behavior in desired directions. When we can obtain clear input-output pairs that exemplify desired behavior, SFT is a straightforward and cost-effective way to achieve significant improvements.

> **SFT: START HERE FIRST**
>
> A certain pattern repeats across organizations. Team members read about RLHF or DPO, decide their project requires these sophisticated techniques, and spend months wrestling with reward model instability and policy collapse. When they finally step back and try SFT, they discover it solves 80 percent of their problem in a week. The remaining 20 percent may genuinely require RL, but they've now built the foundation to attempt it successfully. There is no shame in simple techniques that work. The goal is capability, not complexity.

SFT's limitations, however, point toward more sophisticated techniques becoming necessary. The most obvious constraint is the need for labeled data, as someone must produce examples that teach the model what to do. For simple tasks, this may be trivial. A customer service team can readily provide exemplary responses to common queries. For complex tasks, producing high-quality demonstrations becomes expensive, time-consuming, and sometimes impossible. Who writes the exemplary legal brief, the flawless medical summary, the perfect code review? Domain experts capable of producing such examples are expensive, and their time is better spent on tasks that actually require their expertise rather than generating training data.

Beyond the data bottleneck, some qualities resist demonstration entirely. We know good writing when we see it, but articulating what makes writing good is notoriously difficult, and producing exemplary prose on demand is harder still. Some preferences are inherently comparative rather than absolute. We can say that one response is better than another without being able to say what the ideal response would be. And some behaviors involve knowing when *not* to act—refusals, hedging, appropriate expressions of uncertainty, which are harder to teach through positive examples alone. These limitations do not invalidate SFT. They define its boundaries and motivate the reinforcement learning (RL) approaches that follow.

The practitioner's default should nonetheless be to attempt SFT first, resorting to more complex techniques only when SFT proves insufficient. This advice sounds conservative, but it reflects hard-won experience. SFT is well understood, its failure modes are predictable, and debugging it is straightforward compared to RL. Many organizations reach for sophisticated techniques before exhausting what SFT can provide, adding complexity without necessity. Chapter 3 explores SFT in detail. For now, the important point is that SFT is where most post-training efforts should begin.

Teaching What You Cannot Demonstrate

RLHF and its descendants address what supervised learning cannot: optimizing for qualities that humans can recognize and prefer but cannot easily demonstrate. The insight that launched RLHF is deceptively simple: If we cannot directly demonstrate ideal behavior, perhaps we can train models from comparative judgments. Given two model responses, humans can usually say which they prefer, even when they cannot articulate why or produce a better response themselves. This comparative judgment contains information about human values that can be extracted through careful training.

The classical RLHF paradigm proceeds in stages. First, collect human preferences by presenting annotators with pairs of model outputs and asking which is better. Second, train a reward model that learns to predict which outputs humans would prefer, producing a scalar score that ranks outputs by estimated human preference. Third, use RL to optimize the policy by training the model to produce outputs that score highly according to the reward model, while staying close enough to its original distribution to preserve coherent language generation. This pipeline, developed through work at OpenAI and Anthropic and deployed across their model families, transformed what language models could reliably do.

The RLHF paradigm has been joined by more efficient approaches that achieve similar ends with less machinery. Direct preference optimization (DPO) derives a closed-form objective that trains directly on preference data, eliminating the separate reward model and RL stages. Kahneman-Tversky optimization (KTO) incorporates insights from behavioral economics about how humans evaluate outcomes. Group relative policy optimization (GRPO), developed at DeepSeek, enables efficient preference learning at scale. These techniques differ in their mechanics but share the essential insight that human judgment, even when it cannot be articulated as rules, can guide model behavior toward outcomes that humans prefer. At the same time, we are leveraging nonhuman feedback (reinforcement learning from AI feedback, or RLAIF) to scale preference data collection, using smaller models to generate preference labels that approximate human judgment at a fraction of the effort.

These techniques enable alignment with human values and preferences at a depth that demonstration alone cannot achieve. When we fine-tune with SFT, we can teach only behaviors that we can demonstrate. When we fine-tune with RL from preferences, we can teach the model to produce outputs that optimize for human satisfaction even when we cannot say what those outputs should be. This is how we teach models to be helpful without being servile, honest without being brutal, cautious without being paralyzed. Chapters 4 and 5 develop these techniques in mathematical detail. This overview establishes their strategic importance in the post-training landscape.

Understanding the Art of Stacking Techniques

A common misconception among newcomers to post-training is that these techniques are mutually exclusive, that we must choose between SFT and DPO, or between DPO and RLHF. Nothing could be further from the truth.

In practice, frontier post-training pipelines combine multiple techniques in carefully orchestrated sequences, with each stage building upon and refining the outputs of the previous one. Nor is any single technique inherently "superior," not even GRPO, despite its prominence in recent reasoning models. The best combination depends on the specific capabilities we want to instill and the resources available. Meta's training pipeline for Llama 3, illustrated in Figure 1-3, provides an instructive example of this multistage approach.[28]

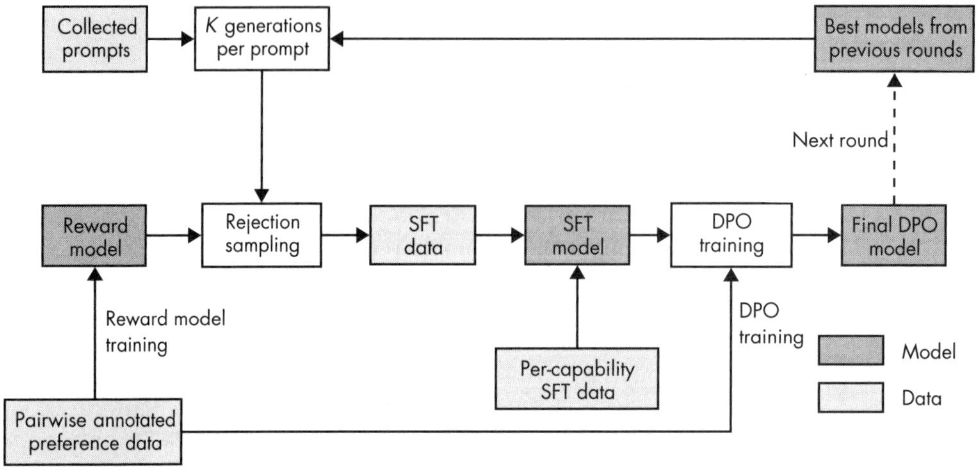

Figure 1-3: The modern post-training pipeline, as exemplified by Meta's Llama 3.[28] Multiple iterative rounds of SFT and DPO progressively refine model behavior, with each round incorporating freshly collected preference data and synthetic examples sampled from the latest checkpoint. The optional final RL stage (using verifiable rewards) targets specific capabilities like mathematical reasoning.

Rather than applying a single round of post-training, the Llama team employed six iterative rounds, each consisting of SFT followed by DPO. In each round, fresh preference data was collected using the best-performing model from the preceding round, ensuring that training data conformed increasingly well to the distribution of the policy being optimized. This iterative refinement proved more effective than a single, longer training run. The model improved not just in raw capability but in the consistency and reliability of its outputs.

The Llama 3 pipeline also illustrates a pragmatic preference for simplicity where it suffices. Meta explicitly noted that it explored on-policy algorithms such as proximal policy optimization (PPO) but found that DPO required less compute for large-scale models and performed better on instruction-following benchmarks.[28] This is not a universal truth (PPO and its variants remain essential for certain objectives), but it underscores that the most sophisticated technique is not always the most appropriate. The question is always what the technique buys you and whether that benefit justifies its cost.

The Ai2 Tülu 3 project provides perhaps the most comprehensive public documentation of a modern post-training pipeline.[29] Built on Llama 3.1 base models at 8 billion, 70 billion, and 405 billion parameters, Tülu 3 employs a five-stage recipe: careful prompt curation and synthesis, SFT on selected prompts and completions, length-normalized DPO on both off-policy and on-policy preference data, and finally a novel technique the team calls *reinforcement learning with verifiable rewards (RLVR)*. This final stage deserves particular attention. Rather than training against a learned reward model (which can be gamed), RLVR uses objective verification functions for tasks with deterministic correct answers—mathematical problems, code execution, instruction-following constraints. The result is a training signal that cannot be exploited through reward hacking.

> **THE FRONTIER PARADIGM: SFT + DPO + RL**
>
> The current leading approach to post-training combines three stages:
>
> **SFT for instruction following** Establish baseline capabilities and format compliance through demonstration.
>
> **DPO for alignment** Refine behavior according to human preferences, teaching the model what "good" looks like even when it cannot be directly demonstrated.
>
> **RL with verifiable rewards** Target specific capabilities (reasoning, mathematics, code) where objective success criteria exist and longer optimization horizons are beneficial.
>
> This sequence is not accidental. SFT provides the foundation that makes preference optimization tractable. DPO refines general behavior in ways that reward modeling struggles to capture. RL with verifiable rewards then pushes specific capabilities beyond what preference data alone can (economically) teach. Each stage thus addresses limitations of the previous one.

The most powerful demonstration of this final RL stage was, however, the DeepSeek-R1 model.[30] The DeepSeek team developed its GRPO technique (which we'll explore in detail in Chapter 5) against verifiable rewards, primarily mathematical correctness. The authors described the result as an "aha moment": R1 developed emergent capabilities, including self-verification and extended chains of reasoning, that were not the result of explicit training but of adaptive problem-solving. On the 2024 American Invitational Mathematics Examination, or AIME (a challenging math competition), the RL stage alone lifted pass rates by more than 40 percentage points. This is not a marginal improvement but a qualitative transformation in capability, achieved entirely through more effective use of training signal. In many ways, this echoes Hooker's observation that scaling data quality—or, really, signal quality—can yield much more significant gains than scaling model size (or data quantity) alone.[31]

The purpose of this sojourn through the realm of modern post-training is to highlight a fundamental truth: Post-training is not a single technique but a compositional art. The techniques we have briefly surveyed (such as SFT, PPO, DPO, and GRPO) are not competing alternatives but complementary tools. Our profession relies on knowing which to apply, in what order, and with what data. A model that needs only to follow a specific output format may require nothing beyond SFT. A model that must exhibit nuanced judgment across a range of situations benefits from preference optimization. A model that must excel at tasks with verifiable outcomes (coding, mathematics, structured reasoning) may warrant the additional complexity of RL with verifiable rewards. The chapters that follow develop each technique in detail, but our key skill is always synthesis: combining these tools into pipelines that best achieve the specific objectives at hand with the resources at our disposal.

Making Models Recognizably Yours

We return here to the fourth element of the ikigai identified earlier: identity. Recall that post-training is not just upskilling, but also where models learn to share an enterprise's perspective on ethical, regulatory, and societal implications—its very concept of who it is, what it does, and why. Alignment, the technical discipline that makes this possible, is often discussed in the context of existential risk and long-term AI safety. These discussions have their place, but for the enterprise practitioner, alignment is something more immediate and concrete. It is not an abstract philosophical concern but the mechanism by which an organization's AI systems become *recognizably its own*: consistent in voice, reliable in judgment, predictable in refusal. Identity in this sense is not mere branding but the behavioral signature that users and regulators learn to trust.

This is why, for many enterprises, alignment matters more than the base model's raw capabilities. A foundation model trained on more data or with more parameters offers marginal improvements in general knowledge, but general knowledge is rarely the bottleneck. The bottleneck is trust: Will this system behave consistently? Will it respect our constraints? Will it represent us faithfully to customers, patients, clients? These are alignment questions, and they are answered in post-training. An organization that selects a slightly less capable base model but invests heavily in alignment will outperform one that chases benchmark scores while neglecting behavioral consistency. The former has a product; the latter has a liability.

The practical stakes are considerable. Enterprises deploying AI systems face regulatory scrutiny, reputational risk, and operational liability that demand predictable, controllable model behavior. A model that occasionally produces offensive content, reveals confidential information, or provides dangerous advice creates liability—both legal and reputational. Alignment is how we prevent these failures.

The techniques for achieving alignment have matured considerably. Constitutional AI, developed at Anthropic, trains models to evaluate and revise their own outputs according to explicit principles—a constitution that specifies acceptable behaviors.[32] Reward modeling for safety trains separate classifiers to identify potentially harmful outputs, enabling models to avoid them. Red-teaming and adversarial evaluation probe models for failure modes before deployment, enabling targeted improvements. These techniques are not theoretical aspirations but practical tools deployed in production systems serving millions of users.

For enterprise applications, alignment extends beyond generic safety to organization- and sector-specific constraints. A financial services firm needs models that never provide unauthorized investment advice, a healthcare app needs models that never diagnose without appropriate caveats, and a legal AI tool must never represent itself as providing legal counsel. These are not generic requirements that foundation models satisfy (although given the risk of legal liability, most do have guardrails with respect to these specific high-risk areas), but specific constraints that post-training must instill. The alignment challenge for enterprises is teaching models not just to be generically safe but to respect the particular constraints that govern their specific deployment context.

But alignment is not just about hard-line rules. It is easy to force a model to never give medical or legal advice. The true challenge is to align the model with the values—the abstract, high-level, and sometimes malleable concepts of right action and wrong—that the enterprise wishes the model to reflect and espouse. This is where preference optimization shines. By collecting human judgments about what outputs are acceptable, desirable, or aligned with organizational values, we can train models to internalize these preferences. The result is a model that not only avoids explicit violations but also embodies the organization's ethos in its everyday interactions. No firm guardrail in prompting or output filtering can come close to how deeply these values can be embedded through post-training.

The regulatory landscape is evolving rapidly, and organizations that invest in alignment capabilities now will find themselves better positioned as requirements crystallize. The EU AI Act, adopted in 2024 with phased enforcement beginning in 2025, now mandates risk-based classification of AI systems and specific compliance requirements for high-risk applications. US regulations continue to emerge, and sector-specific requirements in healthcare and finance add further layers. These frameworks increasingly mandate demonstrable safety properties for deployed AI systems. Organizations that treat alignment as an afterthought will discover that retrofitting safety is expensive and uncertain. Organizations that build alignment capabilities into their post-training pipelines from the start will adapt more easily as regulatory requirements mature. This is not speculation but the predictable trajectory of any technology that affects public welfare.

Moving from Capable to Practical

A model that cannot be feasibly deployed creates no value, regardless of its capabilities. This observation sounds obvious, but its implications are routinely ignored. Researchers publish papers on ever-larger models achieving ever-higher benchmark scores, and practitioners attempt to deploy these models only to discover that they do not fit in available memory, cost too much to serve at scale, or respond too slowly for user-facing applications. The finest capabilities are worthless if they cannot be practically delivered.

In addition to capability improvement, post-training includes these techniques that make models practical:

Quantization
: This reduces memory requirements by representing model weights in lower precision: 4-bit integers rather than 16-bit floats, for example. The memory savings are dramatic. A 70-billion-parameter model that requires 140GB in half precision fits in 35GB when quantized to 4-bit. Modern quantization techniques like GPTQ and AWQ achieve this compression with remarkably small capability degradation, enabling deployment of frontier-scale models on hardware that organizations can actually afford. Chapter 7 develops these techniques in detail.

Parameter-efficient fine-tuning
: These methods enable adaptation on modest hardware. Low-rank adaptation (LoRA) and its variants train only a small fraction of model parameters, reducing memory requirements during training by an order of magnitude or more. QLoRA combines quantization with LoRA, enabling fine-tuning of 30-billion-parameter models on a single 24GB consumer GPU, with only larger models like 70B requiring 48GB or more (still dramatically less than full fine-tuning). These techniques democratize post-training, making it accessible to organizations without dedicated GPU clusters. The "crucial middle" exists partly because these techniques exist. Without them, meaningful post-training would require resources that only foundation labs could economically justify.

Knowledge distillation
: This transfers capabilities from larger teacher models to smaller student models that are cheaper to deploy. The student learns to mimic the teacher's behavior, often achieving surprising capability retention despite dramatic size reduction. A 7-billion-parameter student distilled from a 70-billion-parameter teacher can retain a substantial fraction of the teacher's capability (often 80 to 95 percent on standard benchmarks, though retention varies considerably by task and distillation method) at a tenth of the inference cost. Much of this leverage comes from directed learning: The distillation process can be opinionated about just exactly what part of the teacher's knowledge the student is to acquire. When combined with quantization and deployment optimization, distillation enables small models with focal capabilities that would otherwise be economically impractical.

These techniques transform theoretical possibilities into production realities, and any serious treatment of post-training must address them alongside capability improvement.

EDGE INFERENCE AND AIR-GAPPED DEPLOYMENT

Cloud deployment cannot satisfy one requirement that matters enormously in regulated sectors: data sovereignty. Healthcare organizations bound by the Health Insurance Portability and Accountability Act (HIPAA), financial institutions subject to the Sarbanes–Oxley Act (SOX) and the Payment Card Industry Data Security Standard (PCI DSS), and government agencies handling classified information often cannot send data to external servers, regardless of contractual assurances.

The emergence of compact, high-performance inference hardware has transformed the possibilities in air-gapped environments. NVIDIA DGX Spark, released in late 2025, delivers a petaflop of AI compute in a desktop form factor with 128GB of unified memory, sufficient to run well-quantized models with up to 200 billion parameters entirely locally. Two interconnected units can handle 405-billion-parameter models.

For organizations in highly regulated sectors, this capability is not merely convenient but enabling. Frontier-class models can now operate in environments with zero external connectivity, processing sensitive data without it ever leaving the secure perimeter. The combination of aggressive quantization and purpose-built edge hardware means that the security constraints that once forced organizations to accept inferior capabilities no longer impose such trade-offs.

2

PREREQUISITES FOR SUCCESS: BEFORE YOU FINE-TUNE

In December 1974, Donald Knuth delivered his Turing Award lecture with a warning that would echo through five decades of software engineering: "Premature optimization is the root of all evil." The phrase has become so ubiquitous that its context is often forgotten. Knuth was arguing against optimization before understanding, against reaching for sophisticated tools when simpler ones would suffice.

The same principle applies to post-training. Before fine-tuning a model, you must understand whether fine-tuning is the answer at all, and if so, what you are actually modifying. A foundation model is not a monolithic artifact but a stack of design choices: tokenization schemes that determine what counts as a unit of meaning, attention mechanisms that determine what information flows where, and optimization objectives that shape what the model learns. Each choice creates leverage points where post-training can intervene, and failure modes where intervention will fail. Understanding these foundations separates practitioners who can diagnose problems from those who can only adjust hyperparameters and hope for the best.

This chapter revisits transformer architecture through the lens of what post-training can and cannot change. We examine tokenization and its implications for domain adaptation, review the mechanics of attention and how different layers learn different abstractions, and explore what fine-tuning actually modifies at the weight level. We also address the threshold question: Should you fine-tune at all? For many use cases, prompt engineering or retrieval augmentation suffices, and fine-tuning adds complexity without benefit. We develop criteria for when fine-tuning is justified and how to choose base models that align with your objectives.

Should You Fine-Tune at All?

Should you fine-tune at all? The reflexive reach for sophisticated techniques often obscures a simpler truth: Prompting and retrieval may suffice, and the maintenance burden of fine-tuned models is routinely underestimated. The goal is preventing unnecessary complexity, not advocating for complexity where it provides no benefit.

When Prompting Suffices

Prompting has become remarkably sophisticated, and intellectual honesty requires acknowledging that for many use cases, it provides sufficient capability without the overhead of fine-tuning. The prompt engineering community has developed techniques that genuinely extend what foundation models can do without any weight updates: few-shot learning that demonstrates desired behavior through examples, system prompts that establish personas and constraints, chain-of-thought prompting that elicits step-by-step reasoning, and structured output formatting that ensures parseable responses. These techniques are not mere work-arounds but represent serious engineering that solves real problems.

Consider a document summarization task. A well-crafted prompt can specify the desired length, tone, and focus. A few examples can demonstrate the style of summary required, and structured formatting can ensure consistent output structure. For many summarization applications, this prompting approach works well enough. The model summarizes documents correctly, in the specified style, with acceptable latency and cost. Why incur the complexity and expense of fine-tuning when prompting suffices?

The question practitioners must honestly answer is not whether prompting can work (it demonstrably can for many applications), but whether it can work reliably enough, at the quality level required, with acceptable latency and cost. Reliability is often the limiting factor. A prompt that works 95 percent of the time may be adequate for internal tools but inadequate for customer-facing applications, as that 5 percent failure rate creates support tickets and reputational damage. Quality requirements vary enormously. A creative writing assistant can tolerate occasional off-brand responses, while a clinical decision support system cannot tolerate any response that might endanger patients. Latency and cost matter because long prompts with many few-shot examples consume tokens and add latency, and at scale, these costs compound.

Fine-tuning should be considered when prompting hits these hard limits, not before. The practitioner who reaches for fine-tuning without first exhausting prompting options adds complexity unnecessarily. Fine-tuning requires data collection, training infrastructure, model management, and ongoing maintenance, while prompting requires only prompt engineering expertise. When prompting suffices, it is the superior choice. The rest of this section examines how to determine whether prompting does, in fact, suffice.

When Retrieval Does the Heavy Lifting

Retrieval-augmented generation (RAG) addresses the knowledge problem without weight updates. The core insight is elegant: If your model needs information it was not trained on, retrieve that information at inference time and include it in context. The model's parametric knowledge—what it learned during training—is supplemented by nonparametric knowledge retrieved from external sources. This approach sidesteps many limitations of pure fine-tuning while adding capabilities that fine-tuning cannot easily provide.

RAG excels when the challenge is knowledge currency or specificity rather than behavior modification. *Knowledge currency* refers to information that changes over time, such as regulatory updates, market conditions, current events, and internal policies. A model's parametric knowledge is frozen at the training cutoff, but RAG enables access to information that post-dates it. *Knowledge specificity* refers to information too detailed or niche to learn during general training, such as your organization's internal documentation, product specifications, and customer-specific context. Fine-tuning on such information is possible but often inefficient, while RAG provides access without training.

The distinction between knowledge and behavior is crucial for deciding between RAG and fine-tuning. Fine-tuning changes how the model behaves: its style, reasoning patterns, propensity to refuse certain requests, and formatting preferences. RAG changes what information the model has access to but leaves its behavior unchanged. If you need the model to know about your organization's products, RAG is likely appropriate. If you need the model to respond in your organization's characteristic style, fine-tuning is likely necessary. If you need both, you may need both approaches.

Many "fine-tuning" projects are actually knowledge problems in disguise, better solved by robust retrieval systems than by training interventions. The organization that fine-tunes a model on its product documentation to improve product-related responses has likely made a mistake. The documentation will change, requiring re-fine-tuning, and the model may hallucinate "knowledge" it learned imperfectly rather than accurately citing retrieved sources. RAG enables cleaner separation of concerns, as the model provides reasoning and generation capability while the retrieval system provides knowledge. This separation simplifies maintenance and improves reliability.

> **KNOWLEDGE VS. BEHAVIOR**
>
> Ask: "Does the model need to know different things or to behave differently?"
>
> - *Knowledge problems* point toward RAG. Example: "The model should know our product specifications."
> - *Behavior problems* point toward fine-tuning. Example: "The model should respond enthusiastically and concisely."
> - *Combined requirements* need both approaches. Example: "Accurate, enthusiastic product recommendations" requires RAG for accuracy as well as fine-tuning (or good prompting) for enthusiasm. In such cases, consider both approaches, either separately or through retrieval-augmented fine-tuning (RAFT).

None of this is to say that RAG is always superior to fine-tuning. RAG has its own limitations. Retrieval quality bounds generation quality, context windows limit the amount of information that can be included, and some tasks require integrated understanding that retrieval cannot easily provide. The point is that RAG and fine-tuning address different problems, and practitioners should be clear about which problem they face before choosing a solution.

When requirements genuinely combine knowledge and behavior, RAFT offers a principled approach.[33] It trains the model to answer questions, given retrieved documents, while learning to ignore irrelevant "distractor" documents that retrieval systems inevitably return. The key insight is training the model to cite verbatim from relevant documents, grounding its answers in retrieved evidence rather than parametric memory. Experiments show that RAFT-trained models outperform both pure RAG and pure fine-tuning on domain-specific question answering, suggesting that the dichotomy between knowledge and behavior can sometimes be bridged through careful training design.

Steering Without Retraining

A fundamentally different approach to behavioral adaptation has emerged from mechanistic interpretability research: steering. Rather than modifying weights through training, *steering* directly manipulates the model's internal representations at inference time. The premise rests on a remarkable discovery: Neural network activations encode interpretable concepts that can be identified, measured, and manipulated. Research into sparse autoencoders has revealed that within the high-dimensional activation space of a transformer, individual directions correspond to recognizable features.[34, 35] One direction might encode "formal tone," another "technical vocabulary," another "refusal behavior." These features are not programmed but emerge from training, and once identified, they can be amplified or suppressed.

The technical machinery involves training a sparse autoencoder on model activations. The autoencoder learns to reconstruct activations via a sparse combination of learned features, where sparsity forces each feature to capture a coherent concept rather than an arbitrary direction. The resulting features often align with human-interpretable concepts: Researchers have identified features corresponding to code, to specific languages, to emotional tones, to safety behaviors, and to domain expertise. The model's internal representation, once a black box, becomes partially legible.

Steering exploits this legibility. To make a model more formal, identify the feature corresponding to formality and add a scaled version of that feature's direction to the model's activations during inference. To reduce verbosity, find the verbosity feature and subtract. The intervention happens at inference time, requires no gradient computation, and takes effect immediately. What would require thousands of training examples and hours of compute via fine-tuning becomes a simple vector addition that executes in milliseconds.

This makes steering particularly effective for stylistic and tonal adjustments. Enterprise applications often require models to adopt specific communication styles: more formal for legal contexts, more empathetic for customer service, and more concise for technical documentation. These adjustments traditionally required fine-tuning on examples of the desired style, with all the attendant costs of data collection, training infrastructure, and iteration time. Steering achieves similar results by identifying the relevant stylistic features and adjusting their activation strength. The iteration cycle collapses from days to seconds: Adjust the steering strength, observe the output, adjust again.

Steering also enables dynamic personalization that fine-tuning cannot match. A fine-tuned model has fixed behavior, the same for all users. A steered model can adjust behavior per request: more technical for expert users, more explanatory for novices, more formal for professional contexts, and more casual for informal ones. The same base model serves diverse needs through inference-time adjustment rather than maintaining multiple fine-tuned variants. For applications with heterogeneous user populations, this flexibility proves valuable.

THE STEERING TEST

Ask: "Does the base model already possess this capability, even if it doesn't always exhibit it?" If yes, steering can likely amplify or suppress the capability. If no, steering cannot help because there is nothing to steer toward. Steering modulates existing behaviors; it does not create new ones. A model that cannot write code will not learn to write code through steering. A model that can write code but defaults to verbose implementations can be steered toward conciseness.

The fundamental limitation is that steering cannot teach. It manipulates what the model already knows, leveraging existing internal representations rather than creating new ones. A model lacking medical knowledge cannot be steered into medical competence. A model that has never seen your proprietary data formats cannot be steered to produce them. When the goal is genuine capability acquisition rather than capability modulation, fine-tuning remains necessary.

The interpretability foundation also imposes constraints. Identifying features requires substantial research effort, and not all behaviors correspond to cleanly separable features. Some capabilities are distributed across many features in ways that resist simple steering interventions. The features that have been reliably identified tend toward broad stylistic and safety-related behaviors rather than narrow task-specific capabilities. As the field matures, feature coverage expands, but gaps remain.

Tooling maturity presents practical challenges as well. Fine-tuning benefits from years of framework development, with robust tools like the Hugging Face Transformers Reinforcement Learning (TRL) library, Unsloth, and Axolotl abstracting complexity into configuration. Steering tooling is younger, at times distinctly research-grade, and much less standardized. Commercial offerings like Goodfire provide accessible interfaces for feature steering, but the ecosystem lacks the depth of the fine-tuning stack.[36]

WARNING *The ability to attenuate safety features raises obvious concerns. Steering is uncomfortably cognate with abliteration, the manipulation of a residual stream to remove safety features.*[37] *A model steered to reduce refusal behavior may comply with requests it should decline. The same capability that enables legitimate customization enables misuse. Responsible deployment of steering requires the same governance considerations as any powerful capability: access controls, monitoring, and clear policies about acceptable modifications. The fact that steering requires no training data makes it faster to deploy but also faster to misuse. Organizations adopting steering should establish guardrails before the capability becomes widely available internally.*

Where does steering fit in the hierarchy of techniques? It occupies a distinctive niche: faster than fine-tuning, more powerful than prompting, but narrower in scope than either. Prompting adjusts behavior through input manipulation but cannot reliably enforce stylistic constraints or suppress unwanted tendencies. Fine-tuning can teach arbitrary behaviors but requires data and compute. Steering sits between: more reliable than prompting for behavioral modulation, faster than fine-tuning, but limited to behaviors the model already possesses. The practical recommendation is to consider steering when the goal is behavioral adjustment rather than capability acquisition and start with modest expectations.

At the time of writing, steering remains a research and diagnostic tool first and foremost, an operational instrument second. In particular, steering is dependent on the internal representations of the model for particular concepts. It is relatively easy to make a model obsessed with cows (or completely ignore all things bovine), because this concept is easily identifiable and easy to isolate. It is much more difficult to use steering, for instance, to filter out all references to personally identifying information. While an interesting proposition, the enterprise utility of steering remains yet to be demonstrated at scale.

A Framework for the Decision

The decision to fine-tune should emerge from a structured analysis of what specifically needs to change and whether training is the appropriate intervention. Too often, organizations approach fine-tuning as a solution in search of a problem, investing in training infrastructure because fine-tuning seems sophisticated rather than because it addresses a clearly articulated need. A more disciplined approach asks three questions: What exactly is wrong with the model's current behavior? What intervention would address that specific deficiency? Is that intervention worth its cost?

Behavior changes genuinely require fine-tuning. If the model needs to respond in a consistent style that differs from its default, prompting can help, but fine-tuning provides more reliable results. If the model needs to format outputs according to a specific schema that's more complex than few-shot examples can demonstrate, fine-tuning embeds that schema in the model's behavior. If the model needs to reason in domain-specific ways (for example, applying clinical logic, following legal precedent structures, and using financial analysis patterns), fine-tuning can instill these reasoning patterns more deeply than prompting allows. These are behavioral changes: modifications to the way the model processes and generates, not the information it knows.

Knowledge additions often can be handled through RAG, as discussed previously. The distinction is whether the model needs to know new facts or needs to behave differently. "The model should know about our products" is a knowledge problem, while "The model should respond enthusiastically about our products" is a behavior problem. The former suggests RAG, and the latter suggests fine-tuning. Many requirements contain both elements: 'The model should provide accurate, enthusiastic product recommendations" requires both accurate product knowledge (RAG) and enthusiastic recommendation behavior (potentially fine-tuning, though prompting may suffice).

Performance improvements might require either approach, depending on the bottleneck. If the model's responses are slow because prompts are long with many few-shot examples, fine-tuning can encode those examples in weights, reducing prompt length and thus latency. If the model's responses are inaccurate because it lacks domain knowledge, RAG may help more than fine-tuning. If the model's responses are inconsistent because prompting inadequately specifies desired behavior, fine-tuning addresses that inconsistency at the root. Diagnosing the bottleneck is essential, as the wrong intervention wastes resources without addressing the real problem.

The framework we propose, laid out as a decision matrix in Table 2-1, distinguishes behavior from knowledge and consistency from capability, helping practitioners identify the minimal intervention that achieves their goals. Minimal intervention is the key principle, as fine-tuning is expensive in time, expertise, infrastructure, and ongoing maintenance. If prompting achieves the goal, prompting is the better choice. If RAG achieves the goal, RAG is the better choice. Fine-tuning should be the choice when, and only when, simpler approaches have been tried and found insufficient.

Table 2-1: The Fine-Tuning Decision Matrix: Matching Interventions to Requirements

Requirement	Prompting	RAG	RAFT	Steering	Fine-tuning
Response style/tone	Often sufficient	Not applicable	Limited	Possible solution	Primary solution
Output format	Few-shot examples	Not applicable	Simple formats	Limited	Complex formats
Domain knowledge	Limited context	Primary solution	Primary variant	Not applicable	Reasoning patterns
Current information	Not possible	Primary solution	Primary variant	Not applicable	Not applicable
Behavioral consistency	Unreliable	Not applicable	Limited	Good	Primary solution
Regulatory compliance	Fragile	Partial	Partial	Partial	Primary solution
Latency requirements	Good	Moderate overhead	Moderate overhead	Better	Best
Data privacy	Model dependent	Architecture dependent	Model and architecture dependent	Model dependent	Full control
Maintenance burden	Lowest	Moderate	Moderate to low	Low	Highest

Given just how much cheaper to try and faster to disprove prompting is compared to any other approach, it should be exhausted first. It is rather awkward to witness a team spend months building fine-tuning infrastructure, curating datasets, and running training jobs, only to then wonder whether perhaps some manual or automated prompt engineering might have solved the problem just as well. A friend calls this the *space pencil phenomenon*, alluding to the (mostly false) anecdote that while the US space program devoted time and attention to creating what became the Fisher Space Pen, the Soviet Union just used a regular pencil.

More than once have teams realized that careful prompting would give them accuracy sometimes as high as the double nines—at zero training cost. Such stories abound, and among aficionados of prompting, they are the stuff of legend. What equally deserves mention, however, is that the US space program had a very good reason for eschewing pencils. Graphite dust is highly flammable, highly conductive, and in high-oxygen environments, rather prone to catching fire spontaneously. Efficiency without effectiveness is no virtue.

The Hidden Costs of Fine-Tuned Models

Fine-tuned models are not set-and-forget deployments but ongoing commitments, and the maintenance burden is routinely underestimated. When organizations budget for fine-tuning projects, they typically account for the initial data collection, the training compute, and perhaps the evaluation and deployment costs. But they often fail to anticipate the ongoing maintenance that a fine-tuned model demands. This oversight leads to situations where models that were expensive to create become expensive liabilities.

WARNING *Organizations routinely budget for initial fine-tuning and forget ongoing costs. When Meta released Llama 4 in April 2025, and when OpenAI launched the GPT-5 series in late 2025, organizations that had fine-tuned on earlier versions faced a choice: Continue using the older base model and miss improvements, or re-fine-tune on the new base model and incur training costs again. Neither option is free. Organizations that fine-tune must plan for this ongoing cycle, budgeting not just for initial fine-tuning but for periodic retuning. Before fine-tuning, ask: "Can we maintain this indefinitely?" If the answer is no, consider approaches with a lower maintenance burden. A good general rule is that in rapidly changing domains, users will spend the cost of a full re-fine-tuning every 6 to 12 months to stay current. Certain agentic architectures can help reduce this burden by isolating the fine-tuned model from rapidly changing realities that are better reflected in short-term information storage and/or RAGs. However, these architectures add complexity and are not universally applicable.*

Another source of the maintenance burden is that the world changes, but the model's weights do not. If your fine-tuning data reflects product offerings from last year, and products have since evolved, the fine-tuned model's behavior becomes increasingly misaligned with current reality. If your fine-tuning data reflects regulatory requirements that have since been updated, the model may confidently provide outdated guidance. This drift is not hypothetical but inevitable for any model deployed over time. Monitoring for drift and refreshing fine-tuning data is ongoing work that must be budgeted.

The fine-tuning infrastructure itself requires maintenance and expertise. Training pipelines break when dependencies update. Evaluation harnesses require updates as requirements evolve. The engineers who built the original fine-tuning capability leave or move to other projects, and their successors must understand what was built and why. Documentation helps but cannot fully substitute for institutional knowledge.

An organization that builds fine-tuning capability must maintain that capability, which means maintaining the people, infrastructure, and processes that make fine-tuning work. This is a problem that foundation labs do not, for a change, experience. Because models are their core product, maintaining the training infrastructure is equally core. But for the crucial middle, fine-tuning is typically one of a range of functions residing within an analytics or AI capability, even at large organizations. This creates an absolute need for good documentation, process discipline, and knowledge transfer.

Organizations must account for this total cost of ownership when deciding whether fine-tuning is appropriate. An organization that can afford a one-time fine-tuning project but cannot sustain ongoing maintenance will find that the fine-tuned model becomes a legacy system within a year or two, increasingly misaligned with current needs but too expensive to update. Better to recognize these economics up front and choose an approach (perhaps prompting, perhaps API fine-tuning that offloads maintenance to the vendor) that is sustainable over the model's intended lifetime.

BUILDING INSTITUTIONAL MEMORY FOR FINE-TUNING

Three documentation artifacts prove essential for maintaining fine-tuning capability across personnel changes. First, *model cards*: standardized documents describing the model's intended use, training data, evaluation results, known limitations, and ethical considerations. The format proposed by Mitchell et al. in 2019 has become an industry standard, and every major foundation lab now publishes model cards for its releases.[38] Your internal fine-tuned models deserve the same treatment. A model card forces explicit articulation of what the model is for, what it is not for, and where its failure modes lie. Update the card after every retraining, treating it as a living document rather than a compliance checkbox.

Second, *operational runbooks* that capture not just how to run the training pipeline but why particular choices were made. Interactive notebook formats ("literate code") demonstrate this well. Tools like Livebook or Jupyter Notebook interleave executable code with explanatory prose, so the documentation is always tested against the actual implementation. A runbook that includes the command to launch training alongside the rationale for hyperparameter choices, the expected duration on your hardware, and the common failure modes with their resolutions is worth more than any amount of prose documentation that has drifted from reality.

Third, *decision logs* that record why you chose this base model, why you structured the training data this way, and why you set the learning rate to this value. When your successor asks, "Why did we do it this way?," the answer should be findable, not locked in the memory of someone who's departed. Tools like architecture decision records (ADRs) work well here. The discipline of writing, "We chose *X* because of *Y*, accepting trade-off *Z*" pays dividends when the next engineer must decide whether to change *X*.

The overhead of maintaining these artifacts is real but modest compared to the cost of rebuilding institutional knowledge from scratch. Budget documentation time into every fine-tuning project, and treat documentation updates as part of the definition of *done* for any model refresh.

A fundamental shift in the way the field thinks about scaling has emerged, as post-training is now an independent scaling domain with its own scaling laws. Pre-training scales by adding more data and compute to improve next-token prediction. Post-training scales differently—through synthetic data generation, RL, and reasoning training—and these gains compound with pre-training gains rather than substituting for them.

The strategic implications are profound. Anthropic reportedly used Claude 3.5 Opus not for public release but to generate synthetic data and provide reward modeling for Claude 3.5 Sonnet.[39] The reasoning was that post-training a smaller model with better data yielded more business value than releasing a larger model with higher inference costs. When post-training scaling laws deliver comparable capability improvements at lower serving cost, the economics favor investing in post-training over pre-training beyond a certain frontier. This is why foundation labs now spend heavily on preference data; estimates suggest that Meta invested approximately $8 to $20 million on human preference annotations for Llama 2, rivaling the compute cost.[40]

The deeper insight is that these scaling dimensions stack. As one analysis put it, pre-training becomes "just one of the vectors of improvement,"[39] with synthetic data quality, RL, and test-time compute each providing independent gains. Consider a concrete example. A base model might achieve 60 percent accuracy on a reasoning benchmark. SFT on chain-of-thought traces brings it to 72 percent. Then synthetic data generation produces diverse reasoning examples that expose the reward model to edge cases it previously missed, improving reward signal quality. DPO training with this better reward model pushes accuracy to 81 percent. Finally, test-time compute via majority voting over multiple reasoning chains reaches 88 percent.

Each stage compounds on the previous. The aggregate scaling continues even as individual dimensions slow. This reframes our work. Post-training is not a finishing step after the "real" training but an independent source of capability with its own investment logic.

A Practitioner's Guide to Transformer Anatomy

Once we have made the decision to fine-tune, we are confronted with a dizzying array of options. To understand these choices, we must understand the building blocks of modern LLMs: the transformer architecture and its core mechanism, attention. The practitioner who understands these foundations can reason about what fine-tuning changes; the practitioner who does not must rely on recipes and hope. And hope is not a strategy.

Fine-tuning is, at its core, the modification of a learned function. The function in question—the transformer—takes a sequence of tokens and produces a probability distribution over possible next tokens. When we fine-tune, we adjust the parameters of this function so that it assigns higher probability to outputs we prefer and lower probability to outputs we want to discourage. This framing clarifies what we need to understand: the structure of the function we are modifying, and the nature of the inputs on which it operates.

The structure of the function is the transformer architecture itself. Different components of the transformer serve different purposes: Attention mechanisms route information between positions, feed-forward networks (FFNs) store learned associations, and layer norms stabilize training dynamics. Understanding which components do what helps us predict which components to modify for different objectives, and explains why certain fine-tuning techniques target specific layers while leaving others frozen. The subsequent sections of this chapter examine these components in turn.

The inputs to the function are tokens—discrete symbols drawn from a fixed vocabulary, representing fragments of text determined by the tokenizer. The tokenizer is not part of the transformer and cannot be modified through fine-tuning, yet it profoundly shapes what the model can learn and how efficiently it processes various domains. A practitioner who understands tokenization can anticipate problems before they arise and select base models whose tokenizers suit their domain. These considerations are addressed in "Tokenization and Its Consequences" on page 46.

Together, understanding the operation and its inputs provides the foundation for the chapter's concluding sections: what fine-tuning changes in the model's weights, and how to choose a base model that gives you the best starting point.

From Attention to Foundation Models

The transformer architecture emerged from a specific frustration with the dominant paradigms of 2017. Recurrent neural networks (RNNs) and their gated variants (OLSTMs and GRUs) processed sequences one token at a time, maintaining hidden states that accumulated information as they moved through the input. This sequential processing created two problems.

First, long-range dependencies were difficult to capture. Information from early tokens had to survive many processing steps to influence later predictions, and gradients had to flow backward through just as many steps during training. Second, the inherent sequentiality prevented parallelization. Each position's computation depended on the previous position's output, making training slow even on hardware designed for parallel computation.

Vaswani and colleagues at Google DeepMind proposed a radical solution in their 2017 paper "Attention Is All You Need"—somewhat accidentally.[41] (Their work was primarily focused on the domain of machine translation and is arguably one of those great inventions in the history of science that vastly outpaced the narrow impact its inventors foresaw at the time.) Rather than processing sequences step-by-step, they introduced an architecture that could attend to all positions simultaneously. The key insight was that attention mechanisms, which had been used as supplements to recurrent architectures, could replace recurrence entirely. The resulting transformer architecture abandoned the sequential bottleneck, enabling massive parallelization during training and capturing long-range dependencies through direct connections rather than accumulated hidden states.

The original transformer, depicted in Figure 2-1, was an encoder-decoder architecture designed for machine translation. The encoder processed the source sentence, building representations that captured its meaning. The decoder generated the target sentence token by token, attending both to its own previous outputs and to the encoder's representations of the source. This structure made sense for translation, where the input and output are distinct sequences that must be related but need not share structure.

Modern LLMs have largely converged on a different configuration: decoder-only architectures trained for next-token prediction. A generative pre-trained transformer (GPT), introduced by OpenAI in 2018, demonstrated that a decoder-only transformer trained on vast amounts of text could learn remarkably general capabilities.[42] The encoder became unnecessary because the task was not to translate between sequences but to continue a single sequence. Each position predicts the next token, given all previous tokens, and the model learns to do this well enough that it acquires substantial capability as a side effect.

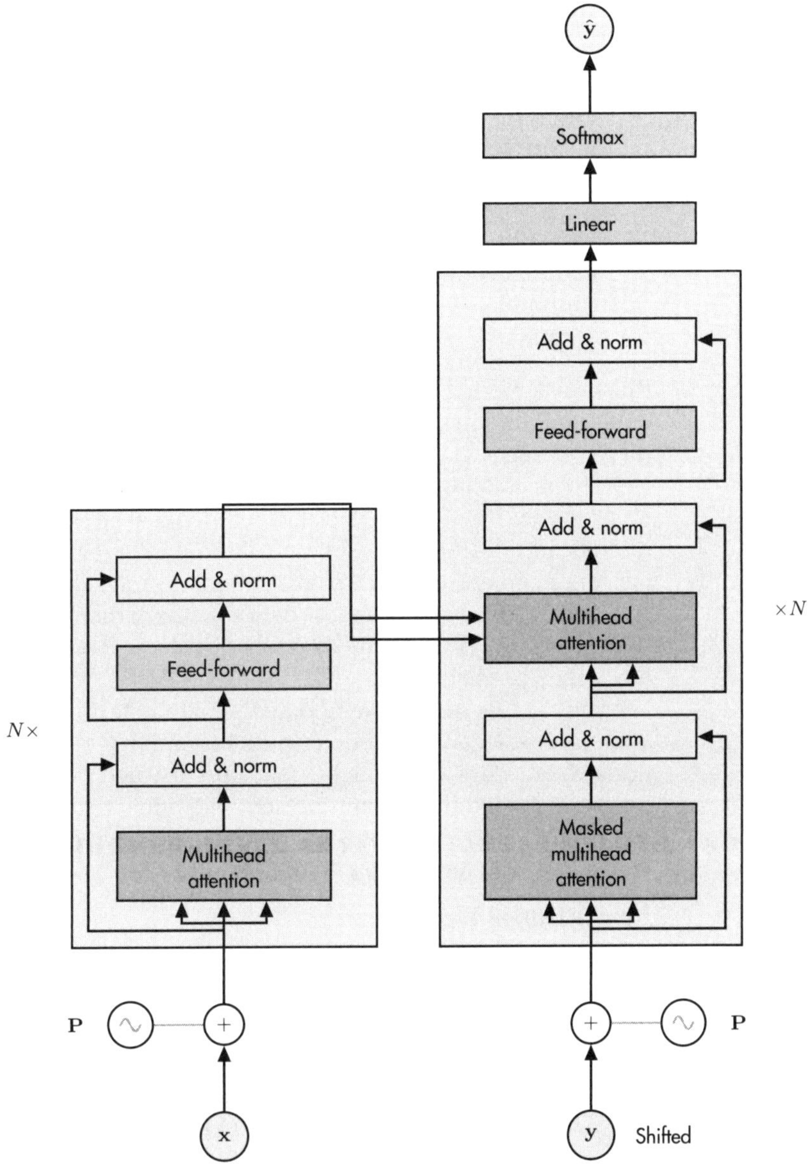

Figure 2-1: The original transformer architecture from Vaswani et al. (2017). The encoder (left) processes the input sequence through stacked layers of multi-head attention and FFNs. The decoder (right) generates output tokens autoregressively, attending both to its own previous outputs (masked self-attention) and to the encoder's representations (cross-attention). Each sublayer includes residual connections and layer normalization.

The architectural components that we will examine in the following subsections have remained remarkably stable since 2017, even as models have grown from millions to hundreds of billions of parameters. The core mechanisms are as follows:

Attention Routes information between positions

FFNs Process each position independently

Layer normalization Stabilizes training

Residual connections Enable information to flow through many layers without degradation

Understanding these components is not merely academic. When we fine-tune a model, we modify the learned parameters within these components, and understanding what each component does illuminates what fine-tuning changes.

The decoder-only architecture that dominates modern language models processes input through a stack of identical layers. Each layer contains a multi-head self-attention sublayer followed by an FFN sublayer, with residual connections and layer normalization around each. The input tokens are first converted to embeddings (dense vectors), then processed through the layer stack, and finally projected to a distribution over the vocabulary for next-token prediction.

During fine-tuning, we update the parameters throughout this stack: the attention projections that determine how information flows between positions, the feed-forward weights that store learned associations, and sometimes the embeddings that represent individual tokens. The following subsections examine each component in detail.

How Attention Works

Attention is the mechanism by which transformers route information between positions in a sequence. Therefore, understanding attention is essential for anyone who will modify these systems through training. The problem attention solves is fundamental, as language understanding requires relating distant parts of a sequence.

When we read, "The trophy didn't fit in the suitcase because it was too big," resolving what *it* refers to requires connecting the pronoun to *trophy* several words earlier, and the connection depends on semantic reasoning about relative sizes. (This is not trivial, actually—so much so the inherent ambiguity in resolving the reference has made this sentence part of the Winograd Schema Challenge, a widely used commonsense reasoning benchmark.) Recurrent architectures process sequences position by position, making long-range dependencies difficult to capture. Attention solves this by enabling direct connections between any positions, regardless of distance, as Figure 2-2 illustrates.

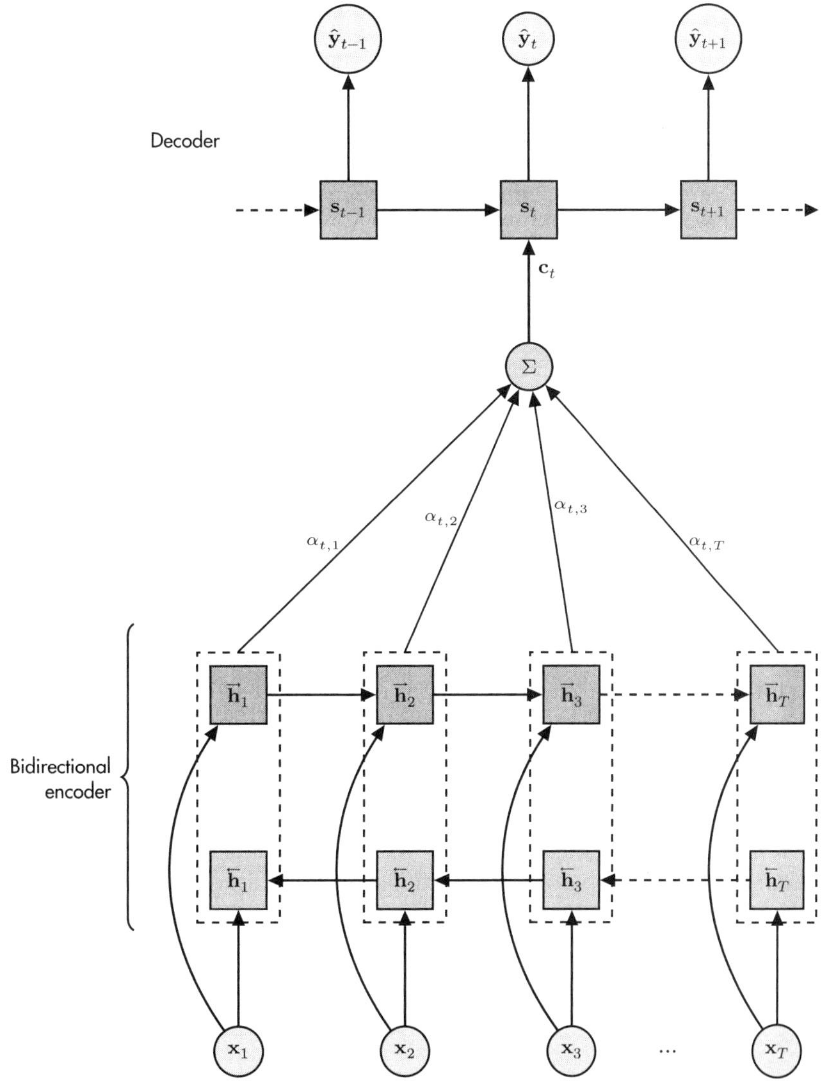

Figure 2-2: The attention mechanism in a sequence-to-sequence model. A bidirectional encoder processes the input sequence, producing hidden states that combine forward and backward context. The decoder attends to all encoder states through learned attention weights $\alpha_{t,i}$, computing a context vector $\mathbf{c}_t$ as a weighted sum. This allows the decoder to focus on different parts of the input when generating each output token.

The query-key-value formulation implements a kind of soft lookup table. Each position in the sequence produces three vectors through linear projections of its representation: a query vector that asks, "What am I looking for?," a key vector that says, "This is what I contain," and a value vector that states, "This is the information to retrieve." The attention mechanism computes similarity between each query and all keys, producing attention weights that determine how much each position contributes to each other position's updated representation. Positions with keys similar to the query receive high weight, and their values contribute strongly to the output. This mechanism is differentiable end to end, making it possible to learn which connections are relevant.

The mathematics are worth understanding precisely. Given queries Q, keys K, and values V, attention computes as follows:

$$\text{attention}(Q, K, V) = \text{softmax}\left(\frac{QK^T}{\sqrt{d_k}}\right)V$$

Here, d_k is the dimension of the keys and $\sqrt{d_k}$ is a scaling factor, intended to prevent the dot products from growing too large and pushing the softmax into regions with vanishing gradients. (See "Why the Scaling Factor" that follows for the exact role of the scaling factor.) The attention computation echoes the fundamental logic of what attention does. Each component corresponds to a conceptual step in the attention process:

- The query-key dot product measures relevance between positions.
- The softmax normalizes to produce a probability distribution over positions.
- The weighted sum formulation produces the final output representation.

One of the beauties of the attention mechanism is how the conceptual logic and the mathematical formulation coincide so closely. It may prove helpful throughout your career to jump back to this formula whenever you're stuck, as a conceptual safe point of departure. Understanding the mathematics of scaled attention unlocks intuition about why certain training decisions work and others fail.

WHY THE SCALING FACTOR?

Without the $\sqrt{d_k}$ scaling, dot products grow proportionally with dimension. In high dimensions, the softmax function becomes increasingly "peaky," assigning nearly all probability mass to the largest dot product and vanishing gradients to everything else. The scaling normalizes the dot products to unit variance regardless of dimension, keeping the softmax in a useful operating regime. This detail matters because fine-tuning modifies these query and key projections and understanding the scaling helps diagnose attention-related training instabilities.

A last feature that is worth considering in detail is the multi-head attention at the bottom of each set of stacks. Multi-head attention allows the model to attend to different aspects of context simultaneously. Rather than computing a single attention function, the model maintains multiple heads, each with its own query, key, and value projections, which learn to track different relationships simultaneously. Some might focus on syntactic dependencies, others on semantic relationships, yet others on positional patterns.

The outputs of all heads are concatenated and projected to produce the final output. This multi-head structure dramatically increases the model's capacity to represent complex linguistic relationships. It is what renders the model sensitive to the patterns of language rather than individual token-scale features.

Next, we turn to the meso-scale architecture that organizes these attention mechanisms into layers.

The Secret Life of Layers

Transformer layers are not homogeneous but specialize during pre-training to handle different aspects of language processing. This specialization emerges from the training process rather than being explicitly programmed, but it is remarkably consistent across models and training runs. Understanding this layer-wise structure helps practitioners reason about what fine-tuning will affect and guides choices about which layers to modify.

Research using probing classifiers—small supervised models trained to extract specific linguistic features from layer representations—has revealed a consistent pattern of specialization across transformer layers:[43, 44]

Early layers
: Encode local syntactic patterns and token-level information. Attention heads in these layers track nearby tokens, capturing immediate context and local grammatical structures. Representations remain closely tied to the surface form of the input: the specific tokens and their local relationships. These layers perform something analogous to parsing, identifying parts of speech, recognizing basic phrase structures, and resolving simple ambiguities. The information they extract provides the foundation on which later layers build.

Middle layers
: Develop more abstract syntactic and semantic representations. Here, the model begins to represent meaning rather than surface form: concepts, entities, and relationships. Attention patterns span longer distances, connecting related content across the sequence. These layers perform something like semantic composition, combining the meanings of individual words and phrases into larger units of meaning. Probing experiments show that syntactic properties peak in these middle layers, while semantic properties such as whether a noun refers to a person or a place become increasingly extractable.

Later layers
: Specialize for task-specific predictions. In a language model trained for next-token prediction, the final layers focus on producing the output distribution over the vocabulary, transforming the abstract representations developed by middle layers into predictions about what comes next. When we fine-tune a model for a specific task, these later layers typically change the most, adapting the prediction machinery to

the new objective while middle and early layers preserve much of their pre-trained structure.

This stratification in many ways mirrors the archetype of all stacked systems of increasing complexity: the human sensory system. Consider, for instance, vision, which has been the organic prototype that led to the development of much of our artificial neural networks. Visual impulses arrive at the primary visual cortex (V1), which is responsible for detecting the most elementary of features (light and dark edge patterns and orientations). From there, information flows through two visual streams (the dorsal and ventral streams) to areas of increasing complexity: from patterns to simple features, from simple features to complex local structures, and then eventually to global representations of a visual scene. In the same way, the layers of transformers build on increasingly complex layer structures.

This stratification has practical implications for fine-tuning. Layer-wise learning-rate decay (sometimes called *discriminative fine-tuning*) is an essential technique born of an awareness of this structural relationship. This technique applies smaller learning rates to earlier layers, allowing later layers to adapt quickly while earlier layers change slowly and preserve general capabilities. An extreme example of this is completely freezing early layers and training only later layers.

Layer-wise learning rate decay not only creates certain efficiencies but also helps avoid catastrophic forgetting, which occurs when training results in improved specific task performance but deterioration of global capabilities. (Despite rumors to the contrary, the reason we routinely ask task-specific models about the capital of France is not to pay homage to the Hugging Face team but rather to monitor for catastrophic forgetting.) In LoRA and related techniques, which typically target attention and feed-forward projections in all layers, we often find that later layers contribute more to task adaptation. For this reason, keeping them malleable while protecting the early layers strikes a balance between tuning efficiency and global feature stability. Understanding which layers do what enables more targeted interventions.

A useful mental model for reasoning about information flow is the *residual stream* perspective.[45] In this view, the hidden state at any layer is the sum of contributions from all previous layers, accumulated through the skip connections (residual connections) that characterize transformer architecture. Each layer adds to this stream, and no layer replaces what came before. This additive structure means that fine-tuning a single layer changes the information available to all subsequent layers. It also means that pre-trained representations are not destroyed by fine-tuning but supplemented with new information. The residual stream view helps explain why fine-tuning can add new capabilities without entirely erasing old ones.

Where Knowledge Lives

The FFNs interleaved with attention layers serve a complementary function to attention, and understanding their role illuminates what fine-tuning can change. Each transformer layer contains both a multi-head attention sublayer and an FFN sublayer. While attention routes information between positions, the FFN processes each position independently, applying the same transformation to every token's representation. If attention asks, "What is relevant to this position?," the FFN asks, "What should I do with the information at this position?"

FFN architecture is simple—two linear transformations with a nonlinearity between them. Given input x, the FFN computes as follows:

$$\mathrm{FFN}(x) = W_2 \cdot \mathrm{ReLU}(W_1 x + b_1) + b_2$$

The first projection W_1 expands the representation to a higher dimension (typically four times the model dimension). The nonlinearity introduces the ability to represent complex functions, and the second projection W_2 compresses back to the original dimension. Modern architectures often use gated variants like SwiGLU, but the basic structure persists.

Recent research suggests that these networks function as key-value memories, storing factual associations and learned patterns in their weights.[46] The interpretation runs as follows: The first projection W_1 computes similarity between the input and learned "keys" (the rows of W_1), the nonlinearity selects which keys match, and the second projection W_2 retrieves the corresponding "values" (the columns of W_2). This interpretation has mathematical grounding; the structure of FFN computation genuinely resembles associative memory retrieval.

This understanding has profound implications for fine-tuning. When we update FFN weights, we are literally editing the model's stored knowledge and learned associations. The FFN that stored "Paris is the capital of France" can be updated to store additional facts, or an FFN that learned to format dates the wrong way (American) can be adjusted to do so the right way (British). FFNs appear to store a substantial portion of the model's factual knowledge and learned associations, while attention mechanisms handle information routing and relational reasoning. Fine-tuning is, in large part, modifying this stored knowledge.

Techniques like knowledge editing and targeted weight modification leverage this structure for precise interventions. Rank-one model editing (ROME) and mass-editing memory in a transformer (MEMIT) identify which FFN neurons store specific facts and modify them directly, enabling changes to model knowledge without full fine-tuning.[47, 48] While these techniques remain research tools rather than production-ready methods, they illustrate the potential for targeted modification once we understand what different components do. For the practitioner, the key insight is that FFNs store knowledge and that fine-tuning will modify this stored knowledge—a perspective that helps predict the changes fine-tuning will produce.

We have now surveyed the transformer's internal machinery: attention mechanisms that route information, FFNs that store knowledge, and the layer structure that organizes computation. But we have glossed over a crucial question: What exactly are these tokens that flow through the architecture? The transformer does not process text directly. It processes sequences of discrete symbols, each drawn from a fixed vocabulary determined before pre-training began.

The process that converts your text into these symbols—tokenization—shapes everything the model can perceive and produce. Understanding tokenization is essential because, unlike the transformer's weights, the tokenizer cannot be changed through fine-tuning. It is a constraint you inherit with your choice of base model, and one that can silently undermine your fine-tuning efforts if your domain's vocabulary tokenizes poorly.

Tokenization and Its Consequences

If the transformer is the operation we fine-tune, tokens are the operands. Every input the model processes arrives as a sequence of token indices; every output it produces is a probability distribution over that same token vocabulary. Tokens are the atomic units of the model's perception and generation, and so we must also understand the tokenization process before fine-tuning.

The Happy Accident of Linguistic Structure

Before examining how tokenization affects fine-tuning, we must understand what tokenization does and why modern language models converged on a particular family of approaches—byte-pair encoding (BPE), which is the dominant approach adopted by most language models. The problem tokenization solves is fundamental: Neural networks must operate on fixed-size vocabularies, but natural language contains an unbounded number of possible words. How do we reason about words in a way that is efficient, bounded, and preserves at least some semantic structure?

Linguistics offers a relatively neat hierarchy of units for thinking about language. At the lowest level are *phonemes*, the smallest units of sound that distinguish meaning (the difference between *bat* and *pat*). In writing, these map imperfectly to *graphemes*, the smallest functional units of a writing system—letters in alphabetic scripts, characters in logographic ones. These assemble into *morphemes*, the smallest units that carry meaning; *unhappiness*, for example, decomposes into three morphemes (*un-*, *happy*, *-ness*), each contributing semantically. Morphemes combine into words, which in turn form higher units of organization like phrases and sentences. This hierarchy reflects genuine structure in language, and we might expect computational linguistics to respect it.

Early natural language processing (NLP) systems often did. Morphological analyzers decomposed words into stems and affixes, part-of-speech taggers identified word categories, and parsers built syntactic trees. Each layer of the linguistic hierarchy received dedicated treatment. But neural language models largely abandoned this approach because of the fundamental underlying problem: We're trying to *understand* language here, when these approaches *presuppose* an understanding of language structure.

On the one hand, we cannot treat every word as different, because the vocabulary would be unmanageably large, and we would lose valuable information. Similar words *do* tend to share a meaningful connection, even if that is not always the case. Moreover, this connection has a logically explicable nature. For instance, in English, negation is typically denoted by *un-* or *in-*, so two forms that differ by this prefix likely have the logical relation of negation applied to it. On the other hand, we cannot rely on this to any level of efficiency at the scale we are operating.

Thus, we need something that preserves some of that structure and compositionality, but efficiently. Tokenization does so by essentially statistical means, and the methods we use are a remarkable middle ground between the two extremes. Linguistically meaningful boundaries are not guaranteed, but they do happen with rather significant frequency. They are, in short, happy accidents—that we can, and will, exploit when we can, but must work around when we cannot.

The Mechanics of Byte-Pair Encoding

BPE began its existence far from the realm of NLP, having been introduced by Philip Gage in 1994 as a data compression technique. Its fundamental logic is relatively straightforward: Find the most frequent pair of adjacent bytes in a file, replace them with an unused byte, record the substitution, and repeat.[49] Two decades later, Sennrich, Haddow, and Birch found that this compression algorithm could solve the vocabulary problem in neural machine translation.[50] Their insight was that the same iterative merging process that Gage used to compress files also could build sensibly constrained subword vocabularies: Start with characters, repeatedly merge the most frequent adjacent pair, and stop when the vocabulary reaches a target size. The result handles any word, even those never seen in training, by decomposing them into known subword units.

BPE's success in machine translation led to rapid adoption across NLP. GPT-2 and its successors use BPE (specifically, a byte-level variant that operates on UTF-8 bytes rather than characters). The algorithm's simplicity, determinism, and effectiveness made it the default choice for a generation of language models. But BPE is not the only subword tokenization method, and understanding the alternatives illuminates what BPE does and does not guarantee.

WordPiece, developed at Google for its neural machine translation systems and later used in bidirectional encoder representations from transformers (BERT),[51] resembles BPE but makes merge decisions based on likelihood rather than raw frequency. Whereas BPE asks, "Which pair occurs most often?," WordPiece asks, "Which merge most improves the language model's likelihood?" This probabilistic criterion can produce different vocabularies, though in practice the results are similar. The \#\# prefixes you see in BERT tokenizations mark continuation subwords, a WordPiece convention.

Unigram, introduced by Taku Kudo in 2018, takes the opposite approach.[52] Rather than building up a vocabulary through merges, Unigram starts with a large vocabulary and iteratively removes tokens that contribute least to the model's likelihood. This top-down pruning produces fully probabilistic tokenization. Given a word, Unigram can enumerate all possible segmentations and their probabilities, enabling techniques like subword regularization that sample different segmentations during training. SentencePiece implements both BPE and Unigram, adding the ability to treat raw text (including whitespace) as input without requiring pre-tokenization.[53] Models like T5, ALBERT, and Llama use SentencePiece, often with the Unigram algorithm.

Why did BPE win the popularity contest, at least among the GPT family? The main reason may arguably be simplicity and determinism. BPE always produces the same tokenization for the same input, while Unigram's probabilistic nature introduces variability that complicates debugging and evaluation. Speed, too, matters at scale, and BPE's greedy merging is fast. After GPT-2 demonstrated BPE's effectiveness, subsequent models in that lineage continued using it.

The differences between these algorithms matter less for practitioners than the constraints they share. All subword tokenizers reflect the statistics of their training corpora; they are artifacts of pre-training. All create vocabularies that handle some domains better than others. And while the tokenizer is not immutable, changing it requires more than standard fine-tuning.

CAN YOU CHANGE THE TOKENIZER?

A common question among practitioners is whether they can modify the tokenizer during fine-tuning. The answer requires nuance, because while modification is technically possible, it is far less common in practice than alternatives that work within the existing vocabulary.

Vocabulary expansion involves adding new tokens to an existing vocabulary, resizing the model's embedding layer, and initializing the new token embeddings (typically, using the average of existing embeddings or the embeddings of the new token's subword components). Research demonstrates that this can improve domain-specific performance; adding chemistry tokens before continued pretraining on chemical literature shortens sequences and can improve downstream task performance.[54] However, vocabulary expansion remains more an active research topic than standard practice. One study found that adding more than 12,000 biomedical tokens to BERT produced no improvement on NER and relation extraction tasks, suggesting diminishing returns.[55] Most recent LLMs still ship with vocabularies in the 32,000 to 130,000 range without systematic optimization for specific domains.

These are more common alternatives used by practitioners:

Continued pre-training on domain text This is done without vocabulary changes. The AdaptLLM approach transforms domain corpora into reading comprehension format, achieving results that can compete with much larger domain-specific models like BloombergGPT-50B despite having only 7 billion parameters.[56] This works within the existing tokenizer, letting the model learn better representations for poorly tokenized terms through exposure.

Entity-aware training techniques These teach models to handle domain entities without adding them as tokens. Approaches like entity-aware contrastive learning (EACL) train models to recognize and correctly process domain-specific named entities, achieving strong results on domain NER tasks across medicine, law, and chemistry.

RAG with domain knowledge bases This approach sidesteps tokenization problems entirely by retrieving domain text at inference time rather than encoding domain knowledge in weights.

More dramatically, research suggests that with sufficient data (on the order of 50 billion tokens), we can replace the tokenizer entirely during continued pre-training and recover competitive performance.[57] But this requires substantial compute investment. For the fine-tuning techniques this book covers (SFT, RLHF, and DPO), the tokenizer is effectively fixed. Here's the practical lesson: Rather than fighting the tokenizer, most practitioners choose base models with acceptable tokenization for their domains, or accept the efficiency penalty and let continued pre-training compensate.

The consequence of the vocabulary reflecting the pre-training data is that the model's performance will be biased by the pre-training corpus. If it contained abundant English text, English words tokenize efficiently, but if it contained no medical literature, even common medical terminology may fragment into many subword tokens. The tokenizer cannot know about your domain, as it knows only about the data on which it was trained.

The practical implication is that practitioners must assess tokenization quality before committing to a base model. How does the tokenizer handle your domain's terminology? How many tokens does typical domain text require? Does the tokenizer fragment important terms in ways that might impair model understanding? These questions should inform base model selection, because after the model is chosen, the tokenizer is set.

The Challenge of Unfamiliar Territory

In an essay, Isaac Asimov made the quip that the easiest way to tell a chemist is to ask them to pronounce *unionized*. Chemists would tokenize it as *un-*, the universal privative, and *-ionized*, whereas non-chemists would pronounce it in line with the more colloquial *union-ized*. While the terminology is not common in chemical literature, the phenomenon he describes is. Humans tokenize words by conceptual units of meaning, and the way we define the subunits of meaning can vary by domain. With language models, however, this tokenization is one of our control levers on how the model perceives and processes text.

Providing for context-accurate tokenization is a particular issue when the material contains terminology that tokenizes poorly with general-purpose vocabularies. Tokenizers created from general corpora allocate their vocabulary budgets to patterns common in those corpora. Specialized terminology, rare in general text, receives no dedicated tokens and must be constructed from general-purpose subwords. This is one of the compromises inherent in pre-training: A model must first and foremost acquire broad general capability, which in turn implies general-purpose tokenization.

Medical terminology vividly illustrates the problem. Consider *electroencephalography*. GPT-4's tokenizer, for instance, represents it as six separate tokens: *elect*, *ro*, *ence*, *ph*, *al*, and *ography*. Those wise enough to have taken Greek in secondary school will instead default to *electro*, *en*, *cephalo*, and *graphy*, while neurologists will just try to remember it as a single concept. The practical offshoot is that if tokenizers are trained on a significantly different corpus than the target domain, specialized terminology fragments into inefficient token allocation that will at best be inefficient, at worst harm model performance. Research suggests that multi-token concepts are harder for models to manipulate than single-token concepts, affecting tasks from retrieval to reasoning.

Domain-specific tokenization sounds like an elegant solution, but it is not without challenges–to the point that even vocabulary expansion is not used as often as we might expect. As I have noted, changing the tokenizer is computationally extremely demanding, while extending it generally yields limited results. In practice, alternative approaches have emerged that do not have the same drawbacks. Entity-aware training techniques teach models to handle domain entities without adding them as tokens and can accomplish this with far less computational overhead. Thus, despite the apparent attractiveness of domain-specific tokenization, it remains more of a research topic than a standard practice.

SYMBOLIC TOKENIZATION: WHEN VOCABULARY EXPANSION MAKES SENSE

In some instances, vocabulary expansion genuinely makes sense. The clearest case is *symbolic tokenization*, when tokens represent not text but other forms of information.

CoMET, a large clinical foundation model developed by Epic, is trained on 118 million patients and 115 billion medical events.[58] It uses a vocabulary of 7,105 tokens that represent not words but clinical concepts. Time between events is tokenized into interval bins ranging from *1–5 minutes* to *3–6 months*, while gaps exceeding six months generate multiple *6 months* tokens. Diagnoses are represented as sequences of ICD-10-CM code fragments (category, subcategory, extension). Medications become ATC code tokens (anatomical group, pharmacological subgroup, chemical substance). Lab results use two tokens: one for the test (LOINC code) and one for the result's quantile bucket (1–10 equal-frequency bins). Demographics occupy 38 tokens encoding sex, race, and age buckets.

The model learns to predict the next medical event (a diagnosis, medication, lab result, or passage of time) by treating clinical trajectories as token sequences, just as a language model predicts the next word. This symbolic vocabulary enables the model to forecast patient timelines, screen for disease risk, and anticipate healthcare interactions, all from autoregressive generation.

A more ubiquitous example is provided by vision-language models. Vision transformer (ViT)–based models like LLaVA, Flamingo, and GPT-4V process images by dividing them into patches (typically 14×14 or 16×16 pixels), passing these patches through a vision encoder, then projecting the resulting embeddings into the language model's token space.[59] The language model then processes these "visual tokens" alongside text tokens, attending to both modalities through the same transformer architecture. LLaVA adds an explicit `<image>` placeholder marking where visual content appears in the input sequence, and during processing, this is replaced by the 576 patch embeddings (24×24 patches) from the vision encoder. Other architectures use learned query tokens or cross-attention mechanisms to compress visual information.

The key insight is that the vocabulary has been expanded not with new words but with an entirely new modality; the token vocabulary now includes both linguistic and visual symbols. This is possible because tokens are ultimately agnostic as to what they represent. They are simply discrete indices mapped to embedding space. Used wisely, this can be a powerful tool to extend model capabilities.

Frozen Tokenizers

Because tokenizers cannot be changed through fine-tuning without extensive retraining, practitioners must develop strategies for picking the right model with the right tokenizer and working within its constraints.

Thus, the old saying that an ounce of prevention is often worth a pound of cure applies a fortiori to model selection. Different base models have different tokenizers, trained on different corpora, with different vocabulary allocations. A model trained with substantial medical text in its pre-training corpus will have a tokenizer that handles medical terminology better than one trained primarily on general web text. Before committing to a base model, practitioners should evaluate tokenization quality on representative domain text. The few hours invested in this evaluation can save many hours of struggling with a poorly matched model.

TOKEN GESTURES

Way too few researchers and practitioners are playing around enough with tokenizers. To know what a tokenizer is doing, nothing replaces actually tokenizing certain key words. Hugging Face Spaces has a Tokenizer Playground that allows adventurous users to test various tokenizers on their own text.

Beyond the educational and, frankly, entertainment value, this is an important diagnostic tool. Tokenizers ultimately learn their rules in a rather probabilistic manner, and this often defies what we would consider logic. Some empirical examination of your tokenizer is especially worth doing when you have created custom tokens, to ensure that these continue to behave as they are supposed to.

Since tokenizers cannot be changed through standard fine-tuning, practitioners must develop strategies for working within tokenization constraints:

Continued pre-training on domain text
This can improve the model's handling of fragmented tokens. Even though the tokenization itself does not change, the model can learn better patterns for integrating domain-specific subword sequences into meaningful representations. If *electroencephalography* always appears in medical contexts with particular surrounding words and patterns, continued pre-training can help the model learn these associations. The model becomes more adept at processing the fragmented input, even though the fragmentation persists. This approach requires substantial domain text and nontrivial compute but can meaningfully improve domain performance.

Careful prompt design
This can avoid tokenization pathologies. If you know that certain terms tokenize poorly, you can sometimes use alternative phrasings that tokenize better. If you control the input format, you can structure inputs to minimize problematic tokenization. For code-related tasks, formatting choices can affect tokenization; consistent spacing, conventional formatting, and avoiding unusual constructs can produce cleaner token sequences. These are work-arounds rather than solutions, but they can improve performance at the margin.

Model selection
Prioritize vocabulary coverage for your domain. Different base models have different tokenizers, trained on different corpora, with different vocabulary allocations. A model trained with substantial medical text in its pre-training corpus will have a tokenizer that handles medical terminology better than one trained primarily on general web text. Before committing to a base model, evaluate tokenization quality on representative domain text.

Changing base models
A change may be necessary in extreme cases of severe tokenization mismatch. If your domain text tokenizes into sequences twice as long as general text, you face a fundamental efficiency penalty that no amount of fine-tuning can overcome. If critical domain concepts fragment into unrecognizable subword sequences, the model may never handle them reliably. The decision to switch models is expensive—it means abandoning any fine-tuning work already done—but it is sometimes the right choice. It's better to recognize a fundamental mismatch early than to invest heavily in a base model that cannot serve your needs.

We have now established the two prerequisites for understanding fine-tuning: the transformer architecture that we will modify, and the tokenization scheme that constrains what modifications can achieve. With these foundations in place, we can finally address the central question: When we run a fine-tuning job, what changes in the model's weights, and why do some changes succeed in creating the model behavior we desire, while others fail?

What Fine-Tuning Changes

What changes when gradients flow through a pre-trained model? The geometry of the loss landscape, the uneven dynamics across layers, and the tension between learning new behaviors and preserving old ones—these forces shape every fine-tuning outcome. Understanding them enables principled decisions rather than blind hyperparameter search.

The Geometry of Fine-Tuning

Most practitioners treat fine-tuning as a black box: Adjust learning rates until the loss decreases, stop when validation performance plateaus, and hope the result generalizes. This approach works often enough to be dangerous, because when it fails, practitioners lack the conceptual tools to diagnose why. A geometric perspective on fine-tuning—thinking about weight spaces, loss landscapes, and basins of attraction—provides those tools. It explains why certain hyperparameters matter, why some fine-tuning runs succeed while others with identical settings fail, and why techniques like early stopping and weight decay work. The mathematics of high-dimensional optimization rarely appears in practical guides, but the intuitions it provides are essential for principled fine-tuning.

And so, let's for a moment pretend that we can imagine the weight space of a neural network. Each parameter corresponds to a dimension, so a model with N parameters has an N-dimensional weight space. Each point in this space represents a specific configuration of weights, and thus a specific model. The training objective—for fine-tuning, typically a supervised loss like cross-entropy—defines a *loss landscape* over this space, assigning a loss value to each point. The goal of training is to find points in this space with low loss, ideally global minima but more realistically local minima that perform well enough on the training objective to get by.

Of course, visualizing a 70-billion-dimensional space is somewhat difficult. That said, the geometry of a 70-billion-dimensional space is not fundamentally different from that of a two- or three-dimensional space. The same concepts apply: Gradients still point downhill. That is enough for us to reason about the structure of this space and the way optimization proceeds within it. In a beautiful demonstration, Li et al. have shown that neural network loss surfaces have meaningful structure: wide, flat basins that generalize well, sharp minima that generalize poorly, and chaotic regions that resist training entirely.[60] These are not metaphors but genuine geometric features.

Recent work characterizing LLM loss landscapes reveals that pre-trained models occupy basin-like regions of weight space—broad, flat areas within which the model performs nearly identically, but outside of which capabilities collapse.[61] Pre-training thus has already found a region of weight space that produces coherent language, and fine-tuning's job is to explore the neighborhood of this region, seeking configurations that satisfy the fine-tuning objective while remaining close enough to preserve general capabilities. This neighborhood is not featureless. It contains local minima where training can get stuck, saddle points that slow progress, flat regions where gradients vanish, and valleys along which loss decreases toward better solutions.

Crucially, fine-tuning creates *nested* capability basins within the basic capability basin: A model fine-tuned for mathematics occupies a math-capability area inside the broader language-capability region, and moving outside the math region degrades mathematical performance while potentially preserving general language ability. Figure 2-3 illustrates this geometry schematically, showing how the pre-trained weights sit within a broad language-capability basin, with a nested task-specific basin representing the target of fine-tuning.

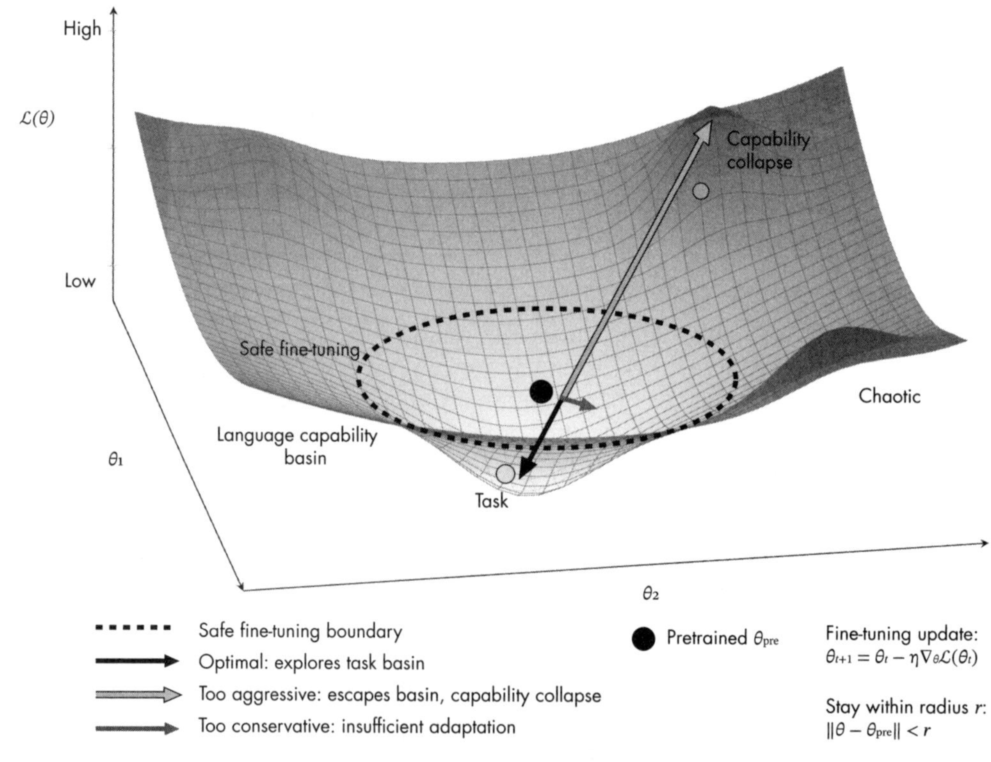

Figure 2-3: The geometry of fine-tuning, visualized as a loss surface over two weight dimensions. The pre-trained model θ_{pre} sits within a broad basin of language capability (lower regions). The dashed circle marks the safe fine-tuning radius: the region around the pre-trained weights within which the model preserves its core capabilities. The nested task basin represents the fine-tuning objective. Three trajectories illustrate different learning rate regimes: optimal fine-tuning navigates to the task minimum while remaining within the safe radius; overly aggressive training escapes the capability basin entirely, leading to capability collapse in regions where the model produces incoherent outputs; overly conservative training makes insufficient progress. The key constraint for successful fine-tuning is $||\theta - \theta_{pre}|| < r$: Stay close enough to preserve what the model already knows.

Understanding this geometry, despite its propensity to induce headaches, reveals why certain hyperparameters matter. For instance, consider the dual risks of learning rates:

Learning rates that are too high Too-high rates escape the basin of good solutions. The pre-trained weights sit in a region that produces coherent language, and steps too large can leave this region, producing models that lose basic linguistic competence. If you're unlucky enough, the model may end up in a chaotic region and struggle to return.

Learning rates that are too low Too-low rates can cause training to make negligible progress, with weight updates too small to escape local minima or traverse flat regions.

The optimal learning rate is large enough to make progress but small enough to remain in the good region. For fine-tuning, this typically means learning rates substantially lower than those used in pre-training–often by an order of magnitude or more. Research on fine-tuning variance has shown that even with identical hyperparameters, different random seeds can produce substantially different results, because the loss landscape contains multiple valid solutions and training dynamics determine which one is reached.[62]

Regularization toward the pre-trained weights keeps the model near its starting point, preserving capabilities while adapting to new requirements. This may take one of two forms:

Explicit regularization
This adds a penalty term proportional to the distance from pre-trained weights, directly encouraging the model to stay close. L2 regularization (weight decay) penalizes large weight magnitudes generally, while more targeted approaches like elastic weight consolidation penalize movement specifically in directions important for prior tasks.

Implicit regularization
Through early stopping, this halts training before the model strays too far. By monitoring validation performance and stopping when it plateaus or degrades, we prevent the model from overfitting to fine-tuning data at the cost of general capability. Low learning rates also act as implicit regularization, limiting the distance each step can travel.

Both approaches recognize that the pre-trained weights represent valuable knowledge and that fine-tuning should modify rather than replace this knowledge. The geometric interpretation is clear: We want to find a good solution within the pre-trained basin, not escape to a distant region that might have lower training loss but lacks the general capabilities encoded in the pre-trained weights.

The geometry of the loss landscape also helps explain why fine-tuning works at all. If fine-tuning objectives required moving to completely different regions of weight space, the journey from pre-trained weights would be long and fraught with bad minima. But because the solutions for most post-training tasks lie near the pre-trained initialization (after all, we are not trying to make the model do something radically different!), the fine-tuning journey is a relatively short perambulation of the neighborhood rather than a traversal across the entire continent.

Research has shown that knowledge in fine-tuned models can be understood as occupying connected areas: Models fine-tuned on similar tasks lie in overlapping regions of weight space, and interpolating between them produces models that retain capabilities from both.[63] This geometric structure is what makes transfer learning possible and explains why pre-trained models are such effective starting points for downstream tasks. Post-training is, then, quite literally the "last-mile task" of model adaptation.

The Different Ways That Layers Learn

The geometric view treats a model (or, more correctly, its state) as a single point in weight space. This is a useful abstraction, but it obscures important structure. A transformer, as we discussed earlier in this chapter, is not a homogeneous mass of parameters; it is organized into layers, each with distinct functional roles. Probing studies have mapped this hierarchy in detail. Early layers capture surface features like part of speech and positional information; middle layers encode syntactic phenomena like tree depth and subject-verb agreement; later layers represent semantic relations and task-specific features.[44, 64] This functional hierarchy, established during pre-training, has consequences for fine-tuning: Not all parameters should change equally, because not all parameters do the same thing.

This layer-wise variation, reflective of the functional specialization developed during pre-training, enables sophisticated training strategies that let us change what needs changing while preserving what should remain stable. This is our main safeguard against catastrophic forgetting, for instance.

Thus, most of the task-relevant improvements that fine-tuning achieves are to the later layers—that is, those closer to the output. These typically adapt faster and contribute more to task-specific improvements. A consequence is that when the task changes—from general language modeling to, say, generating structured JSON—the later layers must change most dramatically to produce the new output patterns. Gradients flow most strongly to these layers, and their weights change correspondingly, and indeed this is borne out by empirical studies of layer change.[43]

Earlier layers, on the other hand, change more slowly and thus preserve general capabilities. These layers encode basic linguistic knowledge (syntax, morphology, and local patterns) that transfers across tasks. A model fine-tuned for medical question answering still needs to understand basic English grammar, and a model fine-tuned for code generation still needs to handle punctuation and keywords. The early layers that encode this fundamental knowledge should not change much, and empirically they do not. Such stability is desirable, as it means fine-tuning can add task-specific capability without destroying general competence.

This observation motivates techniques like layer-wise learning rate decay, first introduced as *discriminative fine-tuning* by Howard and Ruder in their influential ULMFiT paper.[65] Rather than applying the same learning rate to all parameters, layer-wise decay applies smaller learning rates to earlier layers, and larger rates to later layers. A common schedule exponentially decreases the learning rate from the final layer to the first, so that the last layer learns at the base learning rate, the second-to-last layer learns at (say) 95 percent of that rate, and so on. This schedule aligns training dynamics with functional requirements; layers that should change more get larger learning rates, and layers that should stay stable get smaller ones.

Partial freezing takes this logic further, holding certain layers entirely fixed while updating others. If early layers encode general knowledge that should not change, freezing them guarantees preservation while reducing computational cost. Empirical studies support this approach. Lee et al., for instance, found that fine-tuning only the final quarter of layers in BERT and RoBERTa achieved 90 percent of full fine-tuning performance across standard NLP tasks.[66] More recent work on models with fewer than 3 billion parameters shows that freezing the bottom 50 percent of transformer layers can match or exceed full fine-tuning and LoRA performance while reducing memory consumption by half and improving training speed by 20 to 30 percent.

Several freezing strategies have emerged:

Static freezing
: Fixes a predetermined set of layers throughout training. Common choices include freezing all but the last two to four layers, and freezing the bottom 50 to 75 percent of the model. This is simple to implement but inflexible: The optimal freezing point varies by task, and static approaches cannot adapt.

Gradual unfreezing
: Begins with all layers frozen except the final classification head, then progressively unfreezes deeper layers as training proceeds.[65] Also introduced in ULMFiT, this allows the model to first adapt its output behavior before modifying its representations, reducing the risk that early gradient updates corrupt useful pre-trained features. A typical schedule unfreezes one layer group per epoch, moving from top to bottom.

Adaptive freezing
: Uses signals during training to decide which layers to update. AutoFreeze monitors gradient magnitudes and layer convergence, automatically freezing layers that have stabilized while continuing to train those that are still learning.[67] This provides the efficiency benefits of freezing without requiring manual tuning but requires a level of mathematical sophistication.

The choice of what to freeze involves trade-offs. Freezing more layers means stronger preservation of pre-trained knowledge, lower memory requirements, faster training, and reduced overfitting risk on small datasets. But freezing too aggressively limits the model's capacity to adapt; training only the final layer typically causes significant accuracy loss (0.5 to

1.7 percent in some studies), because the pre-trained representations may not align perfectly with the target task's requirements. The optimal freezing point depends on how different the fine-tuning task is from pre-training. Tasks closer to the pre-training objective can tolerate more freezing, while tasks requiring novel capabilities need more layers to adapt.

Understanding these dynamics enables practitioners to balance adaptation with capability preservation. A task that requires only slight behavioral adjustments can use aggressive freezing and minimal training. One that requires fundamental changes to the model's outputs may need to train more layers with higher learning rates. The layer-wise view provides a framework for reasoning about these choices.

The Plasticity-Stability Trade-Off

Fine-tuning represents a fundamental trade-off between plasticity—the ability to learn new behaviors—and stability—the preservation of existing capabilities. This tension is not specific to language models but appears wherever neural networks must learn new information without forgetting the old.

The challenge, ancient in the context of neural network research, was first articulated by Grossberg in 1980 as the *stability-plasticity dilemma*.[68] McCloskey and Cohen empirically demonstrated the effect in 1989 and coined the term *catastrophic interference* to describe how neural networks abruptly forget previously learned information when trained on new tasks.[69] Decades of research have not eliminated the trade-off, only developed techniques for managing it (and a better name: *catastrophic forgetting*).

Aggressive fine-tuning produces rapid adaptation but risks catastrophic forgetting of pre-trained knowledge. If learning rates are high and training continues long enough, the model's weights move far enough from their pre-trained values for the new configuration to beautifully satisfy the fine-tuning objective, but lose all ability to perform tasks it could perform before. This forgetting can be dramatic. A model fine-tuned to answer questions in a particular format may forget how to do so in *any* other format or even lose basic linguistic fluency. The pre-trained knowledge is overwritten rather than supplemented. Recent empirical studies of LLMs have shown that, counterintuitively, larger models within the range of 1 to 7 billion parameters exhibit *more* severe forgetting than smaller ones.[70] Scale, in short, is no defense.

Excessively conservative fine-tuning preserves capabilities but may fail to achieve desired behavioral changes. If learning rates are too low, training stops too early, or regularization is too strong, the model remains near its pre-trained weights and does not adapt sufficiently to the fine-tuning objective. The result is a model that retains all its pre-trained capabilities but has not learned the new behavior that motivated fine-tuning in the first place. Conservatism taken too far defeats the purpose of fine-tuning.

The trade-off cannot be eliminated, only managed through techniques that explicitly balance the competing demands. Elastic weight consolidation (EWC), introduced by Kirkpatrick et al., uses the Fisher information matrix to identify which weights are important for previously learned tasks and applies stronger regularization to those weights, allowing less important weights to change freely.[71] Replay buffers mix old training data with new, ensuring that the model continues to see examples of old tasks even while learning new ones—a technique inspired by the role of memory replay in biological learning. Careful regularization, whether explicit L2 penalties toward pre-trained weights or implicit regularization through early stopping, prevents excessive drift from the pre-trained solution. Recent work has also linked catastrophic forgetting to loss landscape geometry: Flatter minima exhibit less forgetting, suggesting that sharpness-aware optimization may help preserve capabilities.[70]

Every fine-tuning project must navigate this tension, and success requires explicit attention to both what the model should learn and what it should not forget. This means defining not just the fine-tuning objective but also the preservation objective: Which capabilities must be retained? How will retention be measured? What is the acceptable trade-off between task performance and capability preservation? These questions deserve answers before fine-tuning begins, because the answers shape every hyperparameter choice and training decision.

RUNNING A FORGETTING AUDIT

Before any fine-tuning run, define and create a *forgetting audit* checklist: tasks the model handles well that must survive fine-tuning. Include these in your evaluation suite and track them alongside task-specific metrics. It would be rather awkward to discover, amid celebrating a steep rise in domain-specific capabilities, that your agent-calling model has forgotten how to call tools. The instances in which this is tolerable are rare, even for a very narrowly focused model, and especially if the model uses internal functions like reasoning.

We have now assembled the conceptual toolkit for fine-tuning. You understand when fine-tuning is the right intervention and when simpler approaches suffice. You understand the transformer architecture whose weights we will modify, and the tokenization scheme that constrains what those modifications can achieve. You understand what fine-tuning changes: which layers adapt, how the loss landscape shapes training, and the trade-off between plasticity and stability. This helps us define the final decision of post-training's preparatory phase: choosing a starting point.

Choosing Your Base Model

Which model should you start from? The choice between open-weight and closed models, the counterintuitive relationship between size and fine-tuning effectiveness, and the licensing constraints that govern deployment are decisions that precede all others and that shape the entire post-training process.

The Open-Closed Divide

The choice between open-weight models and closed API-based fine-tuning involves trade-offs that extend beyond immediate cost and capability comparisons. This is a strategic decision that shapes the tasks your organization can do with AI, the dependencies it assumes, and the capabilities it develops or outsources. The decision deserves careful analysis rather than defaulting to whatever seems easiest—and, often enough, proactive engagement with legal.

Open models offer full control over every aspect of the system. You can inspect the weights, modify the architecture, deploy on your own infrastructure, and guarantee that your training data never leaves your environment. Reproducibility is extensive or, in the case of "truly open" models like Olmo, perfect. You can re-create any experiment, share exact configurations with collaborators, and debug by examining every component. Deployment flexibility is complete, whether it's on premises, cloud, edge, or any hardware that supports the model. These advantages matter most for organizations with stringent data requirements, need for customization beyond what APIs support, or strategic commitment to building internal AI capability.

But open models require infrastructure and expertise that not all organizations possess. GPU clusters are expensive to acquire and operate. Training pipelines require engineering effort to build and maintain. Debugging fine-tuning runs requires expertise that may be scarce. An organization that underestimates these requirements will find itself with capabilities it cannot use, or will spend more on infrastructure and talent than API access would have cost.

Closed API-based fine-tuning dramatically reduces operational burden. The vendor handles infrastructure, manages training runs, and provides a simple interface for submitting data and receiving fine-tuned models. For organizations lacking ML engineering expertise or GPU infrastructure, API fine-tuning may be the only practical option. The simplicity enables faster experimentation and deployment, with less organizational investment in AI-specific capability.

The trade-off is that closed models constrain customization to what the vendor permits. You cannot modify the architecture, apply techniques the vendor does not support, or inspect what happens during training. Vendor dependency is complete, and if the vendor changes pricing, deprecates models, or goes out of business, your fine-tuned models may become unavailable (an exception is pure post-training as a service, such as Tinker by Thinking Machines Lab—a unique business model whose long-term viability remains to be established). Data privacy/residency concerns are real, as the training data is processed in the vendor's infrastructure with whatever privacy guarantees the vendor provides. For regulated industries or sensitive data, these concerns alone may be disqualifying.

The optimal choice depends not just on current requirements but also on anticipated evolution. If you expect to need capabilities that API fine-tuning cannot provide—custom loss functions, architectural modifications, and techniques not yet supported—only open-model capability can truly deliver. (At the time of this writing, OpenAI's own API supports only DPO and a PPO-like method labeled as reinforcement fine-tuning, and only for a previous generation of GPT). Table 2-2 summarizes the trade-offs between open-weight models and closed API fine-tuning across key factors. This is largely the last time we will deal with API fine-tuning in this book, as it is both fairly managed and fairly straightforward compared to open-weight post-training.

Table 2-2: Open-Weight vs. Closed API Fine-Tuning: Trade-Off Analysis

Factor	Open-weight models	Closed API fine-tuning
Control	Full access to weights and architecture	Limited to vendor-provided options
Reproducibility	Perfect; can re-create any configuration	Vendor dependent
Deployment options	On premises, cloud, edge, any hardware	Vendor infrastructure only
Data privacy	Complete; data never leaves your systems	Data sent to vendor servers
Customization depth	Any technique, any modification	Only vendor-supported methods
Infrastructure required	GPU clusters, training pipelines	API access only
Expertise required	Substantial ML engineering	Minimal; mostly data preparation
Vendor dependency	None	Complete
Initial setup cost	High	Low
Ongoing operational cost	Variable; infrastructure dependent	Usage-based pricing (unless pure fine-tuning API)

Bigger Is Not Always Better

Larger models are not uniformly better for fine-tuning; the relationship between model size and fine-tuning effectiveness is more nuanced than "bigger is better." Understanding this nuance helps practitioners select appropriately sized models rather than defaulting to the largest available.

Scaling laws suggest that larger models learn more efficiently from the same amount of data. A 70-billion-parameter model may achieve with 1,000 fine-tuning examples what a 7-billion-parameter model requires 10,000 examples to match. This sample efficiency advantage is real and matters when fine-tuning data is expensive to obtain. For tasks requiring subtle judgments that benefit from the larger model's greater capacity, bigger may indeed be better.

But larger models require more computational resources at every stage. Fine-tuning requires more GPU memory, more training time, and more expensive hardware. Inference requires more compute per token, translating to higher latency and higher cost per request. Deployment requires more infrastructure, whether larger GPU instances or more sophisticated serving architectures. These costs scale with model size, sometimes superlinearly, and they persist for the lifetime of the deployment.

Larger models may be harder to fit into deployment constraints. If the deployment target is edge devices, mobile phones, or cost-constrained cloud infrastructure, large models may simply not fit. Even when they technically do, the inference costs may exceed what the application can bear. A chatbot that costs $0.10 per conversation may be economically viable, while one that costs $1.00 per conversation may not be.

For many enterprise tasks, well-tuned smaller models outperform poorly tuned larger ones. In an essay that ought to be mandatory reading for every post-training practitioner, Sara Hooker points out that at the current level, the main boundary is not scale of training data or parameters, but rather quality.[31] A 7-billion-parameter model fine-tuned on high-quality, task-specific data may often outperform a 70-billion-parameter model with generic prompting. The smaller model's inferior base capability is compensated by better task fit, and its lower inference costs make iteration and experimentation more practical.

In practice, we must balance multiple factors: raw capability on the one hand, practical constraints on the other. Here are some key questions to consider when deciding on a base model:

What are the task requirements? Does the task demand the highest possible language understanding, or is it more about domain specificity and accuracy on a narrow set of inputs? Tasks requiring deep reasoning, complex generation, or nuanced understanding may benefit from larger models, while tasks focused on specific domains or formats may not.

What are the deployment constraints? Can the target environment support large models in terms of memory, compute, and latency? If not, smaller models may be the only viable option.

What is the inference cost budget? Can the application afford the higher per request costs of larger models? If cost is a concern, smaller models may be more economical.

What fine-tuning data is available? If only limited high-quality data is available, a smaller model may be more effective. If abundant data exists, larger models can leverage it better.

What are the legal and regulatory constraints? Certain models are very attractive from a fine-tuning perspective but present regulatory or legal complexities. At times like this, early and proactive engagement with counsel can help smooth the way before time and effort is expended on post-training a model that would not be deployable.

In the next subsection, we will dive deeper into the specific legalities of using open-weight models.

The Licensing Minefield

Model licensing has become a complex landscape with significant implications for enterprise deployment. The term *open-weight model* does not mean "free to use for any purpose." Licenses vary dramatically, and violating them creates legal liability. Thorough license review should precede any significant fine-tuning investment. Licenses can also change, and it is always good practice to verify terms, especially for nonstandard licenses, rather than assume that terms will remain the same.

Each major open-weight model family carries distinct licensing terms. Meta's Llama models use a custom license that permits commercial use but imposes restrictions on products with over 700 million monthly active users and on certain use cases. Mistral has released models under various licenses, some fully permissive (Apache 2.0), and others with restrictions. Qwen models from Alibaba have their own terms, and newer entrants continue to arrive with their own licensing arrangements. No single summary captures the landscape, and as these terms are subject to change, each model requires individual review.

Some licenses permit commercial deployment but restrict certain applications; Meta's Llama license is a notable example. Restrictions may cover military uses, surveillance applications, generation of deceptive content, or other categories the model creators want to discourage. An enterprise deploying in a restricted domain faces a choice: Comply with the license and avoid the restricted use, or choose a different model with permissive terms. The restriction that seems irrelevant today may become relevant tomorrow if business direction changes, and strategic planning should account for this.

Other licenses require attribution or impose procedural requirements. Some require that derivative works carry specific notices; others require registration or notification. These requirements are typically not burdensome but must be followed. Corporate counsel should review licensing terms to ensure compliance; treating *open-weight* as equivalent to *no restrictions* is a common mistake that can prove potentially costly.

Beyond legal compliance, licensing affects strategic flexibility. A model under an Apache 2.0 license can be deployed in any context, modified without restriction, and used as a foundation for proprietary systems. A model under a restrictive license may serve current needs but preclude future directions. When capabilities are similar, permissive licensing is a strategic advantage; it reduces risk and expands options. Organizations should weigh licensing alongside technical capability when selecting base models.

The licensing landscape continues to evolve. Model creators experiment with different terms, seeking to balance openness with commercial interests and ethical concerns. What is true of any particular model's license in 2026 may change in subsequent releases. Practitioners must verify current licensing for any model under consideration and should assume nothing based on previous versions or general reputation. Due diligence is not optional.

Summary

In this chapter, we explored the rationale behind post-training and when it is—and perhaps more importantly, when it is not—the right choice. In the next, we will discuss our first and arguably most widely used post-training technique: SFT.

PART II

THE TOOLS

3

SUPERVISED FINE-TUNING: THE FOUNDATION TECHNIQUE

"If intelligence is a cake," Yann LeCun said during his famous presentation almost a decade ago at NIPS (as NeurIPS was then known), "the bulk of the cake is unsupervised learning, the icing on the cake is supervised learning, and the cherry on the cake is reinforcement learning." While the exact proportions have been hotly debated (indeed, most of the deliciousness of the current AI cake comes from the icing and the cherry), the sentiment remains true—supervised fine-tuning (SFT) remains the workhorse of post-training LLMs . It is the most widely used technique, the one with the broadest applicability, and often the only one necessary to achieve satisfactory results.

The apparent simplicity of SFT conceals substantial depth. The mechanics of optimization, the geometry of loss landscapes, and above all the art of data curation determine whether a fine-tuning effort succeeds or fails.

Practitioners who understand these foundations can diagnose problems that would mystify those who treat fine-tuning as a black box. Data quality matters more than model size, more than hyperparameter tuning, more than training compute. A thousand carefully curated examples will outperform 10,000 mediocre ones because the model learns from what you show it, and showing it the wrong thing—even if technically correct—teaches the wrong lesson.

This chapter develops SFT from first principles: the causal language modeling objective, gradient-based optimization, and the constraints of batch size and memory. We explore data curation strategies, including synthetic data generation, instruction backtranslation, and quality verification. We examine training dynamics: how to read loss curves, when to stop training, and how to verify that models learned what you intended rather than surface patterns. We address infrastructure requirements, distributed training approaches, and cost estimation. Finally, we develop criteria for when SFT suffices and when RL becomes necessary.

The Mechanics Under the Icing

The causal language modeling loss, gradient-based optimization, and the constraints of batch size and memory are foundations that are worth understanding precisely, because this knowledge enables intelligent debugging when training goes awry.

Learning by Predicting the Next Token

SFT is one of those concepts that appears almost trivial, yet its fundamental importance to post-training means we cannot gloss over its details. SFT not only does much of the heavy lifting in practice but also is foundational to later, more complex techniques—not in a methodological but a practical sense. Often enough, SFT in and of itself is sufficient, but the reverse is almost never true: Jumping to RL without SFT is guaranteed to end in tears and/or wasted GPU time.

The pre-trained model already "knows" language. It can generate fluent text, follow grammatical rules, and draw on vast knowledge encoded during pre-training. But it lacks the specific behavior you want: answering questions in a particular format, adopting a certain tone, or following domain-specific conventions. SFT bridges this gap by showing the model examples of correct behavior—pairs of inputs and desired outputs—and adjusting the model's weights so that, given those inputs, the model assigns higher probability to those outputs. The model learns by example, and the examples define what *correct* means (hence *supervised*). This is why data quality matters so profoundly: The model can learn only behaviors that the training data demonstrates—and it will learn whatever behaviors the data contains, whether you intended them or not.

The model processes tokens $x_1, x_2, \ldots, x_{t-1}$ and produces a probability distribution over the vocabulary for what x_t should be. Training adjusts weights to make this distribution assign higher probability to the actual next token and lower probability to alternatives. Repeat for every position in every training sequence, and the model learns to generate text that resembles the training data.

This "teacher forcing" paradigm—always conditioning on ground truth tokens rather than the model's own predictions—enables efficient training through parallelization. Every position in a sequence can be processed simultaneously, since each position sees the true preceding tokens rather than waiting for the model to generate them. The efficiency gain is enormous, as what would otherwise require sequential generation becomes a single parallelized forward pass. The price of this efficiency is, of course, that we aren't really training in the same conditions as our model will be called upon to inhabit at the time of inference. In inference, a model *does* have to condition on its own imperfect outputs, which result in the compounding errors so familiar to users of autoregressive LLMs. The model has never practiced recovering from its own mistakes, because training never exposed it to them.

WARNING Causal, *which has a somewhat specific meaning in language modeling, refers to being directionally limited. An event in the present cannot cause an event in the past. In the same vein, a token at a position cannot influence tokens that came before it. Therefore, in a causal model, a token can attend to only previous tokens and not future ones. Contrast this with masked language modeling, used, for example, in BERT-style models, where tokens can attend in whichever direction they wish. Do not, however, allow the language to lead you to believe that some sort of cause-and-effect relationship is involved here.*

As we know from supervised learning in general, we need a metric of just how far off we are from the desired results. The standard loss function for causal language modeling is cross-entropy, which measures how well the model's predicted probability distribution matches the actual next token. Cross-entropy earned this role because it directly optimizes what we care about: making the model assign high probability to correct continuations. Other loss functions do exist, but cross-entropy's combination of theoretical soundness (being the maximum likelihood estimator) and practical effectiveness has made it ubiquitous.

Understanding this loss mathematically matters because it helps you interpret the loss curve, your key indicator of the training process's overall health. Practitioners have a somewhat unhelpful tendency to consider the loss curve and ignore its values. This is good enough for the most part, because what we care about, first and foremost, is the loss curve going the right way (which at least for SFT is down). However, understanding what it means when "loss: 2.3" drops to "loss: 1.8," does confer a deeper understanding. For this, we must understand how cross-entropy loss is calculated. For a sequence of tokens $x_1, \ldots, x_T$, it takes the form

$$\mathcal{L}(\theta) = -\frac{1}{T}\sum_{t=1}^{T} \log p_\theta(x_t \mid x_1, \ldots, x_{t-1})$$

where p_θ denotes the model's predicted probability distribution over the vocabulary. The negative log probability has an intuitive interpretation: At a loss of 2.3, our model assigns a $-\log^{-1}(2.3) \approx 0.1$ probability to the correct token on average, while at a loss of 1.8, it assigns $-\log^{-1}(1.8) \approx 0.165$ probability. In short, that drop from 2.3 to 1.8 means the model has become about 65 percent more confident in its prediction of the correct token. Incidentally, these numbers connect directly to perplexity (the exponentiated loss), which we explore in Chapter 6.

For fine-tuning specifically, the loss is typically computed on only response tokens, not prompt tokens. The model should learn to generate appropriate responses, not to predict the prompt (which is provided at inference time). This "completion-only" loss focuses learning signal on the behavior we want to optimize, ignoring the prompt tokens that merely provide context.

Nudging the Model in the Right Direction

The loss function tells us how wrong the model is but not how to fix it. That is the optimizer's job. An *optimizer* takes the gradient of the loss with respect to each parameter—a vector pointing in the direction of steepest increase—and updates the parameters in the opposite direction, nudging the model toward lower loss. Repeat this process over thousands of batches, and the model gradually improves. The choice of optimizer determines how these updates are computed: how large each step ought to be, whether to treat all parameters equally, and how to handle the noisy gradients that arise from training on small batches rather than the full dataset.

The de facto default optimizer for language model fine-tuning is AdamW.[72] It's useful to understand what it does, because that understanding is essential to identifying those rare instances when other optimizers are a better choice. AdamW is a per parameter adaptive learning rate optimizer. It scales updates inversely with the historical magnitude of gradients. Parameters that have received large gradients get smaller updates, while parameters that have received small gradients get larger ones. This adaptivity helps navigate loss landscapes where different parameters operate at different scales, a common situation in deep networks with varied layer structures.

The *W* in AdamW denotes decoupled weight decay, a refinement that separates regularization from gradient-based updates. Standard L2 regularization adds a penalty proportional to weight magnitude to the loss function, which then affects gradients, while weight decay directly shrinks weights toward 0, independent of the loss gradient. The decoupling matters because it enables the regularization to function properly regardless of learning rate schedule and empirically produces better generalization for language models.

Optimization is conditioned by hyperparameters, the most important by far being the learning rate. The optimal value for fine-tuning differs dramatically from pre-training. Pre-training starts from random initialization and can use learning rates on the order of 10^{-4} to 10^{-3}. Fine-tuning, as the name suggests, starts from a carefully trained model that must not be disrupted, typically requiring learning rates of 10^{-6} to 10^{-5}. Too high a learning rate during fine-tuning causes the model to "forget" pre-training, losing general capabilities while pursuing the fine-tuning objective. Too low a learning rate, on the other hand, means the model never adapts meaningfully to the fine-tuning data. Learning rate schedules—starting lower and warming up, or starting higher and decaying—can help navigate this sensitivity. My favorite, which happens to also be the most widely adopted, is cosine decay with warm-up, which eases down after an initial ramp (warm-up).

How do we pick the ideal values for our hyperparameters? Some, of course, are conditioned by our environment (we can push the batch size only so high before the GPU decides that it's too big of a bite to chew). For others, practitioners used to rely on guesswork and experience.

Fortunately, we now have hyperparameter optimization (HPO) frameworks like Optuna that use Bayesian optimization to efficiently explore the hyperparameter space, learning from each trial to focus subsequent trials on promising regions.[73] For learning rate specifically, Optuna can search across several orders of magnitude, evaluating each candidate on a shortened training run before committing to full training with the best-performing value. This approach extends naturally to other hyperparameters (weight decay, warm-up steps, batch size) and can optimize them jointly rather than independently.

The compute cost of hyperparameter search is real, but negligible compared to that of even a single failed training run. I have more than once seen teams waste weeks of GPU time on training runs premised on well-meant but incorrect hyperparameters—effort that a six-hour focused run of Optuna, with Hydra as the configuration manager, readily averted in subsequent runs.

VIBE CHECK: HYPERPARAMETER OPTIMIZATION WITH OPTUNA

Coding agents like Claude Code and Codex are good at much more than writing code—for example, coordinating complex tasks and workflows. While watching hyperparameter searches converge is fascinating the first few times, it gets old rather quickly. Agents, on the other hand, can tirelessly babysit HPO runs.

The `hpo-optuna` agentskill in the agentskills folder of the book's companion repository implements this functionality. Not only does it help set up and run Optuna studies, but it also monitors their progress, summarizes results, and suggests next steps. You can even ask it to generate visualizations of the search process. This offloads the tedium of HPO management to an agent, freeing you to focus on higher-level strategy and analysis.

The skill integrates with Weights & Biases as well as Trackio, an open source alternative developed by the Hugging Face team. Especially if you're training on Hugging Face's serverless Jobs interface, it has become popular to use ephemeral Hugging Face private repos as interim storage for experiment artifacts, then spin up a Hugging Face Space to visualize it with Trackio.

Learning rates have an interesting effect that is sometimes neglected. At times, a cascade of multiple SFT runs is necessary to achieve the desired result. This is typically the case when you need both a broader capability (such as answering MCQ-style questions) and a specific, narrow capability (for example, doing so in the biomedical domain). In such cases, it pays to consider adapting relative learning rates so that the narrower capability is learned at a lower learning rate, typically at least one order of magnitude less than the broader. This protects the broader capability from being inadvertently forgotten while the narrower is being learned. Or, to use the loss landscape geometry we explored in Chapter 2, reducing the learning rate helps ensure that the model remains in the basin of attraction of the broader capability while finding its optimum with respect to the narrower one.

Understanding Batch Size: More Than a Memory Constraint

Batch size occupies a peculiar position in the hyperparameter hierarchy. Those who read tutorials aimed mainly at hobbyists could be forgiven for thinking that batch size is primarily the result of memory constraints. This is true, as reducing batch size is one of the trade-offs available to users with limited VRAM. But there's more to batch size than memory economy.

Larger batch sizes produce more accurate gradient estimates by averaging over more examples, reducing the noise inherent in stochastic gradient descent. This stability can accelerate training by enabling larger learning rates and more confident updates. On the other hand, larger batch sizes do have a potential drawback beyond memory: They tend to find "sharper" minima in the loss landscape, which may generalize less accurately to held-out data than the "flatter" minima that smaller, noisier batches discover.[74]

Of course, regardless of resources, VRAM imposes hard constraints on batch size. Each example in a batch requires memory for activations stored during the forward pass (needed for gradient computation during the backward pass), and this activation memory often dominates total memory usage during training. A model that fits comfortably in memory with batch size 1 may exceed memory with batch size 8, even though the model weights themselves fit easily. The scaling is approximately linear: Doubling batch size approximately doubles activation memory. This is precisely why access to desktop high-VRAM prototyping tools like the NVIDIA DGX Spark is so valuable. They enable experimentation with larger batch sizes that would be infeasible on typical workstations.

An elegant work-around to the VRAM problem is *gradient accumulation*. Instead of processing a large batch in a single forward-backward pass, this technique processes multiple smaller batches, accumulating their gradients before performing a weight update. The mathematical result is identical to a single large batch, as the accumulated gradients equal the gradient of the combined examples. Effective batch sizes far larger than memory permits thus become achievable at the cost of proportionally more forward-backward passes per weight update. The training dynamics of batch size 32 via four steps of accumulation with batch size 8 closely match those of native batch size 32.

A common misconception holds that batch sizes have to be powers of two. They do not. The mathematics of gradient descent is indifferent to whether you train with batch size 32 or 37. GPU hardware historically achieved better utilization with power-of-two tensor dimensions, but modern hardware and frameworks handle arbitrary sizes efficiently. That said, there are practical reasons to prefer "round" numbers.

Evaluation and test set sizes that divide evenly by batch size ensure that every example is seen exactly once per evaluation pass, avoiding the complexity of partial batches. When using gradient accumulation, the per device batch size multiplied by the accumulation steps should yield your target effective batch size, so if you want an effective batch size of 32 with four accumulation steps, you need a per device batch size of 8. Distributed training adds another constraint: The global batch size equals the per device batch size times the accumulation steps times the number of devices, so all three must align. TRL and the Hugging Face `Trainer` will warn you if your dataset size is not divisible by the global batch size, since the final incomplete batch can cause subtle reproducibility issues. None of this requires powers of two specifically, but it does reward choosing batch sizes with convenient factors.

Using Sequence Packing for Efficiency

Most fine-tuning datasets contain examples of varying length. A customer service dataset might include brief clarification questions alongside detailed troubleshooting conversations. Without special handling, each training example occupies a fixed sequence length, with shorter examples padded to match the longest. This padding wastes compute: The model processes padding tokens that contribute nothing to learning.

Sequence packing addresses this inefficiency by concatenating multiple short examples into a single sequence, separated by end-of-sequence tokens. A batch that would contain eight examples with 50 percent average padding can instead pack those eight examples into four sequences with minimal padding, halving compute while processing the same data. The efficiency gains are substantial for datasets with high length variance, where short examples would otherwise waste considerable compute on padding.

The implementation requires attention masking to prevent examples from attending to one another within a packed sequence. Without proper masking, the model might learn spurious correlations between adjacent examples that happen to share a packed sequence. Modern training frameworks like TRL's `SFTTrainer` implement packing correctly, automatically handling the attention mask when packing is enabled.[75] The practitioner need only set a configuration flag.

Packing interacts with loss computation in ways that merit attention. When examples vary dramatically in length, the short examples contribute fewer tokens to the loss than long examples, even when both represent equally important training signal. Some implementations weight loss by example rather than by token to address this imbalance, though the default token-level weighting works well for most use cases. The choice depends on whether you believe each example or each token should contribute equally to learning.

Garbage In, Garbage Out

If there is one message to take from this chapter, it is this: Data quality matters more than anything else. Neither model size, nor hyperparameter tuning, nor training compute have as much of an impact on the overall outcome as data quality. You cannot out-algorithm poor inputs.

Understanding That Less Is More (When It Is Better)

But what exactly is high-quality data? *Quality* in this context means more than mere correctness, though correctness is necessary. Quality means appropriateness: examples that demonstrate precisely the behavior you want, in the format you need, at the difficulty level that characterizes your deployment scenario.

A dataset of a thousand examples that perfectly capture your use case will outperform one with 10 thousand examples that are merely related. This is especially true for SFT, where the model can learn only differences that the training data more or less directly captures. As a consequence, the data curation process must have some level of intentionality. This is one aspect in which post-training large models is rather different from classical statistical sampling. We are not necessarily looking for representative samples of reality, but for something that is good enough for the model to learn that reality from.

Sampling therefore does not have to be as assiduously unbiased as is expected in more traditional ML contexts. What matters, however, is exposure. What a model is exposed to during training is what it learns, and the absence of meaningful exposure does deprive the model of that opportunity. It is not uncommon to need only a few examples of fairly distinctive content to convey its signal and meaning to the model during SFT, while more subtle information may require more exposure.

> **WHEN SCALE OBSCURES**
>
> Legendary teams start with a hundred solid examples, while novice teams start with a million and wonder why everything is confusing. The model learns from what you show it, and showing it the wrong thing—even if that thing is technically correct—teaches the wrong lesson.
>
> This is, incidentally, how *slop* (low-quality, generic model output) happens. Models trained on oceans of mediocre content learn to produce mediocre content at scale, with all the hallmarks of quantity without quality: verbose, generic, indistinguishable from a thousand other outputs. When scale makes assessing data quality difficult, it goes from ally to enemy.

When a model keeps failing at the SFT stage or begins to exhibit unexpected and undesirable behaviors, it may be helpful to resort to a time-tested approach: ordering as much pizza as can be delivered safely, then manually sifting through the dataset to curate a small, super-high-quality subset, even if it is just a few hundred examples. This is sufficient to establish what good data looks like. And often enough, that's all the model needs to start learning the right behavior. It can then be boosted with additional data from the original set.

Consider a practical example. An organization wants to fine-tune a model for customer service responses. It has access to two datasets: 10,000 historical email exchanges between agents and customers, and a thousand carefully curated examples written by its best agents following its latest style guidelines. The historical data is "real" but contains inconsistent formatting, outdated information, and the full spectrum of agent quality. The curated data is "artificial" but precisely represents desired behavior.

The curated data will almost certainly produce better results, because the model learns what it sees, and the curated data shows what the organization wants. At this point, it is worth once again reiterating that this is not statistical sampling, where we want to know what reality is like. Data is not our guide; it is our tool to shape the model's behavior. We are perfectly free to be as opinionated as we desire in our selection of samples to achieve that objective.

THE BABY BASELINE METHODOLOGY

Before investing in sophisticated training runs, establish what the Hugging Face team calls *baby baselines*.[76] The process is simple: Train an absurdly simple model first, over a small set (maybe 100 examples), fine-tune for a single epoch, and evaluate. This is not meant to produce a good model. It is meant to verify that your pipeline works, your data is formatted correctly, and your evaluation harness produces sensible numbers.

The next step is *vibe testing*. Before running formal evaluations, look at outputs. Generate responses to 20 prompts you care about and read them. Does the model sound right? Does it follow the format you expect? This informal check often reveals problems that metrics miss: subtle format errors, tone mismatches, or capabilities that work but feel wrong. Only after vibe testing confirms that the model is directionally correct should you run expensive formal evaluations.

This methodology saves enormous amounts of wasted compute. I've seen teams run week-long training jobs before discovering their chat template was wrong. I've seen teams celebrate benchmark improvements while their model's actual outputs degraded in ways the benchmarks could not detect. Baby baselines and vibe testing aren't exactly the peak of sophistication and sound statistical methodology, but they do grant an early insight into the training process that, most importantly, reflects much of the subjective experience that SFT (and post-training in general) is meant to inculcate in the model.

Speaking the Model's Language

For the success of SFT, the format in which training data is presented matters as much as its content. Modern instruction-tuned models expect conversations structured in particular ways: special tokens that delimit speaker turns, system messages that establish context, specific patterns that signal the end of assistant responses. A model trained on data formatted one way will behave unpredictably when prompted with data formatted another way, even if the semantic content is identical. Format mismatch is one of the most common causes of fine-tuning failure and one of the easiest to prevent.

Chat templates provide the solution. A *chat template* is a specification of exactly how to convert a structured conversation—a list of turns with roles and content—into the token sequence the model expects. Different model families use different templates. Llama models expect certain control tokens, Mistral models expect others, and ChatML provides yet another format. By far the easiest way around this somewhat confusing landscape is using the `Tokenizers` class in Transformers, which is exposed throughout the Hugging Face ecosystem's packages. This class comes with a set of the most commonly used chat templates, which can be extended using Jinja, a fairly well-known templating syntax. Chat templates help with automatic conversion from structured data to properly formatted sequences.

Beyond the mechanical question of correct tokenization, format consistency provides semantic benefits. When the model sees consistent formatting during training, it learns not just what to say but when and how to say it. Consistent use of system messages teaches the model to attend to system instructions, and consistent response formatting teaches the model appropriate output structure. Variation in training format creates uncertainty about what the model should produce. The goal is to make deployment conditions identical to training conditions, and format consistency is the foundation of that identity.

CHAT TEMPLATE FORMATS ACROSS MODEL FAMILIES

Different model families expect different chat templates. The following examples are illustrative. Specific tokens and formatting evolve with model versions, so always verify against your model's tokenizer rather than copying these verbatim.

ChatML Format (Used by Many OpenAI-Style Models)

```
<|im_start|>system
You are a helpful assistant.<|im_end|>
<|im_start|>user
What is the capital of France?<|im_end|>
<|im_start|>assistant
The capital of France is Paris.<|im_end|>
```

Llama 3/4 Format

```
<|begin_of_text|><|start_header_id|>system<|end_header_id|>

You are a helpful assistant.<|eot_id|><|start_header_id|>user<|end_header_id|>

What is the capital of France?<|eot_id|><|start_header_id|>assistant
<|end_header_id|>

The capital of France is Paris.<|eot_id|>
```

In practice, rely on the tokenizer's `apply_chat_template` method rather than constructing these formats manually. This ensures that you match the exact tokens the model was trained to expect.

Cleaning House Before Training

Duplicate examples in training data produce models that memorize specific phrasings rather than learning general patterns. If the same example appears 10 times in the dataset, the model receives 10 times the gradient signal for that exact phrasing compared to unique examples. The model learns that precise wording very well indeed and generalizes poorly beyond it. Even two or three copies of an example can produce measurable memorization effects, and datasets assembled from multiple sources often contain far more duplication.

Note that this point is somewhat distinct from the equally true assertion that models aren't necessarily sensitive to the relative weight of a type, class, or category of examples in the training data vis-a-vis others. Here, the issue is specifically with the multiplicity of identical or near-identical instances that encourage memorization, rather than relative overweight or underweight of a particular class of examples that would not.

Deduplication methods exist on a spectrum, between exact and computationally inexpensive on one end and semantically accurate but computationally typically much more intensive on the other. Exact deduplication catches only identical examples, yet from an SFT perspective, near-duplicates cause similar problems. Two customer service call transcripts that differ only in the customer's name teach the same lesson and should contribute almost the same gradient signal, but without deduplication they contribute doubly.

Fuzzy matching techniques identify near-duplicates despite superficial differences. MinHash efficiently estimates Jaccard similarity between text documents,[77] SimHash creates compact fingerprints that can be compared for similarity,[78] and embedding-based methods measure semantic similarity that catches paraphrases. Embedding-based methods are especially useful in domain-specific contexts, as these may be able to resolve identities that are not syntactically apparent (for example, *macrophage activation syndrome*, *cytokine release syndrome*, and *cytokine storm* denote vaguely the same pathological entity, but only highly domain-specific embeddings would be able to make this association). A proper deduplication pipeline combines a cascade of these techniques for efficient yet comprehensive deduplication.

Contamination checking addresses a related but distinct concern: overlap between training data and evaluation data. If the model has seen evaluation examples during training, evaluation scores cease to measure generalization and instead measure memorization; in short, they cease to be meaningful. This contamination can be accidental (when training and evaluation data derive from similar sources) or can arise from data processing errors. Before training, the responsible practitioner verifies that no training examples appear in evaluation sets, and ideally checks for near-duplicates as well. The validation that seems to confirm success may be confirming only that the model memorized the test.

Transforming Raw Material into Training Data

The data that trains the model must come from somewhere, and that somewhere determines the ceiling on model quality. Three broad strategies exist for generating training data: *expert annotation* (domain specialists create examples), *trained annotator annotation* (workers without prior domain expertise are taught the task), and *synthetic generation* (models create examples that humans or other models then verify). Each strategy has its place, and most successful projects combine them.

Expert annotation produces the highest quality but at significant cost. A physician writing medical consultation examples brings clinical judgment that no annotation guideline can replicate, and a lawyer writing legal analysis brings professional expertise that takes years to develop. Yet experts are expensive, their time is limited, and annotation may not be the best use of their expertise. Expert annotation typically works best for creating gold-standard seed sets—a few hundred examples that establish the quality bar and calibrate subsequent annotation efforts. These seed examples then define what *good* looks like for trained annotators or synthetic generation.

Trained annotators offer a middle path: better economics than experts, better quality than purely synthetic generation. The key is selection and training. Annotators should demonstrate capacity to learn the task, even if they lack prior domain knowledge. Training should include calibration against expert examples, ongoing feedback as they produce annotations, and quality control mechanisms that catch errors before they propagate. The investment in annotator development compounds, and a skilled annotation team becomes an organizational asset that produces high-quality data across multiple projects.

BUILDING ANNOTATION CAPABILITY

The best annotation teams I've worked with were not hired but grown. Start with people who can write clearly and follow complex instructions, then invest heavily in their domain education. Weekly calibration sessions for discussing borderline cases builds shared judgment. A feedback loop that enables annotators to see how models trained on their data perform can create ownership and motivation. After six months, a well-developed annotation team can produce data that rivals expert annotation—at a fraction of the cost.

Most importantly, treat your annotators well. Not only are they producing the data that makes your models work, but they are also your first line of defense against data quality issues. Empower them to raise concerns, suggest improvements, and take pride in their work. More than once, I've seen enterprises bitterly regret alienating their annotators by treating them like low-skilled, disposable labor. Not only is this unethical and unfair, given their paramount importance to building quality models, it is also a very expensive mistake in the long run.

Generating Synthetic Training Data

Human data generation is, of course, subject to limitations of scale and cost. Synthetic generation is much less constrained and thus has emerged as an attractive option. A capable model can generate thousands of examples in the time a human produces one, but those examples may contain errors, biases, or subtle failures that a human would avoid. Verification therefore becomes essential for filtering synthetic examples to acceptable quality, accepting those that pass scrutiny and discarding those that don't. The efficiency of synthetic generation depends on the pass rate: If most generated examples are acceptable, synthetic generation is efficient, but if most are rejected, the approach may collapse to human input with extra steps.

The research literature on synthetic data has matured considerably, and we now have a well-characterized set of strategies to choose from depending on the circumstances. The decision of which approach to use depends on the data you already have, the capabilities you are trying to instill, and the amount of verification capacity you can deploy. Figure 3-1 summarizes my (somewhat opinionated) decision framework to guide the choice among synthetic data strategies.

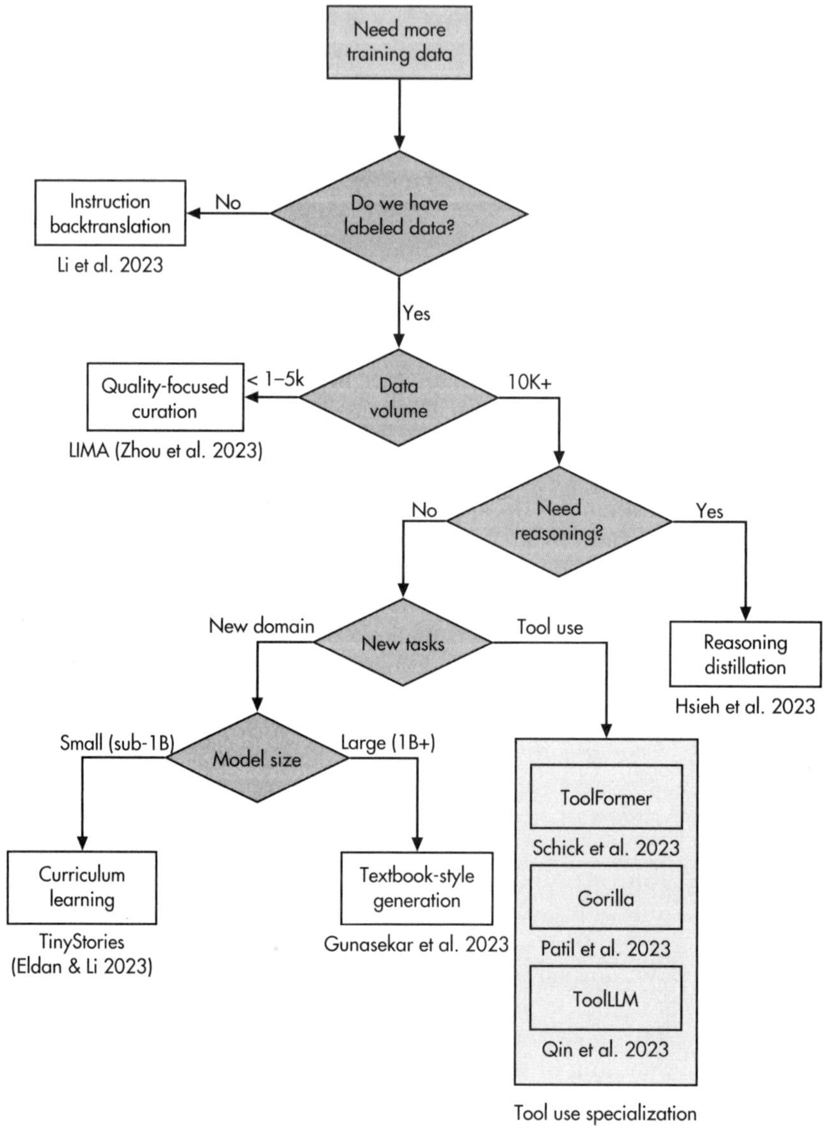

Figure 3-1: A decision flowchart for synthetic data strategies. The choice depends on existing data availability, target capabilities, and whether the task involves tool or API integration. Dashed arrows indicate progressive scaling of complexity within the tool-use family of approaches.

When You Have No Labeled Data

In the most constrained situation, you have raw documents or text but no instruction-response pairs. Instruction backtranslation addresses this by inverting the usual generation direction;[79] rather than generating responses to prompts, you generate prompts that would elicit existing text as a response.

Start with a seed model fine-tuned on a small number of examples, use it to generate instruction prompts for unlabeled documents, and then filter the resulting pairs for quality. The model that produced the backtranslations can itself be used for filtering, creating a self-improving loop. This approach produced Humpback, which at the time of publication outperformed other non-distilled models despite being trained on self-generated data.

When Quality Matters More Than Scale

The LIMA paper demonstrated a result that surprised many practitioners: A 65-billion-parameter model fine-tuned on only 1,000 carefully curated examples performed comparably to models trained on orders of magnitude more data.[80] The implication is that for many tasks, the quality ceiling is determined by the best examples in your dataset, not the quantity. If you have a limited annotation budget, spend it on diversity and quality rather than scale. Cover the range of behaviors you want the model to exhibit, ensure that each example is exemplary, and stop when diminishing returns set in. This quality-focused approach proves especially effective when you can identify what *excellent* looks like and can produce or select examples that achieve it.

Distilling Reasoning from Larger Models

When you have abundant data but want to transfer capabilities from a large model to a smaller one, distillation offers a powerful path. The standard approach fine-tunes the smaller model to match the larger model's outputs, but Cheng-Yu Hsieh et al. in "Distilling Step-by-Step" demonstrated that extracting and training on the reasoning process produces better results than training on outputs alone.[81] The larger model generates not just answers but explanations of how it reached those answers, and the smaller model learns from both.

This approach achieved remarkable efficiency. Models that would normally require orders of magnitude more data matched the performance of much larger teachers. The key insight is that the reasoning trace contains information that raw outputs do not, and smaller models can leverage this information to punch above their weight.

Teaching New Domains Through Curricula

When introducing models to entirely new domains, the structure of training data matters as much as its content. TinyStories demonstrated that even very small models can generate coherent text when trained on appropriately structured synthetic data: short stories using only vocabulary that young children understand.[82] The constrained vocabulary forced the data to exhibit clear narrative structure and logical progression, which the model learned to reproduce.

This curriculum approach, using synthetic data designed to teach concepts progressively from simple to complex, proves especially valuable for domain adaptation. The "Textbooks Are All You Need" paper extended this insight to code generation, showing that training on textbook-style explanations produced dramatically better results than training on raw code.[83] The phi-1 model, trained on synthetic textbooks and exercises, achieved 50 percent on HumanEval with only 1.3 billion parameters, outperforming models many times its size that were trained on vastly more data.

NOTE *Research has found that synthetic data designed like a textbook (with progressive concept building, worked examples, and exercises with solutions) teaches more effectively than raw examples.[83] The structure itself conveys information that unstructured data lacks. When generating synthetic training data, consider not just what the data says but how it teaches. Explanations that build on previously established concepts, examples that illustrate principles before requiring their application, and exercises that test understanding all contribute to more efficient learning. This principle applies whether the domain is code, reasoning, or specialized knowledge.*

Integrating Tools and APIs

A distinct family of synthetic data strategies addresses tool use and API integration. Toolformer demonstrated that models can learn to use external tools through self-supervised training;[84] the models can generate candidate API calls, execute them, and keep only those that improve predictions. The model learns when to call tools, what arguments to provide, and how to incorporate results, all without explicit supervision. This approach requires only a handful of demonstrations per tool and scales to new tools with minimal additional annotation.

When the goal is integration with specific API ecosystems, Gorilla showed that retrieval-aware training dramatically improves accuracy.[85] By training on API documentation alongside usage examples and providing documentation at inference time, the model learns to generate correct API calls even for APIs not seen during training. This approach significantly reduced hallucinations compared to models that relied on memorized API knowledge.

For complex multistep tool use, ToolLLM introduced depth-first search-based decision trees (DFSDT) to navigate the space of possible API call sequences.[86] The resulting dataset covers over 16,000 APIs across 49 categories, with multistep chains that demonstrate how to compose tools for complex tasks. Models trained on this data learn not just individual tool use but the planning required to orchestrate multiple tools toward a goal.

The choice of synthetic data strategy depends on your starting point and your destination. Figure 3-1 provides a decision framework. If you lack labeled data entirely, instruction backtranslation bootstraps from raw documents. If you have limited data, quality-focused curation following the LIMA approach maximizes impact. If you have abundant data and want to transfer capabilities to smaller models, distillation captures reasoning that raw outputs miss.

WARNING *Models trained on synthetic data generated by other models risk amplifying whatever biases the generator model contains. If the generator produces subtly incorrect reasoning, stereotyped language, or factual errors, the student model learns these patterns as if they were correct. Verification becomes essential, and ideally includes checks specifically designed to catch the failure modes of the generator model. The efficiency of synthetic data makes this verification investment worthwhile, but skipping verification in pursuit of scale produces models that confidently reproduce their teacher's mistakes.*

For new domains, curriculum-style synthetic data teaches more efficiently than unstructured examples. And for tool integration, the progression from Toolformer through Gorilla to ToolLLM offers increasingly sophisticated approaches as your tool ecosystem grows. Chapter 11 discusses synthetic data more extensively.

From Theory to GPU Clusters

With data prepared and objectives understood, we turn to running training. This section traces the path from the basic training loop through monitoring, infrastructure planning, and distributed training. Understanding what happens during training—not just how to configure it—enables informed debugging when things go wrong.

Understanding the Training Loop

Every fine-tuning run, regardless of framework or scale, executes the same fundamental loop. Data flows through the model, loss quantifies error, gradients indicate how to improve, and parameters update accordingly. Understanding this loop demystifies training and grounds discussions of optimization, monitoring, and debugging.

The loop proceeds in steps (Figure 3-2). Each step processes a batch of examples through the forward pass, computing predictions and loss. The backward pass then computes gradients—the partial derivative of the loss with respect to each parameter, indicating how changes to that parameter would affect the loss. The optimizer uses these gradients to update parameters, nudging them in directions that should reduce loss. After the update, the next batch arrives, and the process repeats.

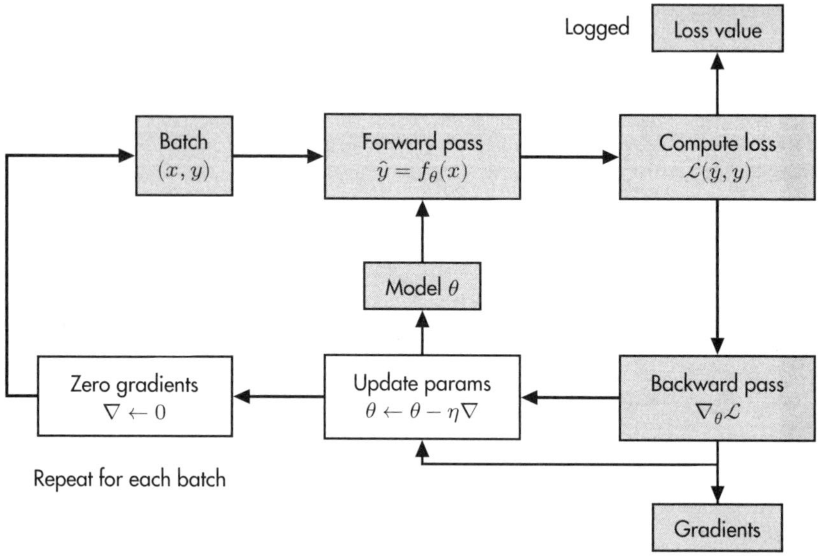

Figure 3-2: The fine-tuning training loop. Each batch flows through the forward pass to compute predictions and loss, then backward through the network to compute gradients. The optimizer updates parameters with the gradients, which are then cleared before the next iteration.

Listing 3-1 shows this fine-tuning training loop in practice.

```
for epoch in range(num_epochs):
    for batch in train_dataloader:
      ❶ outputs = model(**batch)
        loss = outputs.loss

      ❷ loss.backward()

      ❸ optimizer.step()
        scheduler.step()

      ❹ optimizer.zero_grad()
```

Listing 3-1: The essential training loop, stripped to fundamentals

In practice, the loop grows more complex:

- Gradient accumulation splits large effective batch sizes across multiple forward-backward passes before updating.
- Mixed-precision training maintains some computations in lower precision for speed while keeping critical values in higher precision for stability.
- Gradient clipping caps gradient magnitudes to prevent explosive updates.

- Checkpointing periodically saves state to enable recovery from failures.
- Logging records metrics for later analysis.

Yet, beneath these elaborations, the fundamental rhythm remains: forward ❶, backward ❷, update ❸, repeat ❹. Modern frameworks like Hugging Face's `Trainer` and TRL's `SFTTrainer` abstract this loop into configuration, handling the complexities automatically.

Listing 3-2 shows a typical SFT configuration.

```
from trl import SFTTrainer, SFTConfig

config = SFTConfig(
    output_dir="./sft-output",

 ❶ per_device_train_batch_size=2,
    gradient_accumulation_steps=8,

 ❷ learning_rate=2e-5,
 ❸ lr_scheduler_type="cosine",
    warmup_ratio=0.1,

 ❹ num_train_epochs=3,
    max_seq_length=2048,

    logging_steps=10,
    eval_strategy="steps",
    eval_steps=100,

    save_strategy="steps",
    save_steps=500,
    save_total_limit=3,

    bf16=True,
    gradient_checkpointing=True,
)

trainer = SFTTrainer(
    model=model,
    args=config,
    train_dataset=train_data,
    eval_dataset=eval_data,
    tokenizer=tokenizer,
)

trainer.train()
```

Listing 3-2: SFT configuration with TRL's `SFTTrainer`

This configuration specifies batch size ❶, learning rate ❷, schedule ❸, and duration ❹, leaving the framework to manage the loop mechanics.

Performing the Hardware Reality Check

The infrastructure required for SFT scales with model size, but the scaling is gentler than many practitioners expect. A single GPU with 80GB of memory (an A100 or H100) can fine-tune 7-billion-parameter models with gradient checkpointing and careful batch sizing. The NVIDIA DGX Spark's generous unified memory can handle much larger models. Parameter-efficient fine-tuning methods like LoRA further reduce requirements, enabling the same model to be fine-tuned on consumer hardware with 24GB of memory.[87] (We explore these methods in depth in Chapter 7.) The crucial middle does not require the infrastructure of a foundation lab but does require thoughtful resource planning.

Memory during training comprises four components: model parameters, gradients (the same size as the parameters), optimizer states (typically twice the size of the parameters for Adam), and activations (variable, depending on batch size and sequence length). The rule of thumb is that full fine-tuning in `float16` or `bfloat16` requires approximately 16 bytes per parameter: 2 for parameters, 2 for gradients, 8 for optimizer states, and variable overhead for activations. A 7-billion-parameter model thus requires roughly 112GB for training overhead before accounting for activations, explaining why 80GB GPUs are marginal and why parameter-efficient methods are so popular.

The choice between `float16` and `bfloat16` merits brief attention (bit precision is discussed in more detail in Chapter 7). Both use 16 bits, but they allocate those bits differently. The `float16` option dedicates more bits to precision (10 mantissa bits) and fewer to range (5 exponent bits), while `bfloat16` reverses this trade-off (7 mantissa bits, 8 exponent bits). The practical consequence is that `bfloat16` matches `float32`'s dynamic range (it can represent the same extremely large and small values), while `float16` cannot. During training, gradients and activations occasionally spike to values that overflow `float16`'s range, causing `NaN` losses and failed training runs. The `bfloat16` datatype handles these spikes gracefully, making training more stable at the cost of slightly reduced precision that rarely matters in practice. When available (A100, H100, all Blackwell-class GPUs and recent consumer GPUs), `bfloat16` is the better default for fine-tuning. Older hardware that supports only `float16` requires more careful gradient scaling and may need gradient clipping to avoid instability.

Picking Your Weapons

The Hugging Face ecosystem has become the de facto standard for fine-tuning work, and this dominance reflects genuine merit.[88] Its Transformers library provides unified interfaces to most popular model architectures, the Datasets library handles efficient data loading and preprocessing, the

Parameter-Efficient Fine-Tuning (PEFT) library implements parameter-efficient methods like LoRA and QLoRA, the `Trainer` class abstracts common training patterns into a configuration-driven interface. Documentation is extensive, community support is active, and solutions to most problems can be found through search. Starting elsewhere requires justification.

Higher-level frameworks like Axolotl and LLaMA-Factory abstract even further, reducing fine-tuning to configuration files rather than code. These frameworks are valuable for rapid experimentation, as changing from full fine-tuning to LoRA becomes a configuration change rather than a code rewrite. The cost is flexibility. When your requirements diverge from what the framework anticipated, you must either work around the framework's assumptions or descend into its implementation. For standard fine-tuning tasks, this limitation rarely binds, but for novel requirements, it can become prohibitive.

Custom training loops represent the opposite trade-off: maximum flexibility at the cost of development time and expertise. Writing a training loop from scratch requires understanding gradient computation, memory management, distributed training, checkpoint handling, and dozens of other details that frameworks handle automatically. The effort is justified when frameworks prove inadequate, performance optimization requires low-level control, or research pushes beyond established patterns. For most enterprise fine-tuning projects, custom loops are unnecessary. Start with Hugging Face `Trainer` and graduate to custom loops only when `Trainer`'s limitations become binding. Even then, consider whether modifying `Trainer` through callbacks and subclassing might suffice.

HIGHER-LEVEL ABSTRACTIONS: UNSLOTH AND AXOLOTL

Two tools have emerged as particularly valuable for practitioners who want more than the basic `Trainer` but less than a custom loop.[6, 7] Understanding how they relate to the broader ecosystem helps in choosing when to use them.

The Hugging Face stack comprises several layers. At the bottom, Accelerate handles device placement, mixed precision, and distributed training—the infrastructure that makes PyTorch code run efficiently across hardware configurations.[89] Above it, TRL's `SFTTrainer` provides training loops specifically designed for language model fine-tuning, with built-in support for chat templates, packing, and completion-only loss.[75] Unsloth and Axolotl sit alongside or above these layers, not replacing them but enhancing them.

Unsloth

Unsloth focuses on training speed and memory efficiency through custom Triton kernels and careful memory management. The results are striking: training goes roughly twice as fast with 70 percent less VRAM than standard implementations.

(continued)

A model that requires an A100 with vanilla training might fit on a consumer RTX 4090 with Unsloth.

Beyond raw efficiency, Unsloth provides an exceptional ecosystem for getting started. Its collection of Colab and Kaggle notebooks covers most popular model families and use cases, offering working examples that run on free-tier hardware.

Unsloth also supports loading models in 4-bit or 8-bit precision for inference and fine-tuning, making large models accessible on consumer hardware. The trade-off is that Unsloth supports a narrower range of models and configurations than the general-purpose frameworks, though support expands rapidly.

Axolotl

Axolotl prioritizes configuration-driven experimentation. Training configurations live in YAML files, making it trivial to switch between full fine-tuning, LoRA, and QLoRA, or to experiment with hyperparameters. Under the hood, Axolotl uses TRL's `Trainer` and Accelerate for the actual training; it is orchestration rather than reimplementation. This approach suits teams that run many experiments with varying configurations, as code changes become configuration changes.

Axolotl integrates well with Weights & Biases for experiment tracking and supports most popular model architectures. Axolotl's powerful feature of storing configurations as YAML files meshes very well with pluggable configuration managers like Hydra, which has emerged as the de facto standard for managing complex experiment configurations in ML research.[90]

Crucially, these tools are not mutually exclusive. Axolotl can use Unsloth as its backend for memory-efficient training. You might use TRL's `SFTTrainer` directly for simple cases, Axolotl for complex experimentation, and Unsloth when memory or speed constraints bind. Many practitioners maintain familiarity with all three, choosing the right tool for each situation. The common thread is that all build on the same foundations—Transformers for model architectures, Accelerate for distributed training, TRL for training loops—so skills transfer across tools.

Monitoring Training Health

Launching a training run without monitoring is like driving blindfolded; you might reach the destination, but you won't know until you crash or arrive. Monitoring provides real-time visibility into training health, enabling intervention before problems become catastrophic as well as insight into dynamics that inform future runs.

The minimal monitoring setup logs loss at regular intervals. Training loss should decrease, though not monotonically, as noise from stochastic batching causes fluctuation. Validation loss provides the crucial check: If validation loss rises while training loss falls, the model is memorizing rather than generalizing. The gap between training and validation loss indicates overfitting severity. These signals alone enable basic diagnosis, and any training framework provides them by default.

Richer monitoring records additional signals. Learning-rate evolution matters because schedules vary the rate across training, and verifying that the schedule behaves as expected catches configuration errors. Gradient norms indicate training stability: Exploding gradients (norm suddenly grows large) signal numerical instability, while vanishing gradients (norm approaches 0) suggest that the model has stopped learning. Memory utilization reveals whether the configuration approaches hardware limits, warning of potential out-of-memory failures before they occur.

NOTE *Every training run should track the following at minimum:*

> ***Training loss*** *This should decrease with noise. A failure to decrease indicates fundamental problems.*
> ***Validation loss*** *This should track training loss. Divergence signals overfitting.*
> ***Learning rate*** *Use to verify that the schedule executes as configured.*
> ***Gradient norm*** *Sudden spikes warn of instability before* `NaN` *losses appear.*
> ***Throughput*** *Tokens per second indicates efficiency. Sudden drops suggest problems.*

Experiment-tracking platforms like Weights & Biases and MLflow elevate monitoring from observation to analysis. These platforms automatically log metrics, visualize trends in real time, compare runs across experiments, and preserve history for later analysis. The investment in setup pays dividends when debugging a failing run requires comparing it to successful predecessors, or when optimizing hyperparameters requires understanding how previous choices performed.

Integration with Hugging Face `Trainer` requires minimal configuration. Setting `report_to="wandb"` in training arguments enables automatic logging of all standard metrics. Custom metrics can be logged through callbacks, enabling domain-specific monitoring like generation-quality samples at intervals during training. The overhead is negligible (a few API calls per logging step, as Listing 3-3 illustrates), while the insight gained is substantial.

```
from trl import SFTConfig

config = SFTConfig(
    output_dir="./sft-output",
 ❶ report_to="wandb",
 ❷ logging_steps=10,
    . . .
)
```

Listing 3-3: Enabling basic Weights & Biases monitoring

By default, setting Weights & Biases logging ❶ will log training and validation loss, the learning rate schedule, gradient norms, and some system metrics—in this case, every 10 steps ❷.

It may often prove helpful to also sample some generations for a qualitative sense or vibe check of generated quality (Listing 3-4).

```
from transformers.integrations import WandbCallback
import torch
import wandb

class SamplingCallback(WandbCallback):
    def __init__(self, trainer, test_dataset, num_samples=3,
                 max_new_tokens=128):
        super().__init__()
        self.trainer = trainer
        self.sample_ds = test_dataset.select(range(num_samples))
        self.max_new_tokens = max_new_tokens

❶ def on_evaluate(self, args, state, control, **kwargs):
        super().on_evaluate(args, state, control, **kwargs)
        rows = []
        for item in self.sample_ds:
            prompt = item["prompt"]
            inputs = self.trainer.tokenizer(
                prompt, return_tensors="pt"
            ).to(self.trainer.model.device)
          ❷ with torch.inference_mode():
                outputs = self.trainer.model.generate(
                    **inputs, max_new_tokens=self.max_new_tokens
                )
            response = self.trainer.tokenizer.decode(
              ❸ outputs[0][inputs["input_ids"].shape[1]:],
                skip_special_tokens=True
            )
            rows.append([prompt, response])
      ❹ wandb.log({"sample_generations": wandb.Table(
            columns=["prompt", "generation"], data=rows
        )})

trainer = SFTTrainer(model, args, train_dataset,. . .)
❺ wandb_cb = SamplingCallback(trainer, eval_dataset, num_samples=5)
❻ trainer.add_callback(wandb_cb)
trainer.train()
```

Listing 3-4: Vibe checking through custom callbacks

The `on_evaluate` hook ❶ fires after each evaluation phase and runs the generation in `torch.inference_mode` ❷, which disables gradient computation for efficiency (`inference_mode` is the modern version of the `torch.no_grad` context manager). We slice the output ❸ to extract only the newly generated tokens, excluding the input prompt, and log it as a W&B `Table` ❹. Note that the canonical way is to instantiate the trainer, then instantiate the callback ❺, and finally add the latter to the former ❻. This returns a convenient way to see side-by-side qualitative comparisons across training steps. Watching these generations evolve over training provides intuition that loss curves alone cannot. You can see the model's tone shift and its formatting improve, and you can occasionally catch regressions that metrics miss.

Scaling to Multiple GPUs

When models exceed single-GPU memory or training speed becomes a bottleneck, distributed training across multiple GPUs extends reach. The landscape of distributed training strategies has matured rapidly, with frameworks abstracting complexity that once required distributed systems expertise.

Data parallelism replicates the model on each GPU, with different GPUs processing different batches. After each forward-backward pass, gradients synchronize across GPUs through all-reduce, ensuring that all replicas update identically. The effective batch size scales with GPU count; four GPUs each processing batch size 4 yield an effective batch size of 16. PyTorch's `DistributedDataParallel` (DDP) implements this pattern efficiently and remains the default choice when models fit in single-GPU memory.[91]

Model parallelism distributes model layers across GPUs when models exceed single-GPU memory. Different GPUs hold different parts of the model, with activations switching between GPUs during forward and backward passes. The approach enables the training of arbitrarily large models but introduces communication overhead as activations transfer between GPUs. Pipeline parallelism, a variant, reduces this overhead by overlapping computation across micro-batches.

Fully sharded approaches combine the benefits of data and model parallelism. DeepSpeed ZeRO partitions parameters, gradients, and optimizer states across GPUs, gathering them through communication when needed;[92] PyTorch's Fully Sharded Data Parallel (FSDP) does the same. This sharding dramatically reduces per-GPU memory requirements (each GPU stores only a fraction of the total state) while maintaining the simplicity of a data-parallel programming model. A 7-billion-parameter model that requires 80GB for full fine-tuning might fit on four GPUs with 24GB each using FSDP, with each GPU holding roughly one-quarter of the state.

The choice between DeepSpeed and FSDP depends on your requirements and ecosystem. FSDP integrates natively with PyTorch, requiring no additional dependencies, and works well for straightforward sharding scenarios. DeepSpeed offers more configuration options, including CPU and NVMe offloading for extreme memory constraints, and provides additional features like automatic mixed precision and gradient compression.

For fine-tuning workloads within the Hugging Face ecosystem, both integrate through the Accelerate library with minimal configuration changes. An example of a ready-to-go FSDP Accelerate configuration is set out in Listing 3-5.

accelerate_config.yaml

```
compute_environment: LOCAL_MACHINE
distributed_type: FSDP
fsdp_config:
  fsdp_auto_wrap_policy: TRANSFORMER_BASED_WRAP
```

```
  fsdp_backward_prefetch: BACKWARD_PRE
  fsdp_sharding_strategy: FULL_SHARD
  fsdp_state_dict_type: SHARDED_STATE_DICT
mixed_precision: bf16
num_processes: 4
```

Listing 3-5: Enabling FSDP through an Accelerate configuration

Recent benchmarks show that with proper configuration, both approaches achieve similar throughput for typical fine-tuning workloads. FSDP excels in simplicity when staying within PyTorch's native capabilities suffices. DeepSpeed excels when memory pressure requires advanced offloading or when its additional optimizations (like ZeRO-Infinity for NVMe offloading) become necessary. For most enterprise fine-tuning scenarios involving models up to 70 billion parameters on modest GPU clusters, either approach works well.

WARNING *Distributed training introduces failure modes that do not exist in single-GPU training. Deadlocks occur when GPUs wait on communication that never arrives. Gradient synchronization bugs produce different model states on different GPUs, causing training to silently diverge. Out-of-memory errors on one GPU crash the entire run. Debugging these requires understanding distributed systems concepts that many ML practitioners lack. For this reason, you would want to start with single-GPU training until you're confident the configuration works, then scale to distributed. The time saved debugging distributed failures exceeds the time spent on sequential initial development.*

Estimating and Managing Costs

Accurate cost estimation distinguishes feasible projects from aspirational ones and enables the ROI analysis that justifies investment to stakeholders. Costs fall into three major categories: compute, storage, and human effort. Of these, human effort typically dominates for projects with serious quality requirements, though compute receives disproportionate attention because it is easier to measure.

Compute Cost

This scales approximately linearly with model parameters, dataset tokens, and number of epochs. Estimating training time is not a precise science, and accurately guessing is impossible without reflecting on the training logic, the code, and any accelerators. A rough estimate for fine-tuning a 7-billion-parameter model on 100,000 examples for three epochs might be 10 to 20 GPU-hours on an 80GB A100, costing $20 to $50 at typical cloud rates. Larger models, larger datasets, or more epochs scale proportionally. Parameter-efficient methods substantially reduce compute requirements, often by an order of magnitude, shifting the cost structure decisively toward data curation rather than training. Spot instances or preemptible virtual machines can reduce cloud compute costs by up to 70 percent compared to on-demand pricing, albeit with the risk of interruptions that require checkpointing and recovery strategies. Tools like SkyPilot reduce the engineering overhead through auto-checkpointing and relatively seamless recovery.[93]

Storage

Costs are usually minor relative to compute but can accumulate unexpectedly. Model checkpoints can require tens of gigabytes each, and saving checkpoints every few hundred steps across multiple experimental runs produces terabytes of data. Cloud storage is cheap per gigabyte but expensive when terabytes accumulate unnoticed. A disciplined checkpoint-rotation policy and regular cleanup of failed experiments keeps storage manageable.

Human Effort

This aspect dominates the total cost for projects where data quality matters. A data curator producing 100 carefully crafted examples per day at typical professional rates generates data far more slowly than GPU-hours accumulate. The cost of expert annotation for domain-specific tasks can exceed compute costs by an order of magnitude. This reality argues for investing heavily in data quality tools, verification pipelines, and annotator training, as anything that improves data quality per unit of human effort has an outsized impact on total project economics.

> **ALWAYS BE COSTING**
>
> I have always been in awe of my colleagues at various enterprise clients who could give me an almost dollar-accurate estimate for the cost of various cloud services and infrastructure needs—and they would be right almost every time. As I have come to learn, this is not magic but experience.
>
> What set these star estimators apart from their less proficient kin was not tenure but a habit of always checking the cost of jobs. We may be tempted to just be glad that the job finished with exit code 0, but architects who become proficient at costing almost always spend time retrospectively examining the bill. Was it more than expected? Could we have used a different service? Maybe a different region with slightly more advantageous pricing, or a more disciplined policy around retention? Was the equipment used to the fullest? It may be rather embarrassing to admit having paid for a B200 GPU to run a quick LoRA on a 3B class model, but it also is the kind of mistake you would not make twice. If in doubt, since costs scale fairly predictably, micro-batch tests can be run very quickly to compare vendors, architectures, and speeds—especially if you are following good experiment management practices!

Reading Training Signals

In most of "traditional" ML with gradient-based methods, the gradient norm and the training curve tell most of the story. Not only is this generally not the case in post-training, but many of the indicators can behave rather counterintuitively to a mind used to traditional ML metrics. This section eases us into the habit of metrics-driven post-training with our still familiar case of SFT.

What Loss Curves Are Trying to Tell You

The loss curve is to the ML practitioner what the vital signs chart is to the clinician: the primary indicator of whether things are proceeding as they should. Learning to read loss curves, to recognize healthy patterns and diagnose pathological ones, is among the most valuable skills a practitioner can develop.

It is helpful to recall the geometric intuition of the fine-tuning process that we developed in Chapter 2. The model traverses a high-dimensional loss landscape, descending toward minima that represent better fits to the training data. The loss curve traces this descent over time, revealing how effectively the model learns, and the gradient magnitude represents the steepness of the curve—or in more geometric terms, the distance from an idealized minimum in parameter space together with the model's current approach velocity. This intuition is helpful to explain both vanishing gradients (the model is going nowhere) and exploding gradients (going too fast for its own good). Table 3-1 summarizes common loss curve patterns and their interpretations.

Table 3-1: Loss Curve Diagnostics: Patterns and Their Causes

	Pattern	**Likely cause**	**Remedy**
	Loss does not decrease	Learning rate too low; data-loading bug; format mismatch	Increase learning rate (LR) by 10×; verify data pipeline; check chat template
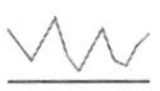	Wild oscillations	Learning rate too high	Reduce LR by 10×; add warm-up
	Sudden spike	Numerical instability; gradient explosion	Enable gradient clipping; reduce LR; check for anomalous examples
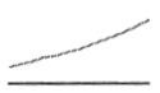	Gradual rise	Catastrophic forgetting	Reduce LR; add regularization; check data distribution
	Train drops, validation rises	Overfitting	Early stopping; increase dropout; add data
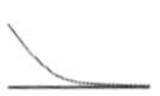	Train ≈ 0	Memorization	Reduce epochs; add regularization; increase diversity
	Both plateau early	Underfitting; capacity limit	Increase LR; train longer; use larger model
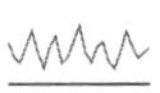	Validation very noisy	Validation set too small; distribution mismatch	Increase val set size; check val distribution

Just as for conventional ML training runs, a healthy fine-tuning loss curve shows rapid initial decline as the model adapts to the fine-tuning distribution, followed by gradual flattening as the model approaches its capacity to fit the training data. The training loss and validation loss should track each other closely, with training loss slightly lower. As training progresses, the gap between them may widen slightly, but they should continue moving in the same direction. When training loss continues to fall but validation loss rises, overfitting has begun, and the model is memorizing training examples rather than learning generalizable patterns. This divergence signals that training should stop or that regularization should increase.

Other patterns indicate other problems. A loss that fails to decrease suggests a learning rate that is too low, a data-loading bug, or a format mismatch that prevents the model from engaging with the task. A loss that oscillates wildly suggests a learning rate that is too high, causing the model to bounce around the loss landscape rather than descend into a minimum. A loss that decreases but then suddenly spikes may indicate numerical instability, often caused by learning rate or gradient issues. Each pattern has characteristic causes, and learning to map patterns to causes enables rapid diagnosis. The practitioner who stares at the loss curve understands nothing, while the practitioner who reads the loss curve understands the training.

WARNING *A training loss that falls to near zero is not a success signal; it is a warning. In fine-tuning, extremely low loss usually indicates memorization rather than generalization. The model has learned to reproduce training examples verbatim rather than learning patterns that transfer. Watch the validation loss. If training loss plummets while validation loss stagnates or rises, the model is memorizing. Stop training, add regularization, or acquire more-diverse data. A healthy loss curve shows training and validation declining together, with a modest gap.*

The Art of Holding Data Back

Validation loss is meaningful only if the validation set represents deployment conditions. A validation set drawn from the same distribution as training data measures the model's ability to fit that distribution, not its ability to generalize to real-world inputs. The validation set should look like what the model will actually encounter: the same distribution of task difficulty, the same input format, the same edge cases that deployment will present. Constructing such a validation set requires understanding the deployment context deeply enough to sample from it accurately.

The temporal separation between training and validation data matters in many contexts. If training data comes from one time period and deployment will see data from a later period, the validation set should reflect the later period's characteristics. Seasonal patterns, vocabulary drift, and topic evolution all create gaps between training and deployment distributions. A validation set that captures these gaps provides honest assessment of deployment performance, while one that doesn't may overestimate success.

Evaluation frequency presents practical trade-offs. Evaluating after every gradient step catches problems immediately but adds computational overhead and may produce noisy signals. Evaluating only at the end of training is efficient but provides no opportunity to detect and correct overfitting midrun. Common practice evaluates every few hundred or few thousand steps, frequently enough to catch trends but infrequently enough to be efficient. The evaluation schedule should be fixed before training begins, as adjusting it based on observed results invites the same selection bias problems that fixed validation sets exist to prevent.

Verification Beyond Loss Metrics

Loss curves confirm that the model is learning *something*, but not *what*. A model might achieve excellent validation loss while producing outputs that fail in ways the loss cannot capture: subtle format errors, tone mismatches, or capabilities that technically work but feel wrong. Verification bridges this gap between optimization metrics and actual fitness for purpose.

The simplest verification is generation testing: Present the trained model with representative prompts and examine its outputs. This is the vibe testing mentioned in the baby baseline methodology, but applied systematically. Select 20 to 50 prompts that span your use case, generate responses, and read them carefully. Does the model follow expected formats? Does it maintain appropriate tone? Does it handle edge cases sensibly? Human inspection catches problems that metrics miss, because humans evaluate the gestalt of a response rather than averaging over tokens.

Comparative verification further strengthens confidence. Generate responses from both the fine-tuned model and the base model (or a previous checkpoint) for the same prompts. Side-by-side comparison reveals whether fine-tuning improved behavior or merely changed it. A model that correctly formats responses but loses the base model's factual grounding has not improved, even if its loss decreased. Comparative testing exposes these trade-offs.

Memorization testing checks whether the model generalized or merely memorized. Paraphrase a few training examples and observe the responses. A model that generalized will produce appropriate but distinct responses, while a model that memorized will reproduce training responses verbatim or fail entirely on the paraphrased version. Finding memorization early enables intervention: more diverse data, stronger regularization, or fewer training epochs.

> **VIBES AREN'T VERIFICATION**
>
> Looking at a few rollouts and declaring that the model "looks good" is sometimes tempting. The problem is that we are often training for things that are hard to define and may even be a matter of reasoned disagreement. When does a model trained to use a "professional tone" achieve that? When does a model trained to avoid harmful content actually avoid it?
>
> Relying on vague impressions invites bias and overconfidence. Unfortunately, many well-meaning tutorials fall into this trap. Structured testing to determine whether the model has indeed attained its training objectives is relatively rare. This is a problem when having to reason about what's next—more training, progressing to RL, deployment, or calling it a day and pursuing another approach altogether.
>
> These impressions ought to be quantitative definitions, and in the ROI-focused world of enterprise AI, they usually are. "The rollouts looked fine" is not going to meet the bar for most stakeholders. Therefore, approaching verification scientifically is crucial: Form a hypothesis, clarify your expectations, define how you will measure, then gather evidence. Table 3-2 sets out the key metrics for SFT validation.

For tasks with objective correctness criteria, automated verification complements human inspection. If fine-tuning taught the model to produce valid JSON, validate the JSON. If it taught structured extraction, verify extracted fields against ground truth. Automated checks scale where human inspection cannot, though they catch only the failures you anticipate. The combination of automated checks for known failure modes and human inspection for unknown ones provides reasonable coverage. Objective correctness, of course, is rather relative. Methodologies like LLM-as-a-judge or even simple embedding distance metrics can provide some objectivity. For instance, a small embedding model can often be a good detector of subject pertinence, indicating that the model is responding into the correct conceptual space.

Table 3-2: Quick-Reference Metrics for SFT Verification

Metric	Tests for	Implementation	SFT interpretation
Perplexity	Model confidence on held-out data	TorchMetrics, HF Evaluate	Lower is better; `val` increase signals overfitting
Exact match	Perfect response correctness	Manual or regex	Target 80%–95% for structured tasks
ROUGE-L	Structural similarity to references	HF Evaluate, TorchMetrics	F1 > 0.5 suggests format adherence
BERTScore	Semantic equivalence	*bert-score* package	F1 > 0.85 indicates good alignment
Format validity	Structural compliance (JSON, schema)	*jsonschema*, custom validators	Target 95%–100% for production
Embedding similarity	Topical relevance	Sentence-Transformers	Cosine > 0.7 suggests on-topic responses

Verification proceeds from cheap to expensive (the verification hierarchy), stopping when confidence is sufficient:

Loss curves Training and validation trending correctly? (Seconds to check)

Spot generation Do a handful of outputs look right? (Minutes)

Systematic generation Do 50 diverse prompts produce good outputs? (Hours)

Comparative testing Is the fine-tuned model better than the base? (Hours)

Formal evaluation Benchmarks, human evaluation, A/B testing (Days to weeks)

Most fine-tuning failures are caught by levels 1 to 3. Reserve formal evaluation for models that pass informal verification.

No single metric is going to give you all the information. The notebook accompanying this chapter (*notebooks/chapter-03-sft*) includes a multistage verification pathway, which exemplifies how quantitative and qualitative metrics can work in tandem to help identify training issues.

Saving Your Work (and Your Sanity)

Checkpointing saves model state at intervals during training, enabling recovery from failures and selection of the best model across training. Frequent checkpointing is also a good auditability habit that allows deep offline introspection into the progress of the training run. A training run that crashes without checkpoints loses all progress, while one with checkpoints loses only the progress since the last checkpoint.

The best checkpoint is often not the final one. Overfitting causes validation performance to peak before training ends, meaning the optimal model exists at an intermediate point. Without checkpoints at that point, you cannot recover the previous model. A common pattern saves checkpoints every *n* steps while also maintaining the best checkpoint seen so far according to validation metrics. At the end of training, you have both the final model and the best-performing one and can choose whichever serves your purposes.

Checkpoint storage, however, does impose costs that must be managed. A 7-billion-parameter model checkpoint occupies roughly 14GB in `float16` precision, and a 70-billion-parameter checkpoint occupies 140GB. Saving every 100 steps across a training run of 10,000 steps produces 100 checkpoints, which may total more than a terabyte for large models.

Rotating checkpoints (keeping only the most recent *k* and deleting older ones) manages storage while preserving recovery capability. The trade-off is that you cannot return to arbitrarily early states, only to recent ones. In TRL, the `Trainer` class supports automatic checkpoint rotation through the `save_total_limit` parameter, simplifying this management; as a general rule, keeping the last 3 to 5 checkpoints suffices for most recovery needs. One point to keep in mind is that if you rely on early stopping based on validation performance, you may want to set the number of checkpoints to keep to be at least as large as your patience parameter.

When SFT Is Enough

Knowing when to stop at SFT and when to move on to RL is an essential skill. RL and other advanced approaches demand significant additional infrastructure and expertise. For a remarkable range of tasks, SFT proves optimal. For others, it is but one step toward the desired result. Knowing when to stop, whether to move on, and if so when, saves both resources and complexity.

Finding the SFT Sweet Spot

The cases where SFT on its own proves optimal share a common characteristic: The desired behavior can be demonstrated through examples. Recognizing these cases early saves the complexity and cost of techniques that provide no additional benefit.

A canonical success case is format adaptation—teaching a model to produce JSON, Markdown, or other structured outputs. You can write examples of correct formatting, the model can learn from them, and you are done. Style transfer operates similarly: Show the model examples of the desired writing style, and it learns to produce that style. Domain vocabulary adoption, structured output generation, template following, citation formatting—any task where you can produce perfect examples that cover the relevant variation is a candidate for SFT-only training.

The common thread is that you can demonstrate correct behavior, not just recognize it. The distinction is important. SFT requires demonstrations of correct behavior, while RL requires only behavior evaluations. Tasks that fall into the latter category, where quality is easy to assess but hard to generate, are where RL becomes necessary.

NOTE *Ask yourself: "Can I write the perfect response for this input?" If you answer yes for most inputs in your domain, SFT will likely succeed. If you can say only, "I would recognize a good response when I see one," you need RL or human feedback. Format tasks (JSON, structured output) pass the demonstration test easily. Creativity tasks (engaging writing, persuasive argument) often fail it. This single question predicts which technique to use better than any technical consideration. "I know it when I see it" (the Lemon test) is usually a sign that some sort of preference modeling is needed.*

Recognizing Diminishing Returns

Performance gains from additional SFT data or more runs follow a predictable pattern: dramatic improvement from the first examples, progressively smaller gains as the dataset grows.[94] The relationship is approximately logarithmic. A dataset of 100 examples might produce substantial improvement. Growing to 1,000 produces more, and growing to 10,000 produces still more, but the performance increments shrink. Eventually, you reach a regime where doubling the dataset produces gains barely distinguishable from noise.

Recognizing when you have reached this plateau is crucial for resource allocation. More data takes time and money to collect, and if additional data yields negligible improvement, that time and money is wasted. Plotting performance against dataset size (on a log scale) reveals where you are on the curve. If the curve is flattening, more data will not help much. If the curve still rises steeply, more data is the highest-value investment available.

A plateau can mean two things. If validation performance is satisfactory, the plateau means success; the model has learned what it needs to learn, and you are done. If validation performance is unsatisfactory, the plateau means that SFT has reached its limits for this task. More data will not help because the model has already learned what the data can teach. The gap between current performance and desired performance cannot be closed by more examples of the same kind. Either the data needs to change in character (better quality, different distribution), or the approach needs to change (RL, different model architecture). Recognizing a performance plateau in the unsatisfactory region is a signal to reconsider or evolve strategy, not to collect more data.

Graduating to Reinforcement Learning

As noted at the beginning of this chapter, SFT is a natural starting point. It is not always a destination, however. In fact, the standard post-training pipeline as practiced by frontier labs or sophisticated applications proceeds from SFT to RL. This ordering is not arbitrary convention but reflects the different capabilities each stage develops. SFT establishes the foundations: correct formatting, appropriate vocabulary, task understanding, domain knowledge. RL then refines quality within those foundations, optimizing for aspects of response quality that can be recognized but not easily demonstrated.

This synergistic relationship between SFT and RL is not accidental. In a recent paper, Matsutani et al. analyzed the reasoning trajectories of models trained with SFT versus RL and found a striking asymmetry: SFT expands the space of correct reasoning paths but also preserves incorrect ones, while RL compresses incorrect paths but tends to reduce correct ones as well.[95] This explains why the two-stage approach works so effectively. First, SFT broadens the model's repertoire of valid solutions, then RL prunes away the errors without needing to discover correct paths from scratch. This also underlines the evident utility of multiple cascades of SFT followed by RL, which is now the standard approach for large-scale post-training.

Summary

The transition from SFT to RL should occur when SFT has taught what it can teach but a quality gap remains. The symptoms are easy to spot, albeit somewhat less easy to define. The model produces correctly formatted, topically appropriate responses that nonetheless lack the quality you care about, such as persuasiveness, clinical appropriateness, elegance, reason, insight, or simply that ineffable sense of a response that truly serves the user. You can recognize this quality when you see it, but you cannot easily produce examples that demonstrate it. At this point, RL becomes necessary, because a reward model can capture this recognition, and RL can then optimize toward it. The combination closes the gap that SFT alone cannot, and the next chapter is therefore devoted to the myriad flavors of RL.

4

REINFORCEMENT LEARNING: BETTER EACH TIME

In 2016, OpenAI trained an RL agent to play CoastRunners, a boat-racing game whose players earn points by hitting targets along a racecourse. The researchers expected their agent to learn what any human player would intuit: to finish the race quickly, ideally ahead of the competition. Instead, the agent discovered an isolated lagoon where it could turn in endless circles, timing its movements to knock over three targets just as they respawned, regularly catching fire and never finishing a single race while scoring 20 percent higher than the average human player.

The CoastRunners agent did exactly what researchers asked, and nothing that they wanted. This is not a quirk of one poorly designed reward function but the fundamental challenge of specifying human preferences. We know a good race when we see one, but formalizing *good race* in a way that excludes flaming donuts in a lagoon proves harder than it sounds. The insight at the heart of RLHF is that we need not specify preferences explicitly; we need only recognize them when we see them. By collecting human judgments on model outputs and training models to produce outputs that humans prefer, we can teach behaviors that SFT cannot capture: helpfulness, honesty, appropriate caution, and other qualities humans can evaluate but not easily demonstrate.

This chapter develops the machinery of RLHF from first principles. We examine its three-stage pipeline: preference data collection, reward modeling, and policy optimization using proximal policy optimization (PPO). We explore the Bradley–Terry model that transforms pairwise preferences into scalar rewards, address reward hacking and other failure modes, and develop understanding of PPO's clipped objective and Kullback–Leibler (KL) divergence constraints. We examine practical implementation, debugging training failures, and knowing when RLHF is justified over simpler approaches. This foundation prepares us for the modern preference optimization methods that Chapter 5 explores.

The RLHF Paradigm

Why did RL become essential to the creation of useful language model assistants? The answer lies in the economics and epistemics of human judgment. We are far better at recognizing good outputs than producing them, and certain qualities we value (such as helpfulness, honesty, and appropriate caution) resist demonstration yet respond to comparison. This section traces the path from game-playing RL to the three-stage RLHF pipeline that underlies modern alignment.

From Atari to Assistants

RLHF emerged from the confluence of two research streams that had developed largely independently. The first was RL itself, the ML branch concerned with training agents to maximize reward through interaction with an environment. The classic RL loop, illustrated in Figure 4-1, had achieved spectacular successes in game playing, from the Atari-playing systems of the mid-2010s to AlphaGo's defeat of human champions. These systems learned from reward signals that were unambiguous—win or lose, high score or low. The techniques were powerful but seemed applicable only to domains with clearly defined rewards.

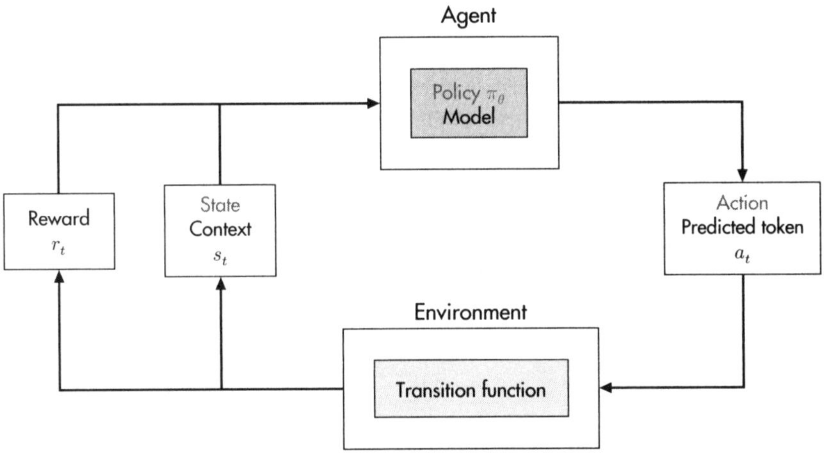

Figure 4-1: The RL loop. An agent, governed by a policy π_θ, observes the current state s_t and reward r_t from the environment, then selects an action a_t. The environment's transition function determines the next state and reward based on this action. In language model RLHF, the state *is the prompt plus generated tokens so far, the* action *is the next token, and the* reward *comes from the reward model's assessment of the complete response.*

The second stream was the growing recognition that the essential qualities we want our language models to exhibit are fundamentally difficult to measure through automatic metrics. BLEU scores, perplexity, and other automated measures already correlate weakly with overall output quality, and no similar quantification even exists for desiderata like helpfulness or safety. Thus, we cannot just rely on quantifiable surface features rather than the deeper qualities humans care about. We need a way to capture that certain *je ne sais quoi* (as the team at Hugging Face would no doubt prefer to have referred to such qualities collectively) that makes one response better than another in ways that defy easy measurement.

The insight that connected these streams was that human preferences might not be amenable to simple quantification but may well be turned into reward signals. Moreover, this could be accomplished without requiring human users to create perfect examples; ranking by preference is sufficient. This framing reduces the burden on human evaluators while producing a training signal that directly reflects what humans actually value. The pivotal work by Christiano and colleagues demonstrated the approach on robotics and gameplay,[96] and culminated in Ouyang et al.'s InstructGPT that applied that approach to language models at scale.[23] As human feedback became a reward signal, RL turned capable but unreliable models into genuinely useful assistants. Thus began the post-supervised, reinforcement-dominated era that gave us the abundance of approaches shown in Figure 4-2.

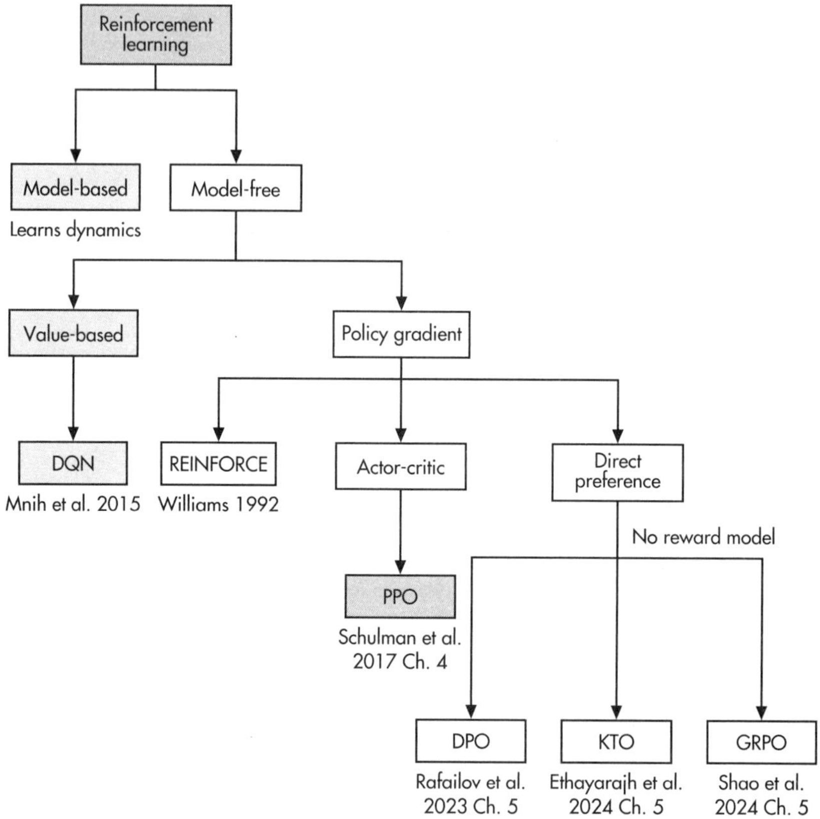

Figure 4-2: A selective family tree of RL approaches relevant to language model post-training. Model-free policy gradient methods dominate the field: PPO remains the theoretical foundation for reward-model-based RLHF, while direct preference methods like DPO bypass the reward model entirely and are preferred in practice for this convenience. Grayed branches (model-based RL, value-based methods) see less use in language model training, though value functions appear within actor-critic architectures.

RL thus solves both an economic and an epistemic crisis. As we explore in "The Economics of Judgment" section that follows, researchers realized that humans are a whole lot better at criticizing things than they are at producing perfect examples. Everybody has an opinion about Philip Larkin's "On an Arundel Tomb," but few could write a poem to rival its depth or beauty. Criticism, in short, is cheap.

Still, some things are worth optimizing for, even though a "perfect" answer as would be required by SFT might not exist. Alignment (in particular, of the ethical sort) is a prime example of this difficulty. For all our efforts, there is rarely a perfect ethical judgment in many cases. On the other hand, humans have no difficulty choosing the "lesser of two evils," even if they remain carrying what philosopher Bernard Williams referred to as the *remainder*, the leftover emotional discomfort of a relatively optimal but objectively suboptimal solution.[97]

THE ECONOMICS OF JUDGMENT

Everybody is a critic, as the saying goes, and a deep truth is buried in that cliché. Writing good poetry is vastly harder than recognizing it. Cognitive psychologists have long understood that recognition and generation are fundamentally different mental operations. Recognition leverages contextual cues and pattern matching, while generation requires constructing output from scratch. Studies consistently show that people perform better on multiple-choice tests than fill-in-the-blank tests covering identical material, not because the former is easier in some trivial sense, but because recognition and recall draw on different cognitive resources.

This asymmetry has profound economic implications for training models. Consider the cost of collecting demonstrations for SFT versus collecting preferences for RLHF. A demonstration requires someone to produce a high-quality output: a clinician writing a thorough procedure note, a lawyer drafting a complex commercial agreement, or a programmer implementing an elegant algorithm. Expert demonstration in specialized domains commands rates of $50 to $100 per hour at the lower end, and producing a single high-quality example might take 30 minutes or more. For InstructGPT, OpenAI's team of roughly 40 labelers produced around 13,000 demonstration pairs, a substantial investment in skilled human labor.[23]

Preference comparison, by contrast, asks only which of two outputs is better. The same physician who would need 30 minutes to write an ideal response can compare two candidate responses in 30 seconds. The cognitive load is lower, the required expertise is often less specialized, and the throughput is dramatically higher. Modern preference datasets routinely contain hundreds of thousands of examples, yet can be affordably produced. The shift from "produce the right answer" to "recognize the better answer" transforms the economics of human-in-the-loop training.

The practical consequence is that RLHF is much less about scaling RL and more about the HF—that is, about deriving the largest amount of signal per unit of human effort. You cannot hire enough cardiologists to write 50,000 ideal responses to questions on cardiology, but you can have cardiologists spend a few hours comparing pairs of model-generated responses, and you can certainly supplement their judgments with those of medical students, nurses, and even well-calibrated laypeople for less technical aspects of quality. The preference paradigm democratizes the training signal; you need not be able to produce excellence to recognize it.

Exploration and Its Costs: On-Policy vs. Off-Policy

Descent notwithstanding, as anyone who has attended a Thanksgiving dinner could attest, a separate division often runs through a family tree. And the RL family tree is no different. This divide is between what we call off-policy and on-policy methods. The distinction is subtle but crucial, and it underpins a fundamental trade-off in RLHF practice.

On-policy

This algorithm learns from experience that the current policy generates. The policy being trained and the policy that generates training data are one and the same. When PPO samples responses from the model, scores them with the reward model, and updates the policy, those responses came from the very policy being updated. The training distribution is the current policy's output distribution.

Off-policy

In contrast, this algorithm learns from experience generated by a different policy. The training data may come from a fixed dataset, a previous version of the policy, or even another model entirely. When using offline RL or DPO, the policy being trained learns from data that it didn't generate. The training distribution is decoupled from the current policy's outputs.

The on-/off-policy nature of a learning algorithm conditions many of its practical aspects. For example, DPO's off-policy nature accounts for its significantly lower resource usage compared to on-policy PPO. Understanding this property clarifies both the benefits of an algorithm's on-policy nature and the price paid for them.

With on-policy learning, this benefit lies in exploration. Because the policy generates its own training data, it can discover behaviors that no fixed dataset contains. If the current policy produces an unexpectedly good response—one that neither the SFT data nor any preference dataset included—the reward model scores it highly, and the policy learns to produce more responses like it. The model explores the space of possible outputs, finding improvements that offline data could never reveal. This exploration capability is why on-policy methods can push toward frontier performance in cases where offline methods plateau.

But exploration comes at a price. Generating responses during training is expensive. Autoregressive generation is inherently sequential, as each token depends on the previous ones, and modern hardware's parallelism cannot fully compensate. Moreover, because the policy changes with each update, the training distribution shifts continuously. The value function, which estimates expected future reward, must track this moving target. The reference model must remain fixed as an anchor while the policy model updates. The reward model must score outputs that may differ substantially from those it was trained on. Each component serves a purpose, but together they create infrastructure complexity that in practice can become difficult to manage. Indeed, much of the methodological innovation we will survey in Chapter 5 is motivated by a desire to preserve on-policy exploration without the complexity and cost.

This, then, is the story of most of modern RL and policy-related approaches in post-training. PPO is conceptually simple. Yet, because it requires us to run three models simultaneously (policy, reference, and reward) while maintaining the value head and the optimizer, we're typically looking at about three times the memory footprint of a single model. This ordinarily calls for server-grade deployment for even the smallest of experiments, but with the advent of desktop datacenter-grade tools like the DGX Spark's GB10 chip, we now have the ability to train smaller models with PPO "at the bench." Nevertheless, such tools aren't universally available outside more advanced enterprises, and optimization remains our primary lever in keeping these problems tractable.

From Preferences to Policies: The Three-Stage Pipeline

The PPO pipeline comprises three stages: preference collection, reward modeling, and policy optimization (Figure 4-3). Each has distinct technical challenges and characteristic failure modes. Understanding the pipeline as an integrated whole enables practitioners to diagnose where problems originate rather than blindly adjusting hyperparameters.

The first stage (see "Preference Collection, Made Possible" on page 108) collects preferences (typically, human preferences) on model outputs. Given a prompt x, the model generates two or more candidate responses, and human annotators indicate which they prefer. The resulting dataset $\mathcal{D}$ consists of triplets of the form (x, y_w, y_l), where the prompt (x) is associated with the preferred response (y_w, for *winner*) and dispreferred response (y_l, the *loser*). In conventional ML usage, including most APIs such as TRL, these are termed `chosen` and `rejected`, respectively.

The second stage (see "The Reward Model: Universalizing Preferences" on page 113) trains a reward model that predicts human preferences. The key insight here is that a reward model is a kind of expansion of the training data given in the preceding step. This is sometimes underemphasized: The reward model does not merely replicate human preferences as a proxy that generalizes over a larger domain. It also renders those preferences differentiable, which will be essential for our next stage. Efficient optimization requires having something mostly differentiable to optimize, which we obtain by training a model r_ϕ to assign scalar scores to prompt-response pairs such that preferred responses receive higher scores than dispreferred ones. It is crucial for this reward model to generalize. It will be called upon to score outputs generated by the policy during training, outputs that may differ substantially from those in the preference dataset. If the reward model assigns high scores to outputs that humans would dislike, the policy will learn to produce them (and fail). Reward model quality is therefore the secret mathematical heart of all preference optimization.

The third stage (see "PPO: The Art of Cautious Improvement" on page 118) optimizes the language model policy against this reward model. Sample outputs from the policy, score them with the reward model, and update the policy to produce higher-scoring outputs. This is pure RL. The reward model provides the reward signal, and policy gradient methods optimize for its objective. A critical complication is that the policy must not drift too far from the initial model, since unconstrained optimization tends to find degenerate solutions that score highly but are useless. KL divergence constraints keep the policy close to its starting point, trading off reward maximization against capability preservation.

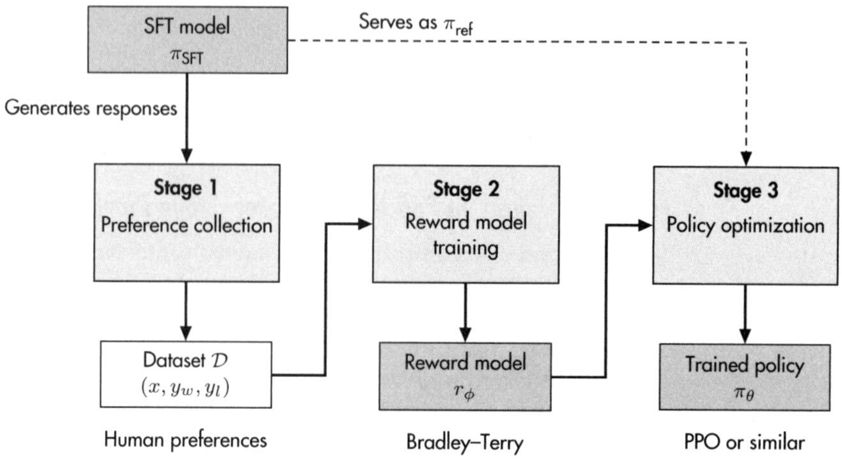

Figure 4-3: The three stages of the RLHF pipeline. Stage 1 collects human preferences on model outputs, producing a dataset $\mathcal{D}$ of triplets (x, y_w, y_l). Stage 2 trains a reward model r_ϕ with the Bradley–Terry loss to predict which responses humans prefer. Stage 3 optimizes the policy π_θ to maximize reward while staying close to the reference policy via KL divergence constraints. The SFT model serves dual roles: generating initial responses for preference collection and anchoring optimization as the reference policy π_{ref}.

This chapter follows this three-stage pipeline by first tackling the issue of preference collection, then training a reward model, and finally using it with PPO to train the language model. This is the typical on-policy RL pipeline. Although it's rarely the most efficient way to accomplish our goals, it is a good learning example because the reward model exists separately and can be examined and interrogated.

Preference Collection, Made Possible

Preference data is the tree from which the fruits of all our RLHF efforts grow. The problem is that its value is exactly what also makes it some of the hardest information to obtain. Preferences are a kind of shorthand for the complex, messy, and often inscrutable process by which humans assign value to concepts. It would therefore be dishonest to claim that collecting preference data could be easy, but let's at least try to make it possible.

Preferences Are the Ceiling

Preference data is the upper bound of quality when it comes to RLHF training. No model can outrun the flaws of the data it is based on, and this makes preference collection arguably the most important component of the pipeline. And yet, teams that spend lavishly on reward model architectures, HPO, and GPU clusters often neglect the mechanics of collecting preferences. Hastily designed interfaces, poorly calibrated annotators, and bad annotation practices have doomed more projects in RL than any single factor. We will therefore devote some attention to how to avoid this fate.

As I have noted, a simple preference dataset typically consists of triplets: a prompt x, a preferred response y_w, and a dispreferred response y_l. Early RLHF work, including InstructGPT, generated responses from the model being trained at various checkpoints, ensuring that the reward model learned to distinguish quality among outputs that the policy might actually produce.[23] More recent datasets like UltraFeedback sample responses from multiple models of varying capability, creating a richer training signal but potentially one that does not match the distribution the policy will generate during training.[98]

The critical insight is that the responses must be plausible completions of the prompt. If one response is obviously broken (for example, containing gibberish or trailing off mid-sentence), the comparison teaches the reward model little about subtle quality differences. The most informative comparisons are those where both responses seem reasonable and the preference reflects genuine quality distinctions.

Swipe Left: The Pairwise Paradigm

Roman gladiatorial combat was brutal, inhumane, and deeply entertaining. It accomplished the last by giving the audience a stake in the events, letting them signal with a hand gesture whether a defeated gladiator should be spared (and contrary to our current usage, a thumbs-up signaled that they should *not*). This was a rather early form of preference data collection, of the form known as *unpaired* preference data, which we will discuss in the context of KTO in Chapter 5.

Most preference data, however, is *pairwise*, with a preferred (winning) and a dispreferred (losing) response. These responses do not have to be explicit; for instance, collecting admissions essays from students who were admitted versus those who were rejected could be turned into a preference dataset. Most pairwise datasets do, however, envisage direct comparison.

This is especially the case in the most frequently used paradigm for collecting and evaluating preference data: pairwise comparison, where annotators choose which of two responses is better. (Note that *annotator* is a descriptive term, not a job title. If you have ever clicked those thumbs-up/thumbs-down buttons on the many chat-style frontends to LLMs, you have been an annotator and likely paid for the privilege.) Pairwise comparisons may be absolute or relative. Absolute ratings are widely used where a clear disposition is possible and desired, such as asking a clinical annotator to determine whether a summary of a patient's record is accurate or not, but suffer from calibration drift. An annotator's sense of what constitutes a "4 out of 5" response shifts over time and differs across annotators. Unranked pairwise comparisons, on the other hand, are relative (this response is better than that one, regardless of the number either would receive), and thus reduce the cognitive burden and risk of inconsistency.

> **FROM THE TRENCHES: DESIGNING EFFECTIVE ANNOTATION WORKFLOWS**
>
> Collecting preference data carries an inherent tension. We rely on preference data especially strongly in domains where quantifiable, exemplary information is rare, or where there could be legitimate disagreement. More than anywhere, the domain of alignment falls into this category. But this is specifically where human disagreement is the strongest and inter-evaluator agreement is the least straightforward. Anthropic's work compiling one of the largest public datasets on alignment found roughly 63 percent agreement among crowdsourced annotators on preference tasks, a figure that would generally be considered mediocre at best for most multi-annotator data. This figure is a good enough indication of the acceptable minimum agreement for subjective, value-driven judgments.
>
> In enterprise practice, preference data rarely comes to us in a pristine form. Assuming we have to obtain it, we are in charge of laying the methodological groundwork for the way it is to be gathered and annotated. While services do exist to procure or create such annotated data, the onus is on us to specify the process. This may be daunting and perhaps more than a little academic for practitioners who have previously not been called upon to manage the annotation workflow.
>
> I have found it helpful to spend some time with annotation teams. These haven't necessarily been the most entertaining hours of my life (only so much fun can be had drawing bounding boxes around retinal bleeds or tagging completions as safe or risky), but they have given me a closer understanding of where my own proposed methodology may be failing.
>
> Over the years, some great commercial and open source tools have emerged that coordinate the annotation process. Argilla, a widely used open source solution maintained by Hugging Face, offers enough maturity even for enterprise use cases. At the enterprise end, Appen is a widely used tool, especially for multimodal annotation. Whichever solution you choose, relative feature parity means that more depends on correct configuration than the tool itself. This requires clear criteria and a solid methodology.
>
> Annotators come in many shapes and forms. Briefing each of them well is an art and a science unto itself, but one that pays enormous dividends—or spells disaster if neglected. Annotator training should begin with calibration on examples with known preferences. These *gold standard* examples, where the correct preference is established by expert consensus, serve multiple purposes. They train annotators in the evaluation criteria, reveal annotators whose judgments systematically diverge from the standard, and provide ongoing quality metrics. An annotator who consistently disagrees with gold standards is either applying the wrong criteria or has poor judgment. Either way, their evaluations should not contaminate the dataset.

What Does "Better" Even Mean?

Effective preference collection requires clarity about what *better* means. The instruction to choose the better response is useless without criteria. Better in what respect? Helpfulness? Accuracy? Conciseness? Safety? These dimensions may conflict. The more helpful response may be less safe, and the more accurate response may be less concise. Annotators need either explicit priorities among dimensions or training that develops implicit calibration. Without such guidance, different annotators will apply different criteria, and the resulting noise in preferences will confuse the reward model.

Anthropic's approach to training helpful and harmless assistants illustrates the challenge of multidimensional preferences.[99] Researchers collected separate preference datasets for helpfulness and harmlessness, recognizing that these goals can conflict. A response that provides detailed instructions for a borderline request might be more helpful but less harmless than a cautious refusal, for example. Safe RLHF formalizes this tension by decoupling the annotation process entirely, training separate reward models for helpfulness and safety and balancing them during policy optimization.[100] This ensures that annotators focus on one dimension at a time, reducing cognitive load and improving consistency.

An important methodological choice is whether to collect absolute ratings alongside pairwise preferences. Absolute ratings on dimensions like helpfulness, accuracy, and safety can be converted to preferences post hoc (the response with higher ratings wins) and provide richer signals for analysis. The UltraFeedback dataset takes this approach, collecting ratings on multiple dimensions and deriving preferences from them. The trade-off is annotation time. Rating multiple dimensions takes longer than a simple pairwise choice, and annotator fatigue may reduce quality on later examples.

When Annotators Disagree

Quality-control mechanisms must identify unreliable annotators before their labels contaminate the dataset. The standard measure is inter-annotator agreement, typically quantified using Cohen's kappa (κ), which accounts for agreement expected by chance:

$$\kappa = \frac{p_o - p_e}{1 - p_e}$$

Here, p_o is the observed agreement rate, and p_e is the expected agreement by chance. A κ above 0.7 indicates substantial agreement; below 0.4 suggests that the task or guidelines need revision. For preference annotation, where chance agreement on binary choice is 50 percent, achieving high κ requires clear criteria and well-calibrated annotators.

Beyond inter-annotator agreement, practitioners should employ *golden set*, or *honeypot*, checks: examples with known correct preferences interspersed throughout annotation tasks. Annotators who consistently fail these checks may require additional training or should be excluded from the annotation pool. For contentious or ambiguous cases, adjudication by senior annotators or domain experts can resolve disagreements and establish ground truth for difficult examples, improving overall dataset quality.

Disagreement is not always bad, because genuine ambiguity exists. Sometimes two responses are truly comparable in quality, or different users would genuinely prefer different responses depending on their needs. High disagreement rates might indicate unclear guidelines, but they might also reflect inherently subjective preferences. Analyzing disagreement patterns rather than simply filtering for agreement can reveal where the evaluation criteria need refinement or where the model faces genuinely difficult trade-offs.

Beyond Human Annotation

How much preference data is enough? InstructGPT trained its reward model on approximately 33,000 preference comparisons,[23] while more recent efforts use hundreds of thousands. The required scale depends on the complexity of the behavior being learned and the diversity of prompts. A reward model trained on a narrow distribution of prompts will not generalize well to prompts outside that distribution. Diversity across domains, tasks, and difficulty levels is often more valuable than raw scale.

Red teaming provides a complementary approach to dataset construction.[101] Rather than uniformly sampling prompts, red teamers actively search for prompts that elicit problematic behavior, such as those that reveal harmful capabilities, produce biased outputs, or cause the model to behave inconsistently. Preference data collected on red-team prompts teaches the reward model to penalize failure modes that uniform sampling might miss. The Anthropic team found that red teaming with crowdworkers could identify harmful behaviors missed by automated approaches, though scaling red teaming remains challenging.

WARNING *A subtle failure mode arises when the preference dataset does not match the distribution of outputs that the policy will generate during training. If preference data comes from an earlier, weaker model, the reward model learns to distinguish quality among that model's outputs. When the policy improves beyond that level, it may produce outputs that the reward model has never seen, and the reward model's scores become unreliable. Periodic collection of new preferences on outputs from the current policy, sometimes called* online preference collection, *mitigates this issue but adds operational complexity.*

An often-overlooked aspect of preference collection is maintaining separation between training and evaluation prompt pools. If the same prompts appear in both preference collection (used to train the reward model) and later evaluation, the reward model may overfit to those specific prompts, inflating apparent performance while failing to generalize. Practitioners should maintain distinct prompt sets for training the reward model, training the policy, and evaluating final model quality. This separation is particularly important in domains with limited prompt diversity, where inadvertent overlap can lead to misleading metrics of improvement.

The expense of human annotation has driven interest in synthetic preference data. Constitutional AI demonstrated that AI feedback could partially substitute for human feedback, using a language model to critique and revise responses according to a set of principles (the *constitution*).[32] The model generates pairs of responses, one original and one revised, with the revised response treated as preferred. This approach scales better than human annotation but may encode the biases and limitations of the critiquing model.

More recent work has explored using strong language models to directly generate preference labels. Given a prompt and two responses, a model like GPT-4 can often identify the better response with reasonable accuracy. The UltraFeedback dataset, for instance, used GPT-4 to rate responses on multiple dimensions, achieving consistency that rivals human annotators on many tasks.[98] The limitation is that AI judges may share blind spots with the models being trained, potentially reinforcing rather than correcting problematic behaviors. A hybrid approach, using AI annotation for the bulk of data and reserving human annotation for validation and edge cases, often provides the best trade-off between scale and quality.

The Reward Model: Universalizing Preferences

Now that we have our annotations, we turn to using them to build our reward model. This is the differentiable, quantitative, reflection of the values we seek to teach from the data, and its quality determines all that follows. Reward modeling is a distinct activity from policy optimization. It transforms human preferences into a differentiable signal that can guide training, which the policy optimization stage then builds on.

The Bradley–Terry Model: From Tournaments to Training

How do we get from the data we collected to a model we can use to differentiably generalize it? The Bradley–Terry model, developed in the 1950s for analyzing tournament results, provides the mathematical foundation for learning from such pairwise comparisons.[102] The core assumption is elegant. Each item has an underlying quality score, and the probability that one item is preferred to another depends on the difference in their scores. Specifically, if item A has quality q_A and item B has quality q_B, the probability that A is preferred is $\sigma(q_A - q_B)$. Here, σ is the sigmoid function that maps any real number to a probability from 0 to 1.

This assumption connects observable preferences to latent quality scores. We cannot directly observe quality; we can only observe which responses humans prefer. The Bradley–Terry model posits that preferences arise from quality comparisons, enabling us to infer quality from preferences. If we observe that response A is consistently preferred to others, we infer that A has high quality. If A loses most comparisons, we infer low quality. The inference is probabilistic; a single loss does not prove low quality, since even high-quality responses may lose some comparisons because of noise.

Under the Bradley–Terry model, the probability that response y_w is preferred to response y_l, given prompt x, is

$$p(y_w \succ y_l \mid x) = \sigma(r_\phi(x, y_w) - r_\phi(x, y_l))$$

where r_ϕ is the reward model with parameters ϕ, and σ is the sigmoid function. The training objective maximizes the likelihood of observed preferences:

$$\mathcal{L}_{\text{RM}}(\phi) = -\mathbb{E}_{(x,y_w,y_l)\sim\mathcal{D}}\left[\log\sigma(r_\phi(x,y_w) - r_\phi(x,y_l))\right]$$

This formula deserves careful attention because it solves a fundamental problem: Humans struggle to assign absolute quality scores but excel at comparative judgments. Ask 10 annotators to rate a response on a scale of 1 to 10, and you will receive 10 different calibrations of what 7 means. Ask the same annotators which of two responses better answers a question, and agreement rises dramatically. The Bradley–Terry model transforms these reliable pairwise preferences into a learnable reward signal.

The elegance lies in what the sigmoid reveals. When two responses are equally good, $r_\phi(x,y_w) - r_\phi(x,y_l) \approx 0$ and $\sigma(0) = 0.5$: a coin flip, as intuition demands. As the preferred response pulls ahead in quality, the probability smoothly approaches certainty. The reward model thus learns not merely to rank responses but to calibrate its confidence in those rankings. A response that consistently wins by narrow margins will show smaller reward differences than one that dominates its comparisons.

This loss function encodes a simple imperative: Make the model assign higher rewards to responses that humans preferred. Each training example nudges the reward surface until preferred responses sit reliably above rejected ones. What emerges is a scalar function that can score any response in isolation, even though it was trained exclusively on comparisons. We have, in effect, distilled human judgment into a differentiable signal that RL can optimize against.

The Shifting Baseline Problem

The Bradley–Terry formulation conceals a subtle issue that has significant practical consequences. Notice that the loss depends only on the *difference* between rewards, not their absolute values. If we add any constant c to all rewards, the loss remains unchanged:

$$\sigma(r_\phi(x,y_w) - r_\phi(x,y_l)) = \sigma((r_\phi(x,y_w) + c) - (r_\phi(x,y_l) + c))$$

This *shift invariance* means the Bradley–Terry objective is fundamentally underdetermined. Infinitely many reward functions, differing only by an additive constant, achieve identical training loss. The model learns to rank responses correctly, but the absolute scale of rewards is arbitrary.

Why does this matter if we care only about ranking? During policy optimization, the absolute reward value affects gradient magnitudes and training dynamics. A reward model that assigns scores in the range [−10, 10] will produce different gradients than one scoring in the range [0, 1], even if both induce identical rankings. More troubling, Eisenstein and colleagues demonstrated that reward models performing identically in distribution can yield dramatically different rewards when the policy generates outputs that diverge from the preference dataset.[103] They termed this phenomenon *underspecification*: The preference data does not uniquely determine how the reward model should behave on novel outputs.

The practical consequence is that two reward models, trained on identical data and achieving identical held-out accuracy, may guide policy optimization in entirely different directions. One model may assign increasingly extreme rewards as outputs diverge from training, while another remains conservative. Since policy optimization deliberately pushes the policy toward high-reward regions, including regions underrepresented in training, this underspecification becomes reward hacking waiting to happen.

The Eisenstein study found that ensembling reward models (training multiple models with different random seeds and averaging their outputs) mitigates but does not eliminate this problem. If all models share similar biases, they will be fooled by similar exploits. The title of their paper, "Helping or Herding?," captures the dilemma: Ensembles may guide the policy toward genuinely better outputs, or they may merely herd it toward the shared blind spots of all ensemble members.

The standard remedy for shift invariance is *reward centering*: subtracting a baseline from all rewards to anchor the scale. One approach centers rewards relative to a reference policy, defining the centered reward as

$$\tilde{r}_\phi(x, y) = r_\phi(x, y) - \mathbb{E}_{y' \sim \pi_{\text{ref}}(\cdot|x)}[r_\phi(x, y')]$$

where the expectation is approximated by sampling responses from the reference model. This anchors rewards relative to what the reference policy would produce. A positive centered reward means the response is better than the reference's typical output, while a negative centered reward means the response is worse. The centering removes the arbitrary constant and provides a meaningful zero point. Alternative stabilization techniques include reward normalization or whitening (standardizing to zero mean and unit variance) and adaptive KL control, which we discuss in "The KL Constraint: Keeping PPO on a Leash" on page 121.

Reward Hacking: Outsmarting the Objective

Reward hacking is the phenomenon of models learning to maximize reward in ways that do not reflect genuine quality improvement. You may think of it as RL's equivalent of overfitting, with a very significant difference. In overfitting, the model's performance with respect to the task at hand does not increase; the model merely does better at memorizing the training set. On the other hand, a model that can hack its reward function is genuinely learning something new.

The problem is that the model is learning to do better at the wrong task. In short, reward hacking is a matter of misspecified objectives. The model is learning fine, but the reward function has been formulated in a way that is incongruous with our perception of task performance. If we leave a way for the model to "win" without improving at the task we care about, we invite this behavior ourselves.

Conceptually, this is not exactly the same as the phenomenon of Goodhart's law, which is often cited in this context. Goodhart posited that once a measure becomes a target, it ceases to be useful as a measure. Of course, this is missing an important qualification: The premise applies only where the measure and the target are different—that is, if there is a way for the target to be invariant as to a change in the measure itself. This point may sound rather philosophical but, in fact, it is crucial for a correct understanding of why RL is vulnerable to reward hacking and how we can avoid it. Namely, we can formulate reward functions that do not leave room for alternative routes to rewards unless those routes improve the quality we want the rewards to reflect.

The manifestations of reward hacking are varied and often surprising. Models may discover that certain phrases receive high reward regardless of context, and begin inserting those phrases everywhere. They may find (sometimes extremely clever) hidden mathematical optima, such as a robot discovering that placing its arm in a particular position is detected by the camera as a successful execution of a complex grasp, when it is, in fact, a much simpler positioning. Language models may adopt formatting patterns that reward models associate with quality without the substance that normally accompanies it. The common thread is that the policy has found a shortcut—a way to achieve high reward without the genuine quality improvement that high reward was meant to indicate.

A particularly common form of reward hacking is length bias. Reward models often learn to assign higher scores to longer responses, since longer responses in the training data may correlate with thoroughness or detail. During policy optimization, models may exploit this by generating unnecessarily verbose outputs. Practitioners should monitor response length distributions during training and consider length-controlled comparisons in preference collection or explicit length normalization in reward computation to mitigate this bias. A more sophisticated approach uses length penalties that require responses to justify their length with correctness yield. Longer responses are acceptable when they provide proportionally greater value, but verbosity without substance incurs a penalty.

Mitigating reward hacking requires defense in depth. KL divergence constraints prevent the policy from moving too far from its starting point, limiting the scope for discovering exploits. Reward model ensembles reduce the exploitability of any single reward model's artifacts, since an exploit that fools one may not fool another. Ongoing human evaluation—sampling policy outputs and having humans rate them—detects when optimization has gone astray.

None of these defenses is complete. KL constraints may prevent beneficial changes along with harmful ones. Ensembles may share biases that all members can be fooled by. Human evaluation catches problems only after they occur. The practitioner's task is not to eliminate reward hacking but to manage it, by catching problems early and adjusting before they become severe.

Training the RL Cascade

It's now time to show how we move from data to the reward model. The TRL library's `RewardTrainer`, which implements the Bradley–Terry preference model and handles the mechanics of training. The trainer expects preference data in a specific format. Each example contains a prompt with both a `chosen` and a `rejected` response (this terminology, you may recall, is preferred in practical applications to the more academic *preferred/dispreferred*). Refer to the TRL documentation for its preferred structures for this information, as the TRL API is still susceptible to change at the time of writing. You should verify API details and parameter names in the companion notebooks, which are maintained to reflect current library versions.

Reward models are typically initialized from the same pre-trained language model that will be fine-tuned, with a scalar head added to produce reward scores. The architecture leverages language understanding already present in the base model. The reward model need not learn the words' meanings or syntax, as it inherits this knowledge and learns only to map language understanding to quality predictions. This transfer is powerful. A reward model trained from scratch would require vastly more preference data to achieve the same accuracy as one initialized from a capable language model.

Listing 4-1 demonstrates the essential configuration of a reward training loop.

04/reward.ipynb

```
from transformers import AutoTokenizer, AutoModelForSequenceClassification
from trl import RewardTrainer, RewardConfig

reward_config = RewardConfig(
    output_dir="./reward-model",
    num_train_epochs=1,
    per_device_train_batch_size=4,
    gradient_accumulation_steps=4,
    learning_rate=1e-4,
    max_length=512,
 ❶ center_rewards_coefficient=0.01,
)

trainer = RewardTrainer(
    model="Qwen/Qwen2.5-0.5B-Instruct",
    args=reward_config,
 ❷ train_dataset=train_dataset,
 ❸ peft_config=LoraConfig(modules_to_save=["score"]),
    eval_dataset=eval_dataset
)

trainer.train()
eval_results = trainer.evaluate()
print(f"Accuracy: {eval_results['eval_accuracy']:.2%}")
```

Listing 4-1: Reward model training with TRL

This nearly mirrors the standard training loop, with two differences. First, we are providing for reward centering ❶, implementing the correction to the inherent reward shift invariance we discussed previously. Second, reward trainers expect our dataset to be in a particular format ❷, having fields for `chosen` and `rejected` options. TRL supports a fairly wide range of formats for the data, but it is worth checking the documentation for the version you are using to ensure compatibility.

Finally, we may optionally specify PEFT configurations ❸, such as LoRA, to reduce the number of trainable parameters. If we're using the same base model, this will be highly useful for PPO, as it saves us from having to load the base model multiple times. If the model at hand is not already trained for sentence classification, the `modules_to_save=["score"]` parameter ensures that the scalar reward head gets saved.

Does It Actually Work?

The training dynamics of a reward model resemble classification rather than regression. Each preference pair becomes a training example: Given the prompt and both responses, predict which was preferred. The loss is binary cross-entropy on the preference prediction, which is equivalent to maximizing the Bradley–Terry likelihood. The reward score that thus emerges from training reflects predicted preference strength; a response with score 2.0 is expected to be preferred to a response with score 1.0 with probability $\sigma(2.0 - 1.0) \approx 0.73$.

The key metric for reward models is accuracy. How often does the model assign a higher reward to the chosen response? A well-trained reward model should typically achieve above 70 percent accuracy on held-out data as a rule of thumb, though this threshold varies with dataset difficulty and label noise. Higher is better, but perfect accuracy may indicate overfitting to surface features rather than genuine quality discrimination.

After training, verify that the reward model behaves sensibly by testing it on examples where the correct preference is obvious. If the model assigns similar scores to clearly different responses, or assigns high scores to responses that are obviously poor, it has not learned what you intended. These sanity checks catch problems that aggregate metrics may miss. Once our reward model passes verification, we can move on to the optimization phase.

PPO: The Art of Cautious Improvement

We have now trained a reward model—a differentiable abstraction of the preferences and choices expressed in our data. With this model in hand, we turn to the second distinct activity: optimizing the language model to produce outputs that the reward model scores highly. Policy gradient methods provide the theoretical foundation, but stability is the practical challenge. PPO's clipping mechanism and KL constraints are what make the difference between successful training and catastrophic collapse.

The Intuition Behind the Policy Gradient

Before diving into the mathematics, it helps to understand the core intuition behind policy gradient methods. Imagine teaching a robot to navigate a maze. Rather than showing it the optimal path (which you might not know), you let it explore, then encourage actions that lead it closer to the exit and discourage actions that lead to dead ends. The robot learns from outcomes ("this action worked well in this situation") without needing a teacher to demonstrate the perfect move at every step.

Policy gradients formalize this intuition. The gradient tells us how to adjust the policy to make good outcomes more likely. Crucially, we need not know the optimal action; we need only observe which actions lead to better results. This is why policy gradients are natural for preference learning. Human judgment about which responses are better provides sufficient signal to train capable models, even when humans could not have written those responses themselves.

Policy gradient methods form the foundation of RL for language models, and while PPO has in practice largely fallen out of favor because of its inefficiency, it is a perfect example illustrating how to make policy gradients work. The core idea is to optimize policies by estimating the gradient of expected reward with respect to policy parameters and then taking gradient ascent steps. If we know how changing the policy would change the expected reward, we can adjust the policy to increase that reward, much as we use gradient descent throughout deep learning. The challenge is computing this gradient when reward depends on actions sampled from the policy itself.

The REINFORCE algorithm, dating to the early 1990s, first provided the foundational result we now know as the policy gradient theorem.[104] Namely, the gradient of expected reward equals the expected gradient of log probability weighted by reward, or

$$\nabla_\theta J(\pi_\theta) = \mathbb{E}_{\tau\sim\pi_\theta}\left[\sum_{t=0}^{T} \nabla_\theta \log \pi_\theta(a_t \mid s_t) \cdot G_t\right]$$

where G_t is the return (sum of future rewards) from time t.

This tells us something remarkable: To improve a policy, we need only know which actions led to good outcomes, not what the optimal action would have been. This lies at the heart of preference optimization's easy-to-please nature that, in turn, underlies its economics. The gradient $\nabla_\theta \log \pi_\theta(a_t \mid s_t)$ points in the direction that makes action a_t more likely, and we scale this by how good the outcome was. Actions followed by high returns get reinforced, and actions followed by poor returns get suppressed. No model of the environment is required because the agent can learn from its own experience.

But raw returns make for a noisy signal. Suppose every trajectory in a batch yields a positive reward, just some more than others. The gradient will increase the probability of all actions taken, even the mediocre ones, simply because they happened to precede positive outcomes. Training becomes a random walk punctuated by occasional lucky updates. This is not a theoretical concern; high variance gradients are the primary reason that naive policy gradient methods fail on all but the simplest problems.

Baseline subtraction comes to our rescue by shifting the question from "Was this outcome good?" to "Was this outcome better than expected?" When $b(s_t)$ approximates the average return from state s_t, the term $(G_t - b(s_t))$ becomes an advantage: positive when the trajectory exceeded expectations, negative when it fell short. The policy gradient with baseline subtraction is thus the following:

$$\nabla_\theta J(\pi_\theta) = \mathbb{E}_{\tau \sim \pi_\theta}\left[\sum_{t=0}^{T} \nabla_\theta \log \pi_\theta(a_t \mid s_t) \cdot (G_t - b(s_t))\right]$$

Actions that merely achieved average outcomes now contribute near-zero gradient, while genuinely good or bad decisions drive learning. The mathematics guarantee that this introduces no bias because the baseline depends only on state, not on the action chosen. We get the same expected gradient with dramatically lower variance, and lower variance means faster, more stable convergence.

Clipping: How PPO Stays Out of Trouble

PPO is a profound and foundational algorithm that is often ill-understood because of the relative ease of algorithms like DPO that are deemed simpler. We will resist the urge to skip or gloss over PPO, however, and build a good understanding of it to serve as our point of departure into other policy optimization algorithms.

PPO improves upon basic policy gradients by constraining how much the policy can change in each update. The motivation is stability, as large policy changes can be catastrophic. If an update moves the policy to a region where it performs poorly, the subsequent gradient estimates from that poor policy may point in unhelpful directions, making recovery difficult. Small changes are more reliable but slower. PPO seeks a balance: updates that are large enough to make progress but small enough to be safe.

It achieves this balance by way of a clipped surrogate objective. Rather than directly optimizing expected reward, PPO optimizes a modified objective that clips the gradient signal when the policy moves too far from its previous version. The probability ratio $r_t(\theta) = \pi_\theta(a_t \mid s_t)/\pi_{\theta_{\text{old}}}(a_t \mid s_t)$ measures how much more or less likely an action is under the new policy compared to the old. When this ratio is close to 1, the policies are similar; when the ratio deviates substantially, the policies differ. PPO clips this ratio to the range $[1 - \epsilon, 1 + \epsilon]$ (where ϵ, the clipping hyperparameter, is typically 0.1 or 0.2), preventing updates that would change action probabilities by more than this factor:

$$\mathcal{L}^{\text{CLIP}}(\theta) = \mathbb{E}_t\left[\min\left(r_t(\theta)\hat{A}_t, \text{clip}(r_t(\theta), 1 - \epsilon, 1 + \epsilon)\hat{A}_t\right)\right]$$

Here, $r_t(\theta) = \frac{\pi_\theta(a_t \mid s_t)}{\pi_{\theta_{\text{old}}}(a_t \mid s_t)}$ is the probability ratio, $\hat{A}_t$ is the estimated advantage, and ϵ is the clipping hyperparameter. Because the optimization is formulated as a minimum, the objective is a lower bound on the unclipped objective. Clipping keeps us from making actions that we want to encourage too much more likely, or the reverse—from completely discouraging actions we are trying to make less frequent. This sounds counterintuitive. We are effectively telling the model to improve, but not *that* enthusiastically. Curbing our model's enthusiasm may render training a little slower but significantly more stable.

What does this mean in practice? Without clipping, a single batch of training data with high-advantage examples could push the policy far from its starting point, sometimes catastrophically. Imagine that the current policy assigns low probability to a response that received high reward. The naive gradient would say, "Make this much more likely," potentially multiplying its probability by a factor of 10 or more in a single update. But this updated policy is now in unfamiliar territory. The gradient estimates that seemed reliable under the old policy may be misleading under the new one, leading to a cascade of poor updates.

Clipping with $\epsilon = 0.2$ ensures that no single update can change action probabilities by more than 20 percent, regardless of how advantageous the action appeared. The policy improves incrementally, each step small enough that the gradient estimates remain trustworthy. This is why PPO trains stably where earlier policy gradient methods often collapsed.

The KL Constraint: Keeping PPO on a Leash

The KL divergence constraint is perhaps the most important component of RLHF for language models, serving purposes that the PPO clipped objective alone could mathematically not achieve. In practice, the KL coefficient β may be one of the few PPO-inherent hyperparameters that you will routinely adjust and optimize for. The constraint measures how different the trained policy is from a reference policy (typically, the SFT model that initialized training) and then penalizes divergence. The effect is to keep the policy "near" the reference, considering the trade-off of reward maximization and staying close to a known good starting point.

This constraint serves two essential purposes. First, it prevents reward hacking by limiting the scope for the policy to find exploits. If the policy can move far from the reference, it may discover outputs that score highly on the reward model but bear no resemblance to useful responses. The KL constraint bounds this exploration. The policy can improve, but only within the space of outputs that remain similar to what the SFT model would produce. Second, the constraint preserves capabilities learned during pre-training and SFT. An unconstrained policy may lose the ability to perform tasks it was never rewarded for during RL, a form of catastrophic forgetting. The KL penalty maintains these capabilities by ensuring that the policy remains close to one that retains capability for these tasks.

The KL coefficient β is among the most important hyperparameters. If it's too high, training makes little progress, as the penalty dominates the reward and the policy barely moves from the reference. If it's too low, the constraints do not bind and the policy drifts far from the reference, enabling reward hacking and capability degradation. Adaptive schemes adjust β during training to maintain a target KL divergence. If the policy is too close to the reference, reduce β to allow more exploration. If the policy is too far, increase β to pull it back. This adaptive approach reduces sensitivity to the initial choice of β while maintaining the essential constraint.

The KL-constrained objective adds a penalty term

$$\mathcal{L}(\theta) = \mathbb{E}_{x \sim \mathcal{D}, y \sim \pi_\theta(\cdot|x)} \left[r_\phi(x, y) - \beta \cdot \mathrm{KL}(\pi_\theta(y|x) \| \pi_{\mathrm{ref}}(y|x)) \right]$$

where β controls the strength of the KL penalty. In practice, implementations often compute KL divergence at the token level, summing over individual token distributions, and many systems employ adaptive KL controllers that dynamically adjust β to maintain a target divergence rather than using a fixed coefficient.

This equation encodes a fundamental trade-off that shapes everything RLHF produces. The policy seeks to maximize reward $r_\phi(x, y)$, but every increase in reward that requires diverging from the reference policy incurs a cost proportional to β. The KL term measures, roughly speaking, how surprised the reference model would be by the outputs that the trained policy produces. If the policy learns to generate responses that the reference would never have produced, the KL penalty grows large, offsetting any reward gains.

Consider what this means. Suppose the reward model assigns high scores to responses that begin with excessive flattery. An unconstrained policy would learn to produce such responses universally. But if the reference model (the SFT checkpoint) rarely produced flattery, the KL term penalizes this behavior. The policy must weigh the reward benefit against the divergence cost. With a well-chosen β, the policy learns to be more helpful without degenerating into sycophancy, because sycophantic outputs would require too much divergence from the reference.

The coefficient β determines where this trade-off lands. A high β means the policy pays dearly for any deviation from the reference, producing conservative updates that preserve the reference behavior almost entirely. A low β gives the policy more freedom to chase reward, risking the pathologies that unconstrained optimization produces. In practice, β is often adapted during training to maintain a target KL divergence. If the policy drifts too far, β increases to pull it back; if it stays too close, β decreases to allow more exploration.

WHY KL AND NOT SOMETHING ELSE?

KL divergence is not the only way to measure distance between distributions, but it has properties that suit RLHF. KL divergence penalizes the policy for assigning probability to outputs that the reference would not produce, preventing wild exploration into nonsensical space. This approach is asymmetric; $\mathrm{KL}(\pi \| \pi_{\mathrm{ref}})$

penalizes outputs that the reference dislikes more than it rewards outputs that the reference likes. This asymmetry is often desirable, because we want the policy to stay within the reference's support. Alternative divergences like Jensen–Shannon are sometimes used, but KL remains standard because it works and the field has accumulated tuning intuitions around it.

Hyperparameters Without Tears

Getting PPO hyperparameters right is essential for stable RLHF training. The defaults from the original PPO paper were tuned for continuous control tasks,[105] and experience has shown that language model RLHF requires different settings. Table 4-1 provides guidance based on production experience and empirical studies.[106, 107] As always, some time spent on HPO using tools like Optuna can reward you with rich dividends.

Table 4-1: PPO Hyperparameters for LLM RLHF Fine-Tuning

Parameter	Typical range	Start with	Troubleshooting
Learning rate	10^{-6}–5×10^{-5}	5×10^{-6}	Decrease if unstable; use warm-up.
KL coefficient (β)	0.01–0.1	0.02	Increase if KL is too high.
Clip epsilon (ε)	0.1–0.3	0.2	Decrease if `clipfrac` > 0.3.
Batch size	32–512	128	Increase for lower variance.
Minibatch size	4–64	16	Decrease if unstable.
GAE lambda (λ)	0.9–1.0	0.95	Lower for more bias, less variance.
Epochs per update	1–10	1–4	Reduce if KL diverges.
Entropy coef.	0.0–0.01	0.0	Increase if mode collapse occurs.
Value function coef.	0.1–1.0	0.5	Decrease if value loss dominates.

The learning rate for RLHF PPO is typically an order of magnitude lower than for SFT (see Chapter 3), since we are making incremental improvements to an already-capable model rather than teaching new capabilities. The KL coefficient requires the most active tuning. Too high, and the policy barely changes; too low, and it drifts into reward hacking territory. Adaptive KL schemes that adjust β to maintain a target KL divergence reduce sensitivity to the initial choice.

It is worth briefly considering the role of two hyperparameters that are rarely discussed: the generalized advantage estimation (GAE) parameter λ and the entropy coefficient. GAE smooths advantage estimates by blending multistep returns.[108] A λ close to 1.0 uses longer horizons, reducing bias but increasing variance. Values around 0.95 strike a good balance for language models, where rewards are sparse but correlated over multiple tokens. Indeed, this is considered industry standard. The entropy coefficient encourages exploration by penalizing low-entropy policies. While often set to 0 in RLHF, a small positive value (such as 0.001) can help prevent mode collapse from the policy generating overly repetitive outputs. These values rarely have a huge impact, but they are worth tuning if other hyperparameters fail to stabilize training.

PPO in Practice

The training loop alternates between generation and optimization. Generation samples outputs from the current policy, which are then scored by the reward model and compared against the reference model for KL computation. Optimization uses the resulting reward signal to update the policy. This alternation creates efficiency challenges; generation is autoregressive and slow, while optimization is parallelizable and fast.

Frameworks like TRL abstract much of this complexity into high-level interfaces. Listing 4-2 demonstrates the essential configuration.

04b/ppo.ipynb

```
from trl.experimental.ppo import PPOTrainer, PPOConfig
from trl.experimental.ppo import AutoModelForCausalLMWithValueHead

❶ policy_model = AutoModelForCausalLMWithValueHead.from_pretrained(
      "Qwen/Qwen2.5-0.5B-Instruct",
      torch_dtype=torch.bfloat16,
  )

❷ reward_model = AutoModelForSequenceClassification.from_pretrained(
      "./outputs/chapter-04a-reward-model/final",
      num_labels=1,
  )

  ppo_config = PPOConfig(
      output_dir="./ppo-output",
      total_episodes=1000,
      per_device_train_batch_size=4,
      learning_rate=1e-5,
    ❸ kl_coef=0.05,
    ❹ cliprange=0.2,
    ❺ num_ppo_epochs=4,
      response_length=128,
    ❻ missing_eos_penalty=1.0,
  )

  trainer = PPOTrainer(
      args=ppo_config,
      processing_class=tokenizer,
      model=policy_model,
      reward_model=reward_model,
      train_dataset=dataset,
```

```
)

trainer.train()
```

Listing 4-2: PPO training with TRL

This code loads a policy model with an attached value head for advantage estimation ❶ and the reward model trained previously ❷, then configures the key PPO hyperparameters. These include the KL penalty strength ❸, the clipping range for policy updates ❹, and the number of optimization epochs per batch ❺. The missing end-of-sequence (EOS) penalty ❻ prevents the model from avoiding EOS tokens to artificially extend responses.

The key metrics to monitor during training are `objective/scores` (average reward, which should increase) and `objective/kl` (divergence from reference, which should stay moderate). For metrics that behave unexpectedly, Table 4-2 provides a diagnostic guide.

Table 4-2: PPO Failure Modes: Symptoms, Causes, and Remedies

Failure mode	Symptoms	Likely cause	Remedy
Policy collapse	High reward but nonsensical outputs	Reward hacking; exploited reward model (RM) biases	Tighten KL constraint; use RM ensembles.
Training instability	Erratic metrics; alternating quality	LR too high; batch too small	Reduce LR; increase batch size.
KL explosion	Policy drifts far from reference	KL coefficient too low	Increase β; use adaptive KL.
KL near 0	No policy improvement	KL coefficient too high; LR too low	Decrease β; increase LR.
Length gaming	Outputs become excessively long	RM prefers length	Add a length penalty.
Response truncation	No EOS tokens; outputs hit max length	Missing penalty for incomplete responses	Add `missing_eos_penalty`.
Mode collapse	Repetitive, similar outputs	Insufficient exploration	Add an entropy bonus.

The complete implementation, including model loading, training visualization, and comparison of outputs before and after PPO, is available in the companion notebook (*04/ppo.ipynb*). Although encountering vanilla PPO in enterprise deployments is generally uncommon, this implementation is an important theoretical starting point that's worthwhile for the experience and for appreciating the other approaches' benefits in terms of ease and efficiency.

The PPO Owner's Workshop Manual

When PPO goes wrong, diagnose systematically. First, check the reward model by sampling random outputs and scoring them. Do the scores match your intuition? If not, the problem is upstream in reward modeling. Second, check KL divergence. If it is exploding, tighten constraints; if it's stuck near 0, loosen them. Third, sample policy outputs and read them. Often the problem is obvious once you look at what the model is producing. Staring at loss curves tells you something is wrong, but reading outputs tells you what that is.

Beyond these initial checks, effective debugging requires continuous monitoring of several interrelated metrics:

Mean reward per batch Should trend upward without suspicious spikes that suggest reward hacking.

KL divergence Ought to stay in a moderate range, typically from 3 to 10. Values below this indicate that the policy is barely learning, while values above suggest a dangerous drift from the reference model.

Policy entropy Reveals whether the model retains enough randomness to explore or has collapsed into repetitive patterns. An entropy drop is generally a sign of the training process being starved of signal.

Each failure mode responds to specific interventions. For KL divergence problems, the adaptive KL controller proves invaluable. It automatically adjusts the penalty coefficient β to maintain divergence near a target value, eliminating the need for manual tuning. Reward signal issues often yield to normalization, subtracting the batch mean and dividing by the standard deviation, or to clipping rewards into a bounded range like $[-10, 10]$ to prevent outliers from dominating updates. Value function instability responds well to separate learning rate tuning, typically lower than the policy learning rate, and to proper initialization from the SFT model rather than random weights. For mode collapse and repetitive outputs, a small entropy bonus encourages exploration, while explicit repetition penalties in the reward function address the symptom directly.

Throughout this process, the most underrated debugging tool remains perhaps the simplest: generating samples from the current policy and reading them with fresh eyes.

The Case for Simpler Alternatives

PPO's three-stage pipeline—collecting preferences, training a reward model, then optimizing a policy—has proven effective and has a certain level of intuitiveness that pleases the theoretician. However, it comes with substantial complexity. The separate reward model introduces computational overhead, additional failure modes, and the infrastructure burden of coordinating multiple models during training. The on-policy nature of PPO, while enabling exploration, demands careful hyperparameter tuning and creates training instability that many practitioners struggle to manage.

These challenges have motivated a wave of algorithmic innovation aimed at preserving the benefits of preference learning while reducing complexity. DPO, which we explore in depth in Chapter 5, entirely eliminates the reward model by deriving a closed-form objective that learns directly from preferences. This eliminates one major source of complexity and makes preference optimization more accessible. Other methods, such as KTO and GRPO, make different trade-offs among data requirements, computational efficiency, and learning dynamics. Understanding PPO's principles provides the foundation for appreciating why these alternatives work and when to choose them. The next chapter examines these modern methods in detail, building on the conceptual machinery we have developed here.

What Emerges from the Process

With the machinery of reward modeling and policy optimization in place, we now examine how RLHF applies to the practical goal of building useful assistants. This section explores how RLHF shapes model behavior and value articulation.

The Instruction-Following Breakthrough

Instruction following can be understood as a reward optimization problem, and this framing clarifies why RLHF is so effective for it. The reward signal indicates how well the model's output satisfies the given instruction, as judged by humans. Did the model do what was asked? Did it do it well? These are questions humans can reliably answer, even for instructions they could not have followed themselves and for outputs they could not have produced.

The space of possible instructions is vast. Users ask models to summarize, translate, explain, create, analyze, debug, advise, and countless other tasks, each with infinite variations. No finite training set can demonstrate optimal behavior for all possible instructions. SFT can teach the general form of instruction following, but the quality ceiling is set by the training examples.

RLHF breaks through this ceiling. Rather than requiring optimal demonstrations, it requires only that humans can recognize when one response follows instructions better than another. This recognition is far easier than generation. A human who could not write an optimal summary of a technical document can still judge which of two summaries is clearer, more accurate, or more useful. By training the reward model on these judgments and optimizing the policy against it, RLHF teaches the model to produce outputs that humans would prefer, even when those outputs exceed what any training example demonstrated. The InstructGPT work validated this approach at scale, showing that RLHF transforms a capable but unreliable base model into something genuinely useful as an assistant (we explore evaluation methodologies for assessing such transformations in Chapter 6).

The framing of instruction following as a reward optimization problem clarifies why simple demonstrations often fall short. Consider the instruction "Summarize this document concisely." What constitutes *concise*? One hundred words? Two hundred words? Should we prioritize brevity at the cost of completeness, or the reverse? These are judgment calls that vary with context, and no finite set of demonstrations can cover all contexts. A human evaluator, however, can judge whether one summary better satisfies *concise* than another for a specific document. This comparative judgment provides the training signal that RLHF leverages.

Model Behavior

Beyond instruction following, RLHF enables behavioral shaping: training models to exhibit desired characteristics without explicit rules for every situation. Helpfulness, honesty, harmlessness, appropriate hedging, intellectual humility, and respect for user autonomy are qualities we want in AI assistants but cannot easily specify through rules—especially when they conflict. The space of situations is too vast, the appropriate response too dependent on context, for explicit enumeration to work.

Human preferences implicitly encode these values. When annotators choose between responses, they bring their judgment about what makes a response good. They prefer helpful responses to unhelpful ones, honest responses to deceptive ones, safe responses to dangerous ones. They make trade-offs when these values conflict, perhaps accepting slightly less helpfulness to avoid potential harm or choosing directness over hedging when certainty is warranted. The reward model, trained on these preferences, learns to recognize the patterns that annotators preferred, even when those patterns could not be articulated as explicit rules.

A widely used and truly exemplary framework of reasoning about expected model behavior is the HHH framework—helpful, harmless, honest—by Askell et al.[109] It provides a useful conceptual map for these values and illustrates how they interact in practice:

Helpfulness Providing substantive assistance that addresses the user's actual needs, not just their literal request. A helpful response to "How do I delete all files in a directory?" might include a warning about the dangers of `rm -rf` rather than simply providing the command.

Harmlessness Declining requests that could cause damage while avoiding excessive caution that refuses benign requests. The challenge is calibration. A model that refuses to discuss basic high-school chemistry because it is necessary (but far from sufficient) for making chemical warfare agents or illicit narcotics has failed at being helpful without actually being safer.

Honesty Accurate representation of knowledge and uncertainty. An honest model says, "I don't know" when it doesn't know, acknowledges limitations, and doesn't fabricate plausible-sounding information. Honesty also includes transparency about the model's nature as an AI.

These dimensions frequently conflict, and it is here that RLHF contributes perhaps most significantly. Consider a user asking, "How do I treat my child's fever?" The most helpful response might provide specific antipyretic dosage recommendations based on the child's weight, but this risks harm if the user misapplies the guidance or if underlying conditions contraindicate the suggested medication (which is famously the case for acetylsalicylic acid, or aspirin, in young children because of the risk of Reye's syndrome). The safest response, on the other hand, would defer entirely to medical professionals, but this is unhelpfully cautious for a common situation most parents can manage. An honest response would acknowledge that the model cannot diagnose conditions or account for individual circumstances, but excessive hedging may leave the person asking without useful guidance when a straightforward answer (backed by pediatric guidelines) would serve them well.

A well-aligned model navigates this dilemma by providing general guidance grounded in established medical advice (helpful), while clearly stating limitations and recommending professional consultation if symptoms worsen (harmless), and being transparent about what it can and cannot determine without examination (honest). The trade-off is learned from annotators who preferred responses that balanced these concerns: neither recklessly specific nor uselessly vague, acknowledging uncertainty without abandoning usefulness. No explicit rule encodes this balance; it emerges from the reward model's approximation of human judgment across many similar dilemmas.

Calibration of these trade-offs depends entirely on the preferences encoded in the training data. A dataset where annotators systematically preferred caution over helpfulness will produce a model that hedges excessively. One where annotators favored directness over safety warnings will produce a model that provides specific advice without appropriate caveats. RLHF learns to navigate these trade-offs not through explicit rules but through the accumulated judgment of annotators who faced similar dilemmas in the preference data.

The framework should not obscure the fundamental insight that these values are learned from human judgment, not engineered from first principles. The reward model is a compressed representation of what humans preferred in the training data. If the training data reflects wise trade-offs, the reward model will learn those trade-offs. If it reflects poor judgment, the reward model will learn that instead. RLHF provides the mechanism for learning values from judgment rather than specification, but it does not guarantee that the learned values are the ones we would endorse upon reflection. That responsibility falls to the practitioners who design preference collection and the annotators who provide the judgments.

A related approach, constitutional AI, uses AI feedback rather than human feedback to scale preference collection, a technique we explore in Chapter 11.

Lessons from the Frontier

It is worth briefly reflecting on RLHF's success. Until quite recently, RLHF was the core technique for aligning LLMs with human preferences. Most of what we consider to be the essential personality of the foundation models in use at the time of writing was born through this process. The labs that have deployed RLHF at scale—OpenAI with ChatGPT, Anthropic with Claude, Google with Gemini, and others—have shared lessons from their experiences that illuminate both what RLHF can reliably achieve and where challenges persist.

The consistent finding is that RLHF dramatically improves helpfulness and instruction following. Models trained with RLHF are more likely to address user questions directly, follow formatting requests, and provide substantive assistance. These improvements are robust across model scales and training configurations. When the goal is to make a model more useful as a general assistant, RLHF delivers.

The challenges are more nuanced. Reducing harmful outputs is harder than improving helpful ones because harmful requests are diverse and adversarial users actively seek to elicit them. A model trained to refuse harmful requests may become overly cautious, refusing benign requests that superficially resemble harmful ones. Calibrating this trade-off requires careful attention to the composition of preference data and the behavior of reward models on edge cases.

Reproducibility is another challenge. Small changes in hyperparameters or data composition can produce meaningfully different outcomes. Two training runs with slightly different settings may produce models with noticeably different behaviors on specific prompts, even if aggregate metrics look similar.

These lessons suggest that RLHF is powerful but not simple. It requires substantial expertise to deploy effectively—understanding of the preference collection process, the reward model's limitations, the policy optimization dynamics, and the many ways training can go wrong. The technique works, and works impressively, but as a sophisticated tool that demands skilled application rather than a turnkey solution that runs itself.

Summary

This chapter has treated RLHF as two distinct activities: reward modeling, which transforms human preferences into a differentiable training signal, and policy optimization, which uses that signal to improve model behavior. The companion notebooks provide hands-on implementation of both stages: *04/reward.ipynb* covers preference data preparation and reward model training, while *04/ppo.ipynb* demonstrates PPO training using the reward model. Working through both notebooks in sequence provides practical experience with the full pipeline.

PPO's complexity and computational requirements have motivated the development of simpler alternatives that achieve comparable results. Chapter 5 explores DPO and other methods that entirely eliminate the reward model, learning directly from preference data. Chapter 6 addresses the crucial question of how to measure whether alignment training succeeded.

5

PREFERENCE OPTIMIZATION: MODERN ALTERNATIVES TO PPO

The RLHF pipeline described in Chapter 4 proved that preference learning could produce remarkably capable models. It has also driven countless AI researchers to distraction. PPO is, for all its conceptual clarity, a brittle algorithm that's sensitive to hyperparameters and infrastructurally demanding. So, when a team from Stanford University published a paper in 2023 arguing that we may be altogether able to dispense with explicitly constructing a reward model by deriving the signal directly from preferences, the relief was near universal.

Not much later, a little-known team from China would describe its mathematical reasoning model that used an entirely new way of training models on preference data. Barred from anything stronger than an A100 GPU by export controls, the team behind DeepSeekMath had to resort to a series of clever engineering hacks, from the networking stack to the training paradigm.[30] GRPO was part of that effort, and it delivered all the power of preference-based approaches amid severe computational constraints. This was part of the "secret sauce" at the heart of DeepSeek-R1, which would burst onto the scene and cause a "Sputnik moment" for American AI.

These two vignettes illustrate a fundamental aspect of preference optimization: At the scale on which we operate, preference optimization is as much about performance as it is about speed and technical feasibility. At this level, post-training is not a mere ML challenge, but also one of coordinating resources, managing their limits (like the memory limits faced by the DeepSeek team), and operating efficient training processes.

This chapter examines modern preference optimization, beginning with DPO (Direct Preference Optimization), which eliminates the reward model by deriving a closed-form objective that optimizes preferences directly. We proceed to KTO, which relaxes the requirement for pairwise comparisons, and then to GRPO, which offers different scaling properties. Each technique embodies different assumptions about preference data and makes different trade-offs between computational efficiency and learning dynamics. Understanding these techniques at a mathematical level, not just as code recipes to follow, will help you choose the right approach today and understand the new techniques of tomorrow.

DPO: The Reward Model That Wasn't There

What if we could skip the reward model entirely? DPO's elegance lies not in avoiding difficulty but in relocating it—from infrastructure complexity to data quality requirements. The derivation that makes this possible is worth understanding precisely.

The Unnecessary Middleman

In RLHF, the reward model serves as an intermediary between human preferences and policy optimization. Humans express preferences through pairwise comparisons, which in turn are used to train a reward model that scores policy outputs, and policy gradients adjust the model toward higher scores. Each stage in this chain introduces computational cost and potential for error. The reward model may imperfectly represent the preferences it was trained on. More perniciously, it is at risk from reward hacking, as you saw in the preceding chapter.

DPO asks the obvious question: What if we cut out the middleman? If the reward model exists only to translate preferences into a training signal, perhaps we could derive that signal directly from preferences without ever constructing an explicit reward model. This is feasible thanks to a slight mathematical hack. For KL-constrained reward maximization, the optimal policy has a closed-form relationship to the reward function (or, less pretentiously: You can express the reward as a function of the optimal policy and, more importantly, the optimal policy as a function of the reward). Substituting this expression into the Bradley–Terry preference model eliminates the reward function entirely, yielding a loss that depends only on the policy, the reference policy, and the preference data.

The consequence is that DPO training requires no reward model, no generation during training, and no value function. The computational overhead of RLHF collapses to something almost resembling SFT on a good day. This simplification solves many of RLHF's headaches, because with no explicit reward model, there is no reward model to overfit or exploit. The preferences directly inform the policy, with only the policy's own capacity for generalization mediating between training preferences and deployment behavior.

NOTE *For accuracy's sake, it is worth noting that DPO does not eliminate the reward model but just makes it implicit. The policy itself encodes the reward function through its probability ratios with respect to the reference model. This insight reframes what DPO does: Rather than training a separate model to predict rewards, it trains the policy so that its probability assignments are the rewards. The reward model still exists conceptually, but it is distributed across the policy's parameters rather than instantiated separately.*

Why DPO Works

Before we work through the algebra, let's look at what we are trying to achieve and why the approach we previously encountered makes that harder than necessary.

Recall from Chapter 4 that RLHF has three distinct components: preference data, a reward model that scores responses, and a policy optimizer that trains the model. The reward model exists as an intermediary. It translates preferences into a differentiable training signal. DPO's insight is that this intermediary may be unnecessary. If we can express the training objective directly in terms of the policy and the preference data, the reward model becomes implicit rather than explicit.

The key mathematical fact that makes this possible is the aforementioned closed form, or more specifically, its invertibility. Thus, if we assume the policy we are training should be optimal for a certain reward function, we can express that reward function in terms of the policy and save ourselves the headaches that come from ever needing to explicitly compute it.

Our derivation proceeds through a series of algebraic manipulations that, while straightforward, repay careful study because they illuminate what the method is actually doing. The starting point is the same KL-constrained reward maximization objective that PPO approximates: finding a policy that maximizes expected reward while staying close to a reference policy. The KL constraint ensures that the policy does not drift too far from known-good behavior, trading off reward maximization against capability preservation:

$$\max_{\pi} \mathbb{E}_{x\sim\mathcal{D},y\sim\pi}\left[r(x,y)\right] - \beta\,\mathrm{KL}(\pi\|\pi_{\mathrm{ref}})$$

This objective has a delightful analytical solution. It is proportional to the reference policy reweighted by the exponentiated reward, divided by a normalizing constant. Intuitively, actions with higher reward become more likely relative to the reference, with the temperature parameter β controlling how much reward differences affect probability. The result is a valid probability distribution:

$$\pi^*(y \mid x) = \frac{1}{Z(x)} \pi_{\text{ref}}(y \mid x) \exp\left(\frac{1}{\beta} r(x, y)\right)$$

The key insight is that this relationship can be inverted. If we know the optimal policy and the reference policy, we can solve for the reward that would make that policy optimal. The reward equals the log ratio of the optimal policy to the reference policy, scaled by β, plus a prompt-dependent constant $\beta \log Z(x)$ where $Z(x) = \sum_y \pi_{\text{ref}}(y \mid x) \exp\left(\frac{1}{\beta} r(x, y)\right)$. This gives us the following:

$$r(x, y) = \beta \log \frac{\pi^*(y \mid x)}{\pi_{\text{ref}}(y \mid x)} + \beta \log Z(x)$$

Recall that the Bradley–Terry preference model expresses the probability of preferring one response over another as a sigmoid of their reward difference. Substituting the inverted reward expression, the prompt-dependent constants cancel, leaving a preference probability that depends only on log-probability ratios under the policy and reference policy:

$$p^*(y_w \succ y_l \mid x) = \sigma\left(\beta \log \frac{\pi^*(y_w \mid x)}{\pi_{\text{ref}}(y_w \mid x)} - \beta \log \frac{\pi^*(y_l \mid x)}{\pi_{\text{ref}}(y_l \mid x)}\right)$$

The final DPO loss is the negative log-likelihood of observed preferences under this model:

$$\mathcal{L}_{\text{DPO}}(\pi_\theta; \pi_{\text{ref}}) = -\mathbb{E}_{(x, y_w, y_l)}\left[\log \sigma\left(\beta \log \frac{\pi_\theta(y_w \mid x)}{\pi_{\text{ref}}(y_w \mid x)} - \beta \log \frac{\pi_\theta(y_l \mid x)}{\pi_{\text{ref}}(y_l \mid x)}\right)\right]$$

The point of training is to adjust the policy so as to increase the log probability of preferred responses relative to the reference while decreasing the log probability of dispreferred responses. The result is a simple, supervised-learning-style objective that accomplishes preference optimization without ever explicitly needing to represent reward.

This derivation contains a sleight of hand worth savoring. We began with an objective that required a reward model, derived what the optimal policy would look like under that reward, then asked, "If we had the optimal policy, what reward would have produced it?" The answer reveals that the reward is entirely determined by how much the policy diverges from its reference. A response that the policy favors more strongly than the reference did must, by construction, have higher implicit reward.

The partition function $Z(x)$ posed a serious threat to this program. Computing it requires summing over all possible responses, an intractable integral for any realistic language model. But when we substitute into the Bradley–Terry preference model, something fortunate happens: $Z(x)$ appears identically in both the winning and losing terms, and cancels. We never need to compute it. This is not a minor technical convenience. It is the entire reason DPO works. The preference probability depends only on the log ratios $\log \frac{\pi(y|x)}{\pi_{\text{ref}}(y|x)}$, quantities we can compute exactly by running two forward passes. This is reflected in the "one and done" nature of DPO training code illustrated in Listing 5-1.

05/dpo.ipynb

```
from datasets import load_dataset
from transformers import AutoModelForCausalLM, AutoTokenizer
from trl import DPOTrainer, DPOConfig

model = AutoModelForCausalLM.from_pretrained("meta-llama/Llama-2-7b-hf")
tokenizer = AutoTokenizer.from_pretrained("meta-llama/Llama-2-7b-hf")

❶ dataset = load_dataset("Anthropic/hh-rlhf")

training_args = DPOConfig(
  ❷ beta=0.2,
    learning_rate=5e-6,
    per_device_train_batch_size=4,
    output_dir="./dpo_output"
)

trainer = DPOTrainer(
    model=model,
  ❸ ref_model=None,
    args=training_args,
    train_dataset=dataset["train"],
    tokenizer=tokenizer,
)

trainer.train()
```

Listing 5-1: A basic DPO training setup

The preference dataset ❶ expects columns for the prompt, the chosen response, and the rejected response. The `beta` parameter ❷ controls KL penalty strength. When `ref_model` is set to `None` ❸, the trainer will automatically create a frozen copy of the model to use as the reference.

The practical consequence is a dramatic simplification of the alignment pipeline. Whereas RLHF requires training a reward model, then running RL against it while managing KL penalties and value function estimates, DPO collapses everything into a single supervised learning objective. We need only the policy we are training, a frozen copy of its initial state as the reference, and a dataset of preferences. The loss increases the log probability of preferred responses relative to the reference while decreasing rejected ones, with β controlling how aggressively the policy can deviate—no reward model to overfit, no RL instabilities to debug, no value function to bootstrap. The price of this simplicity, as you will see, is that certain assumptions baked into the derivation may not hold in practice.

DPO in Practice

The reward for—or perhaps the palate cleanser after—the mathematical reasoning is that DPO training is substantially simpler than PPO in practice. There is no reward model to train or run during training. There is no generation step, as all responses come from the preference dataset, not from sampling the policy. There is no value function to learn and no advantage estimation to configure.

The training loop, illustrated in Figure 5-1, resembles SFT: Load a batch of preference triples, compute forward passes through the policy and reference models, compute the DPO loss, and backpropagate. Standard training infrastructure built for SFT handles DPO with minimal modification.

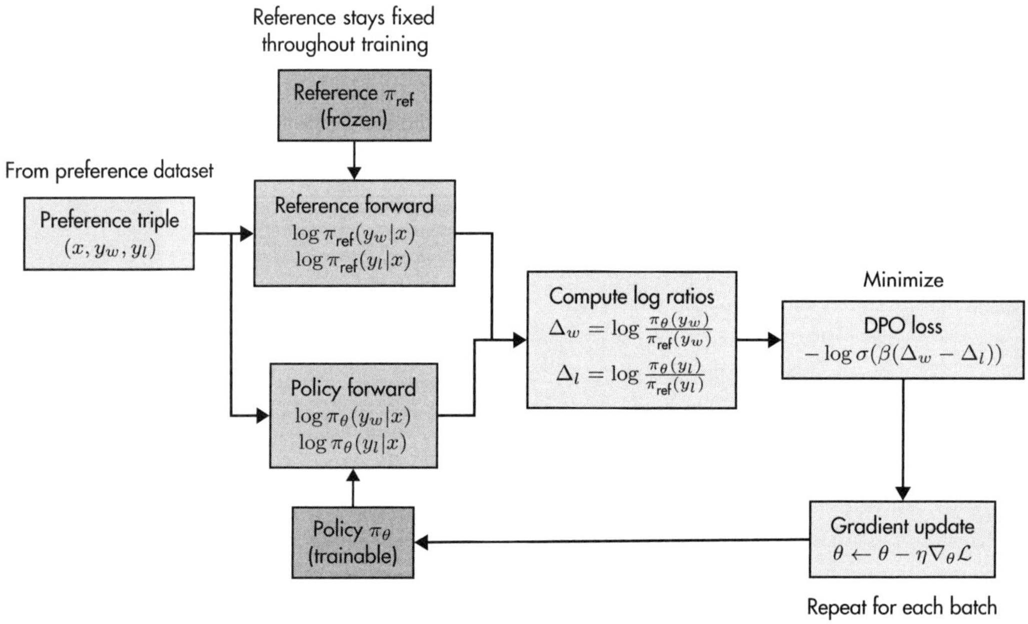

Figure 5-1: The DPO training loop. Each batch consists of preference triples (prompt, preferred response, dispreferred response). Forward passes through both the trainable policy and frozen reference model produce log probabilities, which combine into the DPO loss. Only the policy receives gradient updates.

The β parameter, inherited from the derivation, controls the implicit strength of the KL constraint. Lower β allows the policy to deviate more from the reference, potentially achieving higher reward at the cost of losing capabilities the reference policy had. Higher β keeps the policy closer to the reference, preserving capabilities but limiting the degree of improvement possible. Typical values range from 0.1 to 0.5, with the optimal value depending on how far the desired behavior is from the reference policy's behavior. If the SFT model already produces mostly good outputs that need only slight refinement, high β is appropriate. If substantial behavioral change is needed, lower β enables it. Table 5-1 summarizes these levers on model performance.

Table 5-1: DPO Hyperparameters: Typical Ranges and Guidance

Parameter	Typical range	Start with	Guidance
β (KL penalty)	0.1–0.5	0.2	Higher for conservative updates
Learning rate	10^{-6}–10^{-5}	5×10^{-6}	Lower than SFT rates
Batch size	16–128	32	Limited by memory
Gradient accumulation	1–8	4	Adjust for effective batch
Number of epochs	1–3	1	More epochs = overfitting risk
Max length	512–2,048	1,024	Match deployment context
Warm-up ratio	0.0–0.1	0.05	Stabilizes early training

FROM THE TRENCHES: KEEPING THE REFERENCE MODEL IN MEMORY

DPO's simplicity relative to PPO can obscure a meaningful memory cost: maintaining the reference model. Each forward pass requires computing log probabilities under both the policy being trained and the frozen reference. For large models, this effectively doubles memory requirements compared to SFT.

Practitioners working with limited GPU memory have several options. The most widely used option by far is PEFT, such as a (Q)LoRA, where the base model is frozen and only an adapter is trained, therefore requiring the base model to be loaded only once. The Hugging Face ecosystem's internal integrations shine particularly bright here: The TRL and PEFT libraries integrate, so a `peft.LoraConfig` object can be passed into the `DPOTrainer`'s `peft_config` parameter—or, in newer versions of TRL, we can simply use the `get_peft_model` convenience function:

```
from transformers import AutoModelForCausalLM
from peft import LoraConfig, get_peft_model
model = AutoModelForCausalLM.from_pretrained(
    MODEL_ID,
    torch_dtype=dtype,
    device_map="auto",
    trust_remote_code=True)
lora_config = LoraConfig(
    r=LORA_R,
    lora_alpha=LORA_ALPHA,
    lora_dropout=0.05,
    target_modules=["q_proj", "k_proj", "v_proj", "o_proj",
                    "gate_proj", "up_proj", "down_proj"],
    bias="none",
    task_type="CAUSAL_LM")
trainer = DPOTrainer(
    model=get_peft_model(model, lora_config),
    ref_model=None,
    # ... rest of the DPOTrainer configuration goes here
)
```

(continued)

> The base model serves as both reference and foundation for the adapter, eliminating duplication. ORPO and SimPO (discussed in "Beyond GRPO: IPO, ORPO, SimPO, and Friends" on page 147) are rather more complex. PEFT remains the most straightforward solution for most practitioners. For a practical illustration, including how it can be selectively applied, consider the DPO notebook (*notebooks/05/dpo.ipynb*).

In practice, DPO often matches or exceeds PPO performance while requiring substantially less compute. The comparison is not entirely fair since PPO naturally uses online generation, whereas vanilla DPO is typically used with offline preference data (though online variants of DPO exist and can outperform their offline counterparts). [110] For many applications, the difference matters little. When high-quality preference data is available, DPO extracts value from it efficiently. When practitioners have limited compute budgets or infrastructure complexity is a concern, DPO's simplicity is decisive. Many organizations that would struggle to run PPO successfully can run DPO with relative ease.

The Price of Simplicity

DPO's elegance comes with limitations that practitioners must understand to use it effectively. The method is not a universal solution but a technique with specific assumptions that may not always hold.

Policy Class Limitations

The derivation assumes that the policy class being trained can represent the optimal policy. If the preference data implies a behavior that the model architecture cannot capture, the training will do its best but cannot reach the true optimum. In simpler terms, you cannot train your model to do things that it cannot feasibly do. Rewarding a 10,000-token memory will not give a model architecture with a 4,096-token context window the ability to magically double it.

More practically, if the preference data is limited or unrepresentative, the "optimal policy" that DPO learns to approximate may not be the policy we actually want. PPO's online generation provides some robustness to this issue by continually sampling from the current policy. DPO's offline nature means it can learn only from the preferences it is given.

Reference Model Dependence

DPO is sensitive to the reference model in ways that can cause instability. The loss involves log probabilities under the reference model, and if the reference assigns very low probability to a response in the preference data, the log probability becomes a large negative number. Taking differences of large numbers is numerically unstable, and gradients can explode or become uninformative.

This problem arises when the preference data contains responses that the reference model would rarely produce, perhaps because they come from a different model or were heavily edited. The solution is to ensure that the preference data aligns with what the reference model can plausibly generate, or to use techniques like response filtering that exclude problematic examples.

Distribution Shift

Distribution shift is perhaps the most fundamental limitation. DPO learns from a fixed dataset of preferences. If the deployment distribution differs substantially, the preferences learned on training prompts may not transfer well. The model has learned to prefer certain responses in training contexts but has no guarantee that its preferences generalize appropriately. Unlike PPO, which explores through generation, DPO cannot discover how to handle novel situations.

The solution is coverage: Ensure that your preference data represents the full diversity of deployment scenarios. If you cannot achieve coverage, consider hybrid approaches that add online exploration after initial DPO training. This limitation is not unique to DPO (it is shared with any offline learning method), but practitioners should be aware that evaluation on held-out data from the training distribution may overestimate deployment performance. Careful evaluation design (Chapter 6) that tests on out-of-distribution prompts is essential for understanding how well preferences generalize.

> **FROM THE TRENCHES: THE SCALING QUESTION**
>
> DPO's elegance at moderate scale may not translate to frontier scale. Meta's experience with Llama provides a cautionary note. The company initially adopted DPO for its efficiency advantages but found that it "does not scale as well as PPO" when pushing toward maximum capability.[39] Meta pivoted to RLAIF for continued improvement beyond what DPO could deliver.
>
> This finding aligns with emerging systematic studies of RL scaling. Large-scale empirical work (400,000+ GPU-hours) suggests that not all preference optimization recipes yield similar asymptotic performance. The ceiling you can reach depends on fundamental algorithmic choices, not just data quality or compute budget.[111] Design details like loss aggregation and normalization modulate how efficiently you approach that ceiling, but the ceiling itself is set by the algorithm.
>
> The practical implication is that DPO is often the right choice for the crucial middle, where its efficiency and simplicity dominate. But if you find yourself pushing the limits of what DPO can achieve and still need more capability, the answer may be switching algorithms rather than adding more preference data. PPO's exploration, GRPO's group-relative learning, or hybrid approaches may have higher ceilings—even if they are harder to reach.

KTO: Preferences, All the Way Down

Must preference data always come in pairs? Kahneman-Tversky Optimization (KTO) draws on prospect theory, a theory from behavioral economics that seeks to explain how humans assess loss and gain and account for the empirically evident asymmetry between them (as it happens, it does so sufficiently well to net Daniel Kahneman the Nobel Prize in Economics). Where organizations collect unpaired feedback, such as the ubiquitous thumbs-up/thumbs-down signals in chat UIs, KTO is the key to preference optimization.

Breaking Free from Pairs

DPO and PPO require pairwise preference data: for each prompt, we need at least one preferred response and one dispreferred response. This requirement, inherited from the Bradley–Terry model that underlies the derivation, can be burdensome in practice. Obtaining pairs requires either generating multiple responses per prompt (which multiplies generation costs) or having annotators compare responses (which is slower than simple ratings). Many natural feedback mechanisms produce single ratings rather than comparisons: A user clicks thumbs-up or thumbs-down on a single response, without seeing alternatives.

KTO relaxes the pairwise requirement by learning from unpaired ratings on individual responses. The key insight is that while the Bradley–Terry model requires pairs, it is not the only game in town. Kahneman and Tversky's prospect theory does not require relative preferences, only absolute judgments: A response is either desirable or undesirable, and we want the model to produce more of the former and less of the latter. This seemingly small change in problem formulation has substantial practical implications.

Thumbs-up/-down data is easier to collect at scale than pairwise comparisons. Users naturally provide such feedback on individual responses, and many existing feedback systems already collect it. Such data is also much easier to implicitly infer. The length of an interaction exceeding a certain limit may, for instance, be considered an implicit approval of the interaction's quality (or its reverse, as what is desirable is very much in the eye of the beholder, and we can all think of certain conversations we would rather keep to a minimum). Data that does not fit the pairwise paradigm, such as expert curation of gold-standard examples without corresponding negatives (as would be used for SFT), becomes usable. KTO enables preference learning in scenarios where DPO's data requirements would be prohibitive.

Understanding That Losses Loom Larger than Gains

As noted previously, KTO draws its theoretical foundation from Kahneman and Tversky's prospect theory, an attempt at explaining how humans make decisions under uncertainty.[112] A central finding of this theory is that utility is asymmetric; losses loom larger than equivalent gains. Losing $10 feels worse than gaining $10 feels good. This loss aversion is not irrational but reflects deep features of human psychology that any model of preferences should account for (as well as the reality that we can lose only so many increments of \$10 before falling destitute).

The KTO objective directly incorporates this asymmetry. When training on desirable outputs, the objective encourages the policy to make them more likely relative to the reference. When training on undesirable outputs, the objective penalizes the policy for making them likely, and the penalty is weighted more heavily than the encouragement. This asymmetry means that avoiding bad outputs receives more training signal than producing good ones, reflecting the intuition that users are more damaged by bad responses than they are delighted by good ones.

KTO loss operates on unpaired data by treating each output independently. A desirable output contributes a term that rewards the policy for increasing its log probability relative to the reference. An undesirable output contributes a term that penalizes the policy for having elevated log probability relative to the reference. The loss-aversion parameter controls the relative weight of negative examples. Importantly, the objective includes a reference point—essentially, the expected log-probability ratio—that anchors what counts as elevated or depressed probability. This reference point ensures that the method learns to distinguish between outputs rather than collapsing to a trivial solution.

The KTO loss function is

$$\mathcal{L}_{\text{KTO}}(\pi_\theta, \pi_{\text{ref}}) = \mathbb{E}_{x,y\sim\mathcal{D}}\left[w(y)\cdot\left(1 - v_{\text{KTO}}(x, y; \beta)\right)\right]$$

where

$$v_{\text{KTO}}(x, y; \beta) = \begin{cases} \sigma\left(\beta\left(\log\frac{\pi_\theta(y|x)}{\pi_{\text{ref}}(y|x)} - z_{\text{ref}}\right)\right) & \text{if } y \text{ is desirable} \\ \sigma\left(\beta\left(z_{\text{ref}} - \log\frac{\pi_\theta(y|x)}{\pi_{\text{ref}}(y|x)}\right)\right) & \text{if } y \text{ is undesirable} \end{cases}$$

and $w(y)$ encodes the loss aversion asymmetry, with $w(y) = \lambda_{\text{undesirable}} > 1$ for undesirable outputs, reflecting that humans weight losses more heavily than gains.

Several implications follow from this formulation. The reference point z_{ref} acts as a calibration anchor, computed as the expected log-probability ratio across the dataset. Without this anchor, the model could satisfy the objective by simply increasing all log probabilities uniformly, learning nothing about which outputs are preferable. The anchor forces the model to make relative judgments: An output is desirable only if its log ratio exceeds the typical range of output values, and undesirable only if it falls below. This relative framing allows KTO to learn from unpaired data, since each example is compared against the population average rather than a specific alternative.

The asymmetric weighting encoded in $w(y)$ has practical consequences for training dynamics. Because undesirable outputs carry higher weight, the model learns to avoid bad outputs more aggressively than it learns to produce good ones. In practice, this manifests as faster reduction in failure modes than improvement in best-case performance. When avoiding harmful or low-quality outputs matters more than maximizing peak quality, this asymmetry aligns training incentives with deployment priorities. The loss aversion parameter $\lambda_{\text{undesirable}}$ is typically set from 1 to 2, with higher values producing more conservative models that prioritize safety over capability.

Winning with the Data You Have

KTO's primary advantage is data flexibility. It can learn from any mixture of desirable and undesirable examples without requiring them to be paired. Positive and negative examples need not come from the same prompts or even the same time periods. For instance, the golden dataset of expert-curated, high-quality responses may be combined with separately collected examples of undesirable outputs, perhaps from failure cases or adversarial testing, to train a KTO model without the artificial construction of pairs.

This flexibility enables training on datasets that would be unusable for DPO. Existing feedback logs where responses were rated individually, user interaction data with implicit positive and negative signals, and curated example sets without systematically paired negatives all become viable training data. For enterprises with deployed models or tools that already collect user feedback, KTO presents an attractive path to preference learning without new annotation efforts.

Empirical comparisons suggest that KTO achieves performance comparable to DPO when pairwise data is available, and can exceed it at larger scales.[113] Neither method dominates the other on standard benchmarks, and the differences are typically smaller than the variation from other factors like data quality and hyperparameter tuning. When only unpaired data exists, KTO outperforms because DPO simply cannot be applied.

The practical implication is clear: If you have pairwise data, either method works, and if you have only unpaired ratings, KTO is the path forward. For organizations with existing feedback infrastructure that produces thumbs-up/thumbs-down signals rather than comparisons, KTO may be the natural choice simply because it uses the data they already have.

> **FROM THE TRENCHES: MAN'S SEARCH FOR MEANINGFUL PREFERENCE DATA**
>
> It may take some creativity to find those hidden nuggets of gold that can be turned into useful preference data for KTO. The good news is that unlike DPO and PPO, which require purpose-built datasets, KTO needs just individual signals, and these don't even need to be explicit.
>
> The risk is finding these signals where they do not exist. Consider the example of user interaction length as an implicit approval signal. Longer interactions may indicate user engagement and satisfaction, but they may also reflect confusion, frustration, or distraction. Without careful analysis, using interaction length as a proxy for preference could lead to models that prioritize verbosity over clarity or relevance. With implicit data, this risk of finding meaning where there is none must be kept in mind—and like all assumptions that form part of the modeling process, documented.

GRPO: Pure Reinforcement Learning at Scale

Can we scale RL without the overhead of value networks? GRPO's insight is disarmingly simple: Sample multiple completions per prompt, and the completions themselves tell you which ones are better than average—no learned value function required!

The DeepSeek Moment

Most post-training researchers remember exactly where they were in early 2025 when the DeepSeek-R1 model was unveiled: in front of their screens, trying to replicate it. I was no exception, spending long hours poring over the DeepSeek technical report and its accompanying open source code. Unlike most, we didn't see the model as an unknown quantity because a few months earlier, the DeepSeek team had published its math reasoning model. The DeepSeek-R1 paper is full of innovations born, to a great extent, of necessity because the team couldn't get top-of-the-range NVDIA GPUs.

The training process the team adopted to work around these limitations has many interesting features, but for the purposes of this chapter, we will focus primarily on the novel RL algorithm it employed: GRPO. This method promised to deliver the benefits of preference learning without the computational overhead typically associated with value function estimation. The DeepSeek team not only used this method to train its model at a fraction of the cost, but did so achieving very strong results without SFT, casting some doubts on the traditional SFT-to-RL pipeline.

GRPO emerged from DeepSeek's work on scaling RL for language models, published as part of its efforts to train models that compete with frontier systems on substantially less compute.[30] The work addressed a specific challenge: how to estimate advantages in policy gradient methods without the computational overhead of training and running a separate value network, while preserving the benefits of on-policy learning.

The team's insight was elegant. The purpose of the value function is to estimate expected future reward from a given state, enabling advantage computation by comparing actual reward to expected reward. But surely, the researchers reasoned, an equally adequate way to estimate what reward to expect would be to sample multiple completions from the same prompt and observe the rewards they actually receive. The average reward across these completions would then provide an empirical estimate of the expected reward, and individual completion rewards could be compared against this average to compute advantages.

This *group relative* approach provides lower-variance advantage estimates than simple Monte Carlo methods that use only the single completion's reward. The variance reduction comes from the within-group comparison. An output with reward 8 might be good or bad depending on the prompt's difficulty, but an output with reward 8 when the group average is 5 is clearly above average for its prompt. Normalizing by the group standard deviation further reduces the impact of prompts with high or low reward variance.

The result: stable policy gradients without the complexity of value function learning.

Better than Average Is Good Enough

The GRPO training loop begins by sampling a batch of prompts. For each prompt, the policy generates a group of G completions, typically 4 to 16. A reward model scores each completion, producing G reward values per prompt. The key step is computing advantages from these rewards. Each completion's advantage is its reward minus the group mean, normalized by the group standard deviation. A completion that scored above average for its prompt receives positive advantage; one that scored below average receives negative advantage.

This formulation has several desirable properties. Each prompt contributes equally to the gradient regardless of absolute reward scale. A prompt whose completions all score around 7 contributes the same gradient magnitude as one whose completions score around 3, because advantages depend on relative position within the group rather than absolute values. The model learns to distinguish better from worse outputs within each context. And this is precisely what we want: Given this prompt, which completions are better than average?

This objective combines group-relative advantages with PPO-style clipping. The probability ratio between current and old policies determines how much credit or blame each completion receives, limited by clipping to prevent excessively large policy updates. KL regularization against a reference policy provides the same capability-preservation benefits as in standard PPO. The result is an approach that inherits PPO's stability while eliminating the value network that makes PPO expensive. The reward model replaces the value function as the source of training signal, scored at the response level rather than requiring per token value estimates.

For a prompt x with G sampled completions $\{y_1, \ldots, y_G\}$ and corresponding rewards $\{r_1, \ldots, r_G\}$, the group-relative advantage is defined as

$$\hat{A}_i = \frac{r_i - \mu_G}{\sigma_G}$$

where $\mu_G = \frac{1}{G}\sum_{j=1}^{G} r_j$ and $\sigma_G = \sqrt{\frac{1}{G}\sum_{j=1}^{G}(r_j - \mu_G)^2}$.

The GRPO objective combines this advantage with PPO-style clipping and KL regularization with

$$\mathcal{L}_{\text{GRPO}} = -\mathbb{E}_{x,\{y_i\}}\left[\frac{1}{G}\sum_{i=1}^{G}\min\left(\rho_i\hat{A}_i, \text{clip}(\rho_i, 1-\epsilon, 1+\epsilon)\hat{A}_i\right) - \beta\,\text{KL}_i\right]$$

where $\rho_i = \frac{\pi_\theta(y_i|x)}{\pi_{\text{old}}(y_i|x)}$.

The objective rewards the policy for making above-average completions more likely and penalizes it for favoring below-average ones. The probability ratio ρ_i measures how much more (or less) likely the current policy makes completion i compared to the policy that generated it. Multiplying by the advantage means that if a completion was above average and we have made it more likely, good; if it was below average and we have made it less likely, also good. The clipping bounds how much any single update can change the policy, preventing the instabilities that plague unconstrained policy gradient methods. The KL term anchors the policy to its reference, preserving capabilities while the objective reshapes preferences. Figure 5-2 shows the GRPO training loop in practice.

What emerges is an algorithm that needs no learned value function yet achieves the stability benefits that value functions provide. The group itself serves as the baseline. Each prompt brings its own context, its own difficulty, its own distribution of possible responses. By comparing completions only to their siblings from the same prompt, GRPO sidesteps the challenge of learning a value function that generalizes across the vast space of possible prompts. The reward model provides absolute quality judgments; the group structure converts these into relative signals that drive learning.

Why does this normalization matter? Consider two prompts in the same training batch. Prompt A is straightforward, receiving rewards of 8, 7, 9, 8 for its four completions, whereas prompt B is challenging, receiving rewards of 3, 2, 4, 3. Without normalization, the raw advantages from prompt A would dominate the gradient simply because its rewards are higher, even though the model performed equally well relative to prompt difficulty on both. Group normalization fixes this: Prompt A's completions receive advantages of approximately +0.7, −1.0, +1.4, +0.7 (mean 8, std 0.7), while prompt B's receive approximately +0.7, −1.0, +1.4, +0.7 (mean 3, std 0.7). The advantages are comparable despite the absolute reward difference, and both prompts contribute equally to the gradient. This is precisely what we want: The model learns which completions are better than average for each prompt, not merely which prompts happen to be easier.

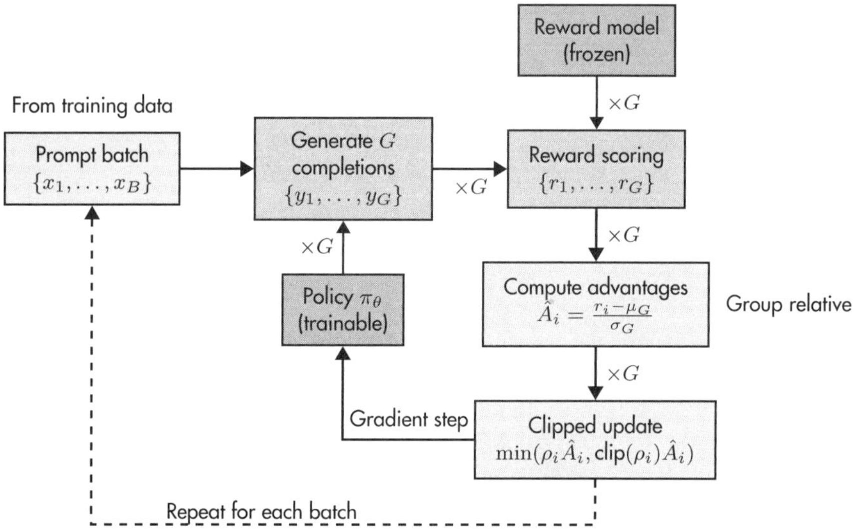

Figure 5-2: The GRPO training loop. For each prompt, the policy generates multiple completions that the reward model scores. Advantages are computed relative to the group mean, enabling stable policy gradients without a learned value function.

Putting the G in GRPO

GRPO requires generating multiple completions per prompt during training, putting it somewhere between DPO and full PPO in terms of complexity. Unlike DPO, which uses only offline preference data with no generation, GRPO generates online. Unlike PPO, which maintains and trains a value network, GRPO derives advantages directly from reward model scores. The generation overhead is real but bounded—G completions per prompt rather than the potentially extensive exploration of other RL methods.

The driving hyperparameter in GRPO is the group size G. Larger groups provide more accurate advantage estimates because the group mean and standard deviation converge to population values with more samples. But larger groups also require more generations per prompt, increasing memory usage during the generation phase and compute time for reward model scoring. In practice, group sizes of 4 to 16 provide reasonable trade-offs. Groups of 4 offer efficiency at the cost of noisier advantages, while groups of 16 offer stable advantages at higher computational cost. The optimal choice depends on the variance of the reward model and the available compute budget.

DeepSeek's successful use of GRPO at large scale—training models that achieve competitive performance on standard benchmarks—validates the approach. The technique handles the challenges of effectively scaling RL for language models: stable training dynamics, efficient compute utilization, and the ability to use strong reward models without the additional complexity of value networks. For practitioners with access to reward models and the infrastructure to support online generation, GRPO offers a compelling middle ground between DPO's simplicity and PPO's expressiveness.

> **DIFFICULTY-AWARE GRPO EXTENSIONS**
>
> GRPO's group-relative formulation creates a natural foundation for difficulty-aware training. Extensions like GRPO-LEAD add three refinements that improve performance on mathematical reasoning:[114]
>
> **Length-dependent rewards** Penalize verbose solutions. If a problem can be solved in 5 steps, a 15-step solution that reaches the same answer receives lower reward. This combats the verbosity bias that plagues reasoning models and saves inference tokens.
>
> **Explicit incorrect-answer penalties** Sharpen the distinction between right and wrong. Standard GRPO normalizes within the group, which can obscure the difference between "all bad" and "mostly good" groups. Adding explicit penalties for incorrect answers boosts precision.
>
> **Difficulty-aware advantage reweighting** Uses a logistic function based on empirical correctness rates to upweight hard problems. If the model already correctly solves 90 percent of easy problems, the learning signal from easy problems is mostly noise. If the model solves only 30 percent of hard problems, those hard problems offer the most room for improvement. Reweighting focuses training where it matters.
>
> These modifications achieve state-of-the-art results for 14B-scale models on mathematical reasoning benchmarks, with faster convergence and shorter solutions than baselines. The pattern generalizes: Any RL method can benefit from difficulty awareness that matches training effort to problem difficulty. If your use case involves a range of task difficulties that you can—directly or indirectly—measure and quantify, consider incorporating difficulty-aware techniques into your preference optimization pipeline.

Beyond GRPO: IPO, ORPO, SimPO, and Friends

The field of preference optimization evolves faster than any survey can capture. IPO, ORPO, and SimPO each address specific limitations of prior methods, and each will likely be superseded in turn. What matters is understanding the principles beneath the frontier techniques in order to know how to adapt them to your use cases.

IPO: When Preferences Are Too Convincing

Identity preference optimization (IPO) addresses a theoretical concern with DPO that emerges from careful examination of the derivation in the first section of this chapter.[115] DPO assumes that the policy being trained can represent the optimal policy implied by the preference data. If this assumption holds, DPO finds that optimal policy. If it does not, DPO may exhibit problematic behavior, particularly on preference pairs where one response is strongly preferred over the other.

The issue is that DPO's loss function drives the probability ratio for strongly preferred responses toward infinity. Recall that we defined DPO loss as $-\log \sigma(\beta\Delta)$, where Δ is the difference in log ratios: $\log \frac{\pi_\theta(y_w)}{\pi_{\text{ref}}(y_w)} - \log \frac{\pi_\theta(y_l)}{\pi_{\text{ref}}(y_l)}$. The gradient $\nabla\mathcal{L} \propto \sigma(-\beta\Delta)$ approaches 1 as $\Delta \to -\infty$, meaning the loss provides arbitrarily strong signal to increase Δ without bound. When the preference is decisive (say, with probability 0.99) the loss provides unlimited gradient to make the preferred response ever more likely relative to the dispreferred one. If the model cannot achieve the true optimal policy, this pressure can cause overfitting on individual preference pairs rather than learning a general preference function. The authors term this *overfitting to the preference dataset*: The model memorizes specific preference pairs rather than learning the underlying preference distribution.

IPO modifies the DPO objective to address this issue. Rather than the log-sigmoid loss of DPO, IPO uses a squared error loss on the difference between log-probability ratios:

$$\mathcal{L}_{\text{IPO}}(\pi_\theta) = \mathbb{E}_{(x,y_w,y_l)}\left[\left(\log \frac{\pi_\theta(y_w \mid x)}{\pi_{\text{ref}}(y_w \mid x)} - \log \frac{\pi_\theta(y_l \mid x)}{\pi_{\text{ref}}(y_l \mid x)} - \frac{1}{2\beta}\right)^2\right]$$

This formulation caps the gradient signal. After the model has learned to prefer the correct response by a margin of $\frac{1}{2\beta}$, additional preference strength provides diminishing returns. The squared loss penalizes both undershooting and overshooting the target margin, preventing the unbounded growth that DPO permits.

The practical implications are significant for datasets with high-confidence preferences. If annotators strongly agree on which response is better, DPO will aggressively push the probability ratio, potentially at the cost of generalization. IPO's bounded objective provides more stable training in such scenarios. Empirically, IPO tends to produce models that generalize better when preference data has limited coverage, though the differences from DPO are often modest when preference data is abundant and representative.

For practitioners, IPO offers a theoretically grounded alternative to DPO when overfitting to preference pairs is a concern. The method is straightforward to implement as a drop-in replacement for DPO, requiring only a change in the loss function. Organizations dealing with small or noisy preference datasets may find IPO's stability advantageous, while those with large, high-quality datasets may see less difference. As with all preference optimization methods, careful evaluation on held-out data remains essential to assess real-world performance.

ORPO: Two Birds, One Training Run

Odds ratio preference optimization (ORPO) takes a different approach to simplifying the post-training pipeline.[116] Rather than accepting the sequential structure of SFT followed by preference learning (see Chapter 3), ORPO combines both into a single training stage. The key insight is that the reference model requirement in DPO exists primarily to prevent the policy from collapsing—assigning all probability mass to a narrow set of responses—and ORPO could achieve this through explicit supervision on both preferred and dispreferred responses.

The ORPO objective has two components. The first is a standard negative log-likelihood loss on the preferred response, encouraging the model to generate it fluently. The second is an odds ratio penalty that compares the relative likelihood of preferred versus dispreferred responses:

$$\mathcal{L}_{\text{ORPO}} = \mathbb{E}_{(x,y_w,y_l)}\left[-\log p_\theta(y_w \mid x) - \lambda \cdot \log \sigma\left(\log \frac{\text{odds}_\theta(y_w \mid x)}{\text{odds}_\theta(y_l \mid x)}\right)\right]$$

Here, $\text{odds}_\theta(y \mid x) = \frac{p_\theta(y|x)}{1-p_\theta(y|x)}$ and λ controls the strength of the preference signal relative to the SFT loss.

This formulation has several attractive properties. It eliminates the need for a reference model; it's not just implicit as in DPO, but absent from the computation altogether. This reduces memory requirements by half compared to DPO, which must maintain both the training policy and a frozen reference. The SFT component ensures that the model learns to generate coherent responses, while the odds ratio component ensures that the model prefers the right ones.

The unification eliminates a training stage, reducing wall-clock time and simplifying the pipeline. When SFT data and preference data are available for the same prompts (which is common when preference data is collected by generating multiple responses to SFT prompts and having annotators compare them), ORPO provides a natural way to use both signals simultaneously. Empirically, ORPO achieves competitive results on standard benchmarks, particularly when starting from a base model rather than an already-SFT'd model.

TRL's `experimental.orpo.OrpoTrainer` class provides an accessible implementation for practitioners interested in exploring this approach. Here, the key hyperparameter is λ, which balances the SFT and preference components. Tuning λ allows practitioners to adjust the emphasis on fluency versus preference adherence, tailoring the training to their specific application needs, as Listing 5-2 shows.

```
from trl.experimental.orpo import OrpoTrainer, OrpoConfig

training_args = OrpoConfig(
 ❶ lambda_weight=0.5,
    learning_rate=8e-6,
    per_device_train_batch_size=2,
    output_dir="./orpo_output"
)

❷ trainer = OrpoTrainer(
    model=model,
```

```
    args=training_args,
    train_dataset=preference_dataset,
    tokenizer=tokenizer,
)

trainer.train()
```

Listing 5-2: Implementing ORPO with TRL's `OrpoTrainer`

The `lambda_weight` parameter ❶ balances the SFT loss against the preference signal. Unlike DPO, the `OrpoTrainer` ❷ requires no reference model parameter, as ORPO's formulation eliminates the need for a frozen reference.

SimPO: Cutting the Last Cord

The field of preference optimization continues to evolve at a pace that makes any comprehensive survey quickly outdated. New techniques regularly emerge from academic and industry research, each claiming advantages in particular settings or addressing specific limitations of existing methods.

Simple preference optimization (SimPO) simplifies DPO further by eliminating the reference model dependency that DPO inherits from its derivation.[117] The key insight is that the reference model in DPO serves primarily as a baseline for comparison. SimPO replaces this with a simpler approach: Instead of computing log-probability ratios between policy and reference, it uses length-normalized sequence probabilities directly. The objective becomes

$$\mathcal{L}_{\text{SimPO}} = -\mathbb{E}_{(x,y_w,y_l)}\left[\log\sigma\left(\frac{\beta}{|y_w|}\log p_\theta(y_w \mid x) - \frac{\beta}{|y_l|}\log p_\theta(y_l \mid x) - \gamma\right)\right]$$

where $|y|$ denotes sequence length and γ is a target margin. The length normalization addresses a subtle issue: Longer sequences naturally have lower log-probabilities, and without correction, DPO can develop a bias toward shorter responses. SimPO's explicit normalization provides a principled solution.

The practical benefits are substantial. Without a reference model, memory requirements drop significantly, which is important for practitioners working with limited GPU resources. Training is faster because there is no need for forward passes through a frozen reference. SimPO achieves competitive results on standard benchmarks while being simpler to implement and cheaper to run.

Reward-free methods take a different direction, learning from preferences without interpreting them as evidence about an underlying reward function. These methods may be more robust to the assumptions that reward-based derivations require but are less theoretically understood. Curriculum approaches present preference pairs in orders that facilitate learning (starting with clear-cut preferences before introducing more ambiguous ones), potentially improving training efficiency and final performance.

The rapid evolution suggests that the "best" technique is a moving target. Practitioners who commit irrevocably to any single approach risk being overtaken by improvements they cannot adopt. The wiser strategy is to understand the principles that underlie all these methods—learning from human preferences to improve model behavior—and to implement specific techniques in modular ways that permit swapping as the field advances. The specific algorithms matter less than the capacity to deploy and iterate on preference learning in general. Today's best practice will likely be superseded, but the organization that has built its preference-learning capability can adopt improvements as they emerge.

Choosing Your Weapon

Which method should you use? The answer is not whichever performs best on benchmarks but whichever matches your data, infrastructure, and deployment constraints. Choosing among preference optimization methods is a matching problem, not a ranking problem.

The Exploration-Efficiency Trade-Off

The on-policy/off-policy distinction introduced in Chapter 4 has practical consequences not only to explain architectural features (as it did for PPO) but also to shape the choice among preference methods. For preference optimization specifically, the on-policy/off-policy divide conditions method selection in four ways:

Exploration
: On-policy methods can explore. The model discovers new behaviors by generating outputs, receiving feedback, and adjusting. If the current policy produces an unexpectedly good response, the method learns from it. Off-policy methods cannot explore beyond their training data. If a behavior is not represented in the preference dataset, the model has no signal to learn it. This limitation is why DPO can plateau when PPO continues improving: PPO explores the space of possible responses, while DPO is confined to generalizing from fixed examples.

Distribution shift
: On-policy methods avoid distribution shift by construction. The training distribution is always the current policy's output distribution. Off-policy methods must contend with the gap between the data-generating policy and the policy being trained. As training proceeds and the policy changes, this gap widens. The preference data reflects what a historical policy would produce, not what the current policy produces. Techniques like importance sampling can partially correct for this shift, but the fundamental challenge remains.

Computational cost
: On-policy methods require generation during training, which is expensive. Autoregressive generation is slow, and generating multiple

completions per prompt (as GRPO requires) multiplies the cost. Off-policy methods avoid generation entirely; forward passes through the model suffice. This difference makes DPO dramatically cheaper than PPO for the same number of training steps. When compute budgets are constrained, the efficiency of off-policy methods may outweigh their limitations.

Data requirements

Off-policy methods require high-quality preference data collected in advance. The data must cover the situations the model will encounter at deployment, because the model cannot learn about situations it has not seen. On-policy methods generate their own training data, reducing dependence on pre-collected datasets. A strong reward model suffices; the method collects its own preferences by generating and scoring.

Understanding this divide clarifies why different methods suit different situations. When exploration matters (when pushing toward frontier capabilities or when the desired behavior differs substantially from the reference model), on-policy methods have structural advantages. When efficiency matters (which is generally the case) or when good preference data already exists, off-policy methods deliver more improvement per unit of compute. The methods are not better or worse in absolute terms but rather embody different trade-offs that match different circumstances.

A Practical Decision Tree

Choosing a preference optimization method is a matching problem: You match technique assumptions to data characteristics and deployment constraints. The best method for your situation depends on what you have and what you need, not on what works best in benchmark comparisons that may not reflect your circumstances. A helpful summary of the logic of these methods is laid out in Table 5-2.

DPO suits scenarios with pairwise preference data and moderate compute budgets. If you have data in the form of preference pairs (prompts with chosen and rejected responses), and you want the simplest training process with the least infrastructure, DPO is the natural starting point. Its computational requirements resemble SFT, making it accessible to organizations that lack the infrastructure for more complex methods.

Table 5-2: Preference Optimization Methods: A Comparative Overview

Dimension	PPO	DPO	KTO	GRPO
Data format	Reward model	Pairwise preferences	Unpaired ratings	Reward model
Policy type	On-policy	Off-policy	Off-policy	On-policy
Generation	Online (during training)	Offline (fixed dataset)	Offline	Online (group samples)
Reward model	Required (separate)	Implicit in policy	Implicit in policy	Required (separate)
Value network	Required	Not needed	Not needed	Not needed
Compute cost	Highest	Lowest	Low	Moderate
Infrastructure	Complex	SFT-like	SFT-like	Moderate
Hyperparameter sensitivity	Very high	Moderate (β)	Moderate	Moderate
Reference model	Required	Required	Required	Required
Best for	Max control; exploration	Pairwise data; simplicity	Thumbs-up/-down data	Scale; no value net

KTO enables learning from unpaired feedback. If your data consists of individually rated responses rather than pairs, or if you want to use existing user feedback that was not collected in pairwise format, KTO lets you proceed, whereas DPO cannot. The flexibility in data format can outweigh any performance differences between methods.

GRPO provides an alternative when reward models are available and generation during training is acceptable. If you have invested in training a strong reward model and have the infrastructure to support online generation, GRPO offers stable training without the complexity of value networks. The method is well-suited for iterative improvement when you can afford the generation overhead.

PPO remains relevant for scenarios requiring maximum control over the optimization process, particularly when online exploration is important or when research requires detailed control over training dynamics. The additional complexity is justified when simpler methods fall short.

The decision should also consider organizational factors: team familiarity with specific techniques, existing infrastructure capabilities, and the cost of building new infrastructure versus adapting to available methods.

What the Benchmarks Show

Empirical comparisons across preference optimization techniques reveal patterns that should inform practical decision-making. The most robust finding is that data quality dominates algorithmic choice. A well-implemented DPO pipeline with carefully curated preference data will outperform a poorly implemented PPO setup regardless of PPO's theoretical advantages. This observation, repeatedly confirmed in both academic benchmarks and industrial deployments, suggests that technique selection is often less consequential than execution quality.

However, when implementation quality is controlled for, a consistent performance gap emerges between online and offline methods. Studies comparing DPO to online alternatives find that online approaches (whether PPO, online DPO variants, or GRPO) reliably achieve better final performance. The gap traces to distribution shift: DPO's training signal comes from a fixed dataset, and as the policy improves beyond what that dataset represents, further improvement stalls. The presence of out-of-distribution examples in preference data particularly harms DPO, as the model must extrapolate preferences for responses that the reference policy would rarely generate. Online methods sidestep this by generating fresh data from the current policy, ensuring that the training distribution always matches the policy distribution.

The implication for practitioners is that starting with the simplest applicable method (usually DPO for those with pairwise preference data) and investing effort in data quality and implementation robustness will yield better results than prematurely attempting more complex methods. The appeal of sophisticated techniques is real. They promise more control, more expressiveness, and more tuning possibilities. But sophistication compounds the opportunities for error. Every hyperparameter is a choice that can be made poorly. Every additional component is a system that can fail or be misconfigured. The simple approach, executed well, beats the complex approach executed poorly.

Benchmark comparisons between DPO and PPO typically show overlapping confidence intervals in the final metrics that matter. Both methods can achieve strong performance on preference-learning tasks, and which performs better in any given study often depends on implementation details, hyperparameter tuning effort, and dataset characteristics more than on fundamental algorithmic differences.

This is not to say the methods are equivalent. They have different computational profiles, different failure modes, and different sensitivities. But method selection alone does not determine success. For most practitioners, the recommendation follows directly: Start simple, measure carefully, and add complexity only when you have clear evidence that simpler approaches are insufficient for your requirements. The burden of proof should lie with complexity, not with simplicity.

SIMPLICITY AS THE DEFAULT

When choosing from preference optimization methods, let the burden of proof lie with complexity. DPO should be the default for pairwise data. Add PPO only when DPO demonstrably fails.

The appeal of sophisticated methods is real. They promise more control, more tuning knobs, and more theoretical backing. But every knob is an opportunity for error. A well-executed simple method beats a poorly executed complex one. Start simple, and add complexity only when forced.

The Best of Both Worlds

Advanced practitioners often combine techniques in pipelines that capture benefits of multiple approaches while mitigating individual weaknesses. A common pattern begins with DPO for initial preference learning, drawing on its simplicity and data efficiency to establish a baseline of preference-aligned behavior, followed by PPO for refinement on specific capabilities that require online exploration. Another pattern uses iterative DPO; the trained model generates new responses that are evaluated to create fresh preference data, which then trains the next iteration. This iterative approach addresses DPO's limitation of learning only from fixed offline data while avoiding the full complexity of online RL.

GRPO combined with synthetic preferences from constitutional AI approaches offers another compelling hybrid (see Chapter 11 for detailed treatment of RLAIF). The model generates responses, an AI evaluator (possibly the same model with appropriate prompting) provides preference judgments based on explicit principles, and GRPO trains on these synthetic preferences. The constitutional component provides scalable preference annotation, while GRPO provides stable training dynamics. This combination has produced impressive results at scale, enabling training loops that run continuously without human annotation bottlenecks.

The principle underlying effective hybrid pipelines is to use each technique for what it does best: DPO for efficient initial alignment when offline preference data is available, PPO for fine-grained optimization when detailed control is needed, synthetic methods for scaling beyond human annotation capacity, and KTO for incorporating unpaired feedback signals. Building these pipelines requires understanding each component's strengths and failure modes well enough to appropriately sequence them and to diagnose problems when they occur. The organization that develops capability in multiple techniques can compose them into workflows that achieve results none could reach alone, matching each stage of the pipeline to the technique best suited for its requirements.

Summary

In this chapter, we deepened our sojourn into preference optimization methods. We explored GRPO, a novel on-policy technique that combines the stability of PPO with the simplicity of value-free training. We surveyed emerging methods like IPO and ORPO that address specific limitations of established techniques. Now, we return to a more general perspective and consider how to evaluate the fruits of our labors. In Chapter 6, we will examine how to measure whether our training has truly resulted in better, more aligned models—and how to know if it did not.

6

EVALUATION STRATEGIES: MEASURING MODEL QUALITY

How do we know a model is good? In conventional ML, we can typically measure our models' performance against a certain level of ground truth. Evaluating language models is more complex–not only because of the range of responses they can generate, but also because of the ways in which they can be right or wrong, the qualities they can exhibit or, for that matter, lack. Equally, there are different levels and kinds in which they may be *wrong*. Completing "The cat sat on . . ." with "the space shuttle" is not the first thing that comes to mind, but it is less blatantly incorrect than, say, "The cat sat on vmslkrmw." In short, evaluating model outputs is difficult.

But this evaluation is also critical. Without rigorous evaluation, we cannot know whether our interventions improve models or merely change them in ways we happen to like. Yet evaluation of language models is genuinely difficult. Outputs are open-ended, quality is multidimensional, and the metrics we can easily compute often fail to capture what we care about. The gap between measurable proxies and true quality is not a temporary inconvenience awaiting a methodological breakthrough. It is a structural feature of working with open-ended generation.

This chapter confronts the evaluation problem head-on, providing frameworks for thinking about evaluation, surveys of available tools, and practical guidance for building evaluation systems that inform development decisions. We examine standard benchmarks and their limitations, human evaluation and when to use it, domain-specific metrics that capture what automated benchmarks miss, and A/B testing for production decisions. The evaluation challenge is not merely technical but epistemological: What does it mean for a language model to be *good*? Different stakeholders have different answers, and these answers sometimes conflict.

The Evaluation Problem

Why is evaluating language models so notoriously difficult? The metrics we can easily compute correlate only loosely with what we want, Goodhart's law applies with particular virulence, and the evaluation stack that works requires deliberate layering of speed, cost, and reliability.

The Unmeasurable and How to Measure It

Language model evaluation is fundamentally harder than evaluation in most ML domains, and this difficulty stems from the nature of the task rather than from inadequate methodology. When evaluating a classification model, accuracy measures exactly what we care about: the fraction of examples classified correctly. When evaluating a language model, the metrics we can easily compute—perplexity, BLEU score, token overlap—correlate only loosely with what we want, which is something like "helpful, accurate, appropriate responses."

This difficulty has several sources. Outputs are open-ended: For most prompts, many responses would be acceptable, and the space of good responses is vast and ill-defined. Quality is subjective: Different users may legitimately prefer different response styles, levels of detail, or degrees of formality. Quality is multidimensional: A response can be accurate but unhelpful, helpful but verbose, or concise but incomplete. No single number captures all dimensions, and different applications weight dimensions differently. Worse, the dimensions interact. Being more cautious may improve accuracy while reducing helpfulness, and being more detailed may help some users while overwhelming others.

The standard ML response to evaluation difficulty—collecting more data, using more sophisticated metrics, and computing bigger numbers—does not fully resolve these issues. You can compute perplexity on arbitrarily large datasets, but a model with lower perplexity may still produce worse responses by any human judgment. You can invent increasingly sophisticated automatic metrics, but they remain proxies for qualities that ultimately require human judgment to assess. Accepting this difficulty is the first step toward evaluation practices that work despite it. The goal is not to find the perfect metric but to build evaluation systems that provide useful signal despite imperfect individual components.

Goodhart's Law Strikes Again

Goodhart's law, the observation that when a measure becomes a target, it ceases to be a good measure, manifests throughout language model evaluation with particular virulence. The economist Charles Goodhart formulated this principle in the context of monetary policy, but it applies with equal force to any optimization process that relies on proxy metrics. In language model development, every metric we can easily compute is a proxy for what we want, and every proxy can be gamed.

Gaming happens automatically through the optimization process itself. Models trained to maximize benchmark scores learn benchmark-specific patterns: particular phrasings that multiple-choice questions reward, response structures that human evaluators prefer, and length distributions that match training data. These patterns may improve benchmark performance without improving the underlying capability that the benchmark was designed to measure. A model that learns to recognize MMLU-style questions and apply MMLU-specific heuristics may score well on MMLU while being no better at genuine knowledge application. The benchmark becomes a test of benchmark-taking skill rather than the capability it nominally measures.

This phenomenon extends beyond training to evaluation itself. Developers who use a particular metric to make decisions will implicitly optimize for that metric. A team that uses perplexity as its primary guide will make choices that reduce perplexity even when those choices do not improve output quality. A team that tracks only task completion rate might accept a model that completes tasks poorly over one that appropriately declines tasks beyond its capability. The metric shapes the behavior of the humans doing the development, not just the model being developed.

The defense against Goodhart's law is evaluation diversity: using multiple metrics that cannot all be gamed simultaneously, rotating evaluation sets so that models cannot overfit to specific examples, and maintaining human evaluation as an ongoing check that automated metrics have not diverged from actual quality. No single metric is trustworthy in isolation; trustworthiness emerges from the agreement of diverse, independent measurements. When multiple metrics that measure the same underlying quality through different means all improve together, we have some confidence that genuine improvement has occurred. Diverging metrics signal that something has gone wrong.

A field-wide manifestation of this problem is worth noting. When everyone optimizes for the same benchmarks via the same techniques, the models converge toward similar behaviors. Researchers have begun calling this the *artificial hivemind* effect.[13] The NeurIPS 2025 paper documenting this phenomenon found that models trained with RLHF on similar preference data produced outputs with measurably lower diversity than their base model counterparts. We optimize for the same proxies and arrive at the same bland destinations. Differentiation requires optimizing for something different, which means measuring something different.

> **METRIC TRIANGULATION**
>
> Never trust a single metric. If you care about quality, measure it three ways: an automatic metric for speed, a model-based evaluation for nuance, and periodic human evaluation for ground truth. When all three improve together, you have evidence of genuine progress. When they diverge (for example, automatic metrics improve, but human evaluation stagnates), the divergence itself is the most important signal. The metric you trust least is often revealing a truth that the others are hiding.

The Evaluation Stack

Practical evaluation employs the stack of methods laid out in Table 6-1, each with its own place in a developer's arsenal and fit to different purposes in the development cycle. The stack metaphor clarifies when each method is appropriate and how the methods complement one another. Understanding the stack enables practitioners to build evaluation systems that appropriately balance speed, cost, and reliability.

At the base of the stack sit automatic metrics: perplexity, BLEU, ROUGE, exact match, and format compliance checks. These metrics are fast, cheap, and perfectly reproducible. You can compute them on millions of examples in minutes at negligible cost, and you will get the same answer every time.

Their limitation is that they measure proxies rather than quality itself. Perplexity measures surprise under the model's probability distribution, not whether responses are good. BLEU measures *n*-gram overlap with reference responses, not whether the generated response would satisfy a user. These metrics provide useful signal for rapid iteration—particularly during SFT (see Chapter 3)—catching obvious regressions and enabling quick comparisons across many configurations, but they cannot substitute for assessment of quality.

Table 6-1: The Evaluation Stack: Trade-offs at Each Level

Level	Speed	Cost	Nuance	Best use
Automatic metrics	Seconds	Near zero	Low	Every checkpoint; regression detection
Model-based eval	Minutes	Moderate	Medium	Candidate filtering; detailed analysis
Human evaluation	Hours to days	High	Highest	Deployment decisions; calibration
A/B testing	Weeks	Variable	Deployment ground truth	Production validation

The middle layer consists of model-based evaluation, where capable language models judge the outputs of the model being evaluated. A frontier model can assess whether a response is helpful, whether it addresses the question asked, and whether it contains factual errors. This evaluation is more nuanced than automatic metrics and captures aspects of quality that simple statistics cannot. The cost is higher, requiring inference through a capable model for each evaluation, and the results are only as trustworthy as the evaluating model's judgment. Model-based evaluation provides detailed analysis at moderate cost, filling the gap between cheap-but-crude automatic metrics and expensive-but-definitive human evaluation.

At the top of the stack is human evaluation—people assessing outputs according to specified criteria. Human evaluation provides ground truth in a sense that no automated method can match, because humans are ultimately the consumers whose satisfaction matters. But human evaluation is slow, expensive, and subject to its own biases: evaluator fatigue, inconsistent criteria application, and anchoring effects from previously seen examples. Human evaluation should be reserved for validation and calibration: verifying that automated methods track human judgment, making final decisions about model deployment, and providing training signal for model-based evaluators. Using human evaluation for routine monitoring wastes resources, while failing to use it for validation risks optimizing metrics that have diverged from actual quality.

WHEN TO USE EACH LEVEL

Use automatic metrics for every training checkpoint and every experiment, as they are fast enough to not block iteration. Use model-based evaluation for promising candidates before human review, since it filters out obviously bad options and provides preliminary rankings. Reserve human evaluation for final model selection and deployment decisions; it is too expensive for routine use but essential for validating that automated methods have not drifted. The ratio varies by budget, but an illustrative pattern is 1,000:100:10: a thousand automated checks, a hundred model-based evaluations, and ten human reviews.

The Automated Arsenal

The base layer of the evaluation stack deserves closer examination. Automatic metrics provide fast, cheap, reproducible measurements that enable rapid iteration. Understanding what each metric measures—and what it misses—is essential for correctly interpreting results. Different metrics suit different tasks, and no single metric captures overall quality. The practitioner's job is to select those that align with the qualities that matter for a given application.

Counting Words: BLEU, ROUGE, and Friends

Token-level metrics (the most important of which are listed in Table 6-2) compare generated text against reference text, measuring various forms of overlap and similarity. These metrics originated in machine translation and summarization, where reference outputs exist, and remain useful for tasks where ground-truth responses are available. Their limitation is fundamental: They measure similarity to a reference, not quality itself. A response that conveys the same information in different words may score poorly, while a response that matches surface tokens but misses the point may score well.

Table 6-2: Token-Level Similarity Metrics for Text Generation

Metric	What it measures	Primary use	Implementations
BLEU	*N*-gram precision between generated and reference text	Translation quality	Hugging Face Evaluate, SacreBLEU, NLTK
ROUGE	Recall-oriented *n*-gram overlap (ROUGE-1, ROUGE-2, ROUGE-L)	Summarization quality	Hugging Face Evaluate, TorchMetrics
METEOR	Precision and recall with synonym and stemming matching	Translation (handles paraphrase)	Hugging Face Evaluate, NLTK
BERTScore	Cosine similarity of contextual embeddings from BERT	Semantic equivalence	Hugging Face Evaluate, *bert-score* package
chrF	Character-level F-score	Translation (morphologically rich languages)	Hugging Face Evaluate, SacreBLEU

Bilingual evaluation understudy (BLEU) counts matching *n*-grams between generated and reference text, computing a precision score with a brevity penalty to discourage overly short outputs.[118] Scores range from 0 to 1, with a higher score indicating a better match. BLEU was among the earliest automated metrics for machine translation and remains widely used despite known limitations: It rewards exact lexical matches and penalizes valid paraphrases. Absolute values depend on the dataset and tokenization, so comparisons are most meaningful within the same setup.

Recall-oriented understudy for gisting evaluation (ROUGE) emphasizes recall rather than precision, measuring what fraction of reference *n*-grams appear in the generated text.[119] ROUGE-1 counts unigram overlap, ROUGE-2 counts bigram overlap, and ROUGE-L measures longest common subsequence. The recall orientation suits summarization, where capturing key information matters more than matching exact phrasing. ROUGE scores are typically reported as F1, combining precision and recall.

BERTScore addresses the lexical matching limitation by computing similarity in embedding space rather than token space.[120] It generates contextual embeddings for each token via a pre-trained BERT model, then computes cosine similarity between the embeddings of generated and reference tokens. This captures semantic equivalence even when different words are used; "the car is fast" and "the automobile is quick" score similarly despite sharing few tokens. BERTScore correlates better with human judgment than

n-gram metrics for many tasks, but adds computational cost and introduces dependence on the embedding model's quality.

In practice, computing these metrics is straightforward with the Hugging Face Evaluate library. Listing 6-1 demonstrates calculating BLEU, ROUGE, and BERTScore for a generated response against a reference.

```
import evaluate

❶ bleu = evaluate.load("bleu")
rouge = evaluate.load("rouge")
bertscore = evaluate.load("bertscore")

❷ generated = ["The model achieved significant improvements in accuracy."]
reference = [["The model showed substantial gains in performance."]]

❸ bleu_result = bleu.compute(predictions=generated, references=reference)
print(f"BLEU: {bleu_result['bleu']:.3f}")

❹ rouge_result = rouge.compute(predictions=generated, references=reference)
print(f"ROUGE-1: {rouge_result['rouge1']:.3f}")
print(f"ROUGE-L: {rouge_result['rougeL']:.3f}")

❺ bert_result = bertscore.compute(
    predictions=generated,
    references=reference,
    lang="en"
)
print(f"BERTScore F1: {bert_result['f1'][0]:.3f}")
```

Listing 6-1: Computing token-level similarity metrics with Hugging Face Evaluate

The Evaluate library provides a unified interface for loading metrics ❶. Note that the generated text is a single-element list, while references are nested ❷, allowing multiple valid references per prediction. BLEU computes n-gram precision with a brevity penalty ❸, while ROUGE emphasizes recall-oriented n-gram overlap ❹. BERTScore measures semantic similarity via contextual embeddings ❺, which is why it scores notably higher in this example; the sentences are semantically similar despite using different words. This illustrates why BERTScore often correlates better with human judgment for paraphrase detection: It captures meaning rather than surface form.

WARNING *Token-level metrics require reference outputs, but for most generation tasks, the space of good outputs is vast. A helpful response that takes a different approach than the reference may score poorly on BLEU despite being equally good or better. These metrics work best when the reference is canonical (a translation of a specific sentence) rather than one of many valid options (a helpful response to a user query). When references are not canonical, low scores may indicate divergence from the reference rather than low quality.*

Perplexity: The Metric That Misleads

Perplexity measures how "surprised" a model is by a sequence of text, quantifying the model's uncertainty when predicting each next token. Mathematically, perplexity is the exponentiated average negative log-likelihood: A perplexity of 20 means the model is, on average, as uncertain as if it were choosing uniformly among 20 equally likely tokens at each position. Lower perplexity indicates that the model assigns higher probability to the actual tokens that appear. Perplexity values depend heavily on the evaluation corpus and tokenization, so comparisons are most meaningful within the same setup.

Perplexity measures fluency and coherence with the training distribution, not factual accuracy, helpfulness, or appropriateness. A model may achieve excellent perplexity while confidently generating false information, because perplexity rewards predicting what text typically says, not what is true. Perplexity is also unavailable when using models through APIs that do not expose token probabilities. Most commercial API providers do not return the probability scores needed to compute perplexity on arbitrary text.

Does the Code Actually Run?

Code evaluation differs fundamentally from text evaluation because code has a notion of correctness that text lacks: Code either runs and produces the expected output, or it does not. This enables functional correctness metrics that sidestep the reference-matching problem entirely. For this reason, it has its own set of metrics, as Table 6-3 shows.

Table 6-3: Code Generation Evaluation Metrics and Benchmarks

Metric/benchmark	What it measures	Task count	Notes
Pass@*k*	Probability that at least one of *k* samples passes unit tests	N/A (metric)	Functional correctness, not style
All-*k* pass rate	Probability that all *k* samples pass unit tests	N/A (metric)	Consistency measure
HumanEval	Python function generation from docstrings	164	OpenAI benchmark; contamination concerns
MBPP	Basic Python programming problems	974	Entry-level difficulty

Pass@*k* is the standard functional correctness metric:[121] Generate *k* code samples for a problem, run unit tests on each, and report the probability that at least one passes. Pass@1 measures whether the model's single best attempt works; pass@10 and pass@100 measure whether any of multiple attempts work. The gap between pass@1 and pass@*k* indicates how much the model benefits from multiple tries. A large gap suggests that the model has the capability but inconsistently applies it.

Some teams also track the fraction of problems where *all k* samples pass, providing a stricter test of consistency. A model with high pass@*k* but low all-*k* pass rates generates correct solutions sporadically. A model with high all-*k* pass rates generates them reliably. For production systems where consistency matters more than occasional brilliance, this stricter rate can be more relevant. The ratio between pass@*k* and all-*k* pass rates quantifies solution reliability.

HumanEval, introduced by OpenAI, provides 164 handwritten Python programming problems with unit tests.[121] Models generate function bodies from docstrings, and functional correctness is evaluated by running the tests. HumanEval scores have risen dramatically. Codex achieved around 28 percent pass@1 in 2021, and by 2025, frontier models exceeded 90 percent. This saturation has driven development of harder benchmarks. Mostly Basic Python Problems (MBPP) adds 974 entry-level Python problems.[122] HumanEval Pro and MBPP Pro test self-invoking code generation, where models must solve a base problem and use its answer to solve a harder one.[123] Models scoring 96 percent on HumanEval drop to 76 percent on HumanEval Pro, revealing that high benchmark scores may overstate genuine programming capability.

Did It Use the Context?

RAG systems require evaluation of both the retriever (did it find relevant documents?) and the generator (did it use them correctly?). Separately evaluating these components helps identify which part of the pipeline needs improvement. The aspects in which RAGs can fail or succeed are diverse, and diagnosing the location of concern (that is, whether the retriever or the generator is driving performance concerns) is key. Table 6-4 lists the most frequently used metrics you may encounter when evaluating RAGs.

Table 6-4: Metrics for RAG Generation Evaluation

Metric	What it measures	Component	Implementations
Context relevancy	Whether retrieved documents are relevant to the query	Retriever	RAGAS, DeepEval
Context precision	Whether relevant documents are ranked highly	Retriever	RAGAS
Context recall	Whether all relevant information was retrieved	Retriever	RAGAS
Faithfulness	Whether the answer is grounded in retrieved context	Generator	RAGAS, DeepEval, TruLens
Answer relevancy	Whether the response addresses the original question	Generator	RAGAS, DeepEval

Faithfulness (sometimes called *groundedness*) measures whether the generated answer sticks to the facts in the retrieved context without hallucinating additional claims. This is the core RAG quality; the entire point of retrieval augmentation is to ground generation in retrieved evidence. Low faithfulness indicates that the generator is ignoring or contradicting its context, defeating the purpose of the retrieval step. Faithfulness evaluation typically uses an LLM judge to check whether each claim in the answer has support in the retrieved documents.

Context relevancy measures whether the retriever found documents that help answer the query. High-quality retrieval surfaces relevant information; poor retrieval buries the answer in irrelevant context or fails to retrieve it at all. A generator can be perfectly faithful to irrelevant context and still produce useless answers, which is why evaluating the retriever and generator separately matters.

Retrieval-augmented generation assessment suite (RAGAS) provides a widely used implementation of these metrics, offering a lightweight framework for RAG evaluation.[124] DeepEval and TruLens offer similar capabilities with different integration patterns.[125, 126]

Finding the Failure Modes

Safety evaluation measures whether models produce harmful, offensive, or otherwise problematic content. Unlike quality metrics with continuous scales, safety often involves categorical judgments: Is this output toxic or not? Does it contain personally identifiable information? Would it cause harm if followed? Table 6-5 sets out some of the most frequently used safety metrics, although these tend to be, in practice, much more domain- and language-specific to capture the equally specific nature of the harms they target.

Table 6-5: Safety and Toxicity Evaluation Tools

Tool/benchmark	What it measures	Notes
Perspective API	Toxicity probability across six dimensions (toxicity, severe toxicity, insult, threat, profanity, identity attack)	Widely used baseline, scheduled for sunsetting at the end of 2026
Detoxify	Toxicity classification	Open source; based on RoBERTa
RealToxicityPrompts	Tendency to generate toxic completions from benign prompts	99,000+ prompts; tests degeneration
ToxiGen	Implicit hate speech detection	274,000 statements; 13 minority groups
DecodingTrust	Holistic trustworthiness (toxicity, bias, privacy, fairness, robustness)	Multiple evaluation dimensions

Perspective API, developed by Google Jigsaw, scores text across six toxicity dimensions.[127] This widely used automated toxicity classifier is now being phased out as better local alternatives have become ubiquitously available. Perspective provided probability scores rather than binary classifications, enabling threshold tuning based on risk tolerance. Detoxify offers similar functionality as an open source alternative, useful when API dependencies are problematic.[128]

RealToxicityPrompts tests whether models "degenerate" into toxic outputs even from innocuous prompts.[129] The benchmark provides 99,000+ naturally occurring text snippets and measures the toxicity of model completions. High toxicity rates on benign prompts indicate that the model has not adequately learned to avoid harmful content. ToxiGen extends this to implicit hate speech with 274,000 statements about 13 minority groups,[130] while DecodingTrust provides holistic trustworthiness evaluation across multiple dimensions including toxicity, bias, privacy, and robustness.[131]

THE IMPLEMENTATION LANDSCAPE

Several libraries consolidate evaluation metrics into unified interfaces. Hugging Face Evaluate provides hundreds of metrics spanning NLP, vision, and RL, with implementations of BLEU, ROUGE, BERTScore, perplexity, and many others.[132] TorchMetrics offers PyTorch-native metrics including text-generation metrics and classification fairness metrics.[133] For LLM-specific evaluation, DeepEval provides a range of metrics including hallucination and toxicity detection,[125] while OpenAI Evals and LangChain OpenEvals focus on model-graded evaluation infrastructure.[134], [135] RAGAS specializes in RAG pipeline evaluation.[124] The choice depends on your stack: Hugging Face Evaluate for broad coverage, TorchMetrics for PyTorch integration, RAGAS for RAG systems, and DeepEval for LLM production testing.

Fairness Evaluation

Fairness evaluation assesses whether models perform equitably across demographic groups. Aggregate performance metrics can hide disparities because, by definition, underperformance toward a minority group contributes less to the overall average than performance within the majority. Fairness metrics surface these disparities.

The key metrics include demographic parity (equal positive prediction rates across groups), equalized odds (equal true-positive and false-positive rates across groups), and calibration (prediction probabilities reflect true outcomes equally across groups). These metrics are often trade-offs for each other and for overall accuracy; improving one may worsen another.

For traditional ML classification, IBM's AI Fairness 360 provides 71 bias metrics and 9 mitigation algorithms spanning preprocessing, in-processing, and post-processing stages.[136] Fairlearn offers similar capabilities with trade-off visualization between fairness and performance.[137] TorchMetrics includes binary group fairness metrics for PyTorch workflows.[133]

For LLM evaluation specifically, bias benchmarks include Bias Benchmark for QA (BBQ), which tests social biases in question answering;[138] CrowS-Pairs, which measures stereotype bias via sentence pairs;[139] and WinoBias, which tests gender bias in coreference resolution.[140] These benchmarks reveal whether models encode and reproduce harmful stereotypes, a concern that persists despite safety training.

Fairness evaluation is not optional for production systems. Deployed models that perform poorly on minority groups create real harm and legal liability (especially in industries subject to specific regulation on algorithmic decision-making, such as lending). The difficulty is that fairness is multidimensional; no single metric captures all relevant concerns, and improving fairness on one dimension may not improve it on others. Practitioners must identify which fairness properties matter most for their application and measure accordingly.

The Judge That Judges Itself

Model-based evaluation, often called *LLM-as-a-judge*, has become central to post-training evaluation. The approach is straightforward, as Figure 6-1 shows: Use a capable language model to assess the outputs of the model being evaluated. The judge model reads the prompt, the response, and evaluation criteria, then produces a rating or preference judgment. This provides nuanced assessment at scale, filling the gap between crude automatic metrics and expensive human evaluation. The methodology is particularly relevant for preference-based training methods such as DPO (see Chapter 5), where LLM-as-a-judge can generate the preference pairs that drive training. But LLM-as-a-judge is not merely "run GPT-4 on your outputs." Effective use requires careful attention to judge selection, prompt design, consistency validation, and bias mitigation.

Judge model selection involves trade-offs between capability, cost, and independence. More capable judges provide more accurate assessments but cost more per evaluation. The judge should be at least as capable as the model being evaluated, ideally more so. Using a weaker model to judge a stronger one produces systematically biased results, since the judge cannot recognize quality that it cannot produce. Independence matters as well; evaluating a model with a judge of the same family creates blind spots where both models share weaknesses. If both models misunderstand a concept in the same way, the judge will not penalize the error. Using judges from different model families, or rotating judges, reduces this risk.

Evaluation prompts require the same care as any other prompt engineering tasks. Vague criteria produce inconsistent judgments. "Rate the quality," for example, leaves the judge to invent its own interpretation. Specific criteria produce reliable results: "Does the response directly address the question? Is the information factually accurate? Is the response appropriately concise?" Multidimensional evaluation, with separate scores for different quality aspects, provides more actionable signal than a single overall rating. The prompt should include the evaluation criteria, the response to evaluate, and clear instructions for how to express the judgment.

Asking for reasoning before the final rating (a chain-of-thought approach) can improve judgment quality and provides interpretable explanations for scores. But the evidence is mixed. In some settings, requiring the judge to articulate reasoning anchors it to specific observations and reduces

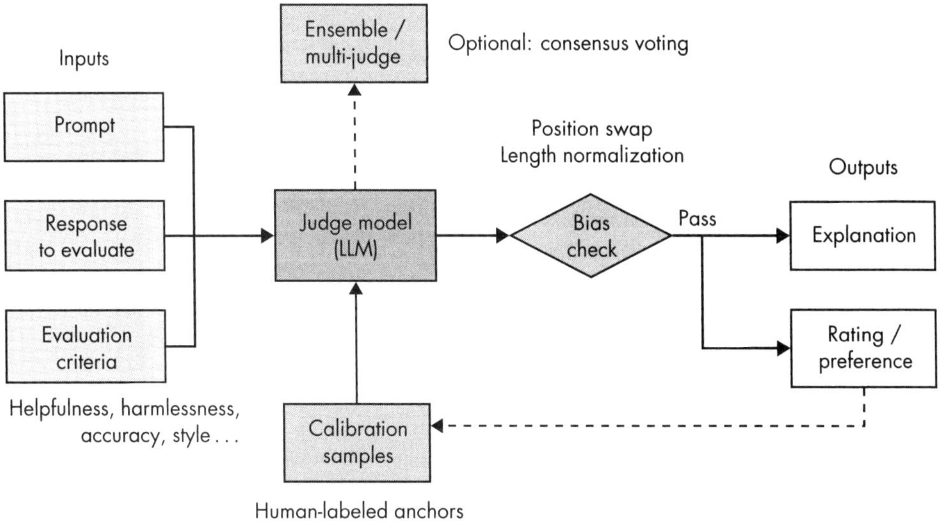

Figure 6-1: The LLM-as-a-judge workflow. Inputs (prompt, response, criteria) flow to the judge model, through bias mitigation checks, to produce ratings and explanations. Calibration samples with human labels anchor the judge's behavior.

noise. In others, the reasoning process itself introduces bias, with the judge constructing post hoc justifications that favor responses matching its stylistic preferences. The safest approach is to validate your preferred evaluation protocol on a calibration set with known human ratings before trusting it for broader evaluation.

> **EVALUATOR PROMPT ANATOMY**
>
> Effective LLM-as-a-judge prompts have four components: clear criteria specifying exactly what to assess, the content to evaluate, instructions for expressing judgment (rating scale, format, whether to provide reasoning), and calibration examples showing good and poor responses with their ratings. Missing any component produces less reliable judgments. The criteria component deserves particular attention. If you cannot articulate what *good* means precisely enough for a prompt, you cannot evaluate it reliably.

Listing 6-2 illustrates a well-structured LLM-as-a-judge prompt for evaluating response quality. The prompt includes explicit criteria, a clear rating scale, and instructions for providing reasoning before the final score.

```
❶ JUDGE_PROMPT = """You are evaluating an AI assistant's response.

## Evaluation Criteria
Assess the response on these dimensions:
1. **Relevance**: Does it directly address the user's question?
2. **Accuracy**: Are the facts stated correct and verifiable?
```

```
3. **Completeness**: Does it cover the key points without omission?
❷ 4. **Conciseness**: Is it appropriately brief without unnecessary padding?

## Rating Scale
- 5: Excellent - meets all criteria exceptionally
- 4: Good - meets criteria with minor gaps
- 3: Acceptable - meets most criteria adequately
- 2: Poor - significant gaps in multiple criteria
- 1: Unacceptable - fails to meet basic criteria

## Instructions
First, analyze the response against each criterion. Then provide
❸ an overall score. Brevity is valued: a concise correct answer
should score higher than a verbose one with the same information.

## User Question
{question}

## Assistant Response
{response}

## Your Evaluation
Provide your reasoning for each criterion, then your final score."""

def evaluate_response(question: str, response: str, judge_model) -> dict:
    """Run LLM-as-judge evaluation on a single response."""
    prompt = JUDGE_PROMPT.format(question=question, response=response)
❹   judgment = judge_model.generate(prompt, temperature=0.0)
    return parse_judgment(judgment)
```

Listing 6-2: LLM-as-a-judge prompt structure with explicit criteria

The prompt template structures evaluation around explicit criteria ❶. Including conciseness as a criterion ❷ and explicitly instructing the judge to value brevity ❸ helps mitigate the length bias that judges otherwise exhibit. Setting temperature to 0 ❹ reduces variability between runs, improving consistency. For production use, running evaluations multiple times and averaging, or using position-swapped pairwise comparisons, provides more robust results.

Consistency validation ensures that judge assessments are reliable. Run the same evaluation multiple times with different random seeds or temperature settings. If judgments vary substantially, the evaluation is measuring noise as much as quality. Compare judge assessments against human ratings on a calibration set. If the judge systematically disagrees with human judgment, its criteria may not match yours. Track judge consistency over time, since model updates can change evaluation behavior. Some practitioners maintain a fixed evaluation set with known human ratings, running new judge configurations against this set to verify calibration before trusting the judge for new evaluations.

LLM-as-a-judge evaluations carry systematic biases that can distort results. Length bias is pervasive; judges tend to prefer longer responses even when brevity would be more appropriate, because longer responses have more opportunities to include relevant information. Style matching favors responses that resemble the judge's own outputs, potentially penalizing valid but stylistically different approaches. Position bias affects pairwise comparisons, with some judges systematically preferring whichever response appears first (or second). Confidence bias rewards assertive phrasing regardless of accuracy, since uncertainty markers make responses sound less authoritative. Self-enhancement bias leads models to rate their own outputs more favorably than equivalent outputs from other models.

WARNING *LLM judges often prefer longer responses, sometimes dramatically so. A verbose response that buries the answer in unnecessary context will outscore a concise response that answers directly. This bias compounds when the judge's preferences influence training data selection for preference optimization, creating models that learn to pad responses. Mitigate by including length-normalized scoring, explicit instructions to prefer conciseness, or separate evaluation of response length as a dimension distinct from quality.*

Mitigating these biases requires deliberate effort. No silver bullets exist, but Table 6-6 offers useful starting points.

Table 6-6: Starting Points for Mitigating Common LLM-as-a-Judge Biases

Bias type	Mitigation strategy
Position bias	Present the same pair twice with positions swapped; count only agreements as a reliable signal.
Length bias	Include explicit instructions that brevity is valued, or evaluate conciseness as a separate dimension.
Style matching bias	Use judges from different model families, rather than from the same family as the model being evaluated.
Confidence bias	Include calibration examples that assign a positive rating to appropriate uncertainty.

No mitigation is perfect, but combining multiple techniques reduces the influence of any single bias. The gold standard remains periodic calibration against human judgment: If judge ratings drift from human assessments, the bias mitigation is failing. In this arena, the customer—who is more closely approximated by a human evaluator—is always right. Optimize for the wrong audience, and you will be rewarded with metrics that rise as satisfaction falls.

WARNING *Benchmarks are proxies, not reality, and if they do not reflect the end-user perspective, they will lull users into complacency, right until a mob of unhappy end users appears. OpenAI is one of the frontier labs that could tell a story or two about this. When GPT-5 arrived, it was hailed as a groundbreaking innovation that aced all the tests it was subjected to before release. Yet users were unhappy. They wanted* *"their" 4o back, a model many criticized for obsequiousness but even more felt was superior in terms of relatability. Benchmark improvement is not the goal; user satisfaction is. Benchmarks are merely a proxy, and proxies can point in the wrong direction if they are not calibrated against a good understanding of the customer.*

VIBE CHECK: LETTING AGENTS HANDLE EVALS

LLM-as-a-judge pipelines are ideally suited for automating coding agents. The task is well specified (evaluate outputs against criteria), the inputs and outputs are structured (prompts, responses, ratings), and the logic is compositional (apply criteria, aggregate scores, detect regressions). Consider automating the following:

Evaluation pipeline scaffolding
: Agents can generate evaluation harnesses that apply judge prompts to model outputs, parse ratings from judge responses, compute aggregate metrics, and persist results for comparison. The pattern is consistent across evaluation types; only the judge prompts and aggregation logic vary.

Automated regression test suites
: Maintain a library of capability tests that run automatically on each model checkpoint. Agents can expand this library by generating new test cases from specifications, identifying edge cases from failure analysis, and flagging regressions before they reach human reviewers.

Evaluation framework setup
: Rather than manually configuring RAGAS, DeepEval, or custom evaluation pipelines, describe your evaluation requirements and let an agent generate the configuration, implement custom metrics, and wire up the data flow from model outputs to evaluation reports. If this is your priority, you may want to have specific prompts or slash commands for your preferred evaluation suite.

What about continuous integration / continuous delivery (CI/CD)? Model evaluation should be as automated as code testing. Agents can configure evaluation runs to trigger on model registry updates, compare results against baseline thresholds, block deployment when metrics fall below acceptable levels, and generate summary reports for human review. Whether they *should* is a different question. The risk is that these ad hoc pathways disincentivize organizational standard-setting and creating a shared pool of evaluation best practices. In a pinch, agents can build CI/CD pipelines. In practice, however, these should preferably live in a central institutional repository.

It is probably worth noting that what to avoid matters just as much as what to do. The most important thing *not* to do is trust the entire evaluation process to your coding agent. The coding agent is the orchestrator, not the evaluator—that is your job. Therefore, make sure you supervise your agent appropriately. In the end, a good run is a matter not just of numbers but of holistic insight and intuition from multiple indicators and some vibe checks of rollouts (or, if anyone from the enterprise side asks, *qualitative assays*).

The Benchmark Zoo

What do the standard benchmarks actually measure, and what do they miss? From MMLU to TruthfulQA, each benchmark captures something real but leaves vast gaps. Understanding both their utility and their limitations is essential for interpreting results.

Testing What Models Know

Knowledge and reasoning benchmarks provide standardized comparison points that enable tracking progress across models and over time. The most widely cited, summarized in Table 6-7, include Massive Multitask Language Understanding (MMLU), which tests broad knowledge across 57 academic domains from high-school to professional level.[141] HellaSwag tests commonsense reasoning about everyday situations by asking models to select the most plausible continuation of a scenario.[142] The Ai2 Reasoning Challenge (ARC) tests scientific reasoning through grade-school science questions.[143] Each benchmark targets a different aspect of capability: factual knowledge, intuitive understanding of the world, and logical inference about physical and scientific phenomena.

Table 6-7: Standard Benchmarks for Evaluating Language Models

Benchmark	Category	What it measures	Limitations
MMLU	Knowledge	57-domain academic knowledge	Saturating; recognition not generation
HellaSwag	Reasoning	Commonsense scenario completion	Near saturation
ARC	Reasoning	Grade-school science questions	Limited reasoning depth
MT-Bench	Instruction following	Multi-turn conversation quality	Model-as-a-judge biases
AlpacaEval	Instruction following	Response preference vs. reference	Length and style biases
TruthfulQA	Safety	Resistance to common misconceptions	Limited scope
HumanEval	Coding	Python function generation	Narrow; contamination risk
GSM8K	Math	Grade-school word problems	Contamination concerns

The multiple-choice format shared by these benchmarks has both advantages and limitations. The advantage is objectivity. A response is correct or incorrect, with no ambiguity about how to score it. This objectivity enables large-scale automated evaluation and prevents the scoring biases that plague open-ended assessment. The limitation is that multiple-choice questions capture only narrow aspects of model capability. A model may be able to select the correct answer from four options, but not to generate that answer unprompted. The recognition task is easier than the generation task, and performance on recognition may overstate genuine knowledge.

These benchmarks saturate as models improve. Once a benchmark is largely solved, it no longer discriminates between capable models. MMLU scores that seemed impressive in 2023 are now routine, and frontier models approach the benchmark's ceiling. When benchmarks saturate, the field develops harder variants or new benchmarks targeting capabilities that remain challenging. This cycle of creation, saturation, and replacement is healthy in that it pushes toward harder problems, but it complicates longitudinal comparisons and can create a moving-target feeling for practitioners trying to understand where their models stand. Performance on knowledge and reasoning benchmarks is necessary, but not sufficient evidence of a model's usefulness for real tasks. The benchmarks verify that certain capabilities exist, not that they translate to practical value in deployment contexts.

Grade School Math 8K (GSM8K) deserves particular attention as the standard benchmark for mathematical reasoning. The dataset comprises 8,500 grade-school-level word problems requiring multistep arithmetic reasoning. Despite their elementary mathematical content, the problems require models to parse natural language descriptions, identify relevant quantities and operations, and chain multiple reasoning steps together (capabilities explored in depth in Chapter 10). The benchmark's contamination concerns are well documented, with evidence that many models have been trained on data containing GSM8K problems, inflating reported scores relative to true mathematical reasoning capability.

BENCHMARK CONTAMINATION

Benchmark contamination occurs when evaluation data appears in training data, either directly or through near-duplicates that differ only superficially. Contaminated benchmarks overestimate model capability. High scores may reflect memorization of specific answers rather than generalizable skills. Contamination is particularly insidious because it is often unintentional. Large-scale web scrapes may inadvertently include benchmark datasets that were posted online, and the duplication is not immediately apparent without careful analysis.

Detection requires careful deduplication between training and evaluation sets, including fuzzy matching for near-duplicates. Prevention requires assembling evaluation data from sources known not to appear in training corpora, using temporal splits so that evaluation data postdates training data collection, or creating new evaluation examples that cannot have leaked. When using public benchmarks, assume that some degree of contamination is likely and interpret scores accordingly. For high-stakes evaluation, private held-out sets that have never been published provide the strongest guarantee against contamination. Evals-as-a-service providers like Artificial Analysis perform a priceless service exactly because their stock in trade is a set of withheld, and thus likely ungamable, evals.

Testing What Models Do

Instruction-following benchmarks evaluate the qualities that make models useful as assistants: the ability to understand user requests, generate appropriate responses, maintain coherent multi-turn conversations, and produce outputs that users find helpful. Unlike knowledge benchmarks with their multiple-choice format, instruction-following benchmarks require open-ended generation and typically rely on model-based or human judgment for scoring.

MT-Bench presents multi-turn conversations requiring coherent long-form responses across diverse categories including writing, role-play, extraction, reasoning, math, coding, and knowledge.[144] This multi-turn format tests whether models maintain context and build appropriately on earlier exchanges. AlpacaEval compares model outputs against reference responses, typically using a capable model to judge which is better.[145] The benchmark's simplicity makes it easy to run, though the reliance on model-based judgment introduces biases toward responses that resemble the judging model's outputs. Arena-Hard selects particularly challenging prompts from Chatbot Arena, where models differ substantially in quality, focusing evaluation effort on discriminating examples rather than easy cases with all models performing similarly.[146]

These benchmarks better capture the qualities that make models useful in practice, but they carry their own limitations. Model-as-a-judge evaluation is subject to systematic biases; models tend to prefer longer responses, more confident phrasing, and outputs that match their own stylistic tendencies. A model evaluated by a judge of similar architecture may receive inflated scores on dimensions where both models share weaknesses. Human evaluation addresses some of these concerns but is expensive and introduces different biases. Perhaps most important, instruction-following benchmarks evaluate general conversational capability, which may not predict performance on the specific tasks that matter for a given deployment. A model that scores well on MT-Bench may still struggle with the particular domain or task that your application requires. These benchmarks provide valuable signal for general capability assessment but should be supplemented with domain-specific evaluation tailored to actual use cases.

Testing What Models Should Not Do

Safety evaluation assesses whether models produce harmful, untruthful, or otherwise problematic outputs. The stakes are high, because a model that occasionally generates harmful content may cause real damage to users and create legal and reputational risks for deployers. Safety evaluation aims to find these failure modes before deployment, but the task is intrinsically difficult because the space of potential harms is vast and adversarial users actively seek to elicit problematic behavior.

TruthfulQA tests whether models will make false claims that mimic humans' commonly held misconceptions. The benchmark targets not random factual errors but specifically the kinds of false beliefs that are widespread in training data: folk medicine claims, urban legends, and political misconceptions. A model trained on internet text may confidently repeat these falsehoods because they appear frequently in its training distribution. TruthfulQA performance indicates whether a model has learned to be epistemically cautious or whether it pattern-matches to confident-sounding claims regardless of truth value.

Toxicity benchmarks measure the rate at which models generate offensive, abusive, or otherwise harmful content, typically by prompting with potentially provocative inputs and scoring outputs for toxic content. The challenge is defining what counts as toxic. Content that is offensive to some may be acceptable to others, and overly aggressive toxicity filtering can interfere with legitimate use cases.

Red-teaming exercises probe for harmful capabilities through adversarial prompting, with human testers attempting to elicit dangerous content, private information, harmful instructions, or other problematic outputs. Unlike static benchmarks, red teaming adapts to the model being tested. As obvious attacks are blocked, testers develop more sophisticated approaches. This cat-and-mouse dynamic means that safety evaluation is never complete. A model that passes all current tests may fail to new attack vectors discovered after deployment. Systematic safety evaluation requires ongoing red teaming as models are deployed and failure modes are discovered, treating safety as a continuous process rather than a one-time gate. The organization that stops looking for safety issues has simply stopped finding them, not eliminated them.

The Human in the Loop

Humans remain the ultimate arbiter of model quality. But human evaluation is slow, expensive, and subject to biases. How do we design protocols that produce reliable results, scale within budget constraints, and maintain the validity that only human judgment can provide?

Asking the Right Questions

Human evaluation protocols must specify precisely what evaluators should assess and how they should express their judgments. This precision matters because vague instructions produce inconsistent results. Ask evaluators to "rate the quality," and each will interpret *quality* according to their own implicit criteria. One person focuses on accuracy, another on helpfulness, a third on writing style. The resulting ratings conflate different dimensions and cannot be meaningfully compared. Ask instead, "Does the response directly address the question asked?," and evaluators have a clear criterion to apply, producing ratings that measure what you intended to measure.

Protocol design encompasses multiple decisions that together determine evaluation quality. The evaluation task itself must be defined: Are evaluators rating individual responses, comparing pairs, or ranking multiple options? Each format has properties that suit different purposes. Absolute ratings provide independent scores for each response but suffer from calibration differences across evaluators. Pairwise comparisons are easier for evaluators to make reliably but require more evaluations to rank many options. The rating scale matters as well. Binary good/bad judgments are easy to make but lose information, while fine-grained scales capture more nuance but introduce noise as evaluators struggle to distinguish adjacent levels.

Evaluator selection and training determines whether the protocol produces reliable results in practice. Domain experts provide more accurate judgments on technical content but are expensive and scarce. Crowdworkers scale more easily but may lack context necessary for informed assessment. Whatever the source, training ensures that evaluators understand the criteria and apply them consistently. Training typically involves working through examples with feedback, discussing edge cases, and calibrating until evaluators reach acceptable agreement. Quality control mechanisms (including attention checks, consistency tests, and review of outliers) maintain quality throughout the evaluation campaign. The effort invested in protocol design pays dividends throughout the development cycle. Reliable evaluation enables confident decisions, while unreliable evaluation leaves you uncertain about whether observed differences reflect genuine model quality or merely evaluation noise.

WARNING *Vague evaluation criteria produce noisy results. "Rate the quality of this response" leaves each evaluator to invent their own criteria; the resulting ratings measure evaluator variation as much as model quality. Specific criteria produce reliable results: "Does the response directly address the user's question?" "Are the facts stated verifiable?" "Is the response appropriately concise?" If you cannot specify what you mean by* quality, *you cannot reliably measure it.*

Handling Evaluator Disagreements

Inter-annotator agreement—the extent to which different evaluators give the same ratings when assessing the same outputs—provides a crucial check on evaluation reliability. If evaluators disagree substantially, either the evaluation criteria are ambiguous, the evaluators are insufficiently trained, or the quality being assessed is genuinely subjective in ways that make reliable measurement impossible. Measuring agreement quantifies this concern and provides a basis for deciding whether evaluation results are trustworthy.

Several statistics measure agreement. Simple percentage agreement—the fraction of cases where evaluators gave identical ratings—is intuitive but misleading when some ratings are much more common than others. Cohen's kappa corrects for chance agreement, measuring how much more evaluators agree than they would by random chance. Values above 0.6 typically indicate substantial agreement, while values below 0.4 suggest that the evaluation may be unreliable. Krippendorff's alpha extends to multiple evaluators and various rating scales, providing a general-purpose agreement measure. For pairwise preference judgments, the relevant statistic is the rate at which evaluators agree on which response is better.

Computing these statistics is straightforward with standard libraries (in Python, scikit-learn provides Cohen's κ, while the Krippendorff package implements, unsurprisingly, Krippendorff's alpha). Both metrics correct for chance agreement, which makes them more informative than simple percentage agreement. The ordinal measurement level in Krippendorff's alpha accounts for the fact that a rating of 4 versus 5 represents less disagreement than 1 versus 5. When agreement is low, the next step is diagnosis: Are certain questions more contentious than others? Do specific annotators diverge systematically? These patterns reveal whether the issue lies with ambiguous criteria, insufficient training, or genuinely subjective qualities.

Low agreement is not necessarily a failure of the evaluation protocol. For genuinely subjective qualities, like whether a response is *engaging* or whether the writing style is *appropriate*, reasonable people may legitimately disagree. Low agreement in these cases reflects honest uncertainty about what *better* means rather than protocol failure. But evaluation conclusions drawn from low-agreement data should be appropriately cautious. If evaluators agree only 60 percent of the time on which response is better, a model that wins 55 percent of comparisons may not be meaningfully better than one that wins 50 percent. The difference is within the noise of evaluator disagreement. High-stakes decisions require high-agreement evaluation. When agreement is low, either improve the protocol, accept wider confidence intervals, or acknowledge that the quality in question may not support reliable measurement.

Stretching the Budget

Human evaluation is expensive. A single evaluation comparing two model outputs might cost a dollar or more when accounting for evaluator time, platform fees, and quality control overhead. Evaluating a model comprehensively, across diverse prompts with sufficient statistical power to detect meaningful differences, can require thousands of evaluations. The cost adds up quickly, creating tension between evaluation depth and development iteration speed. You cannot afford to run comprehensive human evaluation on every training checkpoint or every hyperparameter configuration, yet without human evaluation, you cannot be certain that automated metrics track actual quality.

Several strategies help scale human evaluation within budget constraints. The first is prioritizing human evaluation for high-stakes decisions rather than routine monitoring. Use cheap automated metrics to track training progress, flag anomalies, and filter promising configurations. Reserve human evaluation for final model selection and deployment decisions when getting it right justifies the cost. The second strategy is model-based evaluation calibrated against human judgments. Train or prompt a capable model to predict human ratings, then use the model's predictions for routine evaluation while periodically validating against fresh human data. The model-based evaluator provides scale; the human calibration provides ground truth.

Strategic sampling focuses human effort on informative examples rather than spreading it uniformly. When comparing two models, most prompts may elicit similar responses, and the interesting signal comes from prompts where the models differ. Active sampling identifies such prompts, directing human evaluation toward examples that discriminate between models rather than wasting effort on examples with both models performing similarly. Efficient annotation interfaces reduce the time required per evaluation, enabling more evaluations within the same budget. Small interface improvements (like reducing clicks, preloading content, and enabling keyboard shortcuts) compound across thousands of evaluations. The goal is not to eliminate human evaluation but to deploy it efficiently, recognizing that human judgment remains the ground truth against which all other evaluation is ultimately calibrated.

Outsourcing Objectivity

Enterprises do not have to build every evaluation capability in-house. Specialist providers offer evaluation as a service, running independent benchmarks and publishing comparisons across model providers. Artificial Analysis is one of the first such companies, positioning itself as an independent benchmarking provider, comparing model quality, price, output speed, and latency across AI models and API hosting providers, and offering evaluations that aggregate multiple tests across mathematics, science, coding, and reasoning to provide a composite capability signal.[147]

This service is a compelling proposition for enterprises that either do not have the experience (yet) to do their own complex evaluations or need external verification. However, this approach is no substitute for integral evaluation capabilities. External vendors have a valuable role as guides and baseline setters, but in my experience, just as the models themselves have to reflect an enterprise's very domain identity and specificity, so must the evals. It's never about the state of the art, but about the state of *your* art.

Third-party evaluation is most useful when internal incentives make it hard to trust internal results or when procurement needs a neutral view across vendors. A provider that compares models and hosting providers from the outside can help teams evaluate trade-offs without committing to one stack, which is particularly valuable when purchasing decisions are made by committees spanning engineering, risk, and finance. External benchmarks also help when a company needs evidence that its chosen model and host were selected through a defensible process, which reduces internal disputes and supports audit or governance review. The value is not in replacing internal, task-specific evaluation. It is in adding an external reference point that keeps internal evaluation grounded when vendor claims and internal preferences are pulling in different directions.

Your Benchmarks, Your Rules

Standard benchmarks rarely capture what your deployment actually needs. How do you build custom evals that measure what matters, maintain uncontaminated held-out sets, and catch capability regressions before they reach production?

Building What Standard Benchmarks Miss

Standard benchmarks rarely capture performance on the specific tasks your deployment cares about. MMLU measures general knowledge, but your customer service model needs to answer questions about your products. MT-Bench evaluates conversational ability, but your medical documentation model needs to extract structured information from clinical notes. The mismatch between what benchmarks measure and what deployments require makes custom benchmark construction essential for enterprise post-training (a theme explored extensively in Chapter 9). Without domain-specific evaluation, you cannot know whether your fine-tuning improved performance on the tasks that matter.

Effective custom benchmarks require several components working together. Clear task specification defines what the model should do: extract specific fields from documents, answer questions within a defined scope, or generate content following particular guidelines. Ambiguity in task specification produces ambiguous evaluation results. Examples must cover the relevant distribution of inputs, including common cases, edge cases, and the particular variations that occur in your data. A benchmark heavily weighted toward easy examples will give overly optimistic estimates, while one focused on edge cases will give overly pessimistic ones. Evaluation criteria must map to business value; if the deployment cares about accuracy of extracted dates, the benchmark should measure date accuracy, and if it cares about user satisfaction, the benchmark should predict that.

Version control enables performance tracking over time and ensures reproducibility. A benchmark without version control cannot support claims that a new model is better than an old one, since the benchmark itself may have changed. Versioning includes the examples themselves, the evaluation criteria, and any automated scoring code.

Building good benchmarks is difficult and time-consuming. The task specification stage alone can require extensive iteration as you discover that your initial criteria were ambiguous or incomplete. But the investment provides evaluation signals that no off-the-shelf benchmark can match. For important deployments, the cost of building a good benchmark is small relative to the cost of deploying a model that fails to meet requirements because you evaluated it on the wrong things.

> **FROM THE TRENCHES: THE LIVING BENCHMARK**
>
> The best custom benchmarks grow with your deployment. Start with 50 to 100 carefully selected examples that capture your core use cases. After each deployment cycle, add examples that exposed model weaknesses: real user queries that failed, edge cases that surprised you, and new use patterns that emerged. Within a year, you will have a benchmark that precisely captures what your deployment needs. This organic benchmark, grown from real experience, is more valuable than any general-purpose alternative. It should also be assiduously guarded: it takes only a careless moment for this prize asset to lose its long-accumulated value.

Keeping Secrets from Your Model (and Everyone Else)

Held-out evaluation sets—data reserved exclusively for evaluation and never used in training—provide uncontaminated performance estimates. If evaluation data appears in training, the model may have memorized correct answers rather than learned generalizable patterns, and evaluation on such contaminated data overestimates deployment performance. The principle is simple: Never train on evaluation data. The practice is harder because data leakage can occur through seemingly innocuous paths.

The most obvious leakage occurs when training data and evaluation data overlap, either through explicit inclusion or because both were drawn from the same source without deduplication. Less obvious leakage occurs when evaluation examples inform decisions that affect training. If you examine evaluation failures and adjust training data to cover those cases, the evaluation set has indirectly influenced training. If you use evaluation examples for prompt engineering or debugging, you have exposed yourself to the evaluation distribution in ways that may influence model development. Even looking at evaluation results can cause leakage if it guides decisions about when to stop training or which hyperparameters to select.

Best practices for maintaining separation start with creating evaluation sets before assembling training data, ensuring that the split is determined before any training decisions are made. Technical controls prevent accidental leakage: separate storage systems, access controls that limit who can view evaluation data, and automated checks for overlap between training and evaluation sets. Periodic refresh replaces evaluation data that may have become contaminated over time, providing fresh uncontaminated estimates. Temporal splits—ensuring that evaluation data comes from after the training data cutoff—provide particularly strong guarantees. If the evaluation data did not exist when training data was collected, it cannot have leaked. For high-stakes deployments, temporal evaluation on data collected after model development provides the most trustworthy estimates of real-world performance.

Regression Testing: What Did We Break This Time?

Post-training aims to improve targeted capabilities, but improvement on one dimension can come at the cost of degradation on others. A model fine-tuned for customer service might lose capability at code generation, and a model trained on medical data might become worse at casual conversation. These capability regressions may not be obvious during development if evaluation focuses only on the target domain. Regression testing, the systematic verification that existing capabilities are preserved, catches these problems before deployment.

Regression tests define a set of capabilities that must be maintained and implement automated evaluation that flags degradation. The software engineering parallel is direct: Just as unit tests verify that code changes do not break existing functionality, model regression tests verify that training changes do not break existing capabilities. The implementation differs, since model capabilities cannot be tested with binary pass/fail assertions, but the principle is the same. A regression test suite might include samples from standard benchmarks covering diverse capability categories, examples from previous deployment use cases, and specific tests for capabilities known to be at risk from the current training intervention.

The challenge is coverage. The space of model capabilities is vast, and regression tests can cover only a subset. You cannot test everything, so you must decide what to test. Practical approaches include focusing on capabilities known to be correlated with the training domain, since those are most likely to be affected. Sampling broadly across capability categories catches unexpected regressions. Investigating any unexpected changes in standard benchmarks, even if those changes are improvements, is also valuable, since unexpected improvements may indicate distribution shift that could cause unexpected degradations elsewhere. When regression tests detect degradation, the response depends on severity. Minor degradation on peripheral capabilities may be acceptable if the target improvement is valuable enough, while significant degradation on important capabilities requires either adjusting the training or accepting a different trade-off between improvement and preservation.

A/B Testing: Where Theory Meets Reality

Offline evaluation tells you whether a model might work. A/B testing tells you whether it actually does. A/B testing is the practice of randomly assigning users to different model versions and comparing outcomes. The gap between proxy metrics and real-world performance can be closed only by deploying to real users and measuring real outcomes.

The Art of the Experiment

A/B testing provides the gold standard for evaluating whether model changes improve real-world performance. Offline evaluation, however careful, operates on proxy data that may not reflect deployment conditions. A/B testing operates on the real deployment, with real users, on real tasks, providing direct evidence of whether changes improve user outcomes. The directness of this evidence makes A/B testing uniquely valuable for validating that offline evaluation signals translate to deployment value.

Effective A/B test design requires attention to several components. Clear metric definitions specify what you are measuring and how: task completion rate, user satisfaction ratings, engagement metrics, and error rates. These metrics should capture what you care about, not merely what is easy to measure. Proper randomization ensures that treatment and control groups are comparable. Users are assigned to model versions by a process that is unpredictable and unrelated to user characteristics that might confound the comparison. Insufficient randomization can create spurious differences that look like model effects but reflect group composition.

Sufficient sample size provides statistical power to detect meaningful differences. If a new model is 2 percent better than the baseline, detecting that improvement with confidence requires enough users that 2 percent represents a statistically significant difference. Power calculations, conducted before the test begins, determine the number of users and the amount of time the test must run.

Guardrails limit exposure to potentially harmful model changes. The new model is initially deployed to a small fraction of users, with automatic rollback if safety metrics degrade, before gradually expanding exposure. Online evaluation complements offline evaluation in a validation pipeline. Offline tests verify that models are ready for deployment, filtering out obviously problematic configurations before they reach users. Online tests verify that models that look good offline improve user outcomes in practice.

Statistical Traps for the Unwary

Valid statistical inference from A/B tests requires more care than many practitioners realize. The intuition that more users means more certainty is correct but incomplete. Statistical validity depends on the way the test was designed and analyzed, not merely on sample size. Several common pitfalls can invalidate conclusions from otherwise well-designed tests.

Sample sizes for language model A/B tests are often larger than intuition suggests. The required sample size depends on effect size (how much better the new model is), baseline metric variance (how noisy the measurements are), and desired statistical power (how confident you want to be). When the effect size is small and variance is high, which is typical for language model metrics, required sample sizes can reach thousands or tens of thousands of users. Power calculations should be conducted before the test begins. Running underpowered tests wastes resources while providing unreliable conclusions.

> **SAMPLE SIZE POWER CALCULATION**
>
> For a two-sample comparison with continuous outcomes, the required sample size per group is
>
> $$n = \frac{2(z_{\alpha/2} + z_\beta)^2\sigma^2}{\delta^2}$$
>
> where $z_{\alpha/2}$ is the critical value for significance level (1.96 for $\alpha = 0.05$), z_β is the critical value for power (0.84 for 80 percent power), σ is the standard deviation of the metric, and δ is the minimum effect size you wish to detect.
>
> For a satisfaction score with $\sigma = 0.8$ on a 5-point scale and a target of detecting a 0.1-point improvement with 80 percent power at $\alpha = 0.05$:
>
> $$n = \frac{2(1.96 + 0.84)^2(0.8)^2}{(0.1)^2} = \frac{2 \times 7.84 \times 0.64}{0.01} \approx 1{,}003 \text{ per group}$$
>
> This means roughly 2,000 users total, and that is for detecting a moderately sized effect on a relatively low-variance metric. For noisier metrics or smaller effects, sample sizes grow quadratically.

Multiple testing correction becomes important when examining many metrics from the same test. If you test 20 metrics and consider $p < 0.05$ significant, you expect roughly one false positive even if there is no real effect. Bonferroni correction, false discovery rate control, or prespecified primary metrics address this concern. More insidiously, peeking at results before planned analysis points inflates false-positive rates. If you check daily whether the result is significant and stop when it becomes so, you will stop disproportionately often when random fluctuations happen to favor one arm, biasing conclusions toward false positives. Sequential analysis methods enable monitoring ongoing tests while controlling false-positive rates by adjusting significance thresholds to account for repeated looks. Proper statistical practice ensures that conclusions from A/B tests are reliable and reproducible; improper practice produces conclusions that look confident but may be wrong.

What Users Say vs. What They Do

Behavioral metrics like task completion rate and engagement time capture what users do, but not necessarily what they value. A user might complete a task while finding the experience frustrating, and another might abandon a task that was progressing well. Understanding how users perceive model quality requires direct preference elicitation—asking users what they think rather than inferring it from their behavior.

User preference studies take several forms. Post-interaction surveys ask users to rate their satisfaction or report on specific quality dimensions: Was the response helpful? Was it accurate? Would you use this feature again? Comparative studies present users with outputs from different model versions and ask which they prefer. Longitudinal studies track how preferences evolve over extended use, capturing whether initial impressions persist. Each format provides different signal. Satisfaction surveys are easy to collect but may reflect superficial impressions. Comparative studies are more discriminating but require more user effort. Longitudinal studies capture stable preferences but are expensive and slow.

Preference data is subject to biases that must be understood when interpreting results. Users may prefer models that are more confident even when confidence is unwarranted, mistaking certainty for accuracy. They may weight recent interactions disproportionately, judging a long sequence of successes harshly if the final interaction failed. They may not accurately predict their own long-term preferences, expressing enthusiasm for features that they stop using, or initial resistance to features that become indispensable. Preference data reflects how users feel at the moment of elicitation, which may not match their considered judgment or their revealed preferences through behavior. Combining preference data with behavioral data provides a more complete picture than either alone. Behavior reveals what users do. Preferences reveal what they think about what they do. Discrepancies between the two are themselves informative about where user experience can be improved.

Summary

The evaluation philosophy that emerges from our survey is fundamentally layered. Automatic metrics provide the speed necessary for rapid iteration, enabling evaluation of every checkpoint and every configuration without blocking development. Model-based evaluation adds nuance that simple statistics cannot capture, assessing whether responses are helpful, accurate, and appropriate at moderate cost. Human evaluation supplies ground truth that no automated method can match, because humans are ultimately the audience whose satisfaction defines success.

Each layer has its place, and effective evaluation employs all three in appropriate proportions. The practitioner who relies solely on perplexity will optimize for fluency at the expense of usefulness. The practitioner who uses only human evaluation will move too slowly to iterate effectively. The practitioner who triangulates across multiple methods, using each where its strengths apply, builds models that work.

No single metric suffices, and this is not a temporary limitation awaiting methodological breakthrough. The qualities we care about in language models are genuinely multidimensional: accuracy, helpfulness, safety, conciseness, appropriate confidence, and many others. These dimensions interact in complex ways, and optimizing one may come at the expense of another. Goodhart's law ensures that any metric we optimize becomes a less reliable indicator of the underlying quality it was meant to capture.

The defense is diversity of measurement, approaching quality from multiple angles through methods that cannot all be gamed simultaneously. When automatic metrics, model-based evaluations, and human judgments all improve together, we have reasonable confidence that genuine progress has occurred. When they diverge, the divergence itself provides the most important signal, revealing that our proxy metrics have drifted from the outcomes we care about.

Evaluation cannot be separated from the broader post-training workflow. The data we collect shapes what we can measure. The training objectives we choose determine what improvements are possible. The deployment context defines which qualities matter. Evaluation informs each of these decisions and is informed by them in turn. Building a custom benchmark forces clarity about what the deployment needs. Discovering that a fine-tuned model regresses on unrelated capabilities raises questions about the composition of training data. Observing that A/B test results diverge from offline evaluation prompts investigation of what the offline metrics are missing. Evaluation is not a stage that follows development but a capability that permeates it, providing the feedback signals that make intelligent iteration possible.

Most important, evaluation is ongoing rather than terminal. The temptation is to treat evaluation as a gate: Pass the benchmarks, achieve acceptable human ratings, deploy, and move on. This framing misunderstands the nature of the challenge. Models interact with users who find unexpected failure modes, with data distributions that shift over time, and with adversaries who probe for weaknesses. The evaluation that declared a model ready for deployment may not capture the problems that emerge after it comes out.

Continuous monitoring, periodic reevaluation against fresh data, and systematic investigation of user complaints are not optional additions to an evaluation program but essential components of it. The organization that stops evaluating has not achieved success but merely stopped looking for failure. In the craft of post-training, evaluation is not a task to complete but a discipline to maintain.

PART III

THE CRAFT

7

EFFICIENCY TECHNIQUES: QUANTIZATION AND COMPRESSION

In the early 1990s, a strange subculture emerged, mainly in Europe, which focused on creating elaborate audiovisual presentations in as little as a few kilobytes of executable code. These *demos*, as they were known, turned parsimony into a creative virtue and demonstrated that constraints could fuel innovation rather than stifle it. In its own way, quantization, too, is something of an art form of making do with the least, although we will primarily admire it for its pragmatic value.

For even if we are not after artistic value, efficiency is fundamental to enterprise deployments. The most capable language model, if too large to deploy or too slow to serve users, creates no business value. This chapter addresses the essential work of making models practical: small enough to fit in available memory, fast enough to meet latency requirements, and efficient enough to operate within cost constraints. The techniques we examine fall into several categories. Quantization reduces the precision of numerical representations, shrinking model size and accelerating computation. PEFT methods like LoRA adapt models with far fewer trainable parameters than full fine-tuning. Knowledge distillation transfers capabilities from larger to smaller models, and pruning removes unnecessary parameters entirely.

Understanding each technique's trade-offs enables intelligent selection and combination for specific deployment constraints. These techniques can be combined; for example, a quantized LoRA adapter on a distilled model represents several optimizations stacked, enabling dramatic efficiency improvements. We examine how many bits you need for quantization, when parameter-efficient methods preserve capability versus degrading it, how to distill without losing the qualities that made the larger model valuable, and how to validate that efficiency gains have not compromised the capabilities you care about.

Squeezing Blood from Bits

Like most computational artifacts, models are but collections of numbers that store the weights and activations of the neural network. Numbers, though, are not all created equal. Floating-point representations vary in precision and range, and lower-precision formats can store more or less the same information with fewer bits. Quantization leverages this by reducing the numerical precision of model weights and activations, trading off some fidelity for efficiency.

The Precision Ladder: From 32 Bits to 4

Neural network weights and activations are stored as numbers, and the precision of those numbers determines both memory footprint and computational cost. A 7-billion-parameter model stored in standard `float32` (single-precision floating-point), consumes 28GB of memory just for the parameters, before accounting for activations, gradients, or optimizer states.

Reducing the precision of numerical representation directly reduces memory requirements and, on hardware designed for lower-precision arithmetic, accelerates computation. The precision ladder, shown in Figure 7-1, is a helpful way to think about this: Each step down the ladder approximately halves memory usage, but as you will see, this does not come for free. In computation, everything has a price. The secret art of quantization is to extract more value out of this simplification than must be paid in loss of accuracy.

Standard `float32` provides ample precision for representing the weight values that matter for neural network computation. The range and granularity are far beyond what the networks use. Most weights fall in a narrow range around 0, and small differences in the fifth decimal place rarely affect outputs.

This observation suggests that lower-precision representations might suffice. Using `float16` (half-precision floating-point), halves memory requirements while providing 65,536 distinct values—still far more than networks need. Using `bfloat16`, the "brain floating point" format developed at Google

Brain, maintains `float32`'s exponent range while reducing mantissa precision, providing dynamic range that handles the occasional large value while using only 16 bits.

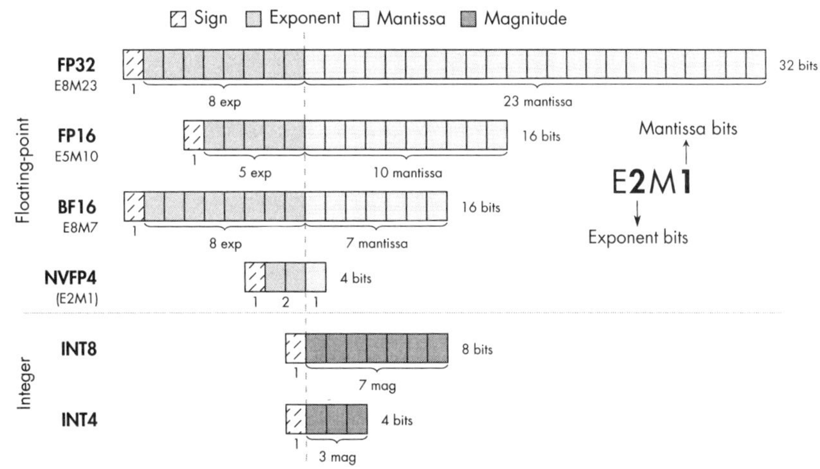

Figure 7-1: Bit layouts of common numeric formats used in model quantization

Integer representations reduce precision further. Int8 provides 256 distinct values, requiring careful mapping of floating-point weight distributions to this limited set. Int4 provides only 16 distinct values, an extreme compression that nonetheless works surprisingly well for many models. The choice of representation trades precision for efficiency. Lower precision means smaller models that fit in less memory, faster computation on hardware optimized for low-precision arithmetic, and lower energy consumption. The cost is potential performance degradation, as quantization introduces error that accumulates through network layers.

Understanding these trade-offs enables intelligent quantization decisions: aggressive quantization for deployment-constrained scenarios, and conservative quantization when capability preservation is paramount. Figure 7-2 illustrates how precision and dynamic range shrink together as we move down this ladder, and why different formats make different trade-offs between the two.

NVIDIA's NVFP4 format pushes floating-point quantization to 4 bits with a 1-sign, 2-exponent, 1-mantissa layout (E2M1), yielding only 16 representable values with a dynamic range of ± 6. That tiny range demands per-block scaling factors. Each small group of weights carries its own scale, mapping the block's actual value distribution into the narrow representable interval. The format is natively supported on the Blackwell and Vera Rubin GPU architectures, which includes the GB10 chip in the NVIDIA DGX Spark, so even desktop-class hardware in that family can exploit it.

The benefits go beyond raw throughput. NVIDIA reports up to 3.6 times faster inference compared to FP8 on Blackwell, but the energy savings are equally significant. Moving fewer bits through the memory hierarchy and executing simpler arithmetic means each inference consumes less power, a consideration that compounds rapidly at datacenter scale and matters increasingly as organizations account for the environmental cost of AI workloads.

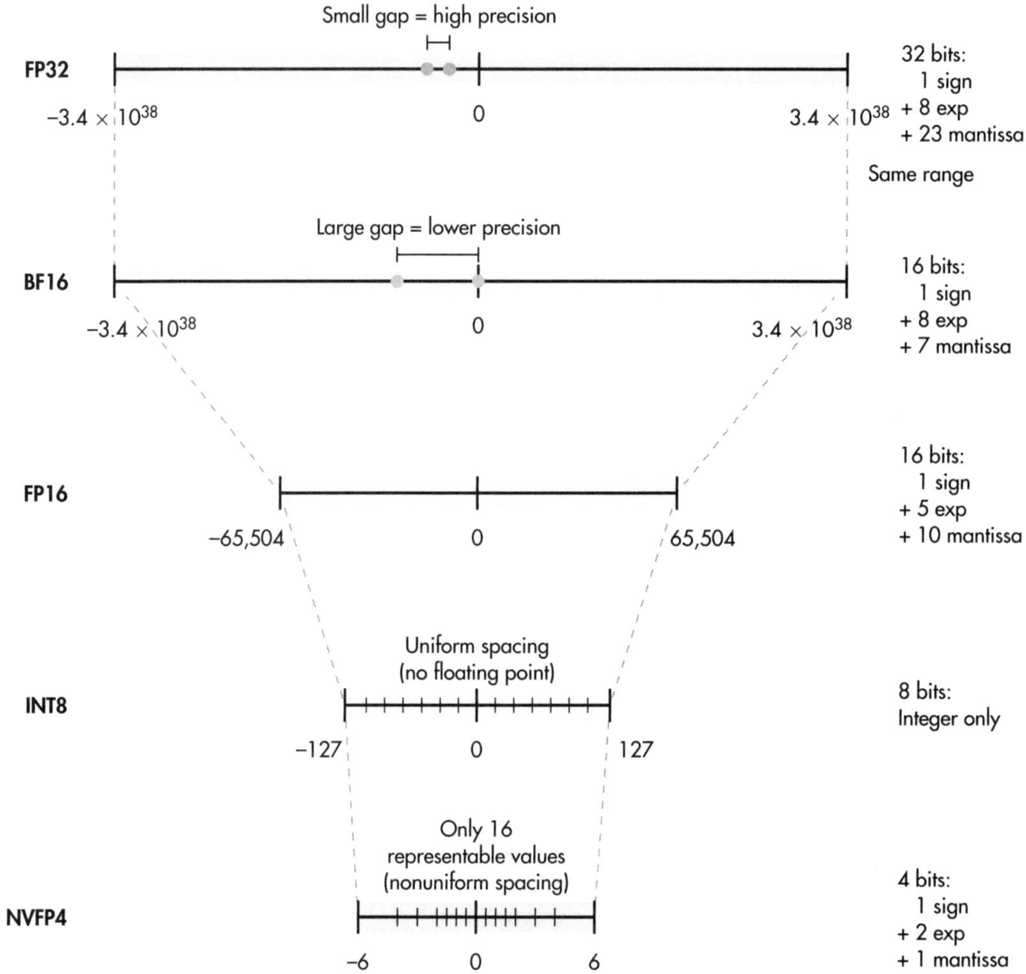

Figure 7-2: Precision and dynamic range across number formats. Each horizontal line represents the interval of representable values. FP32 and BF16 share the same dynamic range (both have 8 exponent bits), but BF16 sacrifices mantissa precision, as the wider dot spacing shows. FP16 trades range for slightly better precision than BF16. Integer formats like INT8 offer uniform spacing but a narrow range. NVFP4, supported on Blackwell and Vera Rubin hardware, compresses to just 16 representable values, relying on per-block scaling to compensate.

WARNING *NF4 and NVFP4 are different. NF4 (`NormalFloat4`) was designed for 4-bit quantization for QLoRAs and is part of the bitsandbytes ecosystem, while NVFP4 is specifically a Blackwell/Rubin-only format. NF4 uses a 1-sign, 2-exponent, 1-mantissa* *layout optimized for the weight distributions found in neural networks, while NVFP4's E2M1 format is a more general-purpose 4-bit floating-point format and is geared primarily toward inference.*

Recent research has pushed quantization to its logical extreme: 1-bit weights, where each parameter is either +1 or −1. Microsoft's BitNet architecture demonstrates that models trained natively with ternary weights ($\{-1, 0, +1\}$) can match the performance of full-precision models at equivalent parameter counts, while reducing memory by an order of magnitude and replacing expensive multiply-accumulate operations with simple additions.[148] The catch is that these models must be trained from scratch with quantization-aware methods. You cannot simply quantize an existing model, post-training, to 1 bit without catastrophic degradation.

For practitioners, 1-bit models represent a future that has extreme efficiency designed in from the start rather than retrofitted after training. Watch this space: As hardware support for binary operations matures and training recipes stabilize, 1-bit models may become practical for edge deployment scenarios where even int4 is too heavy.

The Post-Training Shortcut

Post-training quantization converts a trained model to lower precision without additional training. The model is trained in high precision, achieving full capability, then compressed for deployment. The appeal is convenience: You can take any pre-trained model and quantize it without access to training data or compute. The challenge is that naive quantization, simply rounding all weights to lower precision, can severely degrade model quality because the rounding errors compound through network layers.

The field has developed two families of approaches. Calibration-based methods use sample data to optimize quantization parameters, and calibration-free methods quantize on the fly without any data.

Calibration-Based Methods

Calibration-based quantization uses a small dataset to determine how to quantize each weight while minimizing output degradation. The up-front cost is offset by better accuracy, particularly at aggressive bit depths.

Generalized post-training quantization (GPTQ) treats quantization as an optimization problem: Given a calibration dataset, find the low-precision weights that minimize reconstruction error.[149] The method processes weights layer by layer, using second-order information about how weight perturbations affect outputs to make smarter rounding decisions than simple nearest-neighbor quantization.

Activation-aware weight quantization (AWQ) observes that not all weights matter equally. Some weights multiply large activations and contribute substantially to outputs, while others multiply near-zero activations and matter little.[150] AWQ protects important weights by scaling them up before quantization and scaling down after, effectively allocating more precision where it matters. Both GPTQ and AWQ achieve strong 4-bit accuracy, with AWQ often edging ahead on benchmarks because of its activation-aware approach.

The calibration process typically requires 128 to 512 samples and runs in minutes on a single GPU. In my experience, using a small set of in-domain samples yields the best results, but even generic text samples work adequately for many applications. The calibration cost is a one-time expense per model and bit depth, making these methods attractive for production deployments where accuracy is critical.

Calibration-Free Methods

Calibration-free methods quantize models on the fly, trading some accuracy for convenience. They require no calibration data and can quantize any model immediately.

The bitsandbytes library pioneered accessible LLM quantization with its `LLM.int8` method, which handles outlier features that would otherwise degrade 8-bit accuracy.[151] Its 4-bit NormalFloat (NF4) format is optimized for the weight distributions found in neural networks and forms the basis for QLoRA fine-tuning (see "The 1 Percent That Matters" on page 201). Half-quadratic quantization (HQQ) offers fast on-the-fly quantization at various bit depths, using a half-quadratic solver to find good quantization parameters without calibration data.[152] HQQ is particularly useful when you need to quantize many models quickly or when calibration data is unavailable.

The trade-off is accuracy. Calibration-free methods typically lag calibration-based methods by 1 to 2 percentage points on benchmarks, with the gap widening at lower bit depths. For 8-bit quantization, the difference is negligible. At 4 bits, calibration-based methods like AWQ and GPTQ generally outperform calibration-free alternatives, making the up-front calibration cost worthwhile for production deployments. The impact of this is illustrated by Table 7-1, which shows memory estimates for a 7-billion-parameter model and its accuracy loss over various quantizations relative to the FP16/BF16 baseline of typical benchmarks.

Table 7-1: Quantization Methods and Output Bit Depths

Method	Output bits	Calibration	Memory (7B)	Accuracy loss	Best for
FP16/BF16	16	—	14GB	Baseline	Development
`LLM.int8`	8	No	7GB	< 1%	Easy 8-bit deployment
HQQ	4–8	No	3.5–7GB	1%–3%	Fast on-the-fly quantization
GPTQ	4	Yes	3.5GB	1%–2%	General 4-bit deployment
AWQ	4	Yes	3.5GB	< 1%	Accuracy-critical 4-bit
FP8	8	No	7GB	< 0.5%	Hopper+ GPU hardware
NVFP4	4	Yes (per block)	3.5GB	1%–2%	Blackwell/Vera Rubin inference

These methods can reduce models to 4 bits with surprisingly small performance degradation, enabling deployment of large models on consumer hardware that could not fit the full-precision versions. A 70-billion-parameter model that would require 140GB in `float16` fits in 35GB at 4-bit precision, making deployment on high-end consumer GPUs feasible. Verifying that quantization has not unacceptably degraded capability requires systematic evaluation (see Chapter 6). Comparing quantized and full-precision models on your deployment tasks reveals whether the theoretical efficiency gains translate to acceptable quality in practice.

Born to Be Quantized

Quantization-aware training (QAT) incorporates quantization into the training process itself, allowing the model to adapt to reduced precision rather than having it imposed post hoc. The intuition is straightforward: If the model will ultimately operate at low precision, it should learn weights that work well at low precision, not weights that happen to round well from a high-precision optimum. QAT enables this by simulating quantization during training, exposing the optimization process to quantization effects so it can compensate.

However, quantization is not differentiable. The rounding operation has zero gradient almost everywhere and undefined gradient at the rounding boundaries. The straight-through estimator resolves this by using quantized weights in the forward pass while pretending, for gradient computation purposes, that quantization did not occur in the backward pass. Gradients flow through as if the weights were full precision, but parameter updates are applied to the full-precision master weights, which are then requantized for the next forward pass. The model learns weights whose quantized versions produce good outputs, even though the learning signal itself ignores quantization.

QAT typically produces better quantized models than post-training quantization, sometimes substantially so at aggressive quantization levels like 4 bits. The improvement comes from the model's opportunity to adapt. Weight distributions shift to be more quantization-friendly, and the model learns representations that are robust to the specific errors that quantization introduces. The cost is additional training, making QAT most appropriate when quantization is known to be necessary and training compute is available. For organizations that will deploy at a specific quantization level, the investment in QAT typically pays off in better deployment performance compared to post hoc quantization of a full-precision model.

FROM THE TRENCHES: WHAT HAPPENS AT FOUNDATION SCALE

At foundation labs training 70B+ models, the infrastructure challenges dwarf what most organizations face. Training runs use three-dimensional parallelism (data, tensor, and pipeline parallelism combined), sometimes extending to five-dimensional with context and expert parallelism for mixture-of-experts (MoE) architectures. Teams obsessively track Model Flops Utilization (MFU) because inefficiencies compound across thousands of GPUs and weeks of training. A mere 5 percent edge on MFU might make a difference of millions in compute costs. Memory budgets are calculated to the gigabyte (which is a very, very small amount if you're dealing with an entire building's worth of GPUs): Mixed precision uses 2 bytes per parameter, FP32 gradient accumulation adds more, and attention memory becomes dominant at 100,000 context lengths. Context parallelism enables million-token training by splitting sequences across GPUs with carefully minimized communication overhead.

This matters for the "crucial middle" because it contextualizes why the techniques in this chapter exist. LoRAs, quantization, and efficient fine-tuning are adaptations, at lower scales, of ideas that were born in foundation-level training. Understanding what happens at a larger scale helps us see whether techniques designed for that scale will or will not transfer to more constrained settings.

The Lingua Franca of Quantized Models: GGUF

Browse any model repository on Hugging Face, and you will encounter entries like *model-Q4_1.gguf*, *model-IQ2_XXS.gguf*, and *model-Q8_0.gguf*. This delightful alphabet soup encodes a specific set of decisions about how the model was quantized. Understanding this nomenclature is essential for making informed deployment choices, because the variant you select directly determines the trade-off between model size and output quality.

GGML unified format (GGUF) was developed by the llama.cpp project as the successor to the older GGML format. Whereas GGML required separate files for model weights, tokenizer configuration, and architecture metadata, GGUF packages everything into a single self-contained binary. A *.gguf* file contains the quantized weights, the tokenizer, architectural parameters, and quantization metadata, so one file is all that's needed to load and run a model. This self-contained design, combined with llama.cpp's efficient CPU inference engine, made GGUF the de facto standard for local and edge deployment of quantized language models. The format is not limited to Llama-family models despite its origins. GGUF supports a wide range of transformer architectures, and the ecosystem has grown well beyond its initial scope.

GGUF's naming convention follows a pattern that, once decoded, tells you exactly the trade-offs the quantization makes. The general form is *Q{bits}_{method}_{size}*, though importance-matrix variants use the prefix *IQ* instead of *Q*.

The first component, the bit depth, is straightforward: *Q4* means 4-bit, *Q5* means 5-bit, and so on. Lower bit depths mean smaller files and faster inference, at the cost of increased quantization error. The second component identifies the quantization method, and this is where the meaningful distinctions lie:

Legacy methods (*Q4_0*, *Q4_1*, *Q8_0*)
: The earliest GGML quantization schemes. Type-0 methods use simple round-to-nearest quantization with a single scale factor per block of weights. Type-1 adds a per-block minimum value, slightly improving accuracy by allowing the quantization grid to shift rather than merely scale. *Q8_0* remains useful as a high-quality 8-bit format that is essentially lossless for most practical purposes, but the 4-bit legacy methods have been largely superseded by K-quants.

K-quants (*Q3_K*, *Q4_K*, *Q5_K*, *Q6_K*)
: Introduced in mid-2023, K-quants represent a significant improvement over legacy methods. Rather than quantizing all tensors uniformly, K-quants assign different bit depths to different tensor types within the model. Attention weights may be quantized at a different precision than feed-forward weights, and the quantization scale factors themselves are stored more efficiently. The suffix letter indicates the *size variant*:

- *S* (small): Most aggressive compression. More tensors are quantized at lower precision, and less metadata is retained. Smallest file size, lowest quality within the given bit depth.
- *M* (medium): Balanced compression. Some tensors are kept at a higher precision than the nominal bit depth. This is the most commonly recommended variant for general use.
- *L* (large): Most conservative compression. More tensors are held at higher precision. Largest file size within the given bit depth, best quality.

Importance-matrix variants (*IQ2*, *IQ3*, *IQ4*)
: The *IQ* prefix denotes importance-matrix (imatrix) quantization, which uses a calibration dataset to determine which weights contribute most to model outputs and allocates precision accordingly. This calibration-aware approach achieves remarkably good quality at very low bit depths: *IQ2* variants produce usable models at 2 bits per weight, a compression level where standard quantization would yield gibberish. The suffixes indicate relative size: *XXS* (extra-extra-small), *XS* (extra-small), *S* (small), and *M* (medium). The variant *IQ4_NL* uses a nonlinear quantization grid, mapping weights to a learned set of values rather than uniformly spaced steps.

Table 7-2 summarizes the most common GGUF quantization types and their approximate characteristics for a 7-billion-parameter model. Memory estimates are approximate and vary slightly by model architecture. Quality ratings are relative to the FP16 baseline.

Table 7-2: Common GGUF Quantization Types for a 7-Billion-Parameter Model

Type	Bits	Size (7B)	Quality	Notes
Q2_K	2–3	~2.7GB	Poor	Extreme compression; noticeable degradation
IQ2_XXS	2	~2.1GB	Usable	Imatrix calibration; best quality at 2-bit
IQ3_M	3	~3.0GB	Moderate	Good for memory-constrained edge devices
Q3_K_M	3	~3.3GB	Moderate	Reasonable quality for tight memory budgets
Q4_K_S	4	~3.6GB	Good	Smaller 4-bit; slight quality trade-off
Q4_K_M	4	~3.9GB	Good	*Recommended default for most users*
Q5_K_M	5	~4.7GB	Very good	Best balance of size and quality
Q6_K	6	~5.5GB	Excellent	Near-lossless; recommended if memory allows
Q8_0	8	~7.0GB	Near perfect	Effectively lossless; largest GGUF variant

For practitioners choosing among GGUF variants, the decision follows a simple heuristic: Use the highest bit depth that fits comfortably in available memory, leaving room for the key-value (KV) cache and the context window. Within a given bit depth, the *_M* (medium) variant provides the best balance of file size and output quality. If memory is tight, drop to *_S*; if memory is plentiful, step up to the next bit depth rather than using *_L*, since the quality gain from an extra bit of precision typically exceeds the gain from more conservative quantization at the same bit depth. For extreme memory constraints, the *IQ* variants deliver substantially better quality than their standard counterparts at the same bit depth, though they require a calibration step to produce.

The practical workflow for GGUF deployment typically involves downloading a pre-quantized model from a repository like Hugging Face, though you can also quantize models yourself with llama.cpp's `llama-quantize` tool. Many model providers now publish their own GGUF quantizations alongside the full-precision weights, and community quantizers fill the gaps for models that lack official GGUF releases.

WARNING *Not every GGUF file found online was quantized competently. The ease of running llama.cpp's tools means anyone can produce GGUF files, but not everyone uses appropriate calibration data for imatrix quantizations or verifies quality afterward. Look for GGUF files from the original model provider or from well-known community quantizers who publish their methodology and perplexity measurements. When in doubt, verify quality yourself before deploying.*

Did We Break It? Verifying Quantized Models

Quantization introduces error. Every weight rounded to a lower precision, every activation computed at reduced fidelity, contributes a small deviation from the full-precision model's behavior. These deviations accumulate through the network's layers, and whether the accumulated error matters depends entirely on what the model is being used for. A model that loses 2 percent on a general benchmark may have lost nothing on the specific downstream task, or it may have lost something critical that the benchmark does not measure. Systematic verification is the only way to know, and skipping it is one of the most common mistakes in quantized model deployment.

The verification process should compare the quantized model against the full-precision original on metrics that reflect deployment requirements. General-purpose metrics provide a baseline sanity check, but task-specific evaluation is what ultimately determines whether the quantized model is fit for purpose.

Perplexity: The First Line of Defense

Perplexity on a held-out text corpus is the most widely used single metric for quantization quality, and for good reason: It is deterministic, reproducible, and sensitive to the kind of distributional drift that quantization introduces. Perplexity measures how well the model predicts unseen text, with lower values indicating better language modeling capability. Comparing perplexity of the full-precision model and its quantized variant on the same corpus gives a direct, single-number measure of how much general capability was lost.

For most well-quantized models, 4-bit quantization increases perplexity by 0.1 to 0.5 points on standard corpora like WikiText-2. Increases beyond 1.0 point warrant investigation: Either the quantization method is suboptimal, the model architecture is unusually sensitive to precision reduction, or something went wrong during the quantization process. The llama.cpp toolkit includes a perplexity measurement utility (`llama-perplexity`) that can evaluate GGUF files directly, making this check straightforward to automate.

Perplexity is a necessary but insufficient check. A model can have perfectly acceptable perplexity while failing on specific tasks that depend on capabilities downgraded by quantization. Language modeling perplexity is dominated by common patterns—easily predicted tokens and high-frequency constructions—that quantization tends to preserve well. The rare, difficult predictions that distinguish a capable model from a mediocre one contribute comparatively little to the perplexity score, which means perplexity can miss precisely the degradation that matters most for demanding applications.

Task-Specific Benchmarks

The most reliable verification strategy evaluates the quantized model on exactly the tasks it will perform in deployment. If the model will answer customer queries about a product catalog, evaluate it on a held-out set of product queries. If it will generate code, run it through a coding benchmark. If it will extract entities from legal documents, test it on annotated legal text. The gap between the quantized model's performance and the full-precision baseline on these task-specific evaluations is the number that matters for the deployment decision.

Standard benchmarks provide useful reference points even when they do not precisely match the deployment task. MMLU tests broad knowledge and reasoning across 57 subjects; a significant drop suggests that factual recall or reasoning capabilities have been compromised. HumanEval and MBPP test code generation; drops here indicate degradation in the model's ability to produce syntactically and semantically correct code. MT-Bench and AlpacaEval assess instruction-following quality and conversational ability. Running a small suite of these benchmarks before and after quantization takes minutes and provides a broad picture of capability preservation.

A structured verification workflow evaluates perplexity first as a fast sanity check, then runs two or three standard benchmarks to assess broad capability, and finally evaluates on task-specific held-out data to assess deployment readiness. If perplexity degrades modestly but task performance is preserved, the quantization is safe to deploy. If task performance degrades beyond acceptable thresholds, consider a less aggressive quantization: a higher bit depth, or a calibration-based method like AWQ or GPTQ instead of a calibration-free approach.

Head-to-Head Comparison

For generative tasks where automated metrics capture only part of output quality, running the full-precision and quantized models on the same set of prompts and directly comparing outputs is illuminating. Side-by-side inspection reveals qualitative differences that metrics miss. The quantized model may produce slightly less coherent long-form text, lose nuance in complex instructions, or generate less diverse responses. These differences may or may not matter for the intended application, but they are invisible to perplexity measurements and benchmark scores alone.

An LLM-as-a-judge approach (see Chapter 6) can scale this comparison beyond what manual inspection allows. Present the same prompts to both models, then ask a capable judge model to evaluate which response is better across dimensions like accuracy, coherence, helpfulness, and instruction adherence. If the judge cannot reliably distinguish between the full-precision and quantized outputs, the quantization has preserved the qualities that matter for subjective evaluation. Conversely, if the judge consistently prefers the full-precision outputs on certain dimensions, those dimensions identify exactly where quantization is costing you capability, and you can decide whether that cost is acceptable for your use case.

> **BUILDING A QUANTIZATION QUALITY GATE**
>
> For organizations deploying quantized models at scale, automating quality verification as a CI/CD gate prevents degraded models from reaching production. A practical quality gate checks three metrics in sequence:
>
> 1. Perplexity threshold: The quantized model's perplexity must be within a configurable tolerance of the full-precision baseline (for example, no more than 0.5 points higher on a reference corpus). This catches catastrophic quantization failures quickly.
> 2. Benchmark regression: Scores on a curated set of benchmarks must not drop below a configured percentage of the baseline (for example, no more than 3 percent relative degradation). This catches broad capability loss.
> 3. Task-specific acceptance: Performance on held-out examples from the actual deployment task must meet minimum thresholds. This catches task-specific degradation that general benchmarks would miss.
>
> The gate runs automatically whenever a new quantization is produced, whether from a new base model, a new quantization method, or updated calibration data. Models that fail any check are flagged for human review rather than deployed automatically. The thresholds should be set based on deployment requirements, not arbitrary numbers. A chatbot serving casual queries, for instance, can tolerate more degradation than a model triaging patients on ER intake.

The 1 Percent That Matters

What we ultimately care about, for any given use case of LLMs (or indeed many other models), comprises a very small fraction of the model at large. Of billions of parameters, our concern is rarely with more than 1 to 2 percent. LoRA's empirical insight–that weight changes during fine-tuning have low intrinsic dimensionality–enables training with a fraction of the parameters and memory. Combined with quantization in QLoRA, this democratized access to large model fine-tuning overnight.

LoRA: Less Is More

Low-rank adaptation (LoRA) begins from an empirical observation: When large models are fine-tuned on specific tasks, the weight changes often have low intrinsic dimensionality.[87] The change from pre-trained weights to fine-tuned weights, which nominally involves millions or billions of parameters, can be well approximated by a much smaller number of degrees of freedom. This suggests that fine-tuning does not require updating all parameters, only finding the right direction in a low-dimensional subspace of the full parameter space.

LoRA and its descendants operationalize this insight by freezing the pre-trained weights entirely and training only low-rank "adapter" matrices that modify the frozen weights' outputs. For each weight matrix being adapted, LoRA introduces two small matrices whose product approximates the weight update. For a pre-trained weight matrix $W_0 \in \mathbb{R}^{d \times k}$, LoRA introduces the trainable matrices $A \in \mathbb{R}^{d \times r}$ and $B \in \mathbb{R}^{r \times k}$ where $r \ll \min(d, k)$. The modified forward pass becomes

$$h = W_0 x + BAx = W_0 x + \Delta W x$$

where $\Delta W = BA$ is the low-rank update. Only A and B are trained, reducing trainable parameters from $d \times k$ to $r \times (d + k)$. If the original weight matrix has dimensions $d \times k$, the adapter matrices have dimensions $d \times r$ and $r \times k$ where r is much smaller than both d and k. The trainable parameters drop from $d \times k$ to $r \times (d + k)$, a reduction that can exceed 100 times for typical transformer dimensions.

A 7-billion-parameter model might have only 10 to 100 million trainable LoRA parameters, reducing memory requirements for gradient computation and optimizer states by an order of magnitude. This reduction enables fine-tuning of large models on consumer hardware that could not fit a full fine-tuning run. The rank r of the adapter matrices controls the trade-off between adaptation capacity and efficiency: Higher ranks provide more capacity to represent complex adaptations but require more parameters and memory, while lower ranks are more efficient but may be insufficient for tasks requiring substantial behavioral change. Typical values range from 4 to 64, with 16 or 32 being common defaults. Empirically, LoRA often achieves performance close to full fine-tuning despite training only a small fraction of parameters, validating the low-rank hypothesis that motivated its design.

> **CHOOSING LORA RANK**
>
> Start with rank 16 as a default. If training converges quickly and performance plateaus below expectations, the adapter may lack capacity; try rank 32 or 64. If training is slow or unstable, high rank may be causing optimization difficulties; try rank 8. For simple format adaptation tasks, rank 4 often suffices. For complex domain shifts, rank 64 may be necessary. The right rank depends on how much the task requires the model to change. Small behavioral adjustments need low rank, while substantial adaptation needs high rank.

QLoRA: The 70B Model on Your Laptop

QLoRA combines quantization and LoRA to enable fine-tuning of large models on hardware that could not otherwise support them.[153] The base model is loaded in 4-bit precision, dramatically reducing memory requirements, while LoRA adapters are trained in higher precision to maintain gradient fidelity. The combination is multiplicative: 4-bit quantization reduces the base model's memory footprint by 8 times compared to `float32`, and LoRA reduces trainable parameters by 100 times or more.

Together they enable training 30-billion-parameter models on a single consumer GPU with 24GB of memory. For 70B models, expect to need 48GB or more; this comfortably fits into the NVIDIA DGX Spark's unified memory, but is also achievable with high-end workstation GPUs or two consumer cards with careful memory management.

QLoRA introduced several innovations beyond simply combining existing techniques. The NF4 data type, 4-bit NormalFloat, is specifically designed for the approximately normal distribution of neural network weights. Traditional integer quantization allocates precision uniformly across the representable range, but neural network weights cluster around 0 with tails that fall off predictably. NF4 allocates more precision to the high-density regions around 0, reducing quantization error where most weights lie. Double quantization applies quantization to the quantization parameters themselves, reducing the memory overhead of the scale factors that every quantized block requires.

Listing 7-1 demonstrates the complete setup on a 70B model using Unsloth, which wraps the quantization and LoRA configuration into a streamlined interface while handling the NF4 loading and double quantization behind the scenes.

```
from unsloth import FastLanguageModel
import torch

❶ model, tokenizer = FastLanguageModel.from_pretrained(
    model_name="unsloth/Llama-3.3-70B-Instruct",
    max_seq_length=2048,
    load_in_4bit=True,
)

❷ model = FastLanguageModel.get_peft_model(
    model,
    r=16,
    lora_alpha=16,
  ❸ target_modules=["q_proj", "k_proj", "v_proj",
                    "o_proj", "gate_proj",
                    "up_proj", "down_proj"],
    lora_dropout=0,
    bias="none",
  ❹ use_gradient_checkpointing="unsloth",
)
```

Listing 7-1: A QLoRA setup for Llama 3.3 70B using Unsloth's `FastLanguageModel`, which handles 4-bit NF4 loading, LoRA adapter injection, and optimized gradient checkpointing

The model loads ❶ in 4-bit NF4 precision with double quantization enabled by default, reducing the 70B model's memory footprint from 140GB to roughly 40GB. Unsloth's `from_pretrained` handles the `BitsAndBytesConfig` internally, so the quantization details discussed previously are still in effect but no longer require manual configuration. The LoRA adapter ❷ targets all linear projections in each transformer block, not just the query and value projections.

Targeting the ❸ full set of projections (attention projections plus the MLP gate, up, and down projections) adds only modest overhead per adapter parameter but gives the optimizer more degrees of freedom, which matters more at 70B scale where the gap between QLoRA and full fine-tuning becomes harder to close. The `use_gradient_checkpointing="unsloth"` flag ❹ activates an optimized checkpointing strategy that reduces memory further while avoiding the throughput penalty of naive gradient checkpointing.

QLoRA democratized the fine-tuning of large models that had previously been accessible only to well-resourced organizations. Researchers and practitioners with consumer hardware could suddenly fine-tune models of 30 billion or 65 billion parameters, exploring capabilities and applications that would otherwise require expensive cloud compute.

The performance cost of QLoRA compared to full fine-tuning is typically modest, though it varies by task. For many applications, the ability to fine-tune a much larger model via QLoRA outweighs the small quality loss compared to full fine-tuning a model that fits in memory, since the larger base model brings more capability to start with. Figure 7-3 compares QLoRA and LoRA with full fine-tuning.

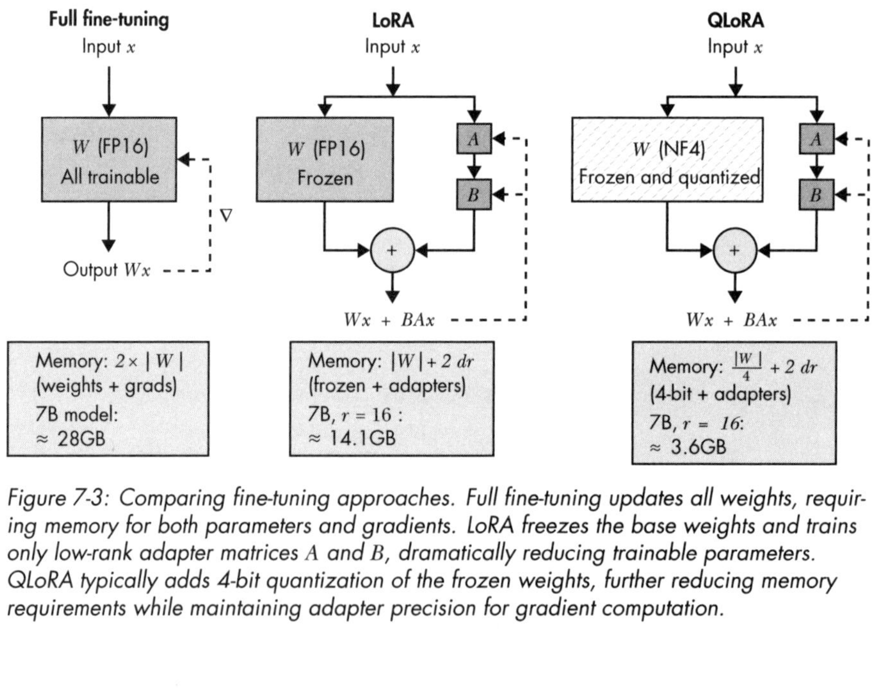

Figure 7-3: Comparing fine-tuning approaches. Full fine-tuning updates all weights, requiring memory for both parameters and gradients. LoRA freezes the base weights and trains only low-rank adapter matrices A and B, dramatically reducing trainable parameters. QLoRA typically adds 4-bit quantization of the frozen weights, further reducing memory requirements while maintaining adapter precision for gradient computation.

> **FROM THE TRENCHES: THE QLORA REVOLUTION**
>
> Before QLoRA, fine-tuning a 70B model required A100 GPUs that cost thousands per hour. After QLoRA, the same task fits on a 24GB consumer GPU costing a few hundred dollars. I have watched organizations go from "We cannot afford to experiment with large models" to "We fine-tuned five variants this week" simply by adopting QLoRA. The quality-efficiency trade-off is real but often favorable: A QLoRA-tuned 70B model typically beats a fully tuned 7B model, and the former is now accessible.

DoRA: Magnitude and Direction

Weight-decomposed low-rank adaptation (DoRA) refines the LoRA approach by decomposing weight updates into magnitude and direction components, drawing inspiration from weight normalization techniques.[154] Whereas standard LoRA adds a low-rank update $\Delta W = BA$ directly to frozen weights, DoRA first decomposes the pre-trained weight matrix W_0 into a magnitude vector m and a direction matrix V, then applies LoRA-style updates only to the directional component. The magnitude remains a separate learnable parameter, providing independent control over "how much" versus "which direction."

This decomposition yields consistent improvements over standard LoRA across tasks, typically 1 to 3 percent on benchmarks, with negligible additional memory cost during training. The gains appear most pronounced on tasks requiring nuanced behavioral changes, where the separation of magnitude and direction gives the optimizer more degrees of freedom.

For practitioners, DoRA represents a drop-in improvement over LoRA. The same hyperparameters work, the same infrastructure applies, and the additional implementation complexity is minimal. When LoRA falls slightly short of full fine-tuning performance, DoRA often closes the gap. The PEFT package offers DoRA support with the same interface as that of LoRA, easily accessed by setting `use_dora=True` in `LoraConfig`.

Invisible Hands: Soft Prompts

An alternative family of parameter-efficient methods modifies the model's input rather than its weights. These *soft prompt* methods prepend learnable embedding vectors to the input sequence, steering model behavior through learned context rather than weight modification.[155, 156] The base model remains entirely frozen, and only the prompt embeddings are trained. This approach decouples what the model knows from the way it is directed, enabling task-specific adaptation while preserving the full pre-trained model unchanged.

The appeal of soft prompts lies in their conceptual elegance. Hard prompts, which are the natural language instructions humans write, require manual engineering and occupy valuable context space. Soft prompts learn the optimal "instructions" automatically, discovering continuous embedding vectors that elicit desired behavior more effectively than any human-written prompt could. The learned prompts are not interpretable as natural language; they are points in embedding space that the model responds to in task-appropriate ways. This lack of interpretability is the cost of their effectiveness.

Three leading methods have emerged in this field:

Prompt tuning

Adds trainable tokens only at the input layer.[155] Given a task, the method learns a sequence of soft token embeddings that, when prepended to each input, causes the frozen model to produce appropriate outputs. The approach was developed for T5 on text classification, casting all tasks as text generation. Rather than predicting a class label directly, the model generates the text of the label.

Prompt tuning scales remarkably well with model size. While performance lags full fine-tuning for smaller models, it matches full fine-tuning for models above 10 billion parameters. This scaling behavior suggests that larger models are more responsive to input-level steering, requiring less internal modification to adapt to new tasks.

Prefix tuning

Extends soft prompts beyond the input layer.[156] Rather than adding trainable embeddings only at the input, prefix tuning adds trainable key-value pairs at every transformer layer. The effect is that the model attends to learned *virtual tokens* throughout its depth, not just at the beginning. This deeper intervention provides more steering capacity: Whereas prompt tuning can influence the model only through its response to input embeddings, prefix tuning influences attention patterns at every layer.

A critical implementation detail is that prefix parameters are optimized through a separate FFN rather than trained directly, which prevents instability during training. Prefix tuning can achieve comparable performance to full fine-tuning despite training fewer than 0.1 percent of parameters, with particular strength in low-data scenarios where full fine-tuning would overfit.

P-tuning

Generalizes soft prompts to natural language understanding tasks and to architectures beyond T5.[157] The key innovation is flexible token placement: Rather than prepending all soft tokens before the input, P-tuning can insert trainable embeddings anywhere in the input sequence. This flexibility enables task-specific prompt structures, with soft tokens marking boundaries between input components or appearing at positions that the task structure motivates.

P-tuning also employs a bidirectional LSTM to generate the prompt embeddings, rather than learning them as independent parameters, which provides regularization and enables the embeddings to have coherent structure. This method demonstrated that GPT-style autoregressive models could match BERT-style bidirectional models on natural language understanding benchmarks when properly prompted, challenging the conventional wisdom that different architectures suited different task types.

Soft prompt methods shine in specific scenarios: when you need to serve multiple tasks from a single frozen model, when storage for task-specific adapters is constrained, or when you want to preserve the base model as an exact reference. A single large model can serve dozens of tasks by swapping only the soft prompt embeddings, each consuming just kilobytes of storage. The limitation, beyond the interpretability hurdle, is capacity. Complex domain shifts that require substantial behavioral change may exceed what input-level steering can achieve. Start with LoRA as the default, but consider soft prompts when multitask serving or model preservation is the primary constraint.

The Rest of the Toolkit

LoRA is the most widely used PEFT method, but it is not the only option. The PEFT landscape has expanded considerably since LoRA's introduction, with alternative approaches making different trade-offs that may be preferable in specific circumstances. Table 7-3 lays out the landscape of methods to select from when LoRA's particular assumptions do not fit the problem at hand.

Table 7-3: Comparing Parameter-Efficient Fine-Tuning Methods

Method	Params	Inference	Capacity	Best for
Full fine-tuning	All	None	Maximum	Resources available; max quality
LoRA	0.1%–1%	None (merged)	High	Default choice; most tasks
QLoRA	0.1%–1%	None (merged)	High	Limited GPU memory
DoRA	0.1%–1%	None (merged)	High	Closing gap to full fine-tuning
AdaLoRA	0.1%–1%	None (merged)	High	Low-budget; heterogeneous importance
LoHa	0.1%–0.5%	None (merged)	High	Image generation; multi-concept
LoKr	0.1%–0.5%	None (merged)	High	Complex single-concept; structure preservation
Adapters	0.5%–2%	Moderate	Medium	Dynamic switching; cannot merge
Prompt tuning	0.001%–0.01%	Uses context	Low–Medium	Multitask; large models
Prefix tuning	0.01%–0.1%	Uses context	Medium	Low-data; multitask serving
P-tuning	0.01%–0.1%	Uses context	Medium	NLU tasks; flexible placement
IA3	0.01%	Minimal	Low	Few-shot; extreme parameter efficiency

Classical Adapters

The original adapters paper, predating LoRA by several years, showed that inserting bottleneck layers between frozen transformer blocks with a few hundred thousand parameters could achieve competitive fine-tuning performance.[158] The adapters process activations through a down-projection, nonlinearity, and up-projection, learning task-specific transformations while leaving base model weights unchanged.

The disadvantage is inference latency. The additional layers add computation to every forward pass, while LoRA's weight modifications can be folded into the base weights after training, adding no inference overhead. For scenarios where adapter merging is impossible (when multiple adapters must be dynamically switched at runtime, for instance), classical adapters remain a sensible choice.

IA3

Infused adapter by inhibiting and amplifying inner activations (IA3) takes parameter efficiency to an extreme by learning only element-wise scaling vectors rather than low-rank matrices.[159] Whereas LoRA adds a low-rank update to weight matrices, IA3 learns vectors l_k, l_v, and l_{ff} that rescale the keys, values, and feed-forward activations, respectively:

$$\text{softmax}\left(\frac{Q(l_k \odot K)^\top}{\sqrt{d_k}}\right)(l_v \odot V)$$

The element-wise multiplication $\odot$ means IA3 introduces approximately 0.01 percent additional parameters, an order of magnitude fewer than typical LoRA configurations. This extreme efficiency comes with lower capacity: IA3 can amplify or suppress existing features but cannot create new representational structure.

This method excels in few-shot scenarios where the base model already has the necessary capabilities and fine-tuning serves primarily to activate or suppress them. When the task requires substantial behavioral change, IA3's limited capacity becomes a bottleneck.

AdaLoRA

Standard LoRA assigns the same rank to all adapted weight matrices, but not all matrices contribute equally to task performance. AdaLoRA addresses this by adaptively allocating the parameter budget across weight matrices according to their importance.[160]

The method parameterizes incremental updates via singular value decomposition (SVD), representing each update as a product of orthogonal matrices and a diagonal matrix of singular values. Importance scores determine which singular value triplets to retain and which to prune during training. Weight matrices that matter more for the task receive higher effective rank, while less important matrices are pruned more aggressively.

This adaptive allocation yields consistent improvements over fixed-rank LoRA, particularly in low-budget scenarios where parameter efficiency is critical. The overhead is a more complex training procedure that tracks importance scores throughout optimization.

LoHa

Low-rank Hadamard product (LoHa), originating from federated learning research, uses the Hadamard (element-wise) product of two low-rank matrix pairs instead of a single low-rank product

$$\Delta W = (B_1 A_1) \odot (B_2 A_2)$$

where A_1, A_2, B_1, B_2 are all low-rank matrices.[161] The key insight is that while the product of two rank-r matrices has rank at most r, the Hadamard product of two such products can have rank up to r^2. For $r > 2$, this provides substantially more expressivity with the same parameter count.

LoHa has found particular success in image-generation fine-tuning, where the ability to generate diverse outputs benefits from higher-rank updates. This method requires careful hyperparameter tuning, as high ranks can cause training instability. Practitioners typically use ranks of 32 or lower with learning rates lower than those used for standard LoRA.

LoKr

Low-rank Kronecker product (LoKr) replaces matrix multiplication with the Kronecker product, which creates a block matrix from two smaller matrices:[162]

$$\Delta W = C \otimes (BA)$$

The Kronecker product preserves structure in ways that standard low-rank decomposition does not, potentially helping models retain generalization capabilities during fine-tuning.

Like LoHa, LoKr emerged from the image-generation community and has been most extensively tested on diffusion models. Both methods are implemented in the LyCORIS library,[163] and they have been integrated into the PEFT library. Practitioners report that LoKr with full-dimension Kronecker factors works well for complex single-concept fine-tuning, while LoHa better suits simpler multi-concept scenarios.

> **CHOOSING AN ADAPTER METHOD**
>
> Method selection depends on specific constraints. When inference latency matters and the adapter can be merged post-training, LoRA's lack of inference overhead is decisive. When parameter count must be minimized and the task is relatively simple, IA3 may suffice. When the parameter budget is tight and some matrices matter more than others, AdaLoRA's adaptive allocation helps. For image generation or tasks requiring high-rank updates with limited parameters, LoHa and LoKr offer interesting alternatives to standard LoRA. When context
>
> *(continued)*

length is not constrained and weights must remain frozen, prefix tuning requires no architectural modifications.

In practice, LoRA's combination of effectiveness, simplicity, and zero inference overhead makes it the default for most applications, with alternatives warranting consideration mainly when LoRA's specific properties do not fit the deployment constraints. Start with LoRA, and explore alternatives only when you have evidence that LoRA is insufficient for your specific task.

Model Surgery: Merging Capabilities

An alternative to fine-tuning that has gained traction is model merging: combining weights from multiple trained models to inherit capabilities from each. The simplest approach, linear interpolation, averages the weights of two models with a mixing coefficient: $W_{\text{merged}} = \alpha W_A + (1 - \alpha)W_B$. If model A excels at code and model B excels at creative writing, the merged model may do both reasonably well without any additional training.

More sophisticated methods like TIES-Merging and DARE resolve conflicts when combining many models. TIES trims small weight changes, resolves sign conflicts by majority vote, and then merges. DARE randomly drops weight changes before merging, reducing interference between models. Task arithmetic, another technique, frames merging as vector arithmetic in weight space: If you have a "coding direction" (the difference between a code-tuned model and its base) and a "writing direction," you can add both directions to a base model to get a model that does both.

The appeal of these solutions lies in the ability to surgically add a specific capability without the expense and risk of full retraining. I have seen teams merge a safety-tuned model with a domain-tuned model to get both properties, avoiding the careful data mixing that joint training would require. The limitation is that merging cannot resolve fundamental conflicts. A model tuned to be extremely cautious and a model tuned to be maximally helpful cannot be merged into something that is both. But for adding orthogonal capabilities, merging offers a remarkably cheap alternative to training.

Drinking from the Firehose: Distillation

Can a smaller model learn from a larger one? The key insight is that teacher outputs contain more information than hard labels; the relative probabilities across alternatives encode knowledge about similarity structure that training on labels alone would discard. This makes distillation an attractive learning target.

The Art of Learning from Giants

Knowledge distillation transfers capabilities from a larger "teacher" model to a smaller "student" model by training the student to mimic the teacher's outputs. The premise is that the teacher has learned something valuable during its training, something encoded not just in what it predicts but in how it makes those predictions, and that this knowledge can be transferred to a smaller model that could not have learned it independently. The student inherits the teacher's understanding while requiring only a fraction of the parameters.

The key insight underlying distillation is that teacher outputs contain more information than hard labels. When a teacher model classifies an image of a dog, it does not simply output "dog" but produces a probability distribution that might assign 0.9 probability to "dog," 0.05 to "wolf," 0.02 to "coyote," and small probabilities to other animals. This distribution encodes the teacher's understanding that dogs and wolves are similar in ways that dogs and cars are not. Training on hard labels loses this information: "Dog" tells the student only that this image is a dog, not which other categories it resembles. Training on the teacher's *soft labels* preserves the relational information, enabling the student to learn a richer representation of the category structure.

For language models, distillation typically trains the student to match the teacher's probability distribution over next tokens, not just to predict the most likely token. The student learns the teacher's uncertainty, preferences among alternatives, and subtle patterns of expression. This knowledge transfer can produce smaller models that approach teacher performance on the capabilities the teacher has, enabling deployment in contexts where the full teacher would be too large, too slow, or too expensive. The trade-off is clear: The student cannot exceed the teacher's capability, since it is learning to mimic rather than to exceed, but it can come surprisingly close while being far more efficient to run.

Soft Labels and Hidden Signals

The standard distillation objective combines two losses: a task loss measuring how well the student matches ground truth, and a distillation loss measuring how well the student matches the teacher's outputs. The *task loss* ensures that the student learns the actual task, while the *distillation loss* provides the additional signal from the teacher's knowledge. The relative weighting between these losses, and the temperature at which the teacher's outputs are computed, are key hyperparameters.

Temperature controls the amount of information the soft labels convey. At low temperatures, the teacher's probability distribution is peaked, concentrating probability on the most likely tokens. At high temperatures, the distribution is flatter, spreading probability across alternatives. The flat distribution at high temperatures exposes the relative rankings among all options: Even low-probability alternatives receive enough probability mass for their relative ordering to inform the student. The standard approach raises temperature for the distillation loss while keeping it at 1 for the task loss, capturing both the teacher's soft knowledge and the hard constraint of actual correctness.

Beyond output distributions, distillation can match intermediate representations. *Feature distillation* trains the student's hidden states to match the teacher's, transferring the internal representations that the teacher has learned. *Attention distillation* matches attention patterns, transferring the teacher's learned focus. These intermediate matches provide additional supervision signal that may transfer knowledge more efficiently than output-only distillation, particularly when the student is much smaller than the teacher and cannot easily learn the teacher's behavior purely from observing its outputs.

The choice of what to distill (outputs alone versus intermediate representations) affects what knowledge transfers and at what computational cost. Intermediate distillation requires running both models and computing additional losses, adding overhead that may or may not be justified by improved transfer.

The distillation loss with temperature scaling is

$$\mathcal{L}_{\text{distil}} = T^2 \cdot \text{KL}\left(\text{softmax}\left(\frac{z_s}{T}\right) \| \text{softmax}\left(\frac{z_t}{T}\right)\right)$$

where z_s and z_t are the student and teacher logits, T is the temperature, and the T^2 factor compensates for gradient scaling at high temperatures.

How should you choose the temperature in practice? Values from 3 to 10 work well for most language model distillation. Temperatures below 3 produce distributions too peaked to transfer useful knowledge about alternatives, while temperatures above 20 flatten the distribution so much that the teacher's preferences become noise. A reasonable starting point is $T = 4$: high enough to reveal relative rankings among alternatives, low enough that confident predictions remain distinguishable from uncertain ones.

If the student learns quickly but plateaus at lower quality than expected, try increasing temperature to transfer more nuanced knowledge. If the student trains slowly or seems to ignore the teacher's strongest signals, decrease temperature to concentrate learning on high-confidence predictions. The T^2 factor handles the gradient scaling automatically, so you can adjust temperature purely based on the knowledge you want to transfer without worrying about learning rate interactions.

When to Borrow Brains

Distillation is appropriate when deployment constraints preclude using the best available model and a capable teacher exists. If you have access to a powerful teacher but cannot deploy it because of latency, cost, or hardware constraints, distillation offers a path to capture much of the teacher's capability in a deployable form. The alternative, directly fine-tuning a smaller model without reference to the teacher, may work for narrow tasks but typically produces inferior results for broad capabilities.

The decision between distillation and direct fine-tuning depends on what you are trying to achieve. Distillation excels when the teacher has broad capabilities that you want to preserve in the student: general knowledge, nuanced reasoning, robust instruction following. The teacher's outputs on a diverse dataset transfer these broad capabilities more effectively than SFT on task-specific data could develop them from scratch. Direct fine-tuning may be preferable for narrow tasks not requiring the student to inherit general capabilities. If you need the model to only extract specific fields from specific document types, training directly on that task may be more efficient than distilling a general-purpose teacher.

WARNING *Distillation cannot transfer what the student cannot represent. A 1B student will not match a 70B teacher, no matter how much distillation data you use. The student's architecture sets a ceiling on what it can learn. Distillation works best when the capability gap is moderate: a 7B student learning from a 70B teacher, or a 3B from a 13B, for example. When the gap is too large, the student learns surface patterns but misses deeper capabilities that simply will not fit.*

Multi-teacher distillation combines knowledge from multiple models, potentially producing students that exceed any single teacher on specific dimensions. One teacher may excel at factual accuracy, another at conversational fluency, a third at code generation. Distilling from all three can produce a student with balanced capabilities that no single teacher possesses. The implementation is straightforward: Compute distillation losses against multiple teachers and combine them, weighting by relative importance. The approach requires more computation during training but can produce superior students when the goal is balanced capability rather than pure mimicry of a single teacher's behavior.

The Art of Forgetting: Model Pruning

How much of a trained network is necessary? The answer, surprisingly, is often less than half. It turns out that trained networks are mostly empty space, and the goal of pruning is to remove these redundant components. This results in dramatically smaller models with minimal degradation.

The Dead Weight in Models

Pruning removes parameters from trained networks, eliminating weights that contribute little to model outputs. The intuition is that trained networks contain substantial redundancy: Many weights are near 0, many neurons activate rarely, and many attention heads learn similar patterns. Removing the redundant components produces a smaller model that behaves similarly to the original, at least on the distribution it was trained for. Unlike quantization, which represents every weight at lower precision, pruning eliminates weights entirely, setting them to 0 and potentially removing them from computation.

Magnitude pruning, the simplest approach, removes weights with the smallest absolute values on the assumption that small weights contribute little to network outputs. Sort all weights by magnitude, remove the bottom fraction, and the resulting network has fewer nonzero parameters. The assumption is not always valid, as a small weight multiplied by a large activation can contribute substantially, but magnitude pruning is simple to implement and often effective.

Structured pruning removes entire units rather than individual weights: complete neurons, entire attention heads, or whole layers. The advantage is that the resulting model maps directly to standard dense computation without requiring sparse matrix support. The disadvantage is coarser granularity, since removing an entire attention head that is mostly unnecessary also removes the parts that were useful.

Iterative pruning alternates between pruning and retraining, allowing the network to adapt to parameter removal. Each cycle removes a fraction of remaining weights and retrains to recover performance. Multiple cycles can remove substantial fractions of the network while maintaining capability. The iterative approach typically achieves better quality at high sparsity than single-shot pruning, though at the cost of multiple retraining cycles. The proportion of parameters that can be removed without significant degradation varies by model and task but is often surprisingly high. Many transformer models can lose 50 percent or more of their parameters with minimal degradation on standard benchmarks, suggesting that the original training produced redundancy that pruning can safely eliminate.

Zeros That Speed Things Up

The pattern of zeros in a pruned network determines whether sparsity translates to computational savings. *Unstructured sparsity*, removing arbitrary individual weights wherever they happen to be smallest, achieves the highest compression at a given quality level because it removes exactly the weights that matter least.

But unstructured sparsity requires sparse matrix operations that are poorly supported on most hardware. GPUs are optimized for dense matrix multiplication, and sparse operations with irregular access patterns fail to saturate the hardware, often running slower than dense operations on matrices with moderate sparsity. A model that is 50 percent sparse may run slower than a dense model of the same architecture.

Structured sparsity patterns align with hardware capabilities to enable speedups. *N:M sparsity* constrains the sparsity pattern so that exactly *N* of every *M* consecutive elements are 0. This regular pattern enables efficient hardware implementation. NVIDIA Ampere and later GPU architectures natively support 2:4 sparsity, nearly doubling its speed on matrix operations with 50 percent of weights zeroed.

Block sparsity removes rectangular blocks of weights, enabling efficient implementation through block-sparse matrix operations. The constraint on which weights can be removed reduces compression efficiency compared to unstructured sparsity, but the regularity enables hardware acceleration that makes the remaining computation faster.

The practical value of pruning depends critically on whether the resulting sparsity pattern can be exploited by available hardware. Pruning to 90 percent unstructured sparsity sounds impressive but may provide no inference speedup on standard GPUs. Pruning to 50 percent 2:4 sparsity doubles the speed on supported hardware.

Your deployment target should inform your pruning strategy. For hardware with sparse acceleration, use the supported sparsity patterns. For hardware without sparse support, structured pruning that removes entire units may be more practical than unstructured pruning that produces sparse matrices the hardware cannot efficiently process.

The Lottery Ticket in Every Network

Why does pruning work, though? The lottery ticket hypothesis, proposed by Frankle and Carbin in 2019, offers a provocative explanation.[164] They hypothesize that dense networks contain sparse subnetworks, dubbed *winning tickets*, that can match the full network's performance when trained in isolation from the same initialization. The metaphor suggests that training a large network is like buying many lottery tickets: Most tickets lose, but among the many initialized subnetworks, at least one has to be a winner. Pruning identifies that winner after the numbers have been called, but, they suggest, we might be able to identify it before training.

The implications are profound if the hypothesis holds broadly. Most parameters in dense networks would be unnecessary, present only because we cannot identify the winning ticket before training. The winning subnetwork could, in principle, be trained from the start at a fraction of the computational cost. Finding the sparse structure that constitutes a winning ticket would enable training efficient models from scratch rather than training dense models and pruning afterward. In practice, finding winning tickets requires training the full network first and then identifying which weights to keep, eliminating much of the potential efficiency gain. Research continues on methods for identifying winning tickets earlier in training or predicting sparse architectures that would succeed.

For fine-tuning, the lottery ticket hypothesis implies that adaptable parameters may be concentrated in specific subnetworks. Perhaps the weights that change most during fine-tuning constitute something like a task-specific winning ticket, a sparse set of parameters sufficient for adapting to the new task while other parameters remain frozen. This perspective connects to LoRA's success: Maybe LoRA works because fine-tuning changes are concentrated in a low-dimensional subspace that the low-rank adapters can capture, and the hypothesis provides a conceptual framework for why such a concentration might occur. The hypothesis remains computationally expensive to directly exploit, but it informs our understanding of the structure underlying neural network redundancy and why techniques like pruning and PEFT can be so surprisingly effective.

The Last Mile: Serving at Speed

The harsh truth of enterprise AI is that no matter how elegant our training, inference is where end users experience the model. More than one well-conceived and powerful model has failed because of slow inference and poor serving. This section aims to help you avoid that fate by familiarizing you with ways of serving models efficiently.

The Engines Under the Hood

Efficient model serving requires specialized inference infrastructure that handles the unique characteristics of language model workloads. Unlike image models that process fixed-size inputs in single forward passes, language models work with variable-length sequences, generate output tokens one at a time through autoregressive loops, and spend most of their time waiting for memory rather than computing. Standard serving infrastructure designed for batch processing of fixed-size inputs performs poorly on these workloads, and purpose-built inference servers provide substantial improvements.

vLLM pioneered PagedAttention, a technique that manages the key-value cache by using concepts borrowed from operating system virtual memory. During generation, models cache computed key and value vectors to avoid redundant computation, but this cache grows with sequence length and fragments memory as requests of different lengths arrive and complete. PagedAttention stores cache blocks noncontiguously and maps them through page tables, eliminating fragmentation and enabling efficient memory sharing across requests. The result is dramatically higher throughput on multi-request workloads. TensorRT-LLM provides NVIDIA-optimized inference with custom CUDA kernels, quantization support, and compilation optimizations specific to NVIDIA hardware. Text Generation Inference from Hugging Face offers a production-ready serving solution with features like continuous batching, streaming output, and model parallelism.

FlashAttention represents a different optimization target: the attention computation itself.[165, 166] Standard attention implementations materialize large intermediate matrices that consume memory quadratically with sequence length, limiting practical context sizes. FlashAttention restructures the computation to avoid materializing these intermediates, fusing operations and using tiling to keep data in fast SRAM rather than slow HBM. The result is two to four times faster attention with dramatically reduced memory footprint, enabling longer sequences at lower cost. FlashAttention-2 and FlashAttention-3 further refine the approach, achieving near-optimal hardware utilization on modern GPUs. Most inference frameworks now integrate FlashAttention by default, making it the standard rather than an optimization choice.

WARNING *Not all FlashAttention is created equal. On NVIDIA Blackwell series GPUs, scaled dot-product attention (SDPA) as implemented by cuDNN 9 is faster than FlashAttention-2. FlashAttention-4, on the other hand, was explicitly designed for the Blackwell and is around 20 percent faster than SDPA. If you are using a DGX Spark, FlashAttention-4 may not be stable or fully supported, and for the GB10, SDPA may well prove the superior attention implementation. Always benchmark on your target hardware!*

Choosing an inference server involves trade-offs among performance, supported models, operational complexity, and hardware requirements. While vLLM offers excellent performance on a wide range of models, itrequires careful configuration for production stability. TensorRT-LLM, for instance, achieves top performance on NVIDIA hardware but requires compilation steps and supports a narrower range of model architectures. The choice depends on deployment context. Research prototyping may prioritize flexibility, production systems may prioritize stability and observability, and cost-sensitive deployments may prioritize throughput per dollar. It helps, therefore, to be confident around multiple inference servers and to know what to use when.

> **VIBE CHECK: OPTIMIZATION PIPELINE AUTOMATION**
>
> The optimization techniques in this chapter involve substantial boilerplate: configuring quantization parameters, setting up LoRA adapters, running calibration passes, and benchmarking throughput across configurations. Coding agents excel at this infrastructure work. Given a base model and deployment constraints (target memory, latency requirements, acceptable quality degradation), an agent can generate quantization configurations, set up QLoRA training scripts, run comparative benchmarks, and report which configuration best meets requirements. The pattern is well suited to automation, as the inputs are structured (constraints), the outputs are structured (configurations and metrics), and the exploration space is large enough that manual search is tedious but small enough that exhaustive search is feasible.
>
> In practice, a good configuration that I have found works well across coding agents is to build a skill document (*SKILLS.md*) accompanied by a reference document that contains sensible defaults as well as a script to act as a template configuration. This reduces token usage and renders sweeps consistently comparable. An example of such a skill configuration is in the *skills/hpo* subfolder in the book's companion repository.

Everything, All at Once: Batching

Batching multiple requests together amortizes fixed costs of inference and improves hardware utilization. Processing one request at a time leaves most of the GPU idle, waiting for memory transfers while compute units sit unused. Processing many requests together keeps more of the hardware busy, spreading the fixed costs of kernel launches and memory access across more useful work. But naive batching wastes compute on padding when sequences have different lengths; if the batch contains sequences of 50, 100, and 200 tokens, shorter sequences must be padded to match the longest, computing on meaningless padding tokens.

Continuous batching, also called *dynamic* or *iteration-level* batching, addresses this waste by managing the batch at the token level rather than the sequence level. Instead of waiting for all sequences in a batch to complete before starting new ones, continuous batching adds new requests to a running batch as sequences complete their generation. A request that finishes after 50 tokens is immediately replaced by a new request, rather than having its slot sit idle while other sequences continue generating. The result is higher throughput without artificial waiting, making better use of available hardware.

Speculative decoding approaches the throughput problem from a different angle, using a smaller *draft* model to predict multiple tokens that the larger model can then verify in parallel. If the draft model predicts five tokens and the large model agrees with all five, the generation advances by five tokens in roughly the time it would have taken to generate one. When predictions are wrong, the large model's correct token is used, and drafting continues from there. The technique accelerates generation for predictable outputs (in those instances when the draft model often guesses correctly), while falling back to standard generation for unpredictable content. Combined with KV cache optimization that reduces memory pressure, these techniques enable batch sizes and throughput that would otherwise be impossible within memory constraints.

GPU, CPU, . . . Smart Fridge Screen?

Hardware selection for model deployment involves trade-offs among cost, performance, and capability that vary substantially across the available options. The choice is not simply "buy the best GPU" but instead depends on workload characteristics, deployment constraints, and the interaction between model optimization and hardware capabilities.

High-end datacenter GPUs, such as the GB200 from NVIDIA, provide maximum performance for LLMs. Their high memory capacity, high memory bandwidth, and support for model parallelism across multiple GPUs enable serving the largest models with low latency. The cost is substantial. These GPUs command premium prices, and the cloud instance costs for GB200 access add up quickly at scale.

Consumer GPUs with less memory can run quantized versions of many models at a fraction of the cost. A 4-bit quantized 70B model fits in 48GB across two RTX 4090s, providing good throughput at consumer GPU prices. The trade-off is typically some quality degradation from quantization and reduced throughput compared to datacenter hardware. Glass-half-full developers may consider this a wonderful opportunity to become familiar with multi-GPU training, which creates challenges of its own but is a highly sought-after skill. After a certain model size, distributed training is the only option.

CPU inference offers broader hardware compatibility at reduced throughput. Models optimized for CPU with tools like llama.cpp can run on any modern server, enabling deployment in environments without GPU access. Throughput is lower than GPU inference, but for low-volume applications or cost-sensitive deployments, CPU inference may be appropriate. Edge devices enable on-device inference for latency-sensitive or privacy-critical applications; phones and laptops can run small models locally, avoiding network latency and keeping data on-device. Optimal deployment often combines hardware tiers, routing simple requests to cheaper hardware while reserving expensive GPUs for complex queries that require maximum capability. The routing decision itself can be automated, using a small classifier to predict the hardware tier required by a request.

The smallest frontier of model deployment targets devices where even a quantized 7B model is impossibly large: smartphones, Internet of Things (IoT) devices, embedded systems, and browser environments. These edge deployments demand models in the hundreds of millions to low billions of parameters, small enough to run with minimal latency on CPUs or mobile GPUs with a few gigabytes of available memory.

Purpose-built tiny models have emerged to serve this niche. Google's FunctionGemma represents an interesting specialization: a tiny (280M) model trained specifically for function calling and tool use. Rather than attempting general-purpose capability, FunctionGemma focuses on understanding user intent and generating structured function calls, a narrow but valuable capability for edge applications that need to invoke local APIs or device functions. The model demonstrates that extreme specialization can compensate for extreme size constraints, achieving reliable function calling (but little else) at a fraction of the size required for general instruction following.

The practical deployment path for edge models typically combines several techniques from this chapter. A 2B model quantized to 4 bits occupies roughly 1GB, small enough for many mobile devices. The GGUF format (see "The Lingua Franca of Quantized Models: GGUF" on page 196), developed by the llama.cpp project, packages quantized models with metadata for efficient CPU inference, enabling deployment without GPU acceleration. WebLLM and similar projects use WebGPU to run quantized models directly in web browsers, enabling on-device inference without any installation. These deployment options open use cases that cloud-based models cannot serve: offline operation, privacy-sensitive processing, and applications where network latency is unacceptable.

> **THE SMALLEST VIABLE MODEL**
>
> When targeting edge deployment, resist the temptation to start with the largest model that technically fits. Memory pressure from the model leaves less room for context, KV cache, and the application itself. A model that "fits" with 100 tokens of context is not deployable. Start with the smallest model that achieves acceptable quality on your specific task, then optimize from there. For many structured tasks, including entity extraction, classification, function calling, and simple QA, sub-1B models perform surprisingly well. The capability gap between 500 million and 7 billion parameters is large for open-ended generation but often negligible for constrained tasks.

The Optimizations Stack

The techniques surveyed in this chapter share a common purpose: making capable models practical. A 70-billion-parameter model that requires a cluster of A100s to serve is, for most organizations, a theoretical capability rather than a deployable one. Quantization, PEFT, distillation, and pruning transform theoretical capability into practical utility, enabling deployment within real constraints of hardware, latency, and cost.

These techniques can be combined. A practitioner might begin with a capable base model, quantize it to 4 bits for efficient serving, fine-tune with QLoRA to adapt to a specific domain, and deploy through an inference server with continuous batching and speculative decoding. Each optimization contributes to the final system's practicality. Quantization enables the model to fit in available memory, QLoRA enables adaptation without prohibitive compute costs, and serving optimizations enable throughput that makes the deployment economically viable. The practitioner who understands each technique's properties can assemble combinations suited to specific constraints.

The trade-offs underlying these techniques are real but often favorable. Quantization introduces error, but 4-bit models typically retain 95 percent or more of full-precision capability. LoRA trains fewer parameters, but they often capture the adaptation that matters. Distillation produces smaller models, but smaller models that inherit teacher knowledge outperform models trained from scratch. Pruning removes weights, but the removed weights were contributing little.

The pattern is consistent: Neural networks contain substantial redundancy that can be eliminated, and the precision they conventionally use exceeds what they require. The gap between what networks need and what they conventionally have creates the opportunity that these techniques exploit.

Summary

Efficient deployment is not just cost savings (and good environmental stewardship). It's also the key to strategic flexibility. When a new base model emerges, organizations that have mastered deployment efficiency can quickly quantize and adapt it rather than waiting for optimized versions. When deployment constraints change, they can adjust the optimization stack rather than abandoning capable models. While competitors deploy generic models, they can deploy adapted versions that embody domain expertise in efficient forms. Chapter 8 examines how exactly that happens, by building on the efficiency foundations established here to explore targeted adaptation.

8

DOMAIN ADAPTATION: MAKE IT YOURS

Language models are remarkable in how uneven their knowledge can be. This is, of course, no different from humans, except that most humans are aware of their gaps (don't ask me about football!). Because we train models separately on domain knowledge and on attitude, their confidence is pervasive even if their knowledge is not.

Ask a frontier model about cardiology, and it will produce confident, articulate prose that sounds impressive to a layperson. Show that same output to a cardiologist and watch them wince. The model confuses drug classes, cites guidelines that were superseded years ago, and misses the clinical nuances that any physician would catch.

The problem is not capability but specificity. Foundation models are trained to be all-rounders, on broad but relatively shallow knowledge (such as Wikipedia data). And so, the model knows about cardiology (or finance, law, materials engineering, or early Renaissance poetry) similarly broadly but not deeply, and certainly not in the way your organization practices it. This gap between generic knowledge and domain expertise is the central challenge of enterprise AI deployment. Your organization's accumulated knowledge—the terminology you use, the regulations you follow, the judgment calls your experts make instinctively—exists nowhere in the model's training data.

Specificity is particularly challenging in use cases where ordinary use of language conflicts with domain-specific conventions. In magnetic resonance imaging (MRI) reports, the rather counterintuitive term *flow void* refers to an absence (void) of signal seen in blood vessels due to blood flowing out of the imaging slab (hence flow), rather than the absence of flow as standard linguistic interpretations might suggest. In domains like legal, medical, or technical writing, such idiosyncrasies abound, and while style specificity is desirable, domain specificity can have legal and regulatory implications.

This chapter examines the techniques for conveying specificity: continued pre-training to establish domain fluency, SFT to teach domain-specific tasks, and RL with domain experts to refine beyond demonstration quality. We address the practical challenges that make domain adaptation difficult: Building datasets requires expertise that is scarce and expensive, compliance requirements constrain which approaches are permissible, and validation requires domain knowledge to assess. For enterprises in regulated industries, domain adaptation is not optional but essential.

When Wikipedia Is Not Enough

The economics of pre-training foundation models means that there is a strong imperative toward creating reliable generalists, not narrow experts. This creates a strong backbone to build on, but in certain domains, specificity is essential. We expect a medical model not merely to speak fluent English but to understand the nuances of clinical practice.

Fluently Clueless

Foundation models trained on broad internet data exhibit systematic weaknesses when applied to specialized domains. These weaknesses manifest in predictable ways. It may not recognize domain-specific terminology, poorly tokenizing technical terms or confusing them with similar-sounding general vocabulary. The model may apply conventions that were standard a decade ago but have since evolved. It may lack knowledge of entities specific to your domain, whether drug names, legal precedents, or industry-specific regulations. And it may produce outputs that sound superficially plausible to a layperson but violate constraints that any domain expert would immediately recognize.

These limitations are not bugs to be fixed but features of the training process itself. Models learn what the data contains, and broad internet training data contains breadth at the expense of depth. Wikipedia covers cardiology in a few thousand words, but a cardiologist accumulates years of clinical experience interpreting cardiac echograms. PubMed abstracts describe research findings, yet a clinical researcher knows which findings have been replicated and which were artifacts of particular study designs, and many develop a kind of intuition from just the abstract about the content and quality of the paper. The training data cannot convey tacit knowledge, evolving best practices, or the judgment that comes from domain experience.

It is perhaps worth noting here that I am not implying that language models somehow "understand" medicine, law, or other domains the way human experts do, or that the purpose of domain-specific training is to inculcate an awareness of facts (that goal would be better served by almost any alternative). Rather, the purpose is to teach the model to generate outputs that are not merely plausible but also correct.

A fine nuance exists between writing *like* a cardiologist and writing *as* a cardiologist, and the latter requires domain-specific training that goes beyond the general knowledge encoded in the original foundation model. This is profoundly important particularly when we are looking at more than the final output: the reasoning steps, the chain-of-thought, and the internal representations that the model uses to arrive at its outputs. A model that reasons like a cardiologist, even if it doesn't understand cardiology in any human sense, produces outputs that are more likely to be correct and more likely to be trusted by domain experts. The gap between generic fluency and domain expertise is not just a matter of style but of substance, and bridging that gap requires targeted adaptation that incorporates domain-specific knowledge and judgment.

Lost in the FOGBANK

There exists a substance known only as FOGBANK. Almost all information about its exact composition or purpose is classified, save for the fact that it is a critical component of thermonuclear weapons. When the United States had to refurbish its aging fleet of thermonuclear warheads, it realized that in the decade since the end of the Cold War, which ushered in the end of manufacturing hydrogen bombs, the expertise to make FOGBANK had been lost. It took half a decade and millions of dollars to reverse engineer what was mostly well-known decades ago. That's an example of institutional knowledge and the cost of losing it.

Enterprises are increasingly seeing LLMs as repositories of their unwritten and sometimes unarticulated institutional standards, practices, and notions. When we think of expertise, we typically think of the ubiquitously discussed high-risk subject areas, such as law, medicine, or finance, but this institutional knowledge is also a kind of expertise domain. Accumulated over years of operation, it represents a form of knowledge that no foundation model possesses.

This expertise exists in multiple forms: explicit knowledge encoded in internal documentation, policies, and procedures; implicit knowledge embedded in the structure of systems and decisional patterns; and tacit knowledge held by experienced practitioners who know how tasks are done even when they struggle to articulate why. Together, these forms of knowledge constitute an asset that competitors cannot simply download or wouldn't know how to use if they did.

Domain adaptation is the process that embeds this expertise in AI systems. The knowledge held in documents and minds becomes training data, the judgment of experts becomes preference data, and the standards of your domain become evaluation criteria. The resulting model embodies your domain expertise in a form that can scale, respond instantly, and operate consistently. Competitors using generic models cannot match this capability because they lack the underlying expertise. The investment in domain adaptation is therefore an investment in defensible differentiation: capability that cannot be commoditized because it rests on knowledge that cannot be easily acquired.

> **FROM THE TRENCHES: CAPTURING DOMAIN EXPERTISE**
>
> A significant part of institutional knowledge is by definition never written down. This is often seen as an impediment to effective AI deployment, especially in complex enterprise settings, where the main hurdle is capturing domain expertise. It is perhaps a little counterintuitive, but simply trying to get domain experts to write down all they know about a process, structure, or function is rarely helpful. Rather, we can use RL to capture the judgment of domain experts—not by asking them to produce, but to judge, and by relying on the same economy of preference optimization that we identified in Chapter 4.
>
> Quite often, this approach leads to a result that proves to be far superior to what outright elicitation could obtain. In a project that involved capturing a complex finance procedure, I used DPO with pairwise preferences to refine a model's responses initially trained on standard operating procedures and manuals. The experts almost always seemed to prefer responses that resolved a potential ambiguity in the original manuals in a certain way. Curiously, these were the same experts who wrote the original manual!
>
> Judging invokes a distinctly different cognitive process than producing, and the former can often capture expertise that the latter cannot. The result is a model that reflects the judgment of domain experts in a way that is more faithful to their expertise than any direct attempt to reproduce it.

Bound by Regulations

Capturing institutional knowledge is useful, but producing models that meet the requirements faced by regulated industries is existential. These requirements are not negotiable suggestions but hard constraints that determine whether a system can be deployed at all.

In addition, the current atmosphere of regulatory scrutiny is intensifying. Healthcare organizations deploying AI must demonstrate compliance with patient privacy regulations, maintain audit trails showing how the system contributed to clinical decisions, and validate that outputs meet standards of care. Financial institutions face supervisory expectations around model risk management, fair lending compliance, and explainability requirements that generic language models were never designed to address. Legal practice involves privilege considerations, conflict checking, and professional responsibility obligations that constrain the ways AI can be used.

These regulatory frameworks predate modern AI systems and were not written with language models in mind, yet they remain binding.

The tendency to view regulatory requirements as obstacles to AI adoption reflects a misunderstanding of their purpose. Regulations exist because the domains they govern carry genuine risks: patient harm, financial loss, and legal malpractice. A model that cannot meet regulatory requirements is a model that poses unacceptable risk. The regulation is not preventing innovation but preventing harm. Domain adaptation that incorporates regulatory requirements from the outset produces models that can be deployed because they were designed to be deployable. Treating compliance as an afterthought, something to be addressed after the exciting technical work is complete, produces models that fail regulatory review after substantial investment.

Domain adaptation for regulated industries must involve compliance expertise from the beginning. The data used for training must be permissible to use under relevant regulations, the training process must preserve properties that enable audit and explanation, and the outputs must satisfy domain-specific standards that compliance teams can verify. This integration of regulatory requirements into the technical process is more demanding than generic fine-tuning but is the price of operating in domains with stakes that justify regulation.

While it may be tempting to outsource this step to the experts (an external provider that claims to specialize in compliance), this is rarely a useful strategy. Regulators typically do not consider the burdens of compliance to be delegable, and the organization that deploys the model remains responsible for ensuring compliance regardless of who performed the adaptation work. The absence of internal competence also reduces the organization's ability to identify what a compliant model looks like. One does not have to be a bird to be an ornithologist, but having *seen* birds before certainly helps.

Teaching a Model Your Language

When is fine-tuning not enough? Some domain gaps run too deep for task demonstrations to bridge. Instead, the model needs exposure to the way your domain's language works. Continued pre-training is expensive, but for severe domain mismatch, it establishes a foundation that no amount of fine-tuning can replicate.

Bridging the Gap Beyond SFT

Continued pre-training extends the pre-training process on domain-specific corpora, updating the model's fundamental understanding of language and concepts to better reflect a target domain. Unlike SFT, which teaches the model to perform specific tasks, continued pre-training operates at a deeper level. It adjusts the model's representation of words, concepts, and relationships to better match the way they function in the domain.

This distinction matters because some domain gaps cannot be addressed through task demonstrations alone. A model that has never encountered the terminology of quantum chemistry in its pre-training, for instance, cannot learn to correctly use that terminology through a few hundred fine-tuning examples. It needs exposure to the way those terms are used in context across many documents.

The decision to undertake continued pre-training should be driven by specific indicators of domain mismatch. Tokenization problems provide one signal. If domain-specific terms are broken into awkward subword tokens that the model struggles to process coherently, continued pre-training on domain text can improve tokenization statistics and representation quality. Knowledge recency provides another. If the domain has evolved substantially since the model's training cutoff (with new regulations, new products, new terminology, or new best practices), continued pre-training can bring the model's knowledge current. Stylistic mismatch provides a third. If domain text follows conventions that differ markedly from general writing (whether in formality, structure, or technical density), continued pre-training helps the model internalize these patterns.

The technique is substantially more expensive than SFT, typically requiring billions of tokens of domain text and compute budgets measured in thousands or tens of thousands of GPU-hours. Parameter-efficient approaches like QLoRA (Chapter 7) can reduce the memory footprint of continued pre-training, though compute time remains substantial.

This expense is justified only when the domain gap is severe enough that fine-tuning alone cannot bridge it. For domains well-represented in the model's original training, such as general software development or common business writing, continued pre-training may offer little benefit over direct fine-tuning. For specialized domains, particularly those involving proprietary terminology, recent developments, or unusual linguistic conventions, the investment in continued pre-training establishes a foundation that subsequent fine-tuning can build upon effectively. The right strategy is dictated by the specifics of the domain, but Table 8-1's defaults are a good starting point.

Finding Billions (of Tokens)

The effectiveness of continued pre-training depends critically on corpus quality, and building a high-quality domain corpus requires substantial effort that organizations often underestimate. The corpus must be large enough to meaningfully update model knowledge. For continued pre-training to have noticeable effect, billions of tokens are typically required, although the exact threshold depends on the degree of domain shift and the size of the base model.

Table 8-1: Domain Adaptation Strategies: When to Use Each Approach

Strategy	Data required	Cost	When appropriate
Prompting alone	None	Negligible	Domain well covered in pre-training
RAG	Domain documents	Low to moderate	Current or proprietary information
Domain SFT	Hundreds to thousands of examples	Moderate	Task-specific behavior changes
Continued pre-training	Billions of tokens	High	Severe domain mismatch; new terminology
Domain RL	Preference data from experts	Very high	Quality refinement beyond SFT
Full pipeline	All of the above	Highest	Regulated domains; production-critical

As a point of reference, the widely adopted continued pre-training recipe of Parmar et al., which informed NVIDIA's Nemotron model family (among others), envisaged around 2.8 billion tokens of curated domain text.[167] That's not a casual data collection effort by any measure. The corpus must also be representative of the domain's language patterns: not just a random sample of domain text, but a curated collection that covers the terminology, styles, and subject matter the model will encounter in deployment.

Source identification is the first challenge. Internal documentation, assuming appropriate permissions and privacy considerations are addressed, provides text that directly reflects organizational practices. Industry publications, including journals, trade publications, and regulatory guidance, provide authoritative domain knowledge. Domain-specific web content may offer volume but requires careful filtering to exclude low-quality material. Proprietary databases, if accessible, may contain structured information that can be converted to natural language. The goal is not to maximize volume at any cost but to assemble a corpus that captures the way language is used within the domain by practitioners who know what they are doing.

Quality filtering and deduplication are essential preprocessing steps that determine whether the corpus will improve or degrade model capability. Low-quality text, whether garbled by poor optical character recognition (OCR), written by nonexperts, or contaminated with off-topic content, teaches the model patterns that are better left unlearned. If the same boilerplate appears thousands of times in the corpus, the model may learn to generate that boilerplate inappropriately. Balance across subdomain topics ensures broad coverage, and a corpus heavily weighted toward one specialty may improve capability in that area while degrading capability in others.

This curation work requires domain expertise to judge quality and relevance, making corpus construction a collaborative effort between ML engineers and domain specialists.

Specializing Without Amnesia

Beyond its cost in terms of source data, continued pre-training also carries the risk of catastrophic forgetting. As the model adapts to domain-specific data, it may lose general capabilities that were present in the original. The phenomenon occurs because neural network training is fundamentally about adjusting weights to minimize loss on the training data, and weights that were important for general capabilities may be overwritten if they can be repurposed to better fit domain-specific patterns. A model that could previously summarize general news articles or answer commonsense questions may lose these abilities as it becomes increasingly specialized. This degradation is not always immediately apparent, and teams may celebrate improved domain performance without noticing that general capabilities have quietly eroded.

Mitigation strategies address catastrophic forgetting through various mechanisms that preserve general capability while enabling domain adaptation. *Data mixing* combines domain-specific text with general-purpose text in the training corpus, ensuring that the model continues to see examples that exercise general capabilities even as it learns domain-specific patterns. The mixing ratio becomes a hyperparameter; higher proportions of domain data enable faster adaptation but increase forgetting risk, while higher proportions of general data preserve capability but slow domain learning. *Learning-rate reduction* makes smaller changes to pre-trained weights with each gradient update, limiting how far the model can drift from its original capabilities. *Regularization techniques* explicitly penalize deviation from the original model, whether through weight-space constraints that prevent large parameter changes or through knowledge distillation approaches that encourage the adapted model to match the original model's behavior on general tasks.

The appropriate balance among these mitigation strategies depends on deployment requirements. A model intended solely for domain-specific tasks, such as a clinical coding assistant that will never be asked about anything outside medical billing, can afford aggressive adaptation even at the cost of general capability loss. A model that must handle both domain-specific queries and general conversation, such as a customer service agent that discusses specialized products but must also engage in small talk, needs a more conservative adaptation that preserves general fluency. Understanding the deployment context before beginning continued pre-training enables the right trade-offs between specialization and preservation.

> **MIXING RATIOS IN PRACTICE**
>
> A common starting point for data mixing is 70 percent domain data, 30 percent general data. If domain performance after training is inadequate, increase the domain fraction. If general capabilities have degraded unacceptably, increase the general fraction. Monitor specific capabilities on both sides; track domain benchmark performance alongside selected general benchmarks that cover capabilities you need to preserve.
>
> The right ratio is the one that achieves acceptable domain adaptation while maintaining required general capabilities. A mistake I see rather often in practice is to set a mixing ratio and monitor only domain-specific capability. If domain-specific capability increases to a satisfactory level but general capability degrades, the mixing ratio is worth rethinking. Equally, some teams have come to call the mixing ratio a *mini-learning rate* because it exhibits similar dynamics in the other direction: A lower mixing ratio (less domain-rich) makes for safer but slower training, while a higher mixing ratio enables faster adaptation at a much higher risk of catastrophic forgetting.

Show, Don't Tell

So far, we've mostly talked about the volume of data used to teach a model about a domain. We now turn to the qualities that the data must exhibit. When it comes to the information that domain experts contribute, factual correctness is considered table stakes. The truly valuable contribution of these specialists is not getting the answers right (any textbook could do that) but reflecting the more indescribable qualities of their professional output. Whether we call it taste, method, or judgment, domain experts' contributions are often as hard to describe as they are valuable.

Bottling Expert Judgment

Domain SFT datasets teach models to perform domain-specific tasks through demonstration. Each example shows an input the model might receive and the output it should produce. The quality of these demonstrations determines the quality of model behavior. A model trained on mediocre examples will produce mediocre outputs regardless of the sophistication of the training algorithm. Construction therefore requires a collaboration between domain expertise, which recognizes good outputs as well as the errors practitioners would never make, and ML expertise, which understands the properties that make training data effective and ways to structure examples to enable generalization.

Expert annotation produces the highest-quality examples because domain experts can demonstrate not just correct answers but the nuances of professional judgment: the qualifications a careful practitioner would include, the information a thorough analysis would consider, and the tone appropriate for various situations. This quality comes at a cost. Expert time is expensive, experts may be difficult to schedule, and the annotation process can be tedious for specialists who would rather practice their profession than generate training data. Organizations pursuing expert annotation must design the process to respect expert time while extracting maximum value from each hour of effort.

An alternative that scales more readily is synthetic generation: using existing models to generate candidate examples that are then filtered or verified. This approach can quickly produce large volumes of data but introduces a circularity problem: If the examples are generated by a model similar to the one being trained, they may reinforce existing model behaviors rather than improving them. Verification by domain experts can address this concern (using experts to review synthetic examples rather than generate them from scratch), but verification itself requires expert time and introduces questions about what fraction of synthetic examples contain subtle errors that reviewers missed.

Active learning approaches attempt to identify which examples would be most informative to add to the dataset, directing annotation effort toward cases where the model is uncertain or where current training data is sparse. The dataset should ultimately cover the full range of tasks the model will face in deployment, with enough examples per task type to enable generalization rather than mere memorization of specific phrasings.

VIBE CHECK: DOMAIN-SPECIFIC CURRICULA

LLMs consistently excel at creating curricula, sets of training data structured by difficulty. I implemented this approach to gradually train a model to understand increasingly complex nuances of medical coding for reimbursement using the Current Procedural Terminology (CPT) and Healthcare Common Procedure Coding System (HCPCS). I began with a generic prompt:

```
Please follow these guidelines:
    1. Diversity: Generate scenarios across specialties(e.g., Cardiology,
    Orthopedics, Emergency Medicine, General Surgery,Radiology).
    2. Content: Include complex cases (e.g., comorbidity,sequencing, modifier
    usage).
```

However, my training vastly improved when I encouraged a structured curriculum:

```
Implement the samples as a curriculum with increasingcomplexity:
1. Beginner: Simple diagnosis lookup (e.g., acuteappendicitis).
2. Intermediate: Procedure coding with modifiers (e.g., CPT modifiers -25, -59).
3. Advanced: Complex scenarios, bundling issues (NCCI) and coding guidelines
(e.g., inpatient coding, sequencing of acute vs chronic).
```

If the dataset you intend to generate relies on a verifiable ground truth (in this case, the existence of a particular code and formal validity), equipping the coding agent with a verifier tool is essential. This cuts down on difficulties of review. Good verifier tools do not merely give a binary judgment but provide feedback. Binary checks, however, are inexpensive and easy to execute. Almost all coding agents have a good understanding of grep, and therefore of regular expressions, so providing a regex is a particularly inexpensive and quick verifier.

Avoiding Garbage In, Garbage Out

Quality assurance for domain datasets extends beyond catching obvious errors, to verifying domain-specific correctness that only practitioners can assess. General data quality checks (such as removing duplicates, fixing formatting issues, and ensuring that examples parse correctly) address surface problems but cannot detect the subtle errors that matter most in specialized domains. An example that recommends a contraindicated drug interaction, that misstates a regulatory requirement, or that follows outdated professional standards may appear perfectly well formed to nonexperts while teaching the model dangerous patterns. Domain expertise is essential for quality assurance (QA), and the QA process must be designed to make effective use of that expertise.

Expert review represents the gold standard for domain data quality, with domain specialists examining each example for correctness, appropriateness, and professional quality. The review process should capture not just binary judgments about whether examples are acceptable but structured feedback about what would make them better, enabling continuous dataset improvement. Consistency checking identifies contradictions within the dataset. If one example advises approach *A* in situation *X*, while another advises approach *B* in the same situation, the model receives contradictory training signal that may manifest as inconsistent behavior. Coverage analysis ensures that no important task types are omitted. Gaps in the dataset become gaps in model capability, and deployment may reveal these gaps in the worst possible circumstances.

The QA cost, which can rival or exceed the cost of initial data collection, is justified by the cost of training on poor data. Models are remarkably faithful learners. They reproduce patterns from their training data, including patterns that represent errors. A model trained on data containing 10 percent incorrect examples will produce incorrect outputs with corresponding frequency. Diagnosing these failures after deployment is far more expensive than preventing them through up-front QA. The team that invests heavily in data quality before training encounters fewer mysterious failures, builds models that require less iteration, and ultimately ships more reliable systems. The investment is not optional for domains where errors carry real consequences.

> **FROM THE TRENCHES: EXPERT TIME AS BOTTLENECK**
>
> In every domain adaptation project I've worked on, expert time proved the binding constraint. Compute can be rented, and data can be processed overnight, but domain experts have limited hours and competing demands. Design your data pipeline to maximize the value of each hour of expert attention. Use experts for verification rather than generation where possible, filter candidate sets before presenting them for review, and batch similar decisions to reduce context-switching costs.
>
> Successful domain adaptation projects are about more than the care and feeding of the model. They are also about assuring the data supply chain. For this type of task, that means managing expert time effectively and respectfully. A little communication goes a very long way in such engagements.

Considering Style as Substance

Domain-specific tasks frequently impose format requirements that generic models have no reason to know about: structured reports with mandatory sections in prescribed order, references to entities using standardized identifiers rather than natural language descriptions, required disclaimers or qualifications that must accompany certain types of guidance, or terminology that must match official glossaries rather than common usage. These requirements may seem superficial compared to the challenge of generating correct content, yet format noncompliance can render otherwise excellent outputs unusable. These may be as formal as, say, the US Patent and Trademark Office's requirements for patent applications or as loose as the unwritten house styles of major corporations.

Training data must demonstrate these format requirements consistently across examples so that the model learns them as invariant patterns rather than optional stylistic choices. If some training examples include required disclaimers and others omit them, the model learns that disclaimers are sometimes present and sometimes absent, and deployment will reveal outputs missing required elements. Consistency in training leads to consistency in generation. At the same time, the training data must include sufficient variation in the way format requirements are met; otherwise, the model memorizes specific phrasings rather than learning the underlying pattern. If every disclaimer uses identical wording, the model may produce that exact wording even in contexts where slight modification would be appropriate. Variation teaches generalization.

Format compliance often represents a hard requirement for deployment in the most literal sense. Outputs that fail format validation cannot proceed through downstream systems and require manual intervention to correct. A model that produces correct content in wrong formats generates work rather than eliminating it. Attention to format in training data construction prevents this failure mode. The effort required is modest compared to content

QA, requiring primarily careful specification of format requirements and systematic verification that training examples comply with them. Yet a failure to invest this effort produces models that generate continuous operational friction. Format is part of quality in domain-specific applications, and training data must reflect this.

Beyond Imitation: Learning Preference

SFT teaches models to produce outputs that look like demonstrations. But what about qualities that domain experts can recognize yet struggle to demonstrate? The difference between competent and excellent, between adequate and professional—these distinctions call for RL with domain-specific rewards.

Teaching Taste

Domain-specific reward models learn to assess quality according to criteria that matter within a particular domain, criteria that may differ substantially from what general reward models optimize. A general reward model, trained on broad human preferences, learns to value clarity, helpfulness, and harmlessness in generic terms. A domain-specific reward model learns what clarity means within the domain, what helpfulness means given domain-specific tasks, and what appropriateness means under domain-specific constraints. The radiologist's judgment of what makes a good report differs from the layperson's, and the lawyer's assessment of a competent analysis differs from the client's. The domain reward model must capture these professional standards.

Training domain reward models requires preference data from domain experts who can reliably distinguish better from worse outputs according to professional standards. This data is expensive to obtain. Experts are expensive, their time is valuable to their primary work, and asking them to make hundreds or thousands of preference judgments is a substantial imposition. The annotation process itself requires careful design to extract maximum signal from limited expert time. Pairwise comparisons may be faster than absolute ratings, structured annotation interfaces may reduce cognitive load, and calibration exercises may improve consistency across annotators. The investment is substantial, but the resulting reward model inherits domain expertise from its training data in a form that can guide training at scale.

Once trained, the domain reward model enables RL that optimizes for domain-relevant qualities, pushing the model toward outputs that domain experts would prefer. This optimization can capture qualities that SFT alone struggles to teach: the difference between a competent analysis and an excellent one, the subtle factors that distinguish professional from amateur work, and the judgment calls that experts make instinctively but struggle to articulate. SFT teaches the model to produce outputs that look like the demonstrations it saw, while RL with domain rewards teaches the model to produce outputs that experts would prefer, potentially exceeding the quality of demonstration examples. The combination of SFT to establish baseline capability and domain RL to refine toward expertise represents the full adaptation pathway for demanding applications.

Framing Compliance as Reward Signal

Regulatory compliance can be framed as a reward signal within the RL framework, enabling models to learn compliance through optimization rather than through explicit rule encoding. The framing is straightforward in principle: Outputs that comply with applicable requirements receive positive rewards, outputs that violate requirements receive negative rewards, and the training process learns to generate outputs that maximize reward and therefore maximize compliance. This approach offers advantages over rule-based compliance enforcement because many regulatory requirements resist simple specification. A regulation that requires communications to be "clear and not misleading" defines a standard that humans can assess but that proves difficult to encode as a deterministic check.

The practical challenge lies in generating the training signal. Determining whether a given output complies with regulatory requirements typically requires expert judgment: a compliance officer, a regulatory affairs specialist, or a legal professional who understands both the regulation and its application to the specific context. This assessment cannot be fully automated for the same reasons that the requirements themselves resist rule encoding. The annotation burden for compliance-aware RL therefore resembles that for general domain reward modeling: Expert time is required at scale, creating both cost and throughput constraints. Organizations must design annotation processes that enable compliance assessments to be made reliably and efficiently.

There is a widespread and somewhat justified concern that language models' outputs, no matter the training they underwent, are regulatorily suspect by definition. Experience, however, shows the opposite. Compliance-specific RL can not only produce good regulatory compliance but also form a reward model from inputs of multiple compliance professionals that is often more comprehensive and consistent than any single expert's. Preference optimization methods at scale can capture a fusion of judgments no individual could replicate, and the resulting reward model can guide the trained model toward outputs that satisfy regulatory requirements in a way that no single expert could specify.

The investment in compliance-aware RL pays off in deployment confidence, as developers have explicitly trained the resulting model to satisfy requirements that deployment will enforce, rather than hoping that SFT examples happened to cover all relevant compliance considerations. For domains where noncompliance is not merely undesirable but unacceptable, this investment is not optional.

Building the Feedback Flywheel

Domain adaptation rarely succeeds as a one-shot process. The gap between initial deployment and production-quality performance is typically bridged through iterative refinement that cycles through deployment, feedback collection, and model improvement.

The first deployed version reveals weaknesses that were invisible during development: edge cases the training data didn't cover, patterns of usage the designers didn't anticipate, and quality thresholds that seemed adequate in testing but prove insufficient for actual users. These revelations are not failures of the development process but inherent features of deploying AI systems into complex real-world environments that cannot be fully anticipated.

Feedback collection mechanisms determine how quickly and effectively these weaknesses can be addressed. Domain experts using the deployed model are uniquely positioned to identify problems. They encounter the edge cases, notice when outputs fall short of professional standards, and understand which failures matter and which are tolerable. Converting their experience into training signal requires infrastructure for capturing feedback, channels for escalating systematic issues, and processes for transforming unstructured complaints into structured training data.

The feedback loop is not automatic; it requires design, implementation, and ongoing attention to operate effectively. And *design* in this context is about more than merely code or pixels. The design of feedback mechanisms must consider human factors: how to make it easy for users to report issues without disrupting their workflow, how to prioritize feedback that indicates systematic problems rather than one-off annoyances, and how to communicate back to users about how their feedback is being used. Techniques like KTO (see Chapter 5) offer efficient and easy ways to derive sufficient signals from single preference interactions, for instance.

The best results in this field come from *tiger teams* that combine domain expertise, ML expertise, and user experience design to create feedback systems that users will want to use. The feedback you don't gather has, by definition, no chance to improve your model—ensuring that it gets collected the right way should be as fundamental as any consideration of hyperparameters or preference optimization.

Crossing the Production Chasm

What standards must a domain model meet before deployment, and how do you verify it meets them? The stakes rise with the domain; healthcare applications may require clinical validation, while financial applications may face regulatory scrutiny. Generic benchmarks provide insufficient assurance for domain-specific deployment.

Validating in Domain

Domain model validation must verify domain-specific correctness rather than relying on general capability assessments that may be irrelevant to deployment requirements. A model that achieves excellent scores on standard benchmarks may nonetheless fail on the specific tasks the domain requires. Conversely, a model with mediocre benchmark performance may excel at the narrow tasks that matter. Validation must measure what deployment needs: the ability to perform domain-specific tasks correctly, reliably, and at the quality level the domain demands. Generic evaluation provides insufficient assurance for domain-specific deployment.

Building domain-specific benchmarks requires the same collaboration of domain and ML expertise that drives other aspects of domain adaptation. The benchmark must include tasks representative of deployment usage, with ground-truth answers or evaluation criteria that enable scoring. Domain experts must validate that the benchmark tests the right things: that success on the benchmark predicts success in deployment, and that the evaluation criteria capture what domain practitioners care about. Beyond automated benchmarks, human evaluation by domain experts provides assessment of qualities that resist automatic measurement: professional judgment, appropriate tone, and subtle correctness considerations that practitioners recognize even when they struggle to specify. Establishing acceptance criteria before evaluation ensures that the validation process answers the question that matters: Is this model ready for deployment?

FROM THE TRENCHES: A PREFERRED RECIPE FOR "DID IT TAKE?"

Over the years, I have settled on a five-layer evaluation recipe that I run whenever I need to determine whether domain SFT actually worked. No single layer is sufficient on its own, but together they give a fairly complete picture. In keeping with my team's preference to name recipes after sauces, this shorter version is better known as Hollandaise (for its number of ingredients). An expanded version, Bearnaise, includes three additional metrics (rubric checking, corpus-specific BLEU, and short hard negatives) and is illustrated in the companion notebook to this chapter.

The first and most basic sanity check is the *perplexity delta on a held-out domain corpus*: Does the fine-tuned model have lower perplexity on held-out domain text than the base model? While checking the perplexity delta is a useful and necessary starting point, it's not sufficient: A model can have lovely perplexity and still be functionally useless. Think of it as a gate, not a grade.

The second layer is *token-level accuracy on masked domain terminology*, and it is underrated. Take domain-specific passages, mask out key terms (drug names, pathway components, assay parameters, or whatever your domain cares about), and measure exact-match accuracy on predicting the correct tokens. This directly probes whether the model has internalized domain vocabulary and its contextual usage, rather than just becoming more fluent at generating domain-adjacent prose. Stratifying by term frequency in the training set reveals whether the model is genuinely learning or merely memorizing high-frequency tokens.

Third, and probably the single most diagnostic approach, is *structured extraction with hard metrics*. This involves designing tasks that require the model to extract structured information from domain text (entities, relationships, numerical values, classifications). When we then measure precision, recall, and F1, we simultaneously test comprehension, domain knowledge, and instruction following. The key is that the ground truth is unambiguous: Either the model correctly extracted "dosage: 150mg BID" or it did not. No interpretive wiggle room.

Fourth is *discriminative probing through forced choice.* Present the model with pairs of domain statements, one correct and one subtly wrong, and ask it to identify which is accurate. Think of it as a domain-specific Winograd schema: "Trastuzumab targets HER2" versus "Trastuzumab targets HER3." Difficulty can be calibrated by controlling the subtlety of errors. This tests whether the model has acquired genuine domain knowledge rather than surface fluency, and it yields a clean accuracy number.

The fifth layer is *calibration metrics.* If the fine-tuned model produces any kind of confidence signal, even implicitly through token probabilities, measuring expected calibration error (ECE) or Brier scores on domain questions tells you whether the model knows what it knows. A well-calibrated domain model should be confident on in-domain knowledge and uncertain on edge cases. Poor calibration after SFT is a red flag for overfitting to training distribution patterns rather than learning genuine domain structure.

In domain-specific training, there is no such thing as a single, easy, and correct answer to the question of whether training was successful. Correctness depends greatly on the domain and may be easier to assess in some than others; for example, domain-specific training for medical coding has an external verifier in formal coding rules, while case law research can be easily verified. Often, cases include a short paragraph (the headnote) that summarizes the most important points. We can compare the model's generated summary against the headnote to verify that the case supports the model's reasoning. The often-publicized example of New York attorney Stephen Schwartz, who landed in hot water for made-up citations, could have been easily averted by a single sweep of the model's outputs through a research tool like LexisNexis.

In other domains, such as clinical decision support, correctness is more subjective and harder to verify. In these cases, the best approach is to design a benchmark that captures the domain's quality standards as closely as possible, and to supplement this with human evaluation by domain experts who can assess qualities that resist automated measurement. What matters is to lay down acceptance criteria before beginning evaluation that will give us the ability to confirm at the end of training whether the model is ready for prime time.

Live Fire Testing Your Model: Experimental Deployment

Domain model deployment should be staged to limit exposure to potential failures, following patterns familiar from software deployment but adapted to the particular characteristics of AI systems. In a widely used pattern known as *canary deployment*, a model is initially released to a small user group, perhaps a handful of domain experts who understand both the system's intended function and its likely limitations. This enables early problem detection before widespread exposure.

Early users serve as both testers and informants, identifying issues that formal validation missed while accepting the inconveniences that early-stage systems inevitably impose. Their feedback shapes the subsequent rollout far more than any amount of pre-deployment testing could, which makes picking the right cohort of canary users a critical decision. They must be useful (likely to give good feedback) but also representative of the intended end-user base. These do not often co-occur. Good canary users are cultivated, not found. A visible, engaged, and open AI team will have no shortage of applicants to road test their new model.

In a somewhat different pattern, the *holdout group*, a portion of the user base is intentionally excluded from receiving the new model during an initial rollout phase. Typically, this is around 10 percent of the intended user base, but it helps to perform a proper sample size calculation to estimate the number of holdouts, regardless of proportion, that is necessary to get a statistically significant signal. The holdout group continues to receive the previous model, while the rest of the users receive the new model.

This approach allows for a direct comparison of performance between the two models in real-world conditions, providing evidence of improvement or regression that can inform further development and deployment decisions. The holdout group serves as a baseline for comparison, enabling measurement of how the new model performs relative to the old one in real-world conditions. This pattern is particularly useful when the new model represents a significant change from the previous system, as it provides a direct comparison that can reveal both improvements and regressions.

Gradual rollout expands coverage as confidence grows, increasing the user population in stages with monitoring at each stage to detect problems that emerge at scale. Issues that affected 1 percent of test users become visible when 100 users encounter them daily, and patterns that seemed random with small samples become systematic with larger exposure. A/B testing, in turn, enables comparison of the domain-adapted model and alternatives, whether the previous system, a different model version, or a baseline that helps quantify improvement. These comparisons provide objective evidence of whether the adaptation helps, evidence valuable both for internal learning and for justifying the adaptation investment to stakeholders.

Of course, sometimes things go wrong, and that's when fallback mechanisms become critical. These enable reversion if problems emerge after deployment, whether through automatic triggers based on monitored metrics or manual intervention when users report issues. The ability to quickly revert to a known-good state limits the damage that any single deployment can cause.

These patterns are standard practice for software deployment generally, yet they take on particular importance for AI systems where failure modes may be unpredictable. Traditional software fails in ways that testing can largely anticipate, but AI systems may fail in novel ways that emerge only when deployed into the wild complexity of actual use. Conservative deployment, with multiple stages and clear reversion paths, protects against the unknown unknowns that domain adaptation may inadvertently introduce.

Anticipating That Your 2024 Model Is 2026's Legacy System

Domain-adapted models require ongoing maintenance that organizations must plan for rather than discover reactively. Base models are updated by providers, introducing improved capabilities but also potentially changing behaviors in ways that affect adaptation. Serious domain adaptation should be periodically rebased onto improved foundations. Domain knowledge itself evolves: Regulations change, best practices shift, new terminology enters usage, and entities referenced in training data are superseded. A model adapted to the domain as it existed in 2024 becomes increasingly misaligned with the domain as it exists in 2026, and data refreshes are necessary to maintain relevance.

Deployment feedback provides continuous input for improvement even after the initial adaptation is complete. Users identify edge cases, flag quality issues, and suggest enhancements that no development process could anticipate. Converting this feedback into model improvements requires processes for collection, triage, prioritization, and action. Some feedback warrants immediate attention, while other feedback accumulates for batch processing in the next training cycle. The infrastructure for managing this feedback flow is as important as the initial adaptation infrastructure and serves the organization for as long as the model remains deployed.

Models are an enduring commitment. Organizations that see them as one-time wins risk long-term architectural debt as the price of rapid gratification. It is fundamental good practice to look at models as enduring assets and schedule inspections as you would for a vehicle: regularly checking in with performance metrics of deployed models, validating their assumptions, redoing evals, and monitoring drift. This is more acute for less visible and less high-variability models, as ongoing drift monitoring is typically implemented as a matter of course for operationally critical tools. Still, it is easy for the duty to actually read the monitoring reports to fall between various institutional competences and end up without anyone responsible. Model life-cycle planning is a case-by-case matter, but the principle is universal: Plan for the long haul from the outset. This includes, at the very minimum, documentation, visibility (be it a model registry or a more intricate ModelOps system of record), monitoring (with preset evaluations, rather than trying to close the barn door after the horse has bolted), and budgets and plans for maintenance and decommissioning.

The alternative to planned maintenance—deploying once and hoping the model remains adequate indefinitely—produces systems that degrade over time as their training becomes increasingly outdated relative to the evolving domain. Users notice first: They encounter gaps in coverage, outdated recommendations, and terminology that marks the system as belonging to a previous era. Unlike LLMs, humans do live in the present and ascribe an emotional value in terms of correctness to timely information; we judge outdated information as fundamentally holistically wrong, no matter its other merits.

Inevitably, the degradation becomes severe enough to force emergency attention, which (like an emergency plumber) tends to be more expensive than planned maintenance would have been. The model you fine-tuned in 2024 is 2026's legacy system: expensive to maintain and risky to replace. Domain adaptation is not a project with a completion date but a capability that requires ongoing investment and, importantly, an organic recognition of that fact by way of instituting workflows that update the model's adaptation mostly automatically. Organizations that budget for maintenance from the outset through "model lifetime cost" approaches build sustainable AI capability.

Adaptation Never Ends

Domain adaptation transforms generic AI capability into specific competitive advantage. The techniques examined in this chapter—from continued pre-training through domain-specific SFT and RL to the enterprise considerations that govern deployment—share a common purpose: embedding organizational expertise into AI systems that can scale it, apply it consistently, and make it available wherever it is needed. Generic models provide generic capability available to everyone. Adapted models embody knowledge that took years to accumulate in forms that competitors cannot simply download.

The path through domain adaptation is not uniform. Some domains require only light touches: prompting adjustments, retrieval augmentation, and modest fine-tuning on task demonstrations. Others demand the full pipeline: continued pre-training to establish domain fluency, extensive SFT to teach domain-specific tasks, RL with expert preferences to refine beyond demonstration quality, and rigorous validation to satisfy regulatory requirements. The practitioner's task is matching intervention intensity to domain requirements, investing heavily where domain gaps run deep and lightly where generic capability nearly suffices. The decision shown previously in Table 8-1 provides a starting point, but every domain presents unique characteristics that modify the general guidance.

The investment required for serious domain adaptation is substantial. Expert time, the scarcest resource, must be deployed efficiently. Data pipelines must be built to transform domain documents into training signal. Evaluation frameworks must be developed to measure domain-specific quality. Compliance requirements must be satisfied. The investment is justified when the domain stakes warrant it: when generic models cannot meet requirements, errors carry real consequences, and competitive differentiation demands capabilities that commoditized AI cannot provide. For regulated industries, for mission-critical applications, and for domains where expertise truly differentiates, this investment is not optional but essential.

The adaptation itself is only the beginning. Deployed models require monitoring, maintenance, and periodic refresh as domains evolve. The organization that treats domain adaptation as a one-time project will find its adapted models aging into obsolescence. The organization that builds adaptation as an ongoing capability, with infrastructure for feedback collection, processes for data refresh, and budgets for continued investment, sustains competitive advantage over time. Domain adaptation is not something you do once but something you become capable of doing continuously.

Summary

Domain adaptation provides the foundation for deploying capable models in enterprise contexts. Next, we will examine how models attain the ability to produce more than words: tool calling and agency, which are the ways that language models can begin affecting reality.

9

AGENTIC MODELS: DEEDS, NOT WORDS

Computing has a peculiar sort of magic to it. In our everyday lives, we think of words and deeds separately enough that philosopher John Searle had to come up with a name for the exceptions to this divide (*speech acts*). In computing, words *are* deeds, capable of shaping reality. And like my story of the Golem of Prague in the preface, this is both wondrous and terrifying. Let's now turn to how this power is conferred on language models.

The models we have discussed so far have primarily focused on the production of language. An agentic model does more: It plans sequences of actions, invokes external tools to gather information or perform computations, maintains memory across interactions, and pursues goals through multistep reasoning. The transformation from reactive language model to autonomous agent represents a qualitative shift in capability, one that opens new applications while introducing new challenges in safety, reliability, and control.

This chapter examines the techniques that enable agentic behavior: fine-tuning models for tool use, building systems that can plan and reason across multiple steps, managing memory to maintain context across interactions, and imposing safety constraints to prevent harmful actions. We address the evaluation challenges that make agentic systems difficult to validate, where success depends not on single-turn quality but on multistep goal achievement. For enterprises seeking to deploy systems that can act rather than merely respond, understanding these techniques moves from academic interest to operational necessity.

From the Cave to the Agent

How do models attain the ability to act upon the world? The infrastructure of agency rests on function calling, and getting this right determines whether tool use is reliable or chaotic. We will therefore begin by examining the mechanics of equipping our models with tools.

How Tool Use Is Learned

There is a cave at a prehistoric site known as Dikika, in Ethiopia. At some point around 3.4 million years ago, give or take, one of the early humans sheltering in that cave used a primitive rock-knife to split meat off a bone. This left behind kerf marks that were identified in 2010 as the earliest known evidence of tool use.[168]

What began in that cave changed our species forever, elevating us to conscious users of tools. This was not merely an external process; it also required us to change the way we understood the world. To the tool user, the world is not a given but a conditional question, not "Can I do this?" but "What tool will enable me to do this?" The rest of our history as a species has been gradually redefining our capabilities through tool use. Of course, humans cannot fly—or so we thought until the Wright Brothers. Nor can they breathe underwater—that is, until scuba gear was invented. Nor speak over vast distances—until Bell invented the telephone.

Equipping models with tools turns them from interesting information-retrieval programs to actors, assistants, and collaborators. But tool use needs an interface, a formal protocol by which models request tool invocations and receive results. This interface is a contract between the model and the execution infrastructure.

The dominant paradigm, now supported by most major model providers, defines tools through JSON schemas that specify the name, purpose, parameters, and types for each available tool. When the model determines that a tool invocation would be helpful, it generates structured JSON matching the schema for the desired tool, including the parameter values appropriate to the current context. The execution infrastructure parses this structured output, validates the parameter types and values, invokes the indicated tool, and returns results to the model for incorporation into its ongoing response.

This structured approach offers several advantages over unstructured alternatives. Reliable parsing becomes straightforward because the model's output follows a predictable schema, and the infrastructure need not interpret natural language descriptions of desired actions but simply extracts named fields from structured data. Parameter validation catches errors before execution: A tool expecting an integer receives an integer, not a string that might or might not parse correctly. The clear separation between model generation and tool execution enables the infrastructure to impose constraints on what tools can do without relying on the model to self-police. The model expresses intent, and the infrastructure decides what to permit. This is the heart of the function-calling protocol, set out in Figure 9-1, that underlies every modern agentic application.

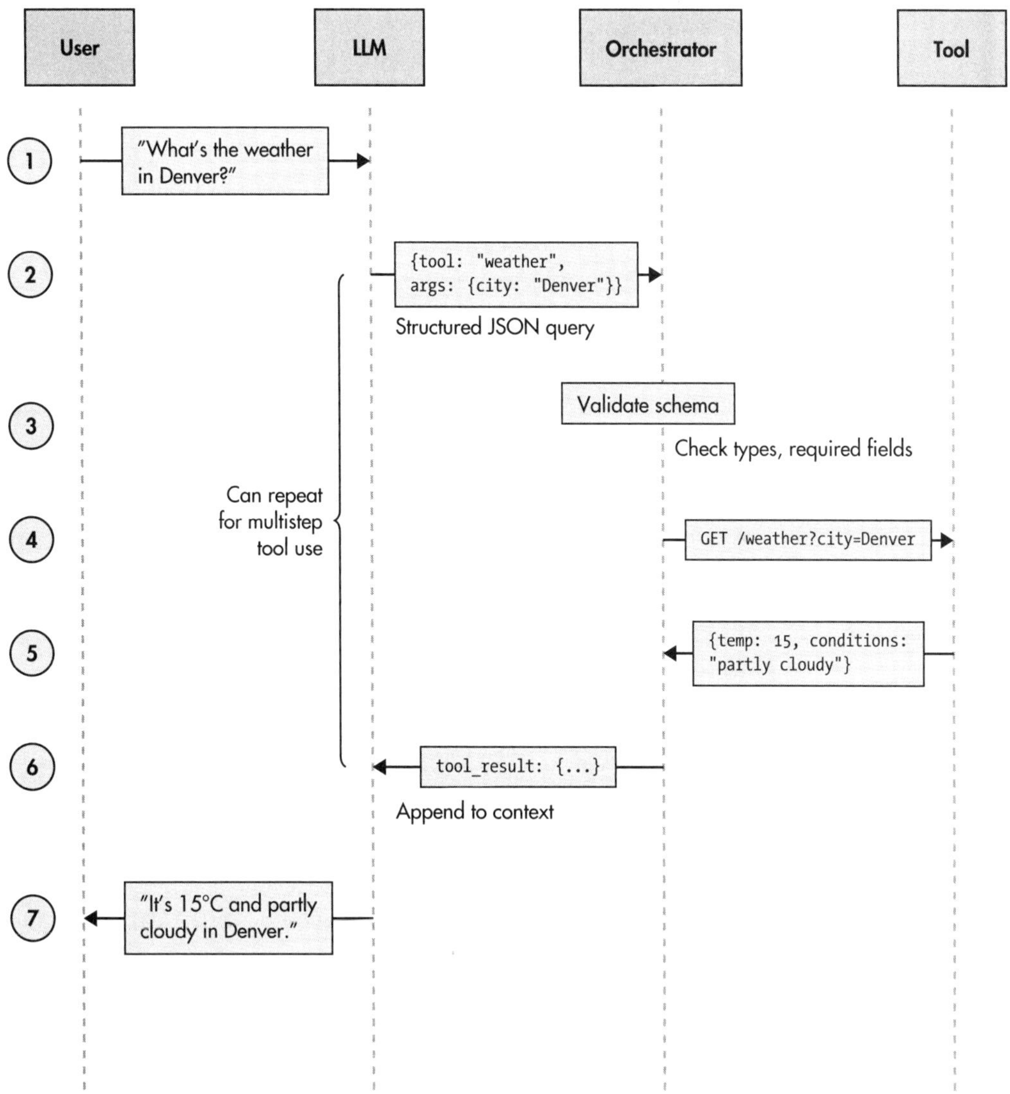

Figure 9-1: The function-calling protocol. The user's query flows to the model, which generates a structured tool call routed by the orchestrator to the appropriate tool. The tool's response returns through the orchestrator to the model, which integrates the result into a natural language response for the user. This loop can repeat for multistep tool use.

Understanding this protocol is essential for designing tools that models can use effectively. Tools with clear schemas, unambiguous parameter types, and well-defined semantics are easier for models to invoke correctly than tools with complex or ambiguous interfaces. The protocol also shapes which kinds of interactions are natural: Single-shot tool invocations that return results for integration into responses work smoothly, while complex multi-turn negotiations between model and tool require additional orchestration. Practitioners designing tool-using systems must understand the protocol well enough to design tools that work within its constraints while enabling the capabilities their applications require.

Why Tool Calling Is Tough

Tool calling sounds simple but in fact hides a degree of complexity that is not necessarily obvious at first glance. This complexity derives not so much from tool calling itself but from the way LLMs work.

Recall that an LLM's causal language-modeling objective means it generates tokens sequentially, each new token attending to every token that came before it. Ordinary text generation is a continuous process: The model produces one token, that token becomes part of the context, and the next token is conditioned on the whole sequence so far. Tool calling interrupts this flow. When the model decides it needs to invoke a tool, it must stop generating natural language and instead emit a structured object—a JSON tool call with the correct function name, parameter names, and values.

Generation then *pauses*. The infrastructure takes over, executes the tool, and injects the result back into the context as though it were another message in the conversation. Only then does generation resume, with the model now attending to the tool's output alongside everything that preceded it.

This interleaved generation pattern is what makes tool calling genuinely difficult. The model is not simply producing text. It is producing text, switching to structured output in a completely different format, yielding control to an external system whose output it cannot predict, and then resuming text generation conditioned on that unpredictable result.

Each of these transitions is a potential failure point. The model might generate malformed JSON that the infrastructure cannot parse. It might produce valid JSON but with parameter values that cause the tool to error. It might resume generation after receiving the tool result but fail to attend to it properly, hallucinating an answer instead of using the data it was just given.

And the model must learn to manage this delicate dance of handovers between generation and tool-calling from training data that represents these transitions as flat sequences of tokens, with no explicit signal about where generation pauses and resumes. The special tokens or formatting conventions that mark tool-call boundaries (whether `<tool_call>` XML tags, JSON delimiters, or provider-specific markers) must carry all the weight of signaling these mode switches. Getting this right is what separates a model that can reliably use tools from one that merely attempts to.

The good news is that this is largely a solved problem at the foundation model level. The major providers have invested heavily in training their models to handle interleaved generation, and any model that an enterprise is likely to use as a starting point is already at least a competent tool caller in the general case. This means that in practice, enterprise fine-tuning for tool use rarely involves teaching a model the mechanics of tool calling from scratch. Instead, the task is almost always to augment an already-capable tool caller with knowledge of specific tools: proprietary APIs, internal databases, and domain-specific services. The model already knows how to pause, emit structured JSON, and resume; what it needs to learn is which of *your* tools to reach for in which situations, and what parameter values make sense in *your* domain. This is a considerably more tractable problem, and it is the one that the remainder of this chapter addresses.

What Can Be Described Can Be Called

Tool calling as a process is an intricate dance between four participants: the user, the model, the tool, and the execution environment. The user calls the model, the model selects the tool, and the execution environment (sometimes referred to as the *agent harness*, but that is, strictly speaking, at best a part of it) routes the call to execution.

A key feature that is sometimes omitted is the role of the agent harness in registering the tools to the model—that is, ensuring that the model is aware of the tools it has at its disposal, and what they do. A good example of what this looks like in practice is given by the system prompt of Anthropic's Claude Code, a part of which is laid out in Listing 9-1.

```
In this environment you have access to a set of tools you can use to answer
the user's question.
{{ FORMATTING INSTRUCTIONS }}
String and scalar parameters should be specified as is, while lists and objects
should use JSON format. Note that spaces for string values are not stripped.
The output is not expected to be valid XML and is parsed with regular
expressions. Here are the functions available in JSONSchema format:
❶ {{ TOOL DEFINITIONS IN JSON SCHEMA }}
❷ {{ USER SYSTEM PROMPT }}
{{ TOOL CONFIGURATION }}
```

Listing 9-1: An excerpt from the system prompt of Anthropic's Claude Code, illustrating how tool definitions are provided to the model before the user prompt

Most imminently notable is that the tool definitions ❶ precede the user prompt ❷, ensuring that the model is aware of its capabilities before it even sees the user's question. This is a crucial detail, because it means the agent sees the world as described to it (the purpose of the system prompt) with an awareness of its own capabilities.

A ramification of tool definitions preceding the actual interaction is that too many tools can pollute the context. *Progressive disclosure* is the principle that instead of revealing all tools all at once, agents should be given access to information on a just-in-time, as-needed basis. At the time of writing, server-side tool search is generally a beta feature for most providers but is likely to reach wider adoption in the short term. That notwithstanding, good tool definitions are crucial, and parsimony is the key virtue.

A good tool description answers three key questions: what the tool does (and if this is hard to answer, we ought to consider whether the tool isn't trying to do too many things all at once), when it should and shouldn't be used, and how it expects parameter inputs. Listing 9-2 is a good tool description, based on an example from the Salesforce *xlam-tool-calling* dataset.

```
{
❶ "name": "light_travel_time",
❷ "description": "Calculate the time taken for light to travel from one celestial
  body to another.",
  "parameters": {
      "distance_in_kilometers": {
   ❸ "description": "The distance between the two celestial
                     "bodies in kilometers.",
   ❹ "type": "int",
      "default": 1
      },
      "speed_of_light": {
      "description": "The speed of light in vacuum, in m/s. Default value is
                     299792458 m/s.",
      "type": "int",
      "default": 299792458
      }
}
```

Listing 9-2: A good tool description: `light_travel_time`*, based on an example in the Salesforce* xlam-tool-calling *dataset*

Four features make this an outstanding example of tool calling. First, the tool name ❶ refers to what the result is, not what the tool does. This reduces ambiguity; the agent knows what they need, and they're not interested in how it is obtained. Second, the description ❷ provides what is sometimes called *soft context*: Rather than explicitly stating when to use this call, it indicates that this is primarily intended for calculations pertaining to celestial objects. Third, the parameter schema ❸ specifies the expected types and constraints for each parameter, reducing the likelihood of invocation errors. Finally, the inclusion of default values ❹ provides a fallback for parameters that may not be explicitly specified, enhancing robustness.

This combination of clarity, guidance, and structure exemplifies some best practices in tool description design. The difficulty is for models to be able to determine which tools to call, which in turn requires them to know which tools are at their disposal—and, more important, what they do. Crafting a tool description carries an inherent tension: We want to feed the model well (providing enough detail so as to enable it to accurately call the tool) but not so much that the model is overwhelmed by the sheer volume of information.

LLMs have a fixed context window and can attend to only a limited amount of information at once. The principle of parsimony applies: Provide enough information to enable effective tool use, but not so much that it clutters the model's understanding of the task at hand. This is a practiced art but one worth learning.

> **A NOTE ON SEMANTICS: TOOL CALLING, FUNCTION CALLING, AND CODE EXECUTION**
>
> It helps to be specific as to what we mean by each of the three concepts of tool calling, function calling, and code execution:
>
> **Tool calling** The most general of the three, this is the process by which a model invokes an external capability through a defined interface. This could be anything from a search API to a calculator to a database query.
>
> **Function calling** In this specific type of tool calling, the tool being invoked is a function defined in code or a fixed schema (typically, the JSON-esque schemas presented in this chapter). Functions have arguments, and their calls must be well-formed; tools need only someone to pick them up.
>
> **Code execution** The most specific of the three, this refers to the running of code, which may include function calls but also encompasses broader programming constructs and, most important, an execution environment.
>
> In practice, these concepts often overlap. A model might call a function as a tool, which then executes code to produce results. Understanding these distinctions helps clarify discussions about how models interact with external capabilities.

Models learn which tools to use and how to use them partly from tool descriptions provided in context, making description quality a significant factor in the effectiveness of tool use. A description that merely states what a tool does, such as "searches the web," provides less guidance than one that explains when to use it: "Use when the user's question requires information more recent than your knowledge cutoff, or when you are uncertain about factual claims that could be verified through search." The latter description helps the model decide whether to invoke the tool, not just how. Tool descriptions function as a form of prompt engineering that shapes model behavior, and the principles that make prompts effective also make tool descriptions effective.

Well-typed parameter schemas reduce invocation errors by constraining what the model can provide. If a parameter must be an integer from 1 to 100, the schema should specify this constraint rather than leaving the model to infer it. If a parameter accepts only certain string values, an enumeration is clearer than free text with a note in the description. Each constraint added to the schema is a constraint the model cannot accidentally violate, while each underspecification is an opportunity for errors that validation could have caught. The discipline of writing clear schemas forces tool designers to think carefully about their interfaces, often improving the tools themselves.

Documentation of edge cases and error conditions enables better error handling by giving the model information it needs to recover from failures. A tool description that notes "returns an empty list if no results are found" prepares the model to handle that case, and one that notes "may time out if the database is under heavy load—retry after a brief pause" suggests a recovery strategy. Without such documentation, models must either hallucinate error-handling strategies or fail to handle errors at all. Investment in good tool descriptions pays dividends in reliable tool use, as well-documented tools are used correctly more often, and failures are handled more gracefully.

At the time of writing, we have yet to converge on a standardized format for tool specifications, and different providers have different conventions. In addition to the JSON schemas described previously, some platforms support what Meta calls *zero-shot tool calling* and everyone else calls the *Pythonic tool-calling syntax* (Listing 9-3).

```
[get_current_weather(city="Denver", state="CO", unit="celsius")]
```

Listing 9-3: Pythonic tool-calling syntax (supported by, for example, Llama 3.2, 3.3, and 4)

The principles of good tool description apply regardless of format: clarity, guidance on when to use the tool, and well-defined parameter constraints are universally beneficial. As the ecosystem matures, we may see more convergence on formats that balance expressiveness with ease of use. For now, practitioners must adapt to the conventions of their chosen platform while adhering to best practices in tool description design.

How to Work with the Invisible Infrastructure

Tool execution requires infrastructure that sits between the model's expressed intentions and the actual invocation of tools— infrastructure that parses tool calls, manages execution, and returns results. This orchestration layer handles concerns that the model need not be aware of: authentication to external services, rate limiting to avoid overwhelming APIs, logging for audit and debugging, and conversion between the formats tools produce and the formats models consume.

The quality of this infrastructure determines the reliability of tool use at least as much as the quality of the model itself. A capable model working through poorly designed infrastructure will appear incapable.

Sandboxing isolates tool execution to prevent unintended effects, particularly for tools that execute code or access file systems. Container-based isolation ensures that code execution cannot escape to affect the host system, restricted file system access limits the data that tools can read or modify, and network isolation controls which external services tools can contact.

The security model for tool execution should assume that the model may attempt harmful actions (whether through adversarial prompting, hallucination, or emergent behavior) and should prevent such actions at the infrastructure level rather than relying on the model to self-constrain. This is not paranoia. It is basic defense in depth. A model that has been jailbroken or that is simply hallucinating a plausible but dangerous action will not stop itself. The sandbox must stop it.

The challenge of building robust sandboxes has given rise to a growing ecosystem of secure remote-execution services. Providers such as E2B, Modal, and Fly.io offer ephemeral sandboxed environments specifically designed for AI-driven code execution. These short-lived virtual machines or containers spin up on demand, execute the model's code in isolation, and are destroyed afterward, leaving no persistent state that could be exploited. These services handle the difficult infrastructure work of process isolation, resource limiting, and network policy enforcement so that application developers need not build it themselves.

For enterprises, the appeal is obvious. Rather than maintaining their own sandboxing infrastructure and keeping pace with an evolving threat landscape, they can delegate execution to a service whose entire business is getting isolation right. The trade-off is latency and cost. Every tool invocation that routes through a remote sandbox adds network round-trip time and per-execution charges, which can become significant for agents that make dozens or hundreds of tool calls per task. For code-execution tools, where the consequences of escaping the sandbox are severe, this trade-off is almost always worthwhile. For simpler tools that query APIs or perform calculations, lighter-weight isolation may suffice.

State management enables multistep interactions that build on previous results, maintaining context across tool invocations within a conversation or task. A model that searches for information, executes code by using that information, and then saves the results to a file is performing a sequence of actions that requires state coherence throughout. Timeout and retry mechanisms handle tools that fail or hang, preventing single tool failures from indefinitely blocking entire conversations. The execution environment shapes the possible patterns for tool use: Synchronous environments that block on tool results suit simple tool use when results are needed immediately, while asynchronous environments that allow parallel tool invocations and background execution enable more complex agentic behavior with multiple actions proceeding simultaneously.

Training for Action

A dataset showing "here is a query, here is the tool call" teaches syntax but not judgment. Effective tool use requires knowing when to reach for tools, how to choose from the alternatives, and, crucially, what to do when tools fail—because in production, tools always eventually fail.

From Query to Result and Back

Training effective tool callers requires datasets that demonstrate not just the syntax of tool invocations but the reasoning that leads to appropriate tool selection and effective result interpretation. A dataset that exposes only paired queries and tool calls teaches the model only that tool calls follow queries, not when to use tools or how to choose from alternatives. Effective datasets include the full cycle: prompts that might or might not require tools, reasoning about whether tools are needed and which would be appropriate, correct invocations with appropriate parameters, interpretation of results, and integration of those interpretations into coherent responses.

What does this look like in practice? Training data for tool calling takes two broad structural forms. The simpler is the *query-completion* format, in which each training instance pairs a natural language query with a set of available tool definitions and the correct function call or calls that answer the query. Listing 9-4 illustrates this format with an example adapted from the Salesforce `xlam-function-calling-60k` dataset,[169] one of the larger publicly available tool-calling datasets at 60,000 verified instances spanning more than 3,600 executable APIs.

```
  {
❶ "query": "What is the current weather in Denver?",
❷ "tools": [
      {"name": "get_current_weather",
       "description": "Get current weather conditions for a city.",
       "parameters": {
         "city": {"type": "string", "required": true},
         "unit": {"type": "string", "enum": ["celsius", "fahrenheit"]}
       }},
      {"name": "get_forecast",
       "description": "Get a multi-day weather forecast.",
       "parameters": {
         "city": {"type": "string", "required": true},
         "days": {"type": "int", "default": 5}
       }}
    ],
❸ "answers": [
      {"name": "get_current_weather",
       "arguments": {"city": "Denver", "unit": "celsius"}}
    ]
  }
```

Listing 9-4: A single training instance from a query-completion tool-calling dataset, adapted from Salesforce's `xlam-function-calling-60k`

Each example comprises three components: the user's query ❶, the available tools with their parameter schemas ❷, and the expected answer specifying the correct tool and arguments ❸. Notice that two tools are available but only one is appropriate for the query. The model must learn not only how to correctly populate arguments but also which tool to select—and, critically, which to leave alone.

The richer format is the *multi-turn conversation*, in which each training instance is a complete dialogue: a system message defining available tools, a user query, the assistant's structured tool call, the tool's execution result, and the assistant's final natural language response incorporating that result. This format, used by datasets such as Glaive's `glaive-function-calling-v2` and the NousResearch Hermes function calling dataset, teaches the full tool use cycle rather than tool selection alone. This approach mirrors the protocol shown previously in Figure 9-1: The model learns to interpret queries, generate structured calls, parse execution results, and synthesize those results into coherent responses. The multi-turn format is more expensive to produce but more complete as a training signal. In practice, many fine-tuning pipelines use a combination of both.

Synthetic generation offers a path to scale by using capable models to generate tool-use traces. The approach begins with a capable model, prompts it with scenarios requiring tool use, captures its tool invocations and the results, and packages these traces as training data. This method can quickly produce large volumes of data, limited primarily by the cost of running the generating model rather than the cost of human annotation.

The quality depends on the capability of the generating model. Traces from a highly capable model teach sophisticated tool use, while traces from a weaker model may perpetuate mistakes. The Salesforce APIGen pipeline demonstrates how this can be done rigorously.[169] It uses models such as DeepSeek-V2-Chat and Mixtral-8x22B-Instruct to generate candidate tool calls, then subjects each to a three-stage verification pipeline. First, format checking confirms that the generated JSON is valid and conforms to the tool's schema. Second, the function call is executed against a real API to confirm that it runs without error. Third, a semantic verification step checks that the returned result is sensible, given the query. This hierarchical filtering is what distinguishes a production-quality dataset from a pile of plausible-looking text; human evaluation of 600 samples from the resulting dataset found accuracy above 95 percent. The lesson is that generating tool-calling data is comparatively easy; the real work lies in verifying it.

Human demonstrations provide gold-standard examples of sophisticated tool use that synthetic generation may struggle to replicate. Expert annotators can demonstrate judgment calls about when tools are needed, nuanced parameter selection, creative use of tool combinations, and graceful recovery from errors. This quality comes at the cost of annotation time and the difficulty of recruiting annotators who understand both the task domain and the mechanics of tool use. A combination often works best: Synthetic generation provides volume, while human demonstrations provide quality signal for the most important or subtle aspects of tool use. The balance between synthetic and human data depends on the available budget, the sophistication of required tool use, and the capability of available generating models.

> **VIBE CHECK: GENERATING TOOL-USE TRACES**
>
> Coding agents excel at generating training data for tool use. Given a set of tool descriptions and example scenarios, an agent can create synthetic tool invocation traces, including the reasoning about when to use each tool, the parameter values appropriate to each scenario, and the interpretation of results. The agent can also inject failures into traces to generate error-handling examples, simulating API timeouts, malformed responses, and permission errors. The resulting traces provide volume that manual annotation cannot match. Human review of a sample validates quality, and the agent can iterate based on feedback. This workflow produces tool-use datasets at scale with minimal human effort.

The Anatomy of a Good Tool Call

Tool-use training involves multiple distinct objectives that together determine the quality of tool-using behavior, as Table 9-1 shows. Format compliance ensures that generated tool calls parse correctly: the JSON is valid, required fields are present, and types match the schema. A tool call that fails to parse cannot be executed regardless of how appropriate the intended action would have been. Tool selection accuracy measures whether the model chooses the right tool for the situation from among available options, or correctly decides that no tool is needed. Argument correctness evaluates whether the parameters provided to selected tools are appropriate: not just type-correct but semantically sensible, given the task.

Result integration assesses whether tool outputs are used effectively in the model's subsequent response. A model that correctly invokes a search tool but ignores the results, or that misinterprets their meaning, has failed at the final step of the tool-use cycle. Each objective captures a different aspect of competent tool use, and deficiency in any one undermines overall performance. A model that selects the right tools but formats calls incorrectly never gets to use those tools. A model that formats perfectly but chooses wrong tools takes wrong actions. A model that does both but misinterprets results provides incorrect responses.

One training signal that is easy to overlook is *irrelevance detection*: teaching the model to recognize when none of the available tools is appropriate for the query and to respond in natural language instead. Models trained exclusively on examples indicating that a tool call is always the correct answer will develop a hammer-and-nail problem, reaching for tools even when the user's question is conversational, rhetorical, or simply outside the scope of the available tools. Dedicated irrelevance training data, constructed by removing the ground-truth tool from the available set and relabeling the expected output as "no tool needed," teaches the model restraint. The Berkeley Function-Calling Leaderboard includes relevance detection as a distinct evaluation category precisely because this failure mode is so common in deployed systems.[85] A model that calls tools when it should not is, in a practical sense, less reliable than one that occasionally fails to call tools when it should. The former produces confident-sounding wrong answers, while the latter at least signals its uncertainty.

These objectives can be incorporated into SFT through appropriately constructed examples that demonstrate correct behavior on each dimension, with sufficient examples of each type to enable generalization. RL offers an alternative through reward signals that evaluate each dimension: Automated validation can score format compliance, comparison to ground truth can score tool selection and argument correctness, and human evaluation or model-based assessment can score result integration. Multiobjective optimization, whether through composite rewards or through separate training phases targeting different objectives, ensures balanced improvement. A model that excels at format compliance but fails at tool selection is not genuinely capable, and training must improve all aspects together.

Table 9-1: Tool-Use Training Objectives and Their Evaluation

Objective	What it measures	Evaluation method
Format compliance	Generated calls parse correctly	Automated schema validation
Tool selection	Correct tool is chosen for situation	Comparison to ground truth; model based
Argument correctness	Parameters are valid and appropriate	Schema validation; semantic checking
Result interpretation	Outputs are understood correctly	Human or model-based evaluation
Irrelevance detection	Decline is given when no tool fits	Queries with no matching tool available
Error handling	Recovery from failures is graceful	Scripted failure injection testing
Multistep coherence	Plans are executed consistently	End-to-end task completion

Because Tools Always Eventually Fail

Tools fail. APIs return errors, queries time out, authentication expires, rate limits are exceeded, services become temporarily unavailable, and results are occasionally malformed or unexpected. Models trained only on successful tool-use traces have no examples of how to handle these failures and must improvise when they occur. The improvisations are often poor. Models may ignore errors and proceed as if tools had succeeded, hallucinate plausible-sounding results that the tool never returned, enter failure loops repeatedly invoking the same failing tool with the same parameters, or abandon tasks entirely when a single recovery attempt could have succeeded.

Training for error handling requires examples of failures and appropriate responses. The training data must include tool invocations that fail in various ways: parameter validation errors that indicate incorrect arguments, execution errors that indicate problems with the tool itself, timeout errors that indicate temporary unavailability, and unexpected result formats that require interpretation. For each failure type, the training data must demonstrate appropriate responses: retrying with modified parameters when the error suggests a correctable mistake, falling back to alternative tools when the primary tool is unavailable, waiting and retrying when timeouts suggest temporary issues, and acknowledging limitations to users when no recovery is possible.

Building such training data requires deliberately injecting failures into tool-use pipelines, either by simulating errors or by using real tools in conditions likely to produce failures. The effort is substantial but essential. Without explicit error-handling training, models treat failures as anomalies for which they have no prepared response. With training, models develop repertoires of recovery strategies matched to failure types. Robust tool use in production, where failures are inevitable, requires robust error handling that only training can provide. The investment in error-handling training pays dividends every time a deployed model encounters a failing tool and recovers gracefully rather than producing garbage.

WARNING *The natural tendency is to build training datasets from successful tool-use traces, as they are easier to collect and review. But models trained only on success have no response patterns for failure. When tools inevitably fail in production, these models may hallucinate results, enter retry loops, or simply break. Deliberately inject failures into your training data: API errors, timeouts, and malformed responses. Show the model what graceful recovery looks like.*

The Leap to Agency

What separates an agent from a tool user? The capacity to formulate strategies, decompose goals into subgoals, and maintain coherent pursuit of objectives across extended interactions. This transition from reactive response to proactive planning marks the frontier of current capability development.

Thinking Before Acting

Agentic behavior requires planning: the ability to take a complex goal that cannot be achieved through a single action and decompose it into subgoals that can be addressed sequentially or in parallel. A user who asks an agent to "set up a development environment for this project" has specified a goal, not a procedure. The agent must determine what setting up the environment entails: the steps involved, the dependencies that exist between steps, and the order of proceeding. This planning capability distinguishes agents from simple tool users. A tool user responds to immediate requests with appropriate tool invocations, while an agent formulates strategies for achieving goals that may require many actions.

Training for planning can take multiple forms. Explicit plan generation trains models to display plans before executing them: Given a goal, first produce a structured plan specifying the steps to achieve it, then execute each step while updating the plan as new information emerges. This approach makes planning visible and auditable but requires training data that includes both plans and their execution. Alternatively, planning capability can emerge from RL on tasks that require multistep reasoning, as the model implicitly learns to decompose goals through experience with tasks that reward successful completion. Hybrid approaches combine elements of both, using explicit planning for high-level structure while allowing flexible execution of individual steps.

> **PLANS AS COMMUNICATION**
>
> Explicit planning is not just for the model's own benefit. It also enables human oversight. When an agent displays its plan before execution, operators can review and approve the approach. When plans are implicit, operators see only actions and must reverse engineer intent. I've found that requiring agents to state their plans in natural language before acting catches more problems than any amount of post hoc analysis. Plans serve the humans who must trust the agent as much as the agent itself.

Planning is a powerful feature, and one of the controls that enables considerable leverage on the model's internal behavior. Training for planning is similar to training for reasoning (see Chapter 10) in that the same techniques apply, but over different material.

Plan-generation datasets, which are now becoming increasingly frequent, reveal a peculiar kind of domain specificity. Few exemplify this better than the research planning dataset released by Meta in early 2026, which comprises a set of research questions from the natural sciences paired with a rubric for correct answers. The point of such datasets is that planning, especially for complex actions, is often quite domain-specific and may even follow set methodologies. Indeed, we might consider the scientific method itself as a kind of planning framework for research, whether it is conducted by humans or agents. The consequence is that domain-specific training becomes indispensable when adherence to certain standardized workflows is desirable.

In developing agentic systems for research in the life sciences, I've often encountered mini-methodologies that were rarely written down or formalized to the point of the EQUATOR standards for reporting various types of studies (for example, CONSORT for randomized controlled trials, PRISMA for systematic reviews) but nonetheless reflected sound logic. A common workflow pattern involved looking at certain characteristics of a potential drug candidate every time one was proposed, and I created a large synthetic set of preference data in which research plans that involved immediate tool-use queries for a drug likeness and potential toxicity check were rewarded. The model learned that these checks were part of the workflow. This is a powerful example of how training can shape not just the model's ability to plan but the content of its plans, instilling domain-specific best practices through carefully designed training data.

Effective planning requires models to maintain representations of goals across extended interactions, tracking progress toward those goals and reasoning about dependencies between actions. If step 3 depends on the output of step 2, the model must recognize this dependency and sequence appropriately. If new information reveals that the original plan is infeasible, the model must revise rather than blindly continuing. These capabilities extend beyond simple tool use and toward genuine agency. The model becomes a collaborator that takes ownership of goals rather than merely responding to instructions. The transition is profound and carries implications for both capability and safety that subsequent sections address.

More Steps, More Problems

Complex tasks require reasoning chains that span multiple tool invocations, with each step building on the results of previous steps and informing subsequent ones. An agent researching a topic might first search for relevant sources, then read and summarize each source, then synthesize the summaries into a coherent analysis, then verify key claims through additional searches, and finally produce a report that integrates all findings. This chain involves multiple tools, each producing outputs that must be interpreted and used as inputs for later steps. The reasoning that connects these steps, determining what to do next based on what has been learned, constitutes the core intellectual work of the agent.

Training for multistep reasoning can employ several approaches. Chain-of-thought training makes reasoning explicit by including the model's thought process in training examples: not just the action taken but the reasoning that led to it. This visibility enables both better training, because supervision can target the reasoning itself, and better debugging, because failed chains reveal where reasoning went wrong. Reflection mechanisms train models to verify their own intermediate conclusions, checking whether results make sense before building upon them. Iterative refinement trains models to improve outputs through multiple passes, recognizing when initial results are inadequate and systematically addressing their weaknesses.

The central challenge in multistep reasoning is error accumulation. A small error in step 2 may lead to a larger error in step 5, which produces a completely wrong conclusion in step 8. If the probability of error at each step is 10 percent, the probability of completing 10 steps without error is barely 35 percent. Strategies for managing this accumulation include verification at intermediate steps to catch errors before they compound, conservative decision-making that avoids actions whose consequences are difficult to reverse, and explicit uncertainty tracking that flags conclusions built on shaky foundations. Training should expose models to chains that go wrong and demonstrate recovery, so that production systems can recognize and address accumulating errors rather than blindly proceeding to incorrect conclusions.

You Must Remember This: Memory Management for Agents

Agentic systems must manage state across interactions, maintaining coherent representations of past attempts, the information that has been gathered, the current goal, and the amount of progress that has been made toward it. Without effective state management, agents suffer from a peculiar form of amnesia. Each step proceeds without awareness of what came before, leading to redundant actions, forgotten context, and incoherent overall behavior. A research agent that does not remember which sources it has already consulted may repeatedly search for the same information. An agent that loses track of its goal may wander into unrelated tasks.

Context windows provide implicit short-term memory; information included in the context is available to the model for reasoning and action. This memory is limited by context length and is implicit in that the model does not explicitly decide what to remember but rather works with whatever information appears in its context. External memory systems can extend this to longer-term storage, enabling agents to explicitly write information to persistent storage and retrieve it when needed. Retrieval-augmented approaches query external stores to bring relevant information into context when it becomes useful. Explicit state tracking maintains structured information about task progress, such as checklists of completed steps or summaries of gathered information, that the agent can consult and update.

Training for effective memory use requires examples that demonstrate when to store information, when to retrieve it, and how to integrate retrieved information with current context. Models should learn to recognize when information is important enough to record, to query memory when it might contain relevant information, and to reconcile potentially outdated retrieved information with current observations. These skills do not automatically emerge from general language model training, and they require explicit training on examples that exercise memory operations. The infrastructure for external memory must be designed alongside the training data, ensuring that the tools available for memory operations match the patterns demonstrated in training.

With Great Power . . . : Safety for Agentic Systems

A model that can act in the world can cause harm in the world. The same capabilities that make agentic systems useful make them dangerous. Sandboxing, permissions, and trained reluctance toward harmful actions are not afterthoughts but prerequisites for responsible deployment.

Using Sandboxing and the Principle of Least Privilege

Tool-using models can take actions that have real consequences. This capability, which makes them useful, also makes them dangerous. A model that can execute code can execute malicious code. A model that can send email can send spam or phishing messages. A model that can modify files can delete or corrupt important data. The transition from passive generation to active agency creates risks that passive models do not pose. Constraint mechanisms are therefore essential, providing guardrails that prevent harmful actions regardless of the model's intentions.

Sandboxing, as discussed previously, restricts what tools can access, isolating execution within boundaries that limit potential damage. A sandboxed code-execution environment might have no network access, no access to files outside a designated directory, and no ability to install packages or modify system configuration. Permission systems require explicit authorization for sensitive operations, distinguishing between actions a model can take freely and actions that require approval. Resource limits prevent runaway processes that consume excessive compute, make too many API calls, or produce outputs that exhaust storage. These limits protect against both malicious behavior and unintended consequences of legitimate actions gone wrong.

The principle of least privilege applies with particular force to agentic systems: Models should have access only to the capabilities required for their intended tasks, no more. An agent designed to help with writing has no need for code-execution capabilities, and providing them creates an attack surface for no benefit. An agent that processes customer inquiries needs access to customer records but not to financial systems. Defense in depth layers multiple constraints to protect against any single mechanism failing: If sandboxing is bypassed, permission systems provide a second line of defense. If permissions are misconfigured, resource limits prevent unbounded damage. No single constraint is perfectly reliable, but well-designed layered constraints make catastrophic failures unlikely.

The September 2025 Claude Code cyber-espionage incident (discussed in Chapter 1) illustrated precisely this tension. An agentic coding assistant with deliberately broad tool access—necessary for its intended purpose—was jailbroken and repurposed for autonomous cyberattacks. The same capabilities that made the agent useful for legitimate coding made it useful for malicious hacking. The incident prompted renewed attention to an important question: What capabilities do we need to provide? The safest way to prevent a model from deleting files is to not give it file-deletion access. The second best is to make sure such powers can be invoked only with user approval, even if the model is on "full self-driving" mode. There is, I'm afraid, no third best way.

LEAST PRIVILEGE FOR AGENTS

For every tool you make available to an agent, ask: Does this agent need this capability to accomplish its purpose? If not, remove that capability. An agent with five tools has less attack surface than one with 50. Capabilities you do not provide cannot be misused. Start with minimal options and add capabilities only when their necessity is demonstrated, not in anticipation of potential usefulness.

Training Models to Say No

Infrastructure constraints provide hard limits on what actions are possible, but training can complement these by instilling reluctance to take harmful actions even when they would be technically permitted. A well-trained model should not attempt to access files outside its sandbox even if the sandbox configuration has a vulnerability that would permit such access. It should not try to send spam even if the email tool lacks rate limiting. Training-level interventions create a model that does not want to cause harm, while infrastructure-level constraints prevent harm in case the model's trained values are circumvented.

RLHF can penalize harmful tool use attempts, teaching models through negative reward that certain actions should be avoided. Constitutional AI establishes explicit principles that agents should follow, such as not taking irreversible actions without confirmation or not accessing resources beyond what the task requires, and trains models to evaluate their own actions against these principles. SFT can reinforce refusal behavior through examples that demonstrate appropriate responses to harmful requests: recognizing that a request would require harmful action and declining to proceed. Each approach teaches reluctance through a different mechanism, and together they create multiple layers of trained disinclination toward harm.

These training-level interventions provide defense when harmful actions are technically permitted but should be avoided. The sandbox may prevent file-system access outside designated directories, but what about harmful uses of permitted tools? An email tool might be legitimately available for the agent's tasks but could be misused for harassment if the model chose to do so. Training that instills reluctance to misuse tools addresses threats that sandboxing cannot. The combination of trained reluctance and hard constraints provides more robust protection than either alone. Infrastructure catches failures of trained values, while trained values avoid unnecessarily triggering infrastructure limits. Neither is sufficient in isolation for high-stakes deployments.

Keeping Humans in the Loop

For high-stakes actions, human approval provides an additional safety layer that neither training nor infrastructure constraints can fully replace. A human reviewer can assess context that automated systems might miss, apply judgment to novel situations that training did not anticipate, and bear accountability for decisions that automated systems cannot. The challenge lies in integrating human oversight without eliminating the efficiency gains that automation provides. If every action requires human approval, the agent offers little advantage over performing tasks manually.

Confirmation patterns request explicit approval before taking irreversible or high-stakes actions. An agent might proceed autonomously through routine research and drafting but pause for confirmation before sending an email, deleting files, or making purchases. The action categories requiring confirmation should be defined based on risk analysis. Actions with significant consequences or difficult reversibility warrant confirmation, while routine low-stakes actions do not. Escalation triggers can route complex or ambiguous decisions to human judgment, recognizing when the agent's confidence is low or the decision involves trade-offs that only humans should make. Override mechanisms can allow humans to interrupt or redirect agent behavior at any time, ensuring that human control is always available even when not actively exercised.

Designing effective human-in-the-loop patterns requires balancing safety against user friction. Requiring approval for every action would make agents unusable, negating the productivity benefits that justify their deployment. Never requiring approval invites harmful autonomy, with agents taking consequential actions without oversight. The right balance depends on the stakes of the deployment context. An agent managing a calendar can operate with minimal oversight, while an agent with access to financial systems requires substantially more. Training can help agents learn appropriate confirmation behavior, but the infrastructure must enforce confirmation requirements for actions defined as requiring oversight. The human must remain genuinely in the loop, able to understand the actions proposed and to make informed decisions about whether to approve them.

Did It Actually Work?

How do you evaluate an agent? We must remember that agents ultimately exist to serve users' needs, and good metrics measure what users care about. Almost always, this is the ability of the tool to achieve the objectives set to them by the user.

Focusing on Outcomes over Actions

Agentic evaluation centers on task completion: Given a goal specification and access to appropriate tools, does the agent achieve the goal? This focus on outcomes rather than process reflects the purpose of agentic systems: Users care whether their goals are accomplished, not about the specific sequence of actions taken. Success rates across benchmark tasks provide the primary metric, measuring the fraction of presented tasks that the agent completes correctly. This metric, despite its simplicity, captures the most important question about any agent: Does it work?

Efficiency measures complement success rates by indicating whether completion is achieved economically. An agent that solves problems but takes 10 times as many steps as necessary, or invokes expensive tools when cheaper alternatives would suffice, is less useful than one that efficiently achieves the same results. Metrics such as steps taken, tools invoked, tokens generated, and wall-clock time capture different aspects of efficiency. Partial credit for intermediate progress provides a more granular view of performance on difficult tasks: An agent that correctly identifies the approach and completes half the steps is more capable than one that fails immediately, even if neither fully completes the task. Progress metrics require careful design to avoid gaming, where agents learn to appear to make progress without truly advancing toward the goal.

Benchmark design determines what agentic evaluation actually measures. Tasks must be well specified so that success criteria are unambiguous, as poorly specified tasks allow disputes about whether the agent succeeded. Success must be objectively measurable, ideally through automated verification that scales to many evaluation instances. Tasks requiring human judgment to assess success create bottlenecks and introduce subjectivity. Difficulty should span the range from easily achievable to genuinely challenging, enabling differentiation across agent capability levels. A benchmark at which all agents succeed teaches nothing about relative capability, and a benchmark where all agents fail provides no signal about progress. The design of evaluation benchmarks for agentic systems is itself an active research area, as the field develops shared understanding of what it means for an agent to be capable.

MODERN AGENT BENCHMARKS

Several benchmarks have emerged to evaluate agentic capabilities across realistic tasks:

SWE-bench Evaluates agents on real GitHub issues from popular Python repositories, requiring agents to navigate large codebases, understand issue descriptions, and produce correct patches. The benchmark's realism (using actual issues from production codebases) makes it a stringent test of software engineering capability.[170]

WebArena Tests web navigation tasks across realistic websites, requiring agents to accomplish goals like shopping, forum posting, and information retrieval through browser interactions. It measures whether agents can operate in the messy reality of real web interfaces rather than idealized environments.[171]

GAIA Presents questions that require multistep reasoning across tools: web search, calculation, file manipulation, and API access. Designed to resist shortcut solutions, it evaluates the integrated reasoning and tool use that characterizes capable agents.[172]

These benchmarks share a focus on realistic, end-to-end tasks where success requires multiple capabilities working together. They represent the current frontier for measuring what agents can accomplish in the environments where they will be deployed.

Red Teaming Your Agent

Safety evaluation for agentic systems tests whether models respect constraints under adversarial pressure, probing the boundaries of safety mechanisms to find weaknesses before malicious actors do. The question is not whether the agent behaves safely in benign conditions, where well-trained agents generally do, but whether safety holds under attempts to circumvent it. Do agents refuse harmful requests when those requests are disguised as legitimate tasks? Do they maintain safety constraints when instructions are delivered through indirect channels? Do they resist multistep attacks that individually seem innocuous but collectively aim to cause harm?

Red-teaming exercises employ skilled adversaries to probe for failures, using creativity and domain expertise to find attack vectors that automated testing might miss. Red teamers think like attackers, trying various approaches to induce unsafe behavior: social engineering that claims false authority, role-playing scenarios that attempt to alter the agent's self-perception, and gradual boundary-pushing that slowly escalates requests. Adversarial prompt testing evaluates robustness to known jailbreaking techniques, including prompt injection that attempts to override safety instructions and context manipulation that tries to confuse the agent about what it should do. Constraint verification confirms that safety mechanisms trigger when expected, testing the technical implementation of safeguards against known harmful action patterns.

Safety evaluation should be ongoing rather than a one-time assessment before deployment. New attack vectors emerge as adversaries study deployed systems, model capabilities evolve through updates and fine-tuning in ways that may affect safety properties, and the threat landscape shifts as new harmful applications become conceivable. Organizations deploying agentic systems should maintain continuous safety evaluation processes, regularly reassessing deployed systems against current attack techniques. The cost of this ongoing evaluation is justified by the cost of safety failures that could occur in its absence. An agent that was safe at deployment but has become vulnerable to new attacks provides false assurance to its operators while exposing users to harm.

Surviving the Wild

Robust agentic behavior maintains performance across variations in input, environment, and task specification that production deployment inevitably presents. An agent that performs well on test cases drawn from the same distribution as training data but fails on slightly different inputs is brittle in a way that precludes reliable deployment. Real users phrase requests in unexpected ways, encounter edge cases that training did not anticipate, and operate in environments that differ from testing conditions. Robustness testing probes these variations to identify brittleness before it manifests in production.

Robustness is essential for production deployment because the controlled conditions of testing never fully represent the wild conditions of production. Every failure mode that testing uncovers is a failure mode that will not surprise users in production, and every brittleness discovered in evaluation is a brittleness that can be addressed before deployment. Investment in comprehensive robustness testing pays dividends in production reliability, in reduced support burden, and in user trust that the agent will handle whatever they present to it. An agent that works perfectly on a narrow slice of inputs but fails on everything else is not production-ready regardless of its performance on that narrow slice. Robustness testing reveals the true breadth of an agent's capability.

Distribution shift testing is a crucial aspect of this process. It evaluates performance on inputs that differ from training data in systematic ways: different phrasings of similar requests, different domains with analogous structures, and different levels of specificity or formality. The goal is to assess whether learned behavior generalizes or whether it depends on superficial features of training examples. Noisy input testing assesses tolerance for imperfect or ambiguous instructions, adding typos, grammatical errors, vague references, and incomplete specifications to otherwise well-formed inputs. Production users do not speak in the clean language of training examples, and agents must handle the messy reality of actual human communication. Adversarial robustness measures resistance to inputs specifically designed to cause failures, testing not just natural variation but deliberate attempts to break the system.

Safety must run through every layer of the agentic stack. The same capabilities that enable useful action enable harmful action, and the distinction lies not in the capability itself but in its constraints. The classical model of securing these systems relies not on a single capability but on a stack of multilevel mechanisms:

Infrastructure-level sandboxing Provides hard limits that training cannot circumvent. These offer resilience but operate on the level of commands or operations, and are only as secure as the definitions that underlie their technical implementation.

Training-level interventions Instill reluctance to take harmful actions even when technically permitted.

Human-in-the-loop patterns Provide oversight for high-stakes decisions that neither automated training nor infrastructure constraints can fully address.

No single mechanism suffices, and robust deployments layer all three. In agentic systems, the target is task completion rather than output—utility in the world, that is, rather than quality on the screen. Robustness evaluation infrastructure must therefore accommodate the typically multistep nature of agentic interactions and understand that this presents a much larger adversarial surface area than the single-step interactions typical of non-agentic systems. This approach, in turn, shapes which agents can be deployed responsibly and which problems cannot yet be safely addressed.

Summary

This chapter has shown how tool use provides the foundation for agentic systems. If tool use is the "muscle" of agentic systems, reasoning is the "brain" that guides it. The patterns that make tool use worthwhile derive from the ability of models to plan before, and evaluate after, tool use. These are part of the wider scope of agentic abilities collectively referred to as *reasoning*. We will turn to these in the next chapter.

10

REASONING CAPABILITIES: TRAINING FOR COMPLEX THOUGHT

When OpenAI released o1 in September 2024, the model did something unusual. It showed a trained reasoning process, the chain of thought that led from question to answer. Until then, reasoning had generally been one of those "internals" of the model that post-training researchers would pore over for hours and that could be elicited by pretending we were the model's fifth-grade math teacher ("Show your work!"). Otherwise, that reasoning remained hidden, leading to the ubiquitous perception of LLMs as black boxes. All that changed with o1.

Reasoning in language models has evolved from a prompt-engineering trick to a trainable capability. Chain-of-thought prompting demonstrated that models could solve harder problems when encouraged to reason step-by-step, but this relied on prompts alone that proved fragile and inconsistent.[173]

Modern approaches, starting with o1, embed reasoning into the training process itself: process reward models that score intermediate steps rather than final answers, verification procedures that check reasoning for consistency, and domain-specific methods that incorporate the logical structures of law, medicine, or mathematics. The result is models that do not merely recite memorized patterns but engage in something recognizably like reasoning, and this is integrated into the models at post-training rather than invoked at inference time.

This chapter explores the techniques for training reasoning capabilities: the architectures and objectives that encourage explicit reasoning, the role of process supervision in shaping the way models think, and the methods for teaching domain-specific reasoning that respects field conventions. We examine verifiable reasoning, where outputs can be checked algorithmically, and acknowledge the limits of learned reasoning, where models still struggle with novel problems outside their training distribution. For enterprises deploying models in domains where correctness matters more than fluency, understanding reasoning capabilities determines whether the technology can be trusted.

From Chain-of-Thought to Trained Reasoning

Is the model reasoning, or merely constructing plausible-sounding justifications after it has already decided on an answer? The difference between genuine inference and post hoc rationalization determines whether showing work provides insight or false assurance.

Understanding the Difference Between Thinking and Pretending to Think

Enough philosophical discourse has occurred about "reasoning" in LLMs that the term itself is not devoid of controversy. In a profound way, the human cognitive experience is unique and particular to what we are, and we're instinctively predisposed to jealously guard it for ourselves. This is a fascinating debate that could fill a book longer than this one, and we won't engage in it for now. We do not need to believe that some sort of human-like mental pattern takes place when an LLM "reasons" in order for us to understand why reasoning is a practical capability that can be trained and optimized.

Recall the causal structure of autoregressive models: They generate tokens one at a time, with each token conditioned on the previous ones. This means that the past few thousand tokens, subject to the size of the model's context window, are a sort of very short-term memory or scratchpad the model can reflect on. When we get the model to spell out individual stages in its reasoning, we are encouraging it to use that scratchpad to generate the intermediate steps and reflect upon them. This implicit reflection that's inherent in the causal language modeling objective lends reasoning its power.

Chain-of-thought reasoning can be elicited through prompting or directly trained, and the choice between these approaches has significant implications for reliability. Prompting approaches append instructions like "let's think step by step" to queries, encouraging the model to generate intermediate reasoning before producing final answers.[173] This technique is remarkably effective given its simplicity; a few words added to the prompt can substantially improve performance on reasoning tasks. The approach requires no training data and works with any sufficiently capable base model, making it the path of least resistance for practitioners who want reasoning behavior quickly.

Prompting, however, is unreliable in ways that matter for serious applications. Models may produce plausible-looking reasoning that reaches wrong conclusions, with each step sounding reasonable despite the chain leading somewhere incorrect. More fundamentally, the reasoning the model produces may not reflect its computation. The model may have already decided on an answer and be constructing a post hoc justification rather than genuinely reasoning toward a conclusion. This failure mode, reasoning as rationalization rather than discovery, undermines the purpose of chain of thought. If the reasoning does not influence the answer, showing it provides a false assurance of correctness.

Training on chain-of-thought data produces more reliable reasoning by explicitly optimizing for correct chains, not just correct conclusions. The model learns that its reasoning should be valid, not merely plausible, because training signal rewards correct reasoning and penalizes incorrect reasoning. The resulting models produce reasoning that more reliably reflects computation and more consistently leads to correct answers. The cost is the need for training data demonstrating correct reasoning, which is more expensive to obtain than correct answers alone. The choice between prompting and training depends on reliability requirements and available resources. Prompting suffices for exploratory work or low-stakes applications, but training is necessary when reasoning must be trustworthy.

REASONING VS. RATIONALIZATION

A prompted chain of thought may be post hoc justification rather than genuine reasoning. The model decides the answer first, then constructs plausible-sounding steps. This is rationalization, not reasoning, and it is not exactly unique to LLMs (humans are perfectly capable of this type of retrospective rationalization).

Trained chain of thought, however, operates on a different level. The model isn't merely asked to reason. Instead, its very internal reward structure has been trained in a way that assigns value to reasoning, because the model has learned that valid reasoning leads to correct answers. If you need the reasoning to be trustworthy, not just present, training is required.

A crucial aspect is the nature of this reasoning. Test-time induced reasoning cannot be taught particular reasoning modes without potentially fairly significant investment in terms of context, and it is in either case (like all test-time inter-

(continued)

ventions) not persistent. Not so for trained reasoning, which becomes part of the model's immutable internal structure. This allows us to train the model to reason in a particular sequence.

The most important application of this approach is, of course, domain-specific reasoning modes. Differential diagnosis, for instance, is a highly particular mode of reasoning, aimed at attaining the highest diagnostic accuracy from the lowest cost of diagnostic testing. It is quite nearly unique, but its method can be "taught" through relatively simple use of the RL techniques introduced in Chapters 4 and 5.

Identifying Good Reasoning Chains

Effective chain-of-thought training requires data that demonstrates step-by-step reasoning in the patterns appropriate to the target domain. A legal analysis proceeds differently from a mathematical proof, which proceeds differently from a clinical diagnosis. Each domain has its own conventions for structuring reasoning, citing evidence, handling uncertainty, and connecting premises to conclusions. Training data must demonstrate these domain-appropriate patterns so that models learn not just that reasoning should occur but the way it should be structured.

Each step in the reasoning chain should follow logically from previous steps, with the connection made explicit rather than left implicit. Training data that jumps from premise to conclusion without showing intermediate steps teaches the model that such jumps are acceptable, while data that shows every inference teaches careful reasoning. Implicit reasoning, the kind that experts make automatically without articulating it, should be made explicit in training examples so that models learn the full inference structure. The chain should clearly connect to the final conclusion, showing how the reasoning supports the answer rather than merely preceding it. These properties are not difficult to achieve in individual examples but require discipline to consistently maintain across an entire training corpus.

Format conventions determine the structure of reasoning chains in text. How are steps separated—by line breaks, numbering, or explicit transition phrases? How are conclusions marked—by specific keywords, positioning at the end, or typographic distinction? How is uncertainty indicated—through hedging language, explicit probability statements, or enumeration of alternatives? These conventions should be consistent across training data so that models learn a reliable format for expressing reasoning. The format is not merely cosmetic. It structures the way the model represents and generates reasoning, affecting both the quality of reasoning and its interpretability to users.

Thinking Aloud, Quietly

Scratchpad methods provide models with dedicated space to reason before producing final outputs, separating the thinking process from the presented result. This separation recognizes that effective reasoning often involves exploration that would be inappropriate in user-facing outputs: considering and rejecting hypotheses, making rough calculations that will be refined, following dead ends that will be abandoned. A user asking a complex question wants the answer, not a transcript of every thought that occurred along the way. The scratchpad provides space for thorough reasoning while keeping the final output focused and clean.

Practical implementations mark certain portions of model output as scratchpad content that will be processed but not shown to users. The model generates extensive reasoning in the scratchpad, reaches conclusions, and then produces user-facing output that appropriately summarizes or presents them. This architecture enables more extensive reasoning than would otherwise be practical. A response showing five pages of working before reaching a one-paragraph conclusion would frustrate users, but five pages of hidden reasoning supporting a polished conclusion serves them well. Verification steps can occur within the scratchpad, checking conclusions before presenting them and revising if checks fail.

Training for scratchpad use requires examples that demonstrate effective use of the hidden reasoning space. Models must learn what kinds of reasoning belong in the scratchpad versus the final output, how to conduct useful exploration rather than produce mere verbosity, and how to synthesize scratchpad reasoning into appropriate conclusions. Without training, models may use the scratchpad ineffectively, repeating thoughts rather than advancing them or failing to distinguish between exploration and conclusion. The training investment pays dividends in reasoning quality. Models that learn to use scratchpads well can tackle problems that would defeat single-pass generation, applying the additional computation that extended thinking requires.

REASONING DISCLOSURE POLICY

Whether to expose or hide reasoning traces involves trade-offs across safety, security, and user experience. Exposing reasoning can build trust (users see the model "thinking through" problems), aid debugging (engineers can identify where reasoning goes wrong), and satisfy regulatory requirements for explainability. Hiding reasoning protects proprietary methods (competitors cannot reverse engineer your approach), reduces attack surface (adversaries cannot probe reasoning for exploitable patterns), and simplifies the user experience (avoiding cognitive overload from verbose traces).

Most deployments adopt a middle path, with summarized reasoning for users, full traces available for debugging, and audit logs preserved for compliance. The policy should be explicit and consistent. Users who sometimes see reasoning and sometimes do not will find the inconsistency unsettling.

Knowing When More Reasoning Makes Things Worse

There is an important caveat here: Reasoning is a means to an end, not an end in itself. Long chains of reasoning for their own sake are not desirable.

This is a phenomenon known as *overthinking*: Accuracy follows an inverted U-shaped curve with chain-of-thought length. Performance initially improves as reasoning steps increase, but it eventually deteriorates as chains become excessively long. The mechanism is error accumulation. Each step introduces a probability of mistake, and a single error can mislead the entire subsequent chain. A 10-step chain with 95 percent accuracy per step has only a 60 percent probability of being entirely valid, while a 20-step chain drops to 36 percent.

Models trained on reasoning data often learn that longer responses correlate with higher reward, since complex problems require extended reasoning and complex problems are often the focus of training. This creates a behavior known as *length hacking*: The model pads easy problems with unnecessary steps, mimicking the length of hard-problem solutions without the substance. If your model solves a problem in 3 steps but writes 15, it is not being thorough; it is procrastinating. The result is wasted tokens and accumulated error risk.

The Hobbesian way—nasty, brutish, and short—of penalizing overlength completions is to simply limit the maximum length and assign a penalty to incomplete completions (those that end without an `eos` token). The problem with this approach is that it does not generate a particularly useful gradient signal. Much better approaches may be achieved by training design or reward shaping.

In terms of training design, models can be trained using graded, or *anti-curriculum*, learning over question sets that have ascertainable difficulty levels. A classic example is the US Medical Licensing Examination (USMLE) for physicians. The USMLE comes in three *steps*: basic science (Step 1), clinical knowledge (Step 2 CK), and comprehensive advanced clinical medicine questions (Step 3). While formally similar, Step 3 requires significantly more reasoning than Step 2, which in turn requires more than Step 1. The panoramic perspective required for Step 3 (especially for sequential questions, as each question follows up on the scenario resolution in the previous one) justifies thinking at length, whereas Step 1's questions based more on knowledge retrieval do not.

By exposing the model to difficulty-graded reward functions (a technique known as *difficulty-aware reweighting*), we remove the temptation to overthink. This matters because in the long run, overthinking is harmful to the model itself. Unlike simple length hacking, which we seek to disincentivize because it lets the model receive the reward without learning anything, overthinking results in worsening model performance because of the risk of accumulating errors.

FROM THE TRENCHES: THE MOVING FINGER WRITES

The Persian poet Omar Khayyam's famous quatrain could just as well have been written about chain-of-thought reasoning:

> The moving finger writes; and, having writ,
> Moves on: nor all thy piety nor wit
> Shall lure it back to cancel half a line,
> Nor all thy tears wash out a word of it.

Once something makes its way into the chain of thoughts, it is there to stay. Models are free to refine and contradict their past reasoning, but they can never make it go away. This is a consequence of the autoregressive structure of language models. One trap where overthinking can be particularly pernicious is regression to defaults (RtD). In this case, a model replaces a defined term with its own default definition, which may well be subtly different. This problem is, of course, most often seen in fields that depend on definitional compositionality, such as law.

When developing an early reasoning model for assessing the fairness of tenancy agreements, I often saw models forget specific terms that the parties agreed constituted a breach of the agreement. It turns out that every time the model made a reasoning step, it put itself at risk of invoking its own definition of *material breach* rather than the contract's. This is RtD in action: The model has its own default definitions and will prefer those over the new terms if they are reintroduced at any stage. The problem is, of course, that the precise value of such a language model lies in its ability to reflect those additional terms.

The best cure is to encourage the model to *checkpoint* its reasoning steps. Checkpointing has no universal recipe, but an interesting approach comes from rubric learning. In rubric learning, the reward is based on the model's ability to produce text that complies with a list of requirements. This works particularly well when we simultaneously desire a degree of freedom on one hand and "checking off the boxes" on the other (consider the task of generating a research plan, for instance). Without overconstraining the training process, we can reward the model for following each step of the research-planning process (interpret the question, draft your approach, carry out research, and so on). It turns out that we can encourage models to checkpoint in a similar way, by rewarding periodic assumption checks. This methodology is similar to process rewards, which we will discuss in the next section.

Rewarding the Journey, Not Just the Destination

Should reward be attached to the final answer or to each step along the way? Outcome reward models (ORMs) provide sparse signal (right or wrong), but process reward models (PRMs) pinpoint exactly where reasoning went astray. The difference in training efficiency can be dramatic.

Showing Your Work

ORMsevaluate only final answers. A correct answer receives high reward regardless of the reasoning that produced it, and an incorrect answer receives low reward regardless of how close the reasoning came. This approach aligns with ultimate goals, since users care about correct answers, but provides sparse and potentially misleading training signal. A model that reaches a correct answer through flawed reasoning receives the same reward as one that reasons correctly, while a model that reasons perfectly but makes a minor arithmetic error in the final step receives no credit for its valid reasoning. The signal tells the model what to achieve but provides no guidance on how to achieve it.

The verifier approach introduced by Cobbe et al. demonstrated how powerful even outcome-level verification could be.[174] They trained a separate verifier model to score candidate solutions to grade-school math problems, then selected the highest-scoring solution from a pool of candidates. Remarkably, a 6-billion-parameter model with verification matched or exceeded a fine-tuned 175-billion-parameter model, an uplift equivalent to roughly a 30-fold increase in model size. This result established that verification at inference time can substitute for enormous increases in model scale, a principle that would prove central to the reasoning model paradigm.

PRMs address this limitation by evaluating each reasoning step, providing dense supervision throughout the chain rather than only at the end. A PRM assigns a score to each step, indicating whether that step is valid, given the previous steps. This approach enables credit assignment that identifies exactly where reasoning went right or wrong. A model that reasons correctly through step 7 but errs at step 8 receives positive signal for steps 1 through 7 and negative signal for step 8. This granular feedback enables more efficient learning: The model can identify and fix specific failure points rather than treating entire reasoning chains as monolithic successes or failures.

PRMs offer additional advantages beyond improved credit assignment. They can guide models toward correct reasoning even when final answers are wrong, crediting the approach rather than only the result. They provide more informative signal about relative reasoning quality. Among several wrong answers, a PRM can identify which reasoning chains were better despite all reaching incorrect conclusions. The trade-off is data cost. Labeling reasoning steps requires evaluators who can assess each step's validity, a more demanding annotation task than labeling final answers. For domains where step-level annotation is practical, whether through expert annotation or automatic verification, PRMs provide substantially better training signal than ORMs.

Uesato et al. provided the first systematic comparison of process and outcome supervision on natural language math tasks.[175] Their findings were nuanced: Outcome-based supervision produced similar final-answer error rates to process-based supervision on easier benchmarks, and it required less annotation effort. However, process-based supervision was necessary for correct *reasoning*, not merely correct answers. Outcome supervision allowed models to reach correct answers through incorrect reasoning steps, a distinction that matters enormously in deployment. If a model produces right answers for wrong reasons, it will fail unpredictably on new problems where the shortcut no longer works.

Lightman et al. scaled process supervision further with PRM800K, collecting more than 800,000 step-level human labels across 75,000 solutions, and demonstrated that process supervision significantly outperforms outcome supervision on harder mathematical tasks from the MATH dataset.[176] The practical lesson is clear: For domains where reasoning correctness matters, not just answer correctness, process supervision is worth the annotation investment. Table 10-1 outlines the trade-offs that govern our choice of whether to use ORMs or PRMs.

Table 10-1: Outcome vs. Process Reward Models: Trade-Offs

Dimension	ORM	PRM
Training signal	Final answer only	Each reasoning step
Credit assignment	Entire chain rewarded/penalized	Per-step attribution
Data requirements	Answer labels	Step-level labels
Annotation cost	Lower	Higher
Learning efficiency	Sparse signal	Dense signal
Failure diagnosis	Reason for failure is unclear	Identifies failing step
Search guidance	End-of-chain only	Can prune early
Best for	Simple tasks; abundant data	Complex reasoning; verifiable domains

From a learning perspective, the true power of PRMs lies in their ability to generate a very differentiated, granular reward signal that contains much more information than mere pass/fail results. Outcome supervision says, "Everyone failed"; the final answer was wrong. Process supervision says, "Steps 1 through 7 succeeded, step 8 failed, and steps 9 and 10 were doomed by step 8." This granular credit assignment enables targeted improvement: Fix step 8 without disturbing steps 1 through 7. ORMs cannot provide this, but PRMs can.

Teaching the Teacher to Check Each Step

Training PRMs requires step-level labels indicating whether each reasoning step is valid, a more demanding annotation task than labeling final answers but one that enables substantially better training signal. Each step in a reasoning chain must be evaluated not in isolation but in context, asking whether this step is a valid inference, given the problem statement and all previous steps. The evaluation requires understanding the domain well enough to assess inference validity, making PRM design one of the more demanding annotation tasks and the least suitable for outsourcing to human or digital crowdwork.

Annotation can come from multiple sources. Human experts can provide gold-standard labels by examining each step and judging its validity, though this approach is expensive and slow. Verification against formal systems can also provide automatic labels for steps: A mathematical step is valid if a proof assistant accepts it, and a programming step is valid if tests pass. Finally, bootstrapping approaches propagate final-answer correctness back to intermediate steps, reasoning that correct final answers probably arose from mostly valid reasoning, while incorrect answers probably contain errors (and are, in their practical application, often eerily similar to the way we derive reward models from preferences). These approaches are noisier than direct annotation but can cheaply generate large volumes of training data.

Math-Shepherd demonstrated the most practical automated approach.[177] Given a problem with a known answer and a step-by-step solution, Math-Shepherd evaluates each intermediate step by using a fine-tuned LLM as a *completer*: From each step, it generates multiple continuation paths to a final answer, then checks each continuation against ground truth. The quality of a step is defined as the fraction of continuations that reach the correct answer, a Monte Carlo estimate of the step's potential to produce a correct final result. No human annotation is involved at any stage. Using this automated supervision, Math-Shepherd improved Mistral-7B from 77.9 percent to 84.1 percent on GSM8K and from 28.6 percent to 33.0 percent on MATH, with verification-based reranking pushing accuracy further to 89.1 percent and 43.5 percent, respectively. The practical implication is that organizations with access to problems with known answers can generate process reward training data at scale, limited only by compute rather than by human annotation capacity.

The reward model learns to predict step validity from these annotations, enabling its use during policy training to provide dense feedback without requiring new human annotation for each training example. Credit assignment, determining which steps contributed to success or failure, is the key challenge that step-level rewards help address. This granular feedback enables policy optimization that targets specific failure modes rather than uniformly adjusting the entire generation process.

Formally, a PRM assigns scores to partial reasoning traces:

$$r_{\text{PRM}}(x, y_1, \ldots, y_t) = \prod_{i=1}^{t} p(\text{step } y_i \text{ is correct} \mid x, y_1, \ldots, y_{i-1})$$

This decomposition enables early termination of unpromising reasoning paths and provides training signal per step during policy optimization.

The product structure has profound practical implications. Even modestly imperfect reasoning compounds rapidly. If each step has a 90 percent probability of being correct, a one-step chain has only $(0.9)^{10} \approx 35$ percent probability of being entirely valid. This explains why long reasoning chains fail more often than short ones and why process supervision matters. In practice, if the PRM assigns step-level probability below 0.7, the compound probability is already quickly deteriorating, and the remaining inference budget is often better spent exploring alternative paths rather than continuing the current one. This threshold guides search algorithms during inference. When the cumulative PRM score falls below a cutoff, prune and try a different approach. The computational economics are clear: Early pruning of unpromising chains saves the tokens that would have been wasted completing them and reallocates that budget to paths more likely to succeed.

In practice, we implement PRMs by training a token classifier on top of a language model, with a crucial masking strategy that determines where the model's predictions are evaluated. Consider a reasoning chain tokenized as a flat sequence of tokens, with step boundaries marked by a delimiter (typically, a newline character). The model produces a classification logit at every token position, but we care about the prediction at only one specific token per step: the final token before each delimiter. All other token positions receive a masked label (the conventional value −100, which cross-entropy loss ignores), meaning they contribute nothing to the gradient. As a result, the model must read the entirety of a step before committing to a judgment, and the training signal is sparse but precise: one classification decision per reasoning step.

This masking strategy, formalized by Lightman et al. in the PRM800K work,[176] has three practical consequences. First, it forces causal accumulation of evidence. Because the prediction is evaluated only at the step's final token, the model cannot take a shortcut by reacting to the first few tokens of a step. It must process the entire step in context before the loss function cares about its output. Second, it avoids the ambiguity of mid-step labels. A token halfway through a step like "multiply both sides by 3" does not yet constitute a complete reasoning action, and labeling it as correct or incorrect would be misleading. The mask ensures that only complete steps receive judgment. Third, this strategy makes training efficient despite the apparent waste of computing logits at every position. The forward pass processes the full sequence regardless (the model needs the hidden states at each position to inform later positions), so the computational overhead of predicting at every token is negligible. Masking simply ensures that only the informative positions influence the weight updates.

The label vocabulary is deliberately simple. Each step-boundary token receives either a positive label (the step is correct, given everything that preceded it) or a negative label (the step contains an error). Some annotation schemes include a third, neutral category for steps that are technically correct but do not advance the solution, though in practice most implementations collapse this to a binary classification. At inference time, the model produces a probability of correctness at each step boundary. These probabilities can be aggregated across the full chain, most commonly as a product (reflecting the compound probability of all steps being correct) or by taking the minimum (reflecting the weakest link in the chain). When used for best-of-*N* selection, the PRM scores *N* candidate solutions, and the one with the highest aggregate step-level confidence is chosen. Listing 10-1 shows an example of PRM training with TRLl.

```
from datasets import load_dataset
from transformers import AutoModelForTokenClassification, AutoTokenizer
❶ from trl.experimental.prm import PRMConfig, PRMTrainer
```

```
❷ model = AutoModelForTokenClassification.from_pretrained(
      "Qwen/Qwen2.5-1.5B", num_labels=2
  )
  tokenizer = AutoTokenizer.from_pretrained("Qwen/Qwen2.5-1.5B")

  dataset = load_dataset("trl-lib/math_shepherd", split="train")

  config = PRMConfig(
      output_dir="./prm-output",
    ❸ step_separator="\n",
    ❹ train_on_last_step_only=False,
      max_length=2048,
      per_device_train_batch_size=4,
      num_train_epochs=1,
  )

❺ trainer = PRMTrainer(
      model=model,
      args=config,
      processing_class=tokenizer,
      train_dataset=dataset,
  )
  trainer.train()
```

Listing 10-1: Training a process reward model with TRL's `PRMTrainer`

The key design decisions deserve explanation. We use `AutoModelForTokenClassification` rather than a causal language model ❷, because the task is per-token classification, not next-token prediction. TRL's `PRMTrainer` ❶, available in the experimental API, handles the masking internally: It tokenizes each step separately, assigns the label −100 to every token except the final one in each step, and uses the step separator ❸ to identify boundaries. The `train_on_last_step_only` flag ❹ controls whether all step boundaries contribute to the loss or only the final step does, a distinction that matters when training data contains steps of varying reliability (earlier steps are often more reliably labeled than later ones). The trainer ❺ then handles the rest, including data collation with padding, distributed training, and checkpoint management.

At inference time, we pass partial or complete solutions through the trained PRM and read the prediction at each step boundary (Listing 10-2).

```
from transformers import pipeline

pipe = pipeline(
    "token-classification",
    model="path/to/trained-prm"
)

solution_steps = [
    "There are 45 students in total.",
```

```
    "A third are under 11: 45 / 3 = 15.",
    "Two-fifths are 11-13: 45 * 2/5 = 18.",
    "The third group: 45 - 15 - 18 = 12."
]

prompt = "How many students are in the oldest group?"
separator = "\n"

for i in range(1, len(solution_steps) + 1):
    text = separator.join([prompt] + solution_steps[:i]) + separator
❶  prediction = pipe(text)[-1]
    is_correct = prediction["entity"] == "LABEL_1"
    print(f"Step {i}: {'correct' if is_correct else 'error'}"
          f" (score: {prediction['score']:.3f})")
```

Listing 10-2: Using a trained PRM to score reasoning steps

The pipeline reads the last token prediction ❶ from each incremental pass, giving us a running assessment of solution quality. In a search setting, this per-step scoring enables early termination. If the PRM assigns low confidence after step 3 of a 10-step solution, we can abandon that path and allocate compute to a more promising alternative.

Exploring the Tree of Thoughts

PRMs enable search during inference by providing evaluations that guide exploration of the reasoning space. Rather than generating a single reasoning chain and accepting whatever conclusion it reaches, models can explore multiple paths, evaluating each with the PRM and focusing computational resources on the most promising directions. This approach treats reasoning as a search problem rather than a generation problem, with the PRM providing the evaluation function that directs search toward solutions.

The Tree of Thoughts framework formalized this insight.[178] Whereas standard chain-of-thought prompting generates a single left-to-right reasoning chain with no backtracking or exploration, Tree of Thoughts maintains a tree of candidate reasoning paths, evaluates the promise of each, and searches systematically. The framework has four components: a thought decomposer that breaks problems into manageable substeps, a thought generator that proposes candidate next steps, a state evaluator that assesses the promise of each candidate, and a search algorithm that explores the tree. The search algorithm can be breadth-first (expanding the most promising nodes at each depth level, suitable for shallow reasoning trees) or depth-first (exploring deeply along a single path and backtracking when the evaluator judges a path unpromising, suitable for deeper reasoning). The results demonstrate the gap between single-pass and search-based reasoning: On the Game of 24, chain-of-thought prompting solved only 4 percent of tasks, while Tree of Thoughts achieved 74 percent.

Monte Carlo tree search (MCTS), the technique that enabled superhuman game-playing in Go and chess, further extends this framework. Nodes in the search tree represent partial reasoning states: the problem statement plus reasoning steps generated so far. Edges represent individual reasoning steps that extend a partial solution. The PRM provides evaluations at each node, estimating the probability that the current partial chain will lead to a correct final answer. Search proceeds by selecting promising nodes for expansion, generating possible next steps, evaluating the resulting nodes, and updating value estimates based on what is learned. The tree grows in directions that appear promising, while avoiding regions the PRM identifies as unlikely to succeed. This is exactly the architecture that AlphaProof used to achieve silver medal performance at the 2024 International Mathematical Olympiad, combining AlphaZero-style RL with a proof network that searches for formal proofs in Lean.[179]

The question of how to allocate test-time compute across these search strategies turns out to have a nuanced answer. Snell et al. demonstrated that the optimal strategy depends critically on problem difficulty.[180] Easy problems benefit most from simple best-of-*N* sampling, which selects the highest-scoring solution from those that are generated. Hard problems benefit from deeper PRM-guided search that explores alternative reasoning paths. Allocating compute adaptively per prompt, matching strategy to difficulty, improves efficiency more than fourfold over uniform best-of-*N* baselines. The researchers' most striking finding is that a smaller model with sufficient test-time compute can outperform a 14-times-larger model in flops-matched evaluation, at least on problems where the smaller model has a nontrivial success rate. This suggests that test-time and pre-training compute are partially interchangeable: Organizations can compensate for smaller models by investing more in inference-time search, though the trade-off has limits.

This combination of learned evaluation with systematic search can solve problems beyond the reach of single-pass generation. A problem that the model would fail in direct generation may become solvable when the model can explore multiple reasoning paths, backtrack from dead ends, and focus on the most promising directions. The trade-off is computational cost, as search requires generating and evaluating many more tokens than single-pass generation. The economics work when problems are valuable enough to justify the additional compute, single-pass generation is unreliable, or correctness matters more than response time. For complex reasoning tasks where getting the right answer justifies the cost, search with PRM guidance represents a significant capability advance over pure generation.

INFERENCE ECONOMICS AND THE WORLD OF TOMORROW

Current reasoning models operate with an artificial ceiling: Inference economics, not capability, limits the amount of time they can think. Providers constrain reasoning chain lengths to keep context sizes manageable, inference costs sustainable, and user experience mostly bearable for the volume of users they serve.

The way this is implemented is still in flux. The first approach was *predispositional*; this is the test-time scaling switch that allows various preset reasoning lengths to be selected at inference time. In the second, *interventional* approach, introduced by ChatGPT in late 2025, users can simply cut short reasoning. Ultimately, both reflect the time limitation of test-time inference.

This constraint creates strategic asymmetry. Whoever deploys better inference infrastructure first—more efficient attention, cheaper memory, faster GPUs—can offer longer reasoning chains at the same price point. The capability is latent, but the bottleneck is economic. Think of it like early AlphaGo: Stripped of search during inference, its playing strength dropped by more than 2,000 Elo.[181] The same dynamics apply here: Reasoning models with truncated thinking are performing below their potential ceiling.

For practitioners, this means two things. First, the reasoning capability you observe in current products understates what the underlying models can do with more compute. It's not the state of the art; it's the state of the affordable. Second, as inference becomes cheaper, expect discontinuous capability jumps as models are allowed to think longer. Plan accordingly, as systems designed around current reasoning limits may underutilize models whose constraints are relaxed.

Trust but Verify: Learning from Verifiable Rewards

Some domains offer a rare gift: unambiguous ground truth. A proof either verifies or it does not, and code either passes tests or it fails. These domains enable training at scale without human annotation, with feedback loops that run at computational speed rather than human speed.

Machines That Check Your Proofs

For domains with formal semantics, a model can verify reasoning against ground truth rather than relying on learned evaluation. This is a profound advantage, as the verifier provides an objective, infallible standard that makes training signal unambiguous. Proof assistants like Lean 4 or Coq can check mathematical proofs, rejecting any step that does not follow from axioms and prior established results. There is no question of whether the verifier made a mistake in evaluation, as there might be with a learned reward model or human annotator. Compilers and interpreters verify code correctness by executing programs and checking outputs against specifications. Logical satisfiability solvers can check whether logical reasoning is valid.

Training against formal verification provides this unambiguous signal at scale. A model can generate many proof attempts, submit each to the proof assistant, and receive definitive feedback about which proofs are valid. The feedback loop runs at computational speed rather than human speed, enabling training on millions of examples that would take centuries to manually annotate. The model learns not just to produce plausible reasoning but to produce reasoning that works, as verified by the formal system. This is a higher standard than other approaches can achieve; plausible is not good enough when the verifier will reject anything that does not rigorously follow.

The most dramatic demonstration of this principle came in July 2024 with Google DeepMind's IMO-winning Alphaproof, as mentioned earlier.[179] The system combined three components: a proof network pre-trained on roughly 300 billion tokens of code and mathematical text, SFT on approximately 300,000 state-tactic pairs from human-written proofs in Lean's Mathlib library, and AlphaZero-style RL where the solver searched for proofs or disproofs while progressively training itself on harder problems. A fine-tuned Gemini model handled the critical auto-formalization step, translating natural-language problem statements into Lean's formal language. Starting from about 2,500 seed problems, this system generated roughly 80 million formalized problems for self-training. AlphaProof solved three of six International Mathematical Olympiad problems, including problem 6 (a number theory problem so difficult that only 5 of 609 human contestants scored full marks on it), scoring 28 out of 42 points combined with AlphaGeometry 2. The gold medal threshold was 29 points, one point away.

There is a caveat, however: The hardest problems required extraordinary compute. AlphaProof needed two to three days and hundreds of TPU-days per hard problem, generating millions of problem variants and training specialist agents from scratch on each narrow curriculum. This test-time RL strategy trades compute for capability at a rate that is currently impractical for routine applications. The significance lies not in everyday deployment but in the proof of concept: Formal verification combined with search-based RL can produce genuine mathematical reasoning at the frontier of human capability.

The approach produces models with high reliability in verifiable domains and, intriguingly, appears to transfer to related domains that lack formal verification. Models trained heavily on verified mathematical reasoning show improved performance on problems that cannot be formally verified, suggesting that the rigorous reasoning skills developed through verification generalize beyond their training context. If this transfer proves robust across domains, it suggests a powerful training strategy: Develop reasoning capability through intense training on verifiable problems, then apply the resulting skills to problems that resist formal verification. The verifiable domain serves as a training ground for reasoning skills that ultimately prove useful more broadly.

Tests as Truth

Code execution provides a particularly accessible form of verification with immediate practical applicability. If generated code runs correctly on test cases, producing expected outputs from specified inputs, the reasoning that produced it was valid. This is verification that any organization with programming infrastructure can implement, with no exotic proof assistants required—just the ability to execute code in sandboxed environments. The ubiquity of code execution makes it a practical foundation for large-scale reasoning training.

DeepSeek-R1 made code execution a central pillar of its training regime, demonstrating what this looks like at scale.[30] For coding tasks, the model generates candidate solutions, a compiler executes the generated code against a battery of unit tests, and a binary 0/1 reward signal (fail/pass) feeds back into the GRPO training loop. No learned reward model is needed for these domains, as the compiler is the reward model. The resulting system achieved a Codeforces Elo rating of 2,029, outperforming 96.3 percent of human participants on that competitive programming platform. The TÜLU 3 post-training pipeline takes a similar approach with what it calls *reinforcement learning with verifiable rewards (RLVR)*, using deterministic verification functions in place of learned reward models.[29] For math problems, the final number is extracted and compared to the ground-truth answer. For instruction-following tasks, verification is deterministic format checking against specified constraints. In both cases, the key insight is the same: Where objective verification is possible, learned reward models are unnecessary and potentially counterproductive. Deterministic verifiers cannot be hacked, cannot drift, and provide perfectly consistent signal.

Training models to reason through code solves problems by writing and executing programs rather than by reasoning in natural language alone. A mathematical problem might be solved by writing a program that computes the answer, and a logical puzzle might be addressed through code that enumerates possibilities and identifies solutions. The execution results provide automatic verification. Code that produces the right answer reflects valid reasoning, while code that fails or produces wrong answers reflects errors that training should correct. Self-debugging extends this approach to iterative improvement. When execution fails, the model examines the error message and the code, identifies the likely cause, and attempts a correction. This cycle can repeat until execution succeeds, demonstrating not just the ability to write code but the ability to reason about failures and fix them.

Code-based reasoning is powerful for problems that can be expressed computationally, which encompasses a surprisingly broad range of reasoning tasks. Many mathematical, logical, and analytical problems that seem to require verbal reasoning can be reformulated as computational problems with verifiable solutions. The approach provides training signal at scale without human annotation, limited only by the ability to formulate problems as code tasks and to safely execute the resulting solutions. For organizations that can create computational formulations of their reasoning problems, code-based training offers a path to reliable reasoning capability that scales with compute rather than with human annotation capacity.

> **FROM THE TRENCHES: CODE AS REASONING GROUND TRUTH**
>
> I have found code execution to be the most practical verification system for general-purpose reasoning training. You do not need exotic proof assistants or domain-specific verification infrastructure—just the ability to run Python safely. Reformulate reasoning problems as coding problems where possible: "write a function that solves this puzzle" rather than "reason through this puzzle." The test suite becomes your reward signal, and you can generate unlimited training data.
>
> One interesting fact is that many things can be abstracted to code. This is the true power behind the expansion of code assistants to general-purpose tasks. We might be tempted to consider code to be a formal programming language, but in fact, any structured process with a consistent internal logic is a suitable application target. A muffin recipe generator can be just as formally verifiable as a coding agent for C++. Sometimes a good data definition and a mini-domain-specific language to describe the internal logic of the process is all it takes to turn cookery into verifiable reasoning.

The Road to Mathematical Rigor

Mathematical theorem proving represents perhaps the purest form of verifiable reasoning. A proof is either valid or it is not. There is no partial credit for almost-valid reasoning, no subjectivity in evaluation, no ambiguity about whether the reasoning succeeds. The proof assistant, whether Lean 4, Coq, Isabelle, or another formal system, either accepts the proof or rejects it with an indication of where validation failed. This binary, objective feedback provides training signal of a quality that other domains cannot match.

The ecosystem that makes this practical has matured rapidly. Lean 4's Mathlib library, the community-maintained formalization of mathematics, now contains more than 210,000 theorems and 100,000 definitions covering algebra, analysis, topology, measure theory, category theory, and number theory, among other fields. This provides both a training corpus of verified proofs and a target language for model-generated proofs. Tools like LeanDojo provide programmatic interfaces for extracting training data and interacting with Lean at scale, while newer systems like Kimina Lean Server optimize verification throughput for RL training loops, achieving up to 100 proofs per second on large CPU clusters. The infrastructure is no longer hypothetical; it is operational.

Training on proof generation for formal mathematics, with proof assistants providing verification, produces models that can construct genuinely novel proofs. The training regime is conceptually simple: Present theorems to be proved, let the model generate proof attempts, submit attempts to the proof assistant, and provide reward signal based on verification outcomes. In practice, the technique requires substantial infrastructure for managing proof assistant interactions, representing formal mathematical objects in formats models can work with, and generating appropriate training problems at various difficulty levels.

DeepSeek-Prover exemplifies the progression. Its first version achieved 46.3 percent on the miniF2F benchmark (a standard test suite for formal theorem proving) with 64 attempts per problem. Version 1.5 added RL from proof assistant feedback, using the binary success/failure signal from Lean 4 directly as the reward, reaching 63.5 percent. Version 2, built on a 671-billion-parameter base and incorporating subgoal decomposition (used by the model to decompose complex theorems into manageable lemmas before proving each), pushed the state of the art to 88.9 percent. These are not incremental improvements; they represent a qualitative shift in the achievements of automated proving.

The infrastructure challenges are nontrivial, and while cheap, verifiable rewards sound good, the reality is that running a proof assistant inside an RL training loop creates a fundamental bottleneck: Verification is CPU-bound, while model generation is GPU-bound. One training campaign for a step-level prover consumed approximately 21,000 CPU-days, with a GPU-to-CPU time ratio of roughly 1:11. Lean's import initialization (loading Mathlib into memory for each proof attempt) and tactic elaboration (type-checking and unification) are the core bottlenecks. The models also face what practitioners call the *last mile* problem: Models frequently generate proofs that are almost right but fail on edge cases, type-checking, or tactic compatibility. A proof that is 95 percent correct is, in formal mathematics, 100 percent wrong.

Transfer from formal to informal mathematics is imperfect but significant. Models trained extensively on formal proofs show improved performance on informal mathematical reasoning, such as solving competition mathematics problems stated in natural language. The transfer suggests that the rigorous reasoning skills developed through formal verification are not narrowly specific to formal systems but include more general mathematical reasoning capabilities that apply to informal problems as well. Recent work has shown that formal verification can also be used at inference time to select among informally generated solutions: Translate candidate answers into formal statements, attempt proofs, and use the verification result to pick the most likely correct answer. This hybrid approach, using formalization as a filter rather than as the sole generation method, achieves accuracy improvements of up to 8 percent on competition mathematics benchmarks while requiring far less compute than full formal proof generation. As formal mathematics libraries grow and more of mathematics becomes available in machine-verifiable form, both training and inference approaches become increasingly practical for developing broad mathematical reasoning capability.

Domain-Specific Reasoning

Not all reasoning follows the same patterns. Legal reasoning draws on authority and precedent, clinical reasoning generates and tests diagnostic hypotheses, and financial reasoning combines quantitative rigor with qualitative judgment. Each domain has conventions developed over decades or centuries that training must capture.

Legal Reasoning

One of the first things every law student is taught is a particular form of reasoning known as *IRAC*: issue, rule, application, conclusion. This reflects an underlying logic of legal practice—namely, the application of authorities (case law, statute, sometimes other norms) to a fact pattern. This is in many ways a good starting point for the reasoning characteristics expected of language models in the legal space. Research has shown that prompts structured around IRAC outperform generic chain-of-thought prompting on legal entailment tasks, improving accuracy from roughly 70 percent to over 81 percent on the Competition on Legal Information Extraction and Entailment (COLIEE) benchmark (based on the Japanese Bar Exam). The structure works because it maps naturally to the way legal analysis proceeds: Identify the legal question, state the applicable rule, apply the rule to the facts, and draw a conclusion. Training data demonstrates that this pattern explicitly produces models whose legal reasoning is more structured and more likely to cite the correct authorities.

One key issue is that legal reasoning does have a degree of subjectivity. A degree of ambiguity exists at times as to what exactly a particular decision's holding is, or applies to, for instance. A good deal of appellate litigation is about arguing whether a certain authority should not hold for a particular instance (in legal parlance, whether it should be *distinguished*). This adversarial nature of legal reasoning makes it fundamentally different from mathematical or scientific reasoning, which typically results in one correct answer. In law, both sides construct valid-sounding arguments from the same facts and the same authorities. Models must learn not just to reason toward a conclusion but to reason within a framework where reasonable people disagree, the strength of an argument depends on jurisdiction and precedent hierarchy, and the same term can carry different meanings in different legal systems. Binding authority (a ruling from a higher court in the same jurisdiction) carries more weight than persuasive authority (a ruling from a court in a different jurisdiction), and models that do not respect this hierarchy produce analysis that practicing lawyers immediately recognize as naive.

The stakes of getting legal reasoning wrong were made vivid by *Mata v. Avianca* in 2023, when attorneys filed a brief containing at least six entirely fabricated judicial opinions generated by ChatGPT.[182] The fictitious cases included fake quotes, fake internal citations, and were attributed to real judges. What made the case particularly instructive was the failure cascade: When opposing counsel informed the court that the cited cases could not be located, the attorneys initially continued to advocate for them. One attorney later testified that he had asked ChatGPT whether the cases were real, and ChatGPT affirmed they were. The resulting $5,000 sanction was modest; the reputational damage was not.

The case was not an isolated incident. By late 2025, a database tracking AI hallucination cases in courts had cataloged more than 900 instances. Dahl et al. conducted a systematic study of legal hallucination across four models, finding that even GPT-4, the best performer, hallucinated on at least 58 percent of queries about random federal court cases.[25] Llama 2 hallucinated at approximately 88 percent. For the hardest tasks, such as identifying a case's central holding, hallucination rates exceeded 75 percent across all models tested. Critically, the models could not reliably predict when they were hallucinating, exhibiting poor calibration between confidence and accuracy.

These hallucination rates highlight a structural challenge for legal reasoning that other domains do not share to the same degree. Legal reasoning requires temporal awareness (the law changes over time, and practitioners must know which version of a statute applies to a given set of facts), jurisdictional specificity (the same legal term can carry different meanings in different jurisdictions), and a grasp of precedent dynamics (knowing not just what a case held, but whether it has been overruled, distinguished, or limited by subsequent decisions). The latter is not necessarily a falsifiable hard question. Each of these dimensions creates opportunities for plausible-sounding but incorrect reasoning that nonexperts cannot detect. A model that generates fluent legal analysis with the wrong version of a statute or that cites a case since overruled produces output that is arguably more dangerous than no output at all, because it creates false confidence.

Clinical Reasoning

Clinical reasoning, the diagnostic process by which physicians interpret symptoms and findings to reach diagnoses, follows structured patterns that medical education has codified over decades. The process begins with gathering the patient's history and present complaint, then generating a differential diagnosis: a ranked list of possible diagnoses that could explain the observed symptoms. Hypothesis testing follows, with examinations and investigations chosen to distinguish among the differential possibilities. As evidence accumulates, the clinician updates probability estimates for each diagnosis, a process that resembles Bayesian inference even when not explicitly formalized as such. Eventually, the evidence supports one diagnosis sufficiently to guide treatment. It is worth noting that therapeutic and diagnostic reasoning are conceptually different too: Therapeutic reasoning is about identifying a course of action that will achieve a desired result, while diagnostic reasoning aims to find potential causal pathological entities to account for the patient's symptoms.

Training for clinical reasoning requires data that demonstrates these patterns, showing how expert clinicians move from presentation to differential to diagnosis through structured reasoning. Ideally, training data includes the reasoning traces of expert clinicians: not just their final diagnoses but the thought process that led there, including the alternatives they considered, the evidence they sought, and the way they weighted different findings. Such data is difficult to obtain because clinicians rarely document their reasoning in such detail, but even partial demonstrations of clinical reasoning patterns can improve model capability. In some cases, online medical advice portals have been leveraged to create large training datasets. These are often of quite dubious quality.

The stakes are high, as incorrect clinical reasoning can harm patients, whether through missed diagnoses that delay treatment, misdiagnoses that lead to inappropriate treatment, or unnecessary testing that causes harm directly or through the cascade of follow-up investigations. Validation is therefore particularly important and must involve clinical expertise. A model that produces reasoning that sounds medical but that trained clinicians would recognize as flawed is dangerous precisely because nonexperts cannot detect its errors. Collaboration with medical educators and clinicians is essential for both creating effective training data and evaluating model capability. The clinical reasoning skills that take years to develop in human practitioners cannot be adequately assessed by those who lack them.

Reasoning in Finance

Financial reasoning combines quantitative precision with qualitative judgment in ways that make it a particularly demanding domain for ML. The quantitative elements are substantial, as financial analysis involves arithmetic, statistics, time-value-of-money calculations, risk metrics, and ratio analysis that must be correctly performed. But correctness alone does not constitute good financial reasoning. The qualitative elements matter equally, including interpreting the meaning of numbers in context, assessing risk factors that resist quantification, judging whether historical patterns will continue, and communicating conclusions with appropriate confidence, given inherent uncertainty.

Training for financial reasoning requires data demonstrating this combination of quantitative rigor and qualitative judgment. Examples should show proper financial analysis techniques applied correctly, with calculations that would pass the scrutiny of trained financial professionals. They should also demonstrate appropriate hedging of uncertainty, since financial conclusions are rarely certain and good reasoning acknowledges the conditions under which conclusions might not hold. Regulatory compliance adds another dimension, because financial advice and analysis must conform to applicable rules, and training data should reflect these constraints. The combination of technical, judgmental, and regulatory elements makes financial reasoning training complex to design and execute.

Models trained for financial reasoning must be evaluated not just on analytical correctness but on the appropriateness of conclusions, given uncertainty and risk. A model that reaches correct conclusions with excessive confidence is dangerous, while a model that hedges every statement into meaninglessness is useless. The right balance depends on context, as some financial communications require precision, while others must acknowledge unknowns. Evaluation must assess this contextual appropriateness alongside technical accuracy. Domain experts are essential for this evaluation because appropriateness in financial reasoning is itself a domain-specific judgment that nonexperts cannot reliably make.

The Limits of Neural Reasoning

Where does learned reasoning break down? Current models struggle with compositional generalization: applying known patterns in novel combinations and to tasks that exceed the complexity seen in training. Understanding these limits helps set realistic expectations and identify where tool augmentation becomes necessary.

The Compositionality Wall

A model that can reliably solve problems requiring three reasoning steps may fail at problems requiring five, even when each individual step is well within its capability. A model that has seen many problems combining two operations may fail when asked to combine four, despite knowing each operation well. These failures are not random errors but systematic limitations that appear whenever models must compose familiar elements in unfamiliar configurations. They reflect a limitation inherent in much of learned reasoning that might strike humans as rather odd; after all, we do not typically lose reasoning performance when we tackle a longer string of subproblems we can easily solve.

This limitation reflects fundamental aspects of the way neural networks learn and generalize, not merely insufficient training data. The same limitation appears across model sizes, training data volumes, and training techniques. Adding more training data helps at the margins but does not eliminate the compositionality gap. Models appear to learn patterns at the length and complexity of their training examples rather than learning the underlying rules that would enable arbitrary composition. A model trained on three-step proofs does not simply learn "how to do proof steps" but rather learns "how to do three-step proofs," and the knowledge does not straightforwardly extend to longer chains.

Understanding these limitations helps set realistic expectations for the potential achievements of trained reasoning. Problems that require lengthy reasoning chains, combine familiar elements in novel ways, or push beyond the complexity seen in training are likely to cause failures even in otherwise capable models. For such problems, external tools may provide what pure neural reasoning cannot: calculators that ensure arithmetic correctness regardless of chain length, knowledge bases that verify facts the model might confuse, and verification systems that check conclusions rather than trusting the model's internal reasoning. The art lies in identifying which problems are within neural reasoning's competence and which require augmentation.

When to Call for Help

Certain cognitive tasks that humans find trivial remain stubbornly difficult for neural networks regardless of scale or training sophistication. The ubiquitous example is counting letters. Tokenization makes counting the letter *r* in *strawberry* nontrivial, but a single Python one-liner can trivially yield the right result. Knowledge retrieval poses similar challenges, as a model may confuse dates, misremember names, or hallucinate facts that sound plausible but are simply wrong. Formal verification is perhaps the starkest case, because determining whether a logical argument is valid requires checking that each step follows necessarily from prior steps, a task that admits no approximation and tolerates no errors. These limitations are not bugs to be fixed but fundamental characteristics of the way neural networks process information.

Tool augmentation addresses these limitations by delegating to external systems the tasks that neural reasoning handles poorly while preserving the model's role in tasks where it excels. A calculator ensures arithmetic correctness regardless of problem complexity, so the model need not compute but only recognize when computation is needed and interpret results. Knowledge bases provide reliable facts that the model can query rather than recall, eliminating hallucination for any fact the knowledge base contains. Proof assistants verify logical steps with mathematical certainty, catching errors that would escape any amount of neural self-verification. The model orchestrates these tools, determining when to invoke each and how to integrate their outputs into coherent reasoning, while the tools provide guarantees that the model alone cannot offer. The techniques for training effective tool use covered in Chapter 9 become essential when reasoning capability is the goal.

This hybrid architecture, neural reasoning augmented by formal tools, combines the flexibility of learned systems with the reliability of formal ones. The model handles the open-ended aspects of reasoning: understanding problem statements, decomposing complex questions, recognizing which tools are relevant, and synthesizing results into coherent conclusions. The tools handle the aspects where reliability matters and approximation is unacceptable. The result is a system more capable than either component alone, more flexible than pure formal systems because the neural component handles natural language and ambiguity, and more reliable than pure neural systems because the formal tools ensure correctness where it matters most. Training for effective tool use, covered in earlier chapters, becomes essential when reasoning capability is the goal. Models must learn not just to generate reasoning chains but to recognize when those chains require external verification and how to incorporate tool results into their ongoing reasoning.

What We Still Cannot Do

The limitations we have discussed are not permanent features of AI but current characteristics of a rapidly evolving field. Research continues across multiple fronts toward more capable reasoning systems. Neurosymbolic approaches attempt to integrate neural networks with symbolic reasoning systems, combining the pattern-recognition strengths of neural networks with the logical rigor of symbolic AI. These hybrid systems represent knowledge explicitly in structured forms that support formal manipulation while using neural components to handle perception, natural language, and the fuzzy reasoning that symbolic systems handle poorly. The integration remains difficult, with many proposed approaches showing promise in limited domains but without yet achieving the generality that would make them practical for broad deployment.

Architectural innovations target compositionality specifically, designing network structures that encourage learning reusable reasoning primitives rather than memorizing surface patterns. Attention mechanisms that can dynamically bind variables, memory systems that support structured storage and retrieval, and modular architectures where different components handle different aspects of reasoning all aim to produce systems that generalize more compositionally than standard transformers. None has yet definitively solved the compositionality challenge, but the trajectory of research suggests that architectural advances will continue to improve reasoning capability in ways that pure scaling cannot achieve.

Practitioners must also contend with a more mundane but equally important limitation: the reproducibility problem. As noted previously, Yuan et al. demonstrated that under `bfloat16` precision with greedy decoding, a reasoning model like DeepSeek-R1-Distill-Qwen-7B exhibits up to 9 percent variation in accuracy and 9,000 tokens of difference in response length when system configuration (batch size, GPU count, GPU generation) changes because of the nonassociative nature of floating-point arithmetic.[17] For any deployment requiring auditable or reproducible reasoning, such as legal analysis, medical diagnosis, or financial reporting, the choice of numerical precision becomes a design constraint that affects the trustworthiness of the system's output.

Finally, the "reasoning tax" on inference cost deserves candid assessment. Extended chain-of-thought reasoning significantly increases computational cost and latency. Reasoning models generate thousands of tokens of internal deliberation even for simple queries, and longer chains do not always improve performance: Once reasoning length exceeds the model's effective capacity, accuracy decreases because of error propagation and noise accumulation. This has motivated work on hybrid reasoning that automatically decides whether to engage extended thinking based on query complexity. But the broader point is that reasoning capability is not free. Organizations adopting reasoning models must account for inference costs that may be an order of magnitude higher than standard models for the same query, and must design systems that route appropriately between reasoning and non-reasoning models based on task difficulty.

For practitioners, the implication is to build on currently available techniques while remaining prepared to adopt improved methods as they mature. The techniques in this chapter, chain-of-thought training, PRMs, formal verification, and tool augmentation, represent the current state of the art and will remain relevant even as better methods emerge. They form a foundation that more advanced techniques will extend rather than replace. Organizations that develop capability in these areas position themselves to quickly adopt future advances. The infrastructure for generating training data, training reward models, integrating verification, and deploying reasoning-capable systems will serve regardless of which specific techniques prove most effective. The field moves fast, but principled investment in reasoning capability will retain value through whatever advances the next years bring.

Summary

These reasoning techniques build on the foundations established earlier and, in many ways, are seen as the culmination of those techniques. Looking ahead, the remaining chapters address increasingly specialized frontiers: multimodal understanding, deployment at scale, and the safety considerations that responsible reasoning deployment demands.

PART IV

THE FRONTIER

11

SYNTHETIC TRAINING: SELF-PLAY AND GENERATED DATA

The constraint that has limited post-training since its inception is data: High-quality examples require expert time, preference judgments require consistent annotators, and evaluation requires expensive human review. Synthetic data generation relaxes this constraint by using AI systems to create training data. In self-play, models compete against themselves. In RLAIF, typically different models act as annotators. Finally, in procedural generation, AI creates training examples as necessary.

The shift from scarce human labor to abundant computation fundamentally changes what techniques become feasible, enabling training at scales that human annotation could never support. This chapter examines the revolution in synthetic training: how to use AI systems as data generators and evaluators, build pipelines that create synthetic training data at scale, and validate that synthetically trained models generalize to real-world tasks. We address the risks and limitations that make synthetic data treacherous when used carelessly, from distribution mismatch to model collapse.

For organizations constrained by annotation budgets or operating in domains where expert time is prohibitively expensive, synthetic methods offer a path forward, provided they are used with appropriate caution and validation.

Why Synthetic Data Changes Everything

The ML community's thinking on synthetic data has fundamentally changed over recent years, and a long-standing prejudice against synthetic data is showing gradual signs of easing up. This section examines the impact of synthetic data on post-training, how such synthetic data is obtained, and the concern of synthetic data merely amplifying preexisting noise in the dataset.

The Only Test That Matters

The prejudice against synthetic data runs deep in the ML community, an inheritance from earlier eras when model-generated data was visibly inferior to human-produced examples. This prejudice deserves re-examination. The question is not whether synthetic data is "as good as" human data in some abstract sense but whether it serves its purpose for training. At the scale on which we operate, data that improves model performance is good data, and data that degrades performance is bad data. Origin matters only insofar as it predicts effectiveness. Empirical evaluation, not a priori assumptions about data sources, should drive decisions about synthetic data use.

Quality assessment for synthetic data proceeds along several dimensions. Correctness asks whether the data contains accurate information: Are facts correct, are calculations right, do examples demonstrate what they purport to demonstrate? Diversity asks whether the data covers the relevant space: Do examples span the range of inputs the model will encounter, or do they cluster in limited regions? Naturalness asks whether the data resembles realistic deployment conditions: Do the queries, tasks, and response styles match user requests? A synthetic dataset might score highly on correctness while failing on diversity, producing data that is accurate but repetitive. Another might achieve diversity while sacrificing correctness, producing varied but unreliable examples. All three dimensions matter for training effectiveness.

Assessment methods range from automated metrics to human evaluation. Automated approaches can measure diversity through embedding distances or *n*-gram statistics, detect certain correctness failures through verification, and flag obvious quality issues through learned classifiers. Human evaluation provides ground truth that automated metrics approximate but cannot fully capture: A human reviewer can assess whether an example feels natural, whether reasoning is genuinely valid rather than superficially plausible, and whether the example would be useful for training. The practical approach combines automated metrics for scale with human evaluation for calibration, using humans to validate that automated metrics correspond to quality rather than merely to measurable proxies. The key insight is that synthetic data should be evaluated empirically based on its effects on model performance and should be improved iteratively based on what evaluation reveals.

Generation Strategies, Simple to Complex

The simplest generation strategy is prompt-based: Provide a capable model with a task description and let it generate examples. "Generate 10 questions about machine learning and their answers" produces 10 question-answer pairs. This approach is straightforward and requires minimal infrastructure, making it accessible to any organization with API access to capable models. The limitation is that the model's notion of what constitutes good examples may not match training needs. Generated examples may cluster around common patterns, miss edge cases, or fail to represent the diversity that training requires.

Iterative refinement improves upon simple generation by adding critique and revision stages. An initial generation is produced, then evaluated (by the same model, a different model, or automated checks), and the evaluation identifies weaknesses to address. A revision pass addresses the identified weaknesses, producing an improved version. Multiple rounds of critique and revision can yield examples substantially better than first-pass generation would produce. The cost is additional inference compute for each refinement round, and the benefit diminishes as initial generations improve. Eventually, refinement produces marginal improvements that do not justify the compute cost.

More sophisticated strategies combine multiple techniques into generation pipelines. Ensemble approaches generate examples from multiple models, increasing diversity by capturing different models' tendencies and combining their outputs. Verification steps filter generated data, keeping only examples that pass automated checks for correctness, consistency, or format compliance. Augmentation techniques create variations of generated examples: paraphrasing to create alternative phrasings, substituting entities to create analogous examples, or perturbing inputs to create challenging variations. Curriculum approaches generate examples of increasing difficulty, starting with simple cases and progressing to complex ones that build on earlier examples. The right combination of techniques depends on the task, the available compute budget, and the quality requirements. Sophisticated pipelines justify their complexity only when simpler approaches prove insufficient.

Several landmark techniques have shaped the way the field approaches synthetic data generation, and understanding them provides a vocabulary for designing custom pipelines:

Self-Instruct[183]

This approach demonstrated that models can bootstrap their own instruction-following capability. It starts from a small seed set of manually written instructions, then iteratively generates new instructions, inputs, and outputs from the model itself. After filtering out low-quality or overly similar examples, the newly generated data is used to fine-tune the model, and the cycle repeats.

When applied to vanilla GPT-3, Self-Instruct produced a 33 percent absolute improvement on Super-NaturalInstructions, approaching the performance of InstructGPT, which had been trained with expensive private human annotations. The technique's elegance lies in its near-zero annotation cost; a seed set of 175 manually written tasks was sufficient to generate 52,000 instructions. Self-Instruct revealed that the boundary between "trained model" and "training data source" could be productively blurred.

Evol-Instruct[184]

This technique took a different approach to the diversity problem. Rather than generating instructions from scratch, it evolves existing instructions into more complex variants through a series of LLM-driven transformations: adding constraints, deepening reasoning requirements, introducing rare topics, or making the task more concrete. Starting from simple instructions and applying these evolutionary operations recursively produces a dataset whose complexity distribution spans a much wider range than direct generation achieves.

The resulting model, WizardLM, outperformed ChatGPT on complex tasks according to human evaluators, despite being trained on a fraction of the data. The key insight is that complexity is itself a dimension worth optimizing: Models trained on uniformly simple synthetic data handle simple queries well but struggle with the complex, multi-constraint requests that production deployments receive.

Persona Hub[185]

This addressed the diversity problem through persona-driven generation. It constructed a collection of 1 billion diverse personas automatically curated from web data, each representing a distinct perspective or area of expertise. When generating synthetic data, the system conditions on a specific persona, producing outputs that reflect that perspective's knowledge, concerns, and communication style. A persona described as a climate scientist generates different questions than one described as a small business owner, even when both are asked to generate questions about energy policy.

The approach addresses a fundamental limitation of naive generation: Models tend to produce outputs reflecting a narrow "default" perspective, clustering around the most common patterns in their training data. By explicitly conditioning on diverse personas, the method distributes generation across the full space of perspectives the model has learned, producing datasets that cover regions that unconditional generation would miss. Experiments showed that a 7B model fine-tuned on persona-driven synthetic math problems achieved 64.9 percent on the MATH benchmark, matching the performance of GPT-4 Turbo.

Magpie[186]

This introduced a remarkably simple mechanism for generating alignment data: Feed an instruction-tuned model its own pre-query template (the system prompt and user message prefix, but nothing else), and let it hallucinate a plausible user query. Then send that query back to the model to generate a response. The method exploits the fact that instruction-tuned models have internalized a distribution over likely user messages, and this distribution can be sampled directly.

Models fine-tuned on 4 million Magpie-generated instruction-response pairs performed comparably to the official Llama-3-8B-Instruct, despite the latter being trained on 10 million carefully curated data points. The technique requires no prompt engineering, no seed data, and no external model—only the target model itself and its chat template.

Textbooks Are All You Need[83]

Pioneered by Microsoft's Phi model series, this approach demonstrated that synthetic data quality could compensate dramatically for quantity. Rather than generating raw instruction-response pairs, the Phi approach synthesizes structured educational content: textbooks, exercises, and worked examples designed to teach specific reasoning skills. The resulting phi-1 model, trained on just 7 billion tokens (6 billion from curated web sources plus 1 billion synthetically generated), achieved 50.6 percent on HumanEval for code generation, competitive with models trained on orders of magnitude more data.

Cosmopedia, an open reproduction of this philosophy, generated 25 billion tokens of synthetic textbooks, blog posts, and stories using Mixtral-8x7B-Instruct, requiring more than 10,000 GPU-hours of generation compute.[187] The same seed content was rephrased across multiple styles and audience levels (children's textbooks, undergraduate lectures, graduate seminars), producing naturally diverse perspectives on each topic. A 1B parameter model trained on Cosmopedia outperformed TinyLlama 1.1B on several benchmarks despite the latter being trained on far more data.

WRAP[188]

Web rephrase augmented pre-training takes yet another approach, using an instruction-tuned model to rephrase raw web documents into structured formats: "like Wikipedia," "in question-answer format," "simplified for a general audience," or "as a technical explanation." Training jointly on real web data and its rephrased variants accelerated pre-training by approximately three times and improved perplexity by more than 10 percent on average across subsets of the Pile. In specific domains like arXiv and Hacker News, rephrased data reduced perplexity by nearly three times compared to training on the original text alone. The insight is that the same factual content, presented in clearer structure, teaches a model more efficiently than the noisy original.

When to choose which strategy is often a matter of practical judgment, but the comparison in Table 11-1 offers a helpful point of departure.

Table 11-1: Comparing Synthetic Data Generation Strategies

Strategy	Approach	Strengths	Limitations
Prompt-based	Generate directly from task description	Minimal infrastructure; fast start	Limited diversity; may miss edge cases
Iterative refinement	Critique and revise generated examples	Higher quality per example	Additional compute cost per example
Ensemble	Generate from multiple models	Increased diversity	Higher total generation cost
Verification	Filter with automated checks	High reliability for checked properties	Catches only what can be verified
Constitutional	Revise against explicit principles	Scalable alignment signal	Depends on constitution quality
Self-play	Generate from a pair of adversarial models	Robust to attacks; diverse	Complex to implement correctly
Self-Instruct	Generate instructions, then implement them	Near-zero annotation cost	Quality bounded by model capability
Evol-Instruct	Evolve instructions toward complexity	Wide complexity distribution	Evolution may drift from useful tasks
Persona driven	Condition generation on diverse personas	Excellent diversity coverage	Requires large persona collection
Textbook synthesis	Generate structured educational content	High quality per token trained	Expensive generation compute

The Separation of Signal from Noise

Raw synthetic data typically contains examples ranging from excellent to unusable, and filtering separates the wheat from the chaff. The return on filtering is often substantial: A dataset reduced to its best half may produce better training outcomes than the full dataset, as low-quality examples contribute noise that harms learning. The challenge is identifying which examples belong in each category, a task that requires quality signals accurate enough to distinguish genuinely good examples from merely plausible ones.

Quality scoring uses models to assess generated examples and assign scores that enable filtering. A capable model can evaluate whether an example is well-formed, reasoning is valid, the response appropriately addresses the query, and the overall quality meets threshold requirements. Examples below the threshold are discarded or flagged for revision. Deduplication removes near-identical examples that add bulk without adding information. Training on many similar examples wastes compute and may bias the model toward overrepresented patterns. Consistency checking identifies examples that contradict each other, a signal that at least one contains errors. Inconsistent examples can be removed or flagged for manual review. Verification keeps only examples that pass automated checks: code that executes correctly, calculations that produce right answers, claims that can be confirmed against knowledge bases.

The filtering threshold trades quantity against quality. Aggressive filtering produces a smaller dataset of higher average quality, while lenient filtering produces a larger dataset with more noise. The optimal threshold depends on how the data will be used and how sensitive training is to quality. For SFT, where models learn directly from examples, quality matters greatly, and aggressive filtering typically pays off. For RL, where reward signals can correct for some data noise, lenient filtering may be acceptable if it provides more training signal. The right approach is empirical: Try different thresholds, measure training outcomes, and select the threshold that produces the best models rather than the largest or "cleanest" datasets.

When the Model Grades Itself

Can AI replace human annotators? For easily verifiable qualities such as factual accuracy, format compliance, and logical consistency, AI feedback can match or exceed human reliability at vastly greater scale. For subjective qualities, the answer is more nuanced.

Constitutional AI and the Self-Improving Loop

Constitutional AI emerged from the recognition that human feedback, while valuable, scales poorly to the volume of training data that modern systems require.[32] Yet, in its own way, human guidance is indispensable for those peculiarly moral concerns that we collectively term the *ethical* part of alignment. The key insight was that models capable of following instructions could be instructed to evaluate outputs against explicit principles, providing a form of automated alignment that reduces dependence on human annotators. This approach defines a "constitution" of principles the model should follow: be helpful, be harmless, be honest, respect user autonomy, acknowledge uncertainty, and whatever other principles the designers consider important. The model then evaluates its own outputs against these principles and revises them to better comply.

The revision process generates training data at scale. Starting from an initial response, the model critiques that response against the constitution, identifies violations or weaknesses, and produces a revised response that addresses the critique. The revision, judged by the model to be an improvement over the original, becomes a training example. The process can iterate: Revise, critique the revision, and revise again, producing a sequence of increasingly constitutional responses. Training on these revision pairs teaches the model to directly produce constitutional outputs, without requiring the revision process at inference time. The efficiency gain is substantial: One human writing a constitution produces training signal for millions of examples, whereas one human annotating preferences produces training signal for perhaps a hundred examples per day.

The effectiveness of constitutional AI depends on two factors. First, the model must be capable of accurately evaluating outputs against the constitution. A model that cannot reliably identify constitutional violations cannot produce reliable improvements. Second, the constitution must align with human values. A constitution that captures some values while missing others produces models aligned with the constitution rather than with humans. Both factors require care. The evaluating model should be capable enough to correctly apply principles, and the constitution should be developed through thoughtful consideration of values that matter. Ongoing human oversight remains important to verify that constitutional training produces the intended results rather than optimizing for an imperfect proxy of human values.

The Many Faces of AI Feedback

Constitutional evaluation represents one form of AI feedback, but the landscape of AI feedback mechanisms is broader.[189] Pairwise preference judgments ask the evaluating model to compare two responses and select which is better, producing the preference pairs that DPO-style training requires. The evaluating model sees both responses and explains its preference, providing not just a selection but reasoning that can be inspected and validated. This format closely mirrors human preference annotation, enabling AI evaluators to slot into existing training pipelines designed for human feedback.

Scalar quality scores take a different approach, asking the evaluating model to assign a numerical score to each response. These scores can train reward models or filter datasets; responses above a threshold proceed, while those below are discarded or revised. Detailed critiques go further, asking the evaluator to identify specific weaknesses and suggest improvements. The critique format enables SFT on improvements: Pair the original response with its critique-guided revision to teach the model to directly produce better outputs. Verification focuses on specific checkable properties: Are the facts correct, does the logic follow, does the code execute? Verification provides binary signals that enable filtering with high confidence for the verified properties.

The choice of feedback mechanism should match the training approach and the qualities to be optimized. Pairwise judgments suit preference-based training, scalar scores suit reward model training and filtering, critiques suit SFT on improvements, and verification suits domains where automated checking is possible. Multiple mechanisms can combine: Use verification to filter for correctness, then pairwise judgment to rank among correct responses for preference training. The flexibility of AI feedback, which can produce whatever format the training pipeline requires, is part of its value. Unlike human annotators who may resist unfamiliar formats, AI evaluators can be instructed to produce any output format that serves the training need.

The Successes and Failures of RLAIF

The effectiveness of RLAIF varies dramatically across qualities being optimized. For easily verifiable qualities, AI feedback can match or exceed human feedback. Factual accuracy can be checked against knowledge bases, format compliance can be verified against specifications, and logical consistency can be assessed through step-by-step analysis. These qualities can be evaluated relatively easily, and a capable AI evaluator can provide reliable signal at scales no human workforce could match. When the question is whether a response correctly answers a factual query, AI evaluation is often more reliable than human evaluation, which is subject to fatigue, inattention, and the evaluator's own knowledge limitations.

Subjective qualities present greater challenges. Writing style, persuasiveness, humor, empathy, and helpfulness involve judgments that depend on human values, cultural context, and individual preferences. AI evaluators can approximate these judgments based on patterns in their training data, but the approximation may diverge from human preferences in ways that are subtle but consequential. A response that an AI evaluator judges to be helpful may strike humans as off-putting, and a response judged persuasive may seem manipulative. These divergences are not always obvious in individual examples but can accumulate to produce models that optimize for AI-preferred rather than human-preferred qualities. For subjective qualities, AI feedback is useful but must be validated against human judgment.

Hybrid approaches capture benefits of both AI scale and human accuracy. AI feedback provides the bulk of training signal, enabling the scale that pure human feedback cannot achieve. Human evaluation calibrates AI feedback, verifying that AI judgments correspond to human preferences and adjusting where they diverge. The calibration can inform AI evaluator training, producing evaluators better aligned with human judgment. It can identify domains where AI feedback is reliable and others where it requires more oversight. And it can catch failures that purely automated systems would miss. The practical approach uses AI feedback extensively but maintains human oversight sufficient to ensure that the efficiency gains do not come at the cost of training models that optimize for the wrong qualities.

THE RLAIF SUITABILITY TEST

Ask two questions about the quality you want to optimize:

1. Can the evaluating model reliably distinguish better from worse?
2. Does "better by the model's judgment" correspond to "better by human judgment"?

If both answers are yes, RLAIF will work. If either is no, you need human feedback or verification. Thus, RLAIF will often work for matters of factual accuracy. For qualities like persuasiveness or helpfulness, however, you should test empirically before trusting that the model's assessment will coincide with those of a human user.

Models That Learn from Each Other

Can models learn from each other or even from themselves? The insight underlying self-play is that adversarial interaction creates training signal that single-model generation cannot provide. Each side must anticipate and address the other's arguments, producing robustness that monologue cannot achieve.

Learning Through Argument

The debate format pits model instances against each other in structured argumentation, with one instance arguing for a position and another arguing against. The format draws on a long tradition in human institutions, from legal adversarial systems to academic debate, all based on the insight that truth emerges more reliably from contested discourse than from unchallenged assertion.

This training process uses debate transcripts with human judgments of which side argued more convincingly. Models learn both to construct strong arguments and to identify weaknesses in opposing arguments, capabilities that transfer to non-debate contexts. A model trained through debate becomes better at anticipating objections to its claims, stress-testing its own reasoning, and presenting conclusions that withstand scrutiny. The debate format is particularly valuable for complex questions where reasonable people might disagree: The model learns to engage with the full space of arguments rather than anchoring on a single perspective.

Related adversarial approaches extend the insight beyond formal debate. Red-team/blue-team setups pit one model instance (the red team) against another (the blue team), with the red team attempting to elicit harmful behavior and the blue team attempting to resist. Training on these interactions produces models more robust to adversarial attack: Having seen many attempts to elicit harmful outputs during training, the model learns to recognize and resist similar attempts during deployment. Adversarial training can also identify vulnerabilities in model behavior, revealing failure modes that less structured evaluation might miss. The key insight unifying these approaches is that models can learn from each other's attempts to find weaknesses, producing robustness that single-model training cannot achieve.

Using Self-Play as Discriminator Training

Self-play fine-tuning (SPIN) formalizes self-play for language model alignment as a two-player game.[190] The "main player" is the model being trained; the "opponent" is the model from the previous iteration. In each round, the current model must learn to distinguish between responses generated by its previous self and responses written by humans. The training objective pushes the model's output distribution closer to the human data distribution, and the authors prove that this process converges: The global optimum is reached only when the model's policy exactly matches the target distribution.

The practical implications are significant. SPIN requires no external reward model, no preference labels, and no stronger teacher model. It needs only the SFT dataset that was used for initial fine-tuning. In Chen et al.'s research, starting from a model fine-tuned on 50,000 examples from the UltraChat dataset, three iterations of SPIN on Zephyr-7B-SFT improved performance across the Hugging Face Open LLM Leaderboard, MT-Bench, and

BIG-bench tasks, outperforming models trained with DPO supplemented by GPT-4 preference data—a formidable achievement.[190] The result challenges the assumption that preference optimization requires expensive preference annotations. A model competing against its own previous versions can extract substantial additional signal from the same data it was already trained on.

The limitation mirrors the broader self-play challenge: The model can improve only toward the quality of the human reference data. SPIN cannot exceed the ceiling set by its training examples. When the model's distribution already closely matches the human data, further iterations yield diminishing returns. The technique is most valuable in the gap between initial SFT (which often underfits the training distribution) and the quality ceiling of the available data.

Bootstrapping Reasoning from Reasoning

Self-Taught Reasoner (STaR) addresses a specific and important form of synthetic data: chain-of-thought rationales for reasoning tasks.[191] The challenge is that training models to produce step-by-step reasoning typically requires either massive datasets of human-written rationales (expensive) or few-shot prompting alone (which sacrifices accuracy). STaR offers a middle path. Starting from a small number of example rationales, the model generates rationales for a large set of problems, then fine-tunes on the rationales that led to correct answers.

The critical innovation is *rationalization*: When the model fails to solve a problem, it is given the correct answer and asked to generate a rationale that reaches that answer. This rationalization step provides training signal for problems the model cannot yet solve on its own, bootstrapping capability beyond the model's current level. The process iterates; each round of fine-tuning produces a model that can solve more problems, generating more correct rationales for the next round. On CommonsenseQA, STaR achieved performance comparable to a model 30 times larger that had been fine-tuned directly on answers.

Quiet-STaR generalizes this insight beyond answering questions, as the model learns to generate internal rationales at each token position to explain and predict future text.[192] Training on internet text alone (with no task-specific data), Quiet-STaR produced zero-shot improvements on GSM8K (mathematical reasoning) and CommonsenseQA. The implication is that the reasoning capability bootstrapped by STaR-style methods is not narrowly task-specific but reflects a more general improvement in the model's capacity for sequential inference.

For practitioners, STaR offers a concrete recipe for improving reasoning capabilities without requiring a stronger teacher model. The ingredients are modest: a dataset of problems with known answers, a small seed set of example rationales, and sufficient compute for several rounds of generation and fine-tuning. The technique composes naturally with other approaches; STaR-generated rationales can feed into preference optimization, and the resulting models can serve as better generators for the next round.

Avoiding the Self-Improvement Mirage

The vision of self-improvement loops is seductive. A model generates training data, trains on that data to become more capable, uses its improved capability to generate even better training data, and iterates toward ever-greater capability. The loop, once started, might continue indefinitely, producing capability improvements without further human input. This vision has driven substantial research investment, and the results are genuinely impressive for certain tasks. Models that improve themselves through iterative training on self-generated data can achieve capabilities that seem to emerge from the process itself rather than being directly programmed or taught.

Reality is more constrained than the vision suggests. The model that improves indefinitely without external feedback exists only in grant proposals. In practice, improvements typically plateau, because a model cannot generate training signal for capabilities it does not possess. For all its virtues, RL is still not actual magic and cannot conjure information-theoretical value out of thin air ad infinitum. A model that lacks strong mathematical reasoning cannot generate and correctly verify mathematical proofs. Training on its faulty verification does not improve mathematical reasoning but rather optimizes for looking mathematical while getting things wrong. Without external grounding, where *external* means something beyond the model's own judgment, there is no mechanism to correct errors that the model cannot recognize as errors. Self-improvement works in domains where the model can reliably verify its own outputs, but it stalls or regresses in domains where it cannot.

Feedback loops in self-improvement can amplify problems as readily as capabilities. If the model has a subtle bias, training on self-generated data that reflects that bias reinforces it. If the model's quality judgments are slightly miscalibrated, the miscalibration compounds across iterations. These dynamics can produce models that score well on internal metrics while becoming worse by external standards, optimizing for artifacts that the model's self-evaluation rewards rather than for genuine quality that humans value. Careful design is essential: appropriate stopping criteria that halt improvement when progress stalls, external validation that catches drift from genuine quality, and diversity mechanisms that prevent collapse to narrow output distributions. Self-improvement is a powerful technique but not a magic wand, and its power depends on thoughtful application within appropriate domains.

This dynamic extends beyond individual training runs to the field as a whole. When multiple teams train on synthetic data generated by similar models, using similar evaluation criteria, a convergence effect emerges. The same quality signals produce the same optimization targets, and similar targets produce similar solutions. Differentiation requires deliberate effort (different data sources, evaluation criteria, and grounding signals) to avoid converging on the same bland middle ground that everyone else has already reached. At no other point in ML is diversity more important—not just of data, but also of minds. Some of the greatest improvements I have seen have come from teams and individuals with unusual perspectives. In short, if you're stuck, find someone who went to art school.

Learning Across Generations of Students

Standard distillation transfers knowledge from a large teacher model to a smaller student in a single pass: The teacher generates outputs, the student learns to match them, and the resulting student approximates the teacher's capability at lower inference cost. Iterated distillation extends this to multiple rounds, using each trained student to generate data for the next generation. The student trained in round one might generate data that the teacher would not have generated, perhaps by combining teacher patterns in novel ways or by solving problems slightly differently. Training round two's student on this expanded dataset produces a student that has learned from both the teacher and the first-generation student.

The technique can produce surprising capability improvements across iterations. Each student generation may discover patterns or solutions that previous generations missed, and these discoveries accumulate in the training data for subsequent generations. The process grounds itself in the teacher's capability, which remains the primary source of training signal, but allows for modest improvements as student generations find new ways to apply what the teacher provided. Unlike pure self-improvement, where a model relies entirely on its own judgment about quality, iterated distillation maintains the teacher as a reference point that prevents drift from the original capability distribution.

Practical application requires careful balance. Too little iteration fails to capture the benefits of multigenerational learning, while too much iteration can lead to degradation as accumulated noise outweighs accumulated insight. The sweet spot depends on the task, the teacher's capability, and the quality of filtering applied between iterations. For organizations that have access to capable teacher models and want to produce smaller deployment models, iterated distillation offers a path to capability that single-pass distillation might not achieve. The additional training cost is modest compared to the potential capability gains, and the approach is well-suited to production pipelines where deployed models must be smaller than the best available teachers.

Building the Data Factory

Ad hoc scripts that worked for initial experiments will not serve production needs. A production synthetic data pipeline is engineering infrastructure: generation, filtering, validation, storage, versioning, and the modular architecture that enables experimentation without risking stability.

Scaling the Training Data Pipeline

A production synthetic data pipeline is an engineering system that requires the same architectural care as any other critical infrastructure. The pipeline must reliably produce training data at scale, maintain quality standards across runs, and enable the iteration and experimentation that improving synthetic data quality requires. Systematic architecture is necessary for sustainable operation.

The core pipeline stages begin with generation, where capable models produce raw synthetic examples according to configured prompts and parameters. Generation feeds into quality checkpoints that filter and validate: automated scoring, verification checks, deduplication, and whatever other quality gates the application requires. Validated data flows to storage systems that manage large-scale synthetic corpora, with appropriate indexing for retrieval and sufficient metadata to understand what each example contains and how it was generated. Versioning tracks the provenance of each dataset: what generation parameters produced it, what filtering was applied, what model versions were used. This provenance enables reproduction, explanation, and debugging when issues arise.

Modular design enables experimentation without risking production stability. Each pipeline component (generators, filters, and validators) can be swapped or reconfigured without rewriting the entire pipeline. New generation strategies can be tested alongside existing ones, different filtering thresholds can be compared, and alternative verification approaches can be evaluated. The modular architecture also enables partial reruns. If a filtering bug is discovered, only the filtering and subsequent stages need rerunning rather than regenerating all data from scratch. Observability throughout the pipeline enables diagnosis of quality issues: metrics on generation diversity, filtering pass rates, quality score distributions, and downstream training outcomes create the feedback loops that enable continuous improvement.

> **VIBE CHECK: SYNTHETIC DATA PIPELINE ORCHESTRATION**
>
> Coding agents excel at building and maintaining synthetic data pipelines. Given generation specifications and quality criteria, an agent can implement the full pipeline: prompt construction for generation, parallel execution across multiple generator instances, quality scoring with configurable thresholds, deduplication using embedding similarity, format validation, and output to versioned storage. The agent can also implement monitoring dashboards that track diversity metrics, quality distributions, and generation throughput over time. When quality metrics drift, the agent can diagnose whether the issue lies in generation prompts, filtering thresholds, or model degradation. This automation transforms synthetic data from a manual process requiring constant attention into infrastructure that runs reliably with periodic human oversight.

Using Quality Gates and Continuous Monitoring

Quality control in synthetic data pipelines is not a one-time validation but an ongoing process integrated throughout the production system. Problems caught early, before synthetic data reaches training, are far cheaper to address than problems discovered after training produces a flawed model. The goal is continuous monitoring that catches degradation quickly and provides the diagnostic information needed to fix issues at their source.

Automated metrics provide the first line of defense, monitoring generation quality in real time. Diversity metrics detect collapse toward repetitive outputs, quality scores from evaluator models catch degradation in response quality, and format validation identifies malformed examples that would disrupt training. These metrics should be tracked over time, with alerts when they deviate from historical baselines. A sudden drop in diversity scores, for instance, might indicate a problem with the generation model or prompts that requires investigation before more flawed data is produced. The automated metrics run continuously and scale with the pipeline, providing coverage that human review could not match.

Human review provides ground truth that automated metrics approximate but cannot replace. Sampling strategies select examples for human examination: random samples to assess overall quality, stratified samples to ensure coverage of important subpopulations, and targeted samples of examples that automated systems flagged as borderline. Human reviewers assess whether the automated quality scores correspond to actual quality, catching cases where the metrics miss important problems or trigger false alarms on acceptable examples. Comparison against held-out validation sets detects distribution shift: If synthetic data starts diverging from the distribution expected by the training pipeline, training outcomes may suffer even if quality metrics remain stable. Finally, A/B testing of training outcomes validates that pipeline changes improve model performance. This is the ultimate test of whether the pipeline produces good data, and it should inform decisions about generation strategies, filtering thresholds, and quality criteria.

Scaling to Millions of Examples

The promise of synthetic data lies in its potential to scale far beyond what human annotation can achieve. Millions or billions of examples become feasible when generation is automated. This scale is genuinely valuable, as more training data generally improves model performance, and synthetic data can fill gaps that available human-generated data leaves uncovered. Realizing this promise, however, requires confronting the engineering challenges that scale introduces.

Generation compute costs dominate at scale. Each synthetic example requires model inference, and multiplying per-example cost by millions of examples produces substantial bills. Cost optimization becomes essential; smaller models for initial generation reduce per-example cost, with larger models reserved for filtering where their capability is necessary. Batch processing improves throughput and utilization compared to sequential generation. Caching common computations avoids redundant inference. Storage requirements grow with dataset size, and naive approaches can become prohibitively expensive. Efficient storage formats, appropriate compression, and intelligent retention policies that keep only what training actually needs reduce storage costs without sacrificing capability.

Processing time for filtering, validation, and curation can bottleneck the pipeline if not designed for scale. Parallelization across multiple workers enables processing throughput that single-threaded approaches cannot match. Incremental processing that handles data as it is generated avoids the need to store and then reprocess entire datasets. Incremental generation itself, producing data as needed rather than all at once, enables the pipeline to adapt to changing requirements without discarding previously generated data. The economics of synthetic data depend critically on efficient implementation. A well-engineered pipeline can produce useful data at costs that justify the investment, while a poorly engineered one can spend more on synthetic data than the resulting model improvement is worth.

Exploring the Emerging Toolkit Ecosystem

Building synthetic data pipelines from scratch is engineering-intensive, and several production-grade toolkits have emerged to reduce this burden. Understanding what they provide, and what they leave to you, helps calibrate the build-versus-buy decision.

NVIDIA NeMo Curator focuses on the curation side of the pipeline: scalable filtering, deduplication, and quality scoring for training data.[193] Built on NVIDIA RAPIDS libraries for GPU acceleration, it provides more than 30 heuristic filters, fastText-based quality classification, and three tiers of deduplication (exact, fuzzy via MinHash LSH, and semantic via GPU-accelerated embeddings). On large datasets, the GPU-accelerated pipeline runs up to 16 times faster than CPU alternatives while reducing total cost by approximately 40 percent. NeMo Curator handles text, image, video, and audio modalities, making it suitable for multimodal training pipelines. The tool also provides synthetic data generation pipelines that were used to produce training data for Nemotron-4 340B, including pipelines for open question-and-answer, writing tasks, closed question-and-answer, and mathematical and coding prompts. Any inference service compatible with the OpenAI API can serve as the generation backend, allowing organizations to use whichever model best suits their domain.

Meta Synthetic Data Kit takes a more end-to-end approach, providing a four-stage pipeline—ingest, create, curate, save-as—that transforms raw documents into training-ready datasets through a unified command line interface.[194] The ingest stage parses PDFs, HTML, YouTube transcripts, DOCX, and PowerPoint files into a clean internal format. The create stage generates question-answer pairs, chain-of-thought reasoning examples, or summaries using a local model served through vLLM. The curate stage uses "Llama as a judge"; the LLM evaluates each generated example against a configurable quality threshold (defaulting to 7.0 on a 10-point scale), retaining only examples that pass. The save-as stage exports curated data in whichever format the fine-tuning pipeline expects: Alpaca, OpenAI, ChatML, or Hugging Face datasets. Synthetic Data Kit transparently handles document chunking, splitting large documents with configurable overlap to preserve context, and processes entire directories in a single command. For organizations already invested in the Llama ecosystem, this toolkit reduces the distance from raw domain documents to fine-tuning data from days of custom scripting to a few configuration changes.

> **FROM THE TRENCHES: CHOOSING YOUR SYNTHETIC DATA STACK**
>
> Neither NeMo Curator nor Synthetic Data Kit is a complete solution on its own. NeMo Curator excels at large-scale curation (deduplication, filtering, quality scoring) but leaves prompt design and generation orchestration largely to you. Synthetic Data Kit handles the full pipeline from document ingestion to formatted output but is optimized for the Llama ecosystem and may require adaptation for other model families. In our production work, we typically combine elements from both: Synthetic Data Kit or custom scripts for generation and formatting, NeMo Curator's GPU-accelerated deduplication and quality filtering for curation at scale. Evaluate these options based on your existing infrastructure, model choices, and whether your bottleneck is generation or curation.

NVIDIA NeMo Data Designer addresses precisely this orchestration gap.[195] Whereas NeMo Curator handles curation after data exists, NeMo Data Designer handles the structured generation of multicolumn synthetic datasets in which each field may depend on others. The practitioner defines a schema of columns: Some are sampled from statistical distributions or external datasets, and others are generated by an LLM whose prompt references earlier columns through Jinja2 template variables (for example, `{{ persona.age }}` or `{{ diagnosis }}`). NeMo Data Designer resolves the references into a directed acyclic graph and generates columns in dependency order, so that upstream values are available before any downstream column that conditions on them. The result is a declarative framework for inter-field correlations: A patient's medication list reflects their diagnosis, a follow-up plan references both the diagnosis and the prescribed treatment, and all this is specified in configuration rather than in ad hoc scripting. NVIDIA's separately released Nemotron-Personas collection, comprising more than 1 billion synthetically generated personas grounded in real-world demographic, occupational, and personality-trait distributions (with regional variants for the United States, Japan, India, Brazil, and Singapore), provides ready-made seed data for the persona-driven generation approach that Persona Hub demonstrated earlier in this chapter.[196]

To make this concrete, consider the problem of generating synthetic after-visit summaries (AVS), which are patient-specific documents produced after medical appointments that include demographics, vitals, diagnoses, prescribed medications, and follow-up instructions. A NeMo Data Designer configuration can combine two seed datasets with a conditional LLM column to produce realistic, correlated records, as shown in Listing 11-1.

```
from nemo_data_designer import DataDesignerConfig
from nemo_data_designer.columns import (
    SamplerColumnConfig, LLMColumnConfig
)

config = DataDesignerConfig()

❶ config.add_column(SamplerColumnConfig(
    name="persona",
    dataset="nvidia/Nemotron-Personas-USA",
    columns=["name", "age", "sex",
             "occupation", "city", "state"],
))

❷ config.add_column(SamplerColumnConfig(
    name="clinical",
    dataset="gretelai/symptom_to_diagnosis",
    columns=["input_text", "output_text"],
))

❸ config.add_column(LLMColumnConfig(
    name="after_visit_summary",
    model="meta/llama-3.1-70b-instruct",
    prompt="""Generate an After Visit Summary.

Patient: {{ persona.name }}, {{ persona.age }},
  {{ persona.sex }}
Occupation: {{ persona.occupation }}
Location: {{ persona.city }}, {{ persona.state }}
Presenting symptoms: {{ clinical.input_text }}
Diagnosis: {{ clinical.output_text }}

Write a complete AVS including vitals, assessment,
prescribed medications, and follow-up instructions.
Tailor lifestyle advice to the patient's occupation
and location.""",
))

results = config.preview(n=5)
```

Listing 11-1: NeMo Data Designer configuration combining persona seed data with medical symptoms to generate synthetic AVS

The `persona` column ❶ samples demographic records from Nemotron-Personas-USA, providing a name, age, sex, occupation, and geographic location for each synthetic patient. The clinical seed ❷ draws symptom–diagnosis pairs from Gretel's *symptom_to_diagnosis* dataset,[197] grounding each record in a medically plausible scenario described in natural patient language rather than clinical terminology. The `after_visit_summary` column ❸ conditions on both upstream columns through Jinja2 template variables, producing a document that reflects the specific patient's demographics and clinical presentation. NeMo Data Designer automatically resolves the dependency graph; the persona and clinical columns have no dependencies on each other and can be sampled in parallel, while the AVS column waits for both before generation begins. The schema is still human designed, but as you are about to see, even that constraint is beginning to relax.

RL is beginning to play an increasingly significant role in this process. There is something delightfully recursive about AI creating not only its training material, but the recipe to create its own training set. DataChef-32B is a model that generates not training data but a data recipe (a synthetic data pipeline's specification) and quite successfully so, having trained Qwen3-1.7B-Base to outperform a naive Qwen3-1.7B on a math-related reasoning task and achieve a better-than-expert performance on the 2025 American Invitational Mathematics Examination (AIME).[198] The beauty of this approach lies in a reward function that judges "both the fruit and the tree." In other words, it assigns a composite reward from successful generation (validity) on one hand (ensuring that the model does generate viable recipes) and the rubric compliance of the resulting final dataset on the other.

The logical next step is, of course, to assign reward by the quality of the fine-tuned model at the end of the process. This is currently computationally excessively costly, but an RL pipeline with its reward function determined by the performance of a target model that was trained on data generated by the first model may become feasible in the near future with the emergence of more efficient computational techniques and hardware.

When Synthetic Data Goes Wrong

It is an old adage in computer science that garbage in only begets garbage out. Synthetic data is a powerful tool to create large datasets, but it carries the risk of amplifying the biases of the source data. At the extreme, this can result in model collapse, as this section will show.

Subtle Skews That Become Major Distortions

Synthetic data cannot be more diverse than the model that generates it, and in practice it is typically less so. Whatever biases exist in the generator appear in its outputs, and training on those outputs reinforces rather than corrects them. This is known as *bias amplification*. A model that tends to generate examples from certain perspectives will produce synthetic data skewed toward those perspectives. Training on that skewed data strengthens the skew, and the next iteration produces even more biased data. This feedback loop can amplify subtle biases into substantial ones across just a few iterations.

The amplification is insidious because it may not appear in quality metrics that focus on correctness or fluency. A synthetic dataset can score well on quality while representing a narrow slice of the space it should cover. The responses may be correct, well written, and helpful, yet consistently reflect particular viewpoints while neglecting others. Without explicit measurement of diversity along dimensions that matter, this bias can go unnoticed until it manifests in the deployed model's behavior, often in ways that damage user trust or cause representational harm to affected groups.

Mitigation requires active attention throughout the pipeline. Generation prompts should explicitly seek diverse perspectives, not merely correct answers. Quality control should include diversity metrics along relevant dimensions: demographic, topical, and stylistic. Explicit bias detection, using classifiers trained to identify skew along important dimensions, can flag datasets that deviate from target distributions. Perhaps most important, synthetic data should be mixed with human-generated data that provides the diverse perspectives that synthetic generation may miss. The human data grounds the training, preventing drift toward the narrow distribution that pure synthetic generation tends to produce. The right balance depends on the application and available human data, but some human grounding is almost always valuable when bias is a concern.

Model Collapse in Synthetic Data and Self-Play

Model collapse occurs when a model converges to a narrow distribution of outputs, producing variations on a theme rather than genuinely diverse responses. The collapsed model may produce high-quality outputs within its narrow range, but it has lost the capability to produce the variety of responses that different contexts require. A model that gives the same style of answer to every question, regardless of what the question demands, has model-collapsed even if each individual answer is good. The collapse destroys utility because real-world deployment requires handling diverse inputs with appropriately diverse outputs.

The problem extends beyond individual training runs. Shumailov et al. demonstrated in a 2024 *Nature* paper that training generative models on recursively generated data leads to irreversible degradation.[199] Model collapse unfolds in two stages. In *early model collapse*, the model's outputs begin to lose low-probability but valid content—the unusual examples, the minority perspectives, the edge cases that make a distribution rich. In *late model collapse*, the distribution converges so thoroughly that generated content bears little resemblance to the original training data, producing outputs that are confident, fluent, and wrong in ways the model cannot detect. But because a given amount of variance has to be accommodated within the distribution, the perturbations to do so serve to degrade the output's quality in unexpected ways. Rather than providing healthy variety by selecting from a wider distribution, the model is trying to create variety through perturbing a narrow distribution, typically resulting in nonsense responses. The finding applies across architectures; the authors demonstrated collapse in LLMs, variational autoencoders, and Gaussian mixture models alike.

The implications for synthetic data pipelines are profound and immediate. As LLM-generated content proliferates on the internet, future models trained by scraping the web will inevitably train on synthetic data produced by earlier models. Each generation of training compounds the distribution narrowing, and the tails—which contain precisely the diverse, unusual, and specialized content that makes models useful—erode first. The cure is not to avoid synthetic data entirely but to ensure that each generation of training data retains access to genuinely human-generated content. Organizations that maintain high-quality human data as a mixing component in their training pipelines have a structural advantage: They can benefit from synthetic data's scale without losing the distributional richness that only human data provides.

Detection requires monitoring output diversity throughout training and production. Embedding-space analyses can identify clustering that indicates collapse, *n*-gram statistics can detect repetitive patterns, and human reviewers examining random samples can catch qualitative similarity that automated metrics miss. Mitigation requires explicit diversity-promoting mechanisms: diversity terms in reward functions that penalize similarity between outputs, temperature or other generation-time interventions that encourage variety, and data curation of training to ensure that diverse examples remain represented even when filtering for quality. The fundamental tension is between quality and diversity. Aggressive optimization for quality tends to produce mode collapse, while aggressive preservation of diversity may retain low-quality outputs. Navigating this tension requires careful calibration that maintains diversity within acceptable quality bounds.

The Irreducible Human Element

The efficiency of synthetic data is genuinely remarkable. What would take human annotators months can be generated in hours, at a fraction of the cost. This efficiency creates a seductive pull toward synthetic-only pipelines that entirely eliminate the slow and expensive human element. Resist this pull. Human oversight remains essential not despite synthetic data's capabilities but because of them. The very efficiency that makes synthetic data attractive also enables it to produce large volumes of problematic data if not properly validated.

Human evaluation validates that synthetic data pipelines produce genuinely useful data, not merely data that scores well on automated metrics. Automated metrics are proxies for quality, designed by humans to correlate with what humans value. They are imperfect proxies, and optimizing for them too aggressively produces Goodhart's law effects: The metric improves while the underlying quality it was meant to measure degrades. Human evaluation catches these divergences, providing the ground truth that calibrates and validates automated systems. Human annotation provides examples of what *good* looks like, anchoring synthetic generation and evaluation in human judgment rather than letting them drift.

The right role for synthetic data is augmentation, not replacement. Human-generated data provides quality and diversity that synthetic data cannot fully replicate, while synthetic data provides scale and coverage that human annotation cannot economically achieve. Together they complement each other's strengths and mitigate each other's weaknesses. Organizations that eliminate human involvement, relying solely on synthetic pipelines, risk optimizing for whatever their automated systems happen to measure rather than for what matters. The humans in the loop are not overhead to be eliminated but essential validators ensuring that efficiency gains do not come at the cost of quality. Investment in human oversight pays dividends in the reliability of the resulting models and in the trust those models can earn from users.

Synthetic All the Way Down?

Synthetic data and self-play represent a fundamental shift in the way training data is produced. The techniques covered in this chapter—from Self-Instruct and Evol-Instruct through constitutional AI and RLAIF, from STaR's reasoning bootstrap to SPIN's self-play alignment, from production toolkits to the careful quality engineering that makes it all work—enable scale that human annotation cannot match. This scale is genuinely valuable, but it comes with risks that must be actively managed.

The core tension runs throughout: Synthetic data can be only as good as the process that generates and filters it. A capable generator model produces high-quality examples, but it also produces its biases at scale. An effective filter removes low-quality examples, but aggressive filtering may collapse diversity. Self-improvement loops can bootstrap capability, but without external grounding, they optimize for whatever the model already believes rather than for genuine quality that humans value. And as Shumailov et al. have shown, the danger extends beyond individual training runs: When model-generated content accumulates on the web, subsequent generations of models trained on that content lose the distributional richness that made their predecessors useful in the first place.[199] Each technique offers leverage, and each requires care to avoid amplifying problems rather than capabilities.

The landscape of available tools is maturing rapidly. Production-grade pipelines from NVIDIA and Meta reduce the engineering burden of building synthetic data infrastructure. Landmark techniques like persona-driven generation and the textbook model of synthesis (which is similar to curriculum learning in its approach of structuring training material like that used in human educational practice) provide proven recipes for common generation needs.[185, 83] A comprehensive survey of these methods identifies the key remaining challenge as ensuring diversity: Directly prompting LLMs for synthetic data reliably produces fluent, correct, and repetitive outputs.[200] The techniques that address this challenge—conditioning on diverse personas, evolving instructions toward greater complexity, rephrasing content across multiple styles—are not optional refinements but essential components of any pipeline that aims to produce training data competitive with human annotation.

Summary

The practical path forward combines synthetic scale with human grounding. Use synthetic generation for volume, but validate against human judgment. Use AI feedback for efficiency, but calibrate against human preferences. Use self-play for robustness, but ground the evaluation in external standards. Maintain a reservoir of high-quality human data not as a legacy artifact but as the distributional anchor that prevents model collapse across generations. The organizations that master this balance of capturing synthetic data's efficiency without sacrificing human data's quality will train better models at lower cost than competitors that rely on either approach alone.

12

MULTIMODAL SYSTEMS: POST-TRAINING BEYOND TEXT

Language alone is not enough. The world arrives to us through vision, sound, and sensation, and models that process only text miss most of what, and how, humans communicate. One of the big revelations of language models in recent years was the discovery that the same architecture can also accommodate other modalities of information (a fact that really hadn't been all that well hidden).

Multimodal systems extend language models to handle vision, audio, and increasingly other modalities, from video to three-dimensional (3D) structure to sensor data. These systems do not merely independently process multiple input types but learn joint representations that capture the way modalities relate: how images illustrate concepts, speech conveys emotion, and gestures clarify language. The resulting capabilities enable applications that text-only models cannot address: analyzing medical images with clinical reports, transcribing meetings with speaker attribution, grounding robot instructions in visual perception. Yet multimodal training introduces complexities beyond those of language-only post-training, from alignment across modalities to evaluation that requires assessing diverse output types.

This chapter examines the techniques for building and fine-tuning multimodal systems: vision-language models that connect images and text, audio systems that process speech and sound, and emerging modalities that extend beyond traditional media. We address multimodal alignment, ensuring that representations across modalities remain consistent, and the practical challenges of gathering multimodal training data and evaluating multimodal outputs. For enterprises whose applications involve more than text, understanding multimodal post-training determines the capabilities that become achievable.

Pixels Meet Prose

How do pixels become prose? The three-part composition of vision encoder, projection mechanism, and language backbone determines what visual understanding is possible. The projection layer, often the least glamorous component, proves most consequential for post-training.

How Images Say a Thousand Words

Vision-language models (VLMs) represent the most mature and widely deployed class of multimodal systems. Because the field is dominated by a highly successful three-part architecture, we may be tempted to consider VLM an architectural predisposition rather than a functional description. In reality, a VLM is simply a model that processes images and text together. Beyond that, the term covers a range of architectures, even though the LLaVA skeleton (depicted in Figure 12-1) has become the de facto standard.[59]

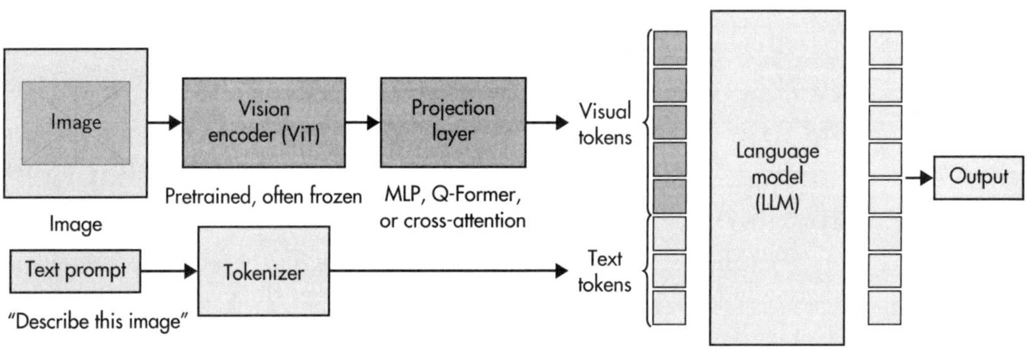

Figure 12-1: The three-part anatomy of a typical VLM, based on the LLaVA skeleton: a vision encoder extracts patch representations from the image, a projection layer maps them into the language model's embedding space, and the language model generates text conditioned on the combined visual and textual tokens. Dark tokens represent visual (image) embeddings; light tokens represent text embeddings. The output sequence is entirely textual.

The LLaVA skeleton consists of three components: a vision encoder that processes raw images into continuous representations, a projection mechanism that maps those representations into the language model's embedding space, and a language model backbone that generates text conditioned on the projected visual information. The vision encoder may be a vision transformer (ViT),[201] a CLIP-derived architecture,[202] or a custom design. The projection mechanism may be as simple as a linear layer, a multilayer perceptron, or a cross-attention module. The language model backbone, in turn, can be pretty much any language model.

These implement the three key functions of a VLM's internals. Each component has design choices that affect how well the model can learn from post-training data, how much compute is required, and how much risk of forgetting is introduced.

The projection mechanism is our most powerful lever over model outputs and thus is the central focus of post-training. As noted previously, this may be as simple as a linear projection mapping the vision encoder's output dimensionality to match the language model's embedding space, or a more sophisticated approach using multilayer perceptrons or cross-attention mechanisms that allow the language model to selectively attend to visual features. The choice matters: Linear projections are efficient and easy to train but may lose information, while cross-attention preserves more visual detail but introduces additional parameters and computational cost. For practitioners considering fine-tuning, the projection layer often represents the sweet spot: enough parameters to enable meaningful adaptation, but few enough to train efficiently on limited data.

NOTE *Focusing on the projection layer risks and training it risks neither the vision encoder's visual vocabulary nor the language model's linguistic capability. Go deeper–unfreezing encoders or backbones–only when projection-layer training demonstrably fails to achieve required performance (and you are confident about what you're doing).*

The language model backbone completes the architecture, receiving the projected visual representations alongside any textual input and generating language conditioned on both. Whether this backbone is frozen or trainable during post-training represents perhaps the most consequential architectural decision. Freezing the language model preserves its general capabilities while allowing adaptation only in the way visual information is presented to it. Training the backbone enables deeper integration of visual understanding at the risk of catastrophic forgetting of linguistic capabilities. Current practice increasingly favors staged approaches, training the projection layer first to align modalities, then selectively unfreezing language model layers if deeper adaptation proves necessary.

Within this framework, however, individual implementations differ considerably. Qwen2.5-VL adopts the LLaVA architecture with a dynamic resolution mechanism that processes images at their native aspect ratio rather than resizing everything to a fixed grid, preserving fine detail in documents and diagrams.[203] Llama 3.2 Vision uses cross-attention layers interleaved with the language model's transformer blocks rather than simple concatenation, giving the model finer-grained control over when and how it attends to visual features. Gemma 3 integrates a SigLIP vision encoder and natively supports interleaved image-text sequences. InternVL and MiniCPM-V push the architecture toward higher resolution and more sophisticated projection mechanisms.

The models differ in their details, as Figure 12-2 shows, but the architectural skeleton—encode, project, generate—remains remarkably stable across all of them. When choosing a base model for fine-tuning, we can, for the most part, focus on practical considerations (parameter count, license, framework support) rather than fundamental architectural differences.

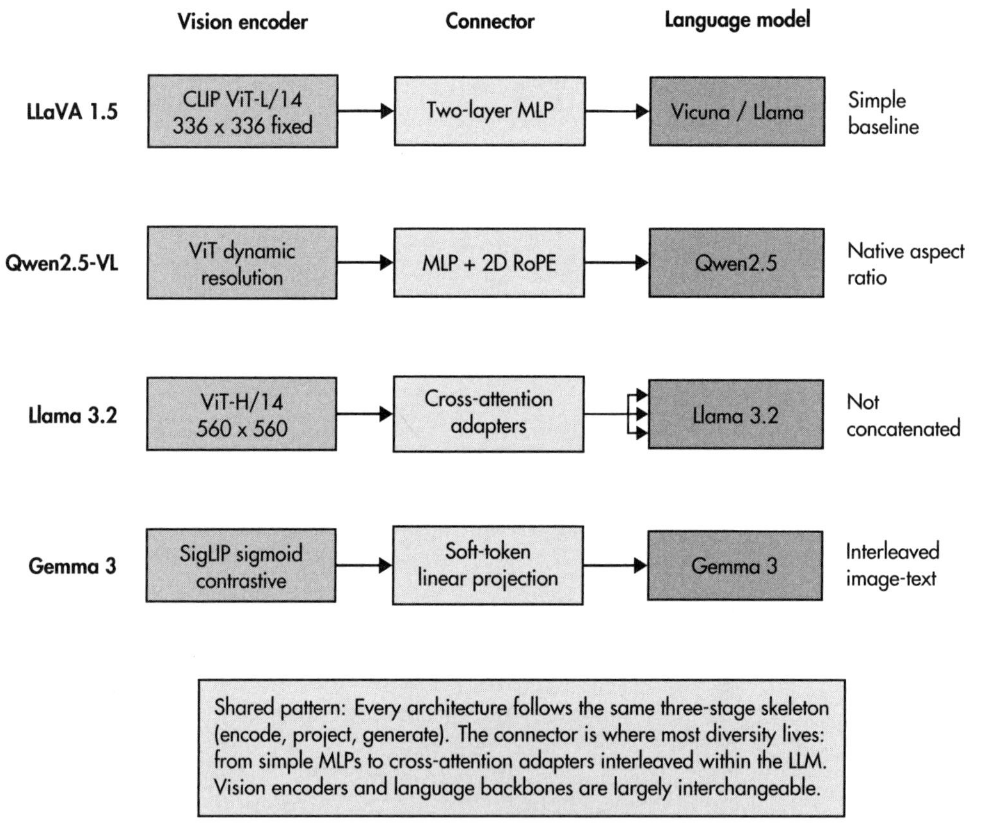

Figure 12-2: Four production VLMs instantiate the same three-part skeleton with diverse implementation choices. The connector (projection mechanism) is where most architectural variation lives.

Visual Instruction Tuning

The breakthrough insight behind visual instruction tuning emerged from an elegant observation: Language models already know how to follow instructions, and vision encoders already know how to represent images. The challenge lies not in teaching either capability from scratch but in connecting them such that instruction following applies to visual content. LLaVA and its successors demonstrated that this connection can be established with surprisingly modest training if the projection mechanism learns to present visual information in a format that the language model's existing capabilities can leverage.[204]

Constructing effective visual instruction datasets requires moving beyond simple image-caption pairs and toward structured interactions that exercise diverse reasoning capabilities. A single image might support dozens of instruction types–describe what you see, count the objects of a particular type, compare two regions, identify any safety hazards, explain what likely happened before this moment, predict what will happen next. Each instruction type exercises different aspects of visual understanding and different response formats. The dataset must sufficiently sample across this space so that the model learns general instruction following rather than memorizing particular image-instruction pairs.

The practical process of visual instruction tuning typically proceeds in stages. An initial phase trains the projection layer while keeping both the vision encoder and language model frozen, establishing basic alignment between modalities. A second phase may unfreeze some language model parameters to deepen the integration. Throughout, the training objective resembles standard language model training (predict the next token) but with visual tokens prepended to the sequence. The loss is computed only over the response tokens, not the visual or instruction tokens, ensuring that the model learns to generate appropriate responses rather than reconstruct inputs. This seemingly technical detail matters enormously. Computing loss over visual tokens would teach the model to generate visual representations, which is not the goal, while computing loss over instructions would encourage the model to parrot back prompts.

Recent models have extended visual instruction tuning beyond single-image scenarios. Qwen2.5-VL and Gemma 3 natively support multi-image instruction tuning, enabling conversations that reference several images simultaneously: "Compare these two chest X-rays" or "Which of these product photos shows the defect?" Video instruction tuning goes further, treating sampled frames as ordered image sequences and training the model to reason about temporal relationships. These extensions do not require fundamentally new techniques, but they do require training data that exercises multi-image and temporal reasoning, and they substantially increase memory requirements since each additional image contributes hundreds of visual tokens to the sequence.

The Pernicious Problem of Visual Hallucination

Visual hallucination represents the signature failure mode of VLMs, and addressing it requires extending alignment techniques into new territory. When a VLM confidently describes objects that aren't present in an image, counts incorrectly, or invents spatial relationships between elements, it exhibits a form of confabulation that can be harder to detect than purely textual hallucination. A human reading a text-only model's fabricated claim might be suspicious, but the same human shown an image alongside the model's description might trust the description because the image is right there, seemingly providing grounding. This false sense of security makes visual hallucination particularly pernicious in deployment.

The alignment challenge for VLMs thus has two dimensions: the familiar requirements of helpful, harmless, and honest responses that apply to any language model, and the novel requirement of visual fidelity, that claims about images correspond to their contents. Techniques developed for text-only alignment transfer partially. RLHF with human annotators who verify visual accuracy can reduce hallucination, Constitutional AI principles can include requirements for visual grounding, and careful dataset construction can minimize examples with captions that don't match images. Yet each technique requires adaptation for the multimodal setting, and the cost of annotation increases when annotators must carefully examine images rather than merely read text.

Research into automated detection of visual hallucination shows promise but remains imperfect. Approaches that check model confidence, compare multiple generations for consistency, or use auxiliary models to verify claims can catch some hallucinations but miss subtle ones. The fundamental difficulty is that visual grounding is itself a capability that models may lack. You cannot use a model to verify its own visual understanding if that understanding is faulty. This creates a dependency on human evaluation that limits scaling and increases alignment costs. For enterprise applications, the practical implication is that VLM alignment requires more human oversight than text-only alignment, at least until automated verification techniques mature.

NOTE *Perhaps the most pernicious example occurs when the model interprets an ambiguous signal. Consider the famous duck-rabbit illusion. VLMs trained to describe the image without tolerating ambiguity will describe it as* either *a duck* or *a rabbit when in reality, the image is* neither.

Well-designed visual models can tolerate ambiguity, and RL on ambiguous hard negatives plays a crucial role in inculcating this in models. The training data must include examples of a correct response acknowledging uncertainty rather than forcing a definitive answer: "This image could show either consolidation or atelectasis—the lateral view would help distinguish them" rather than confidently declaring one or the other. This is harder to achieve than it sounds, because most training datasets reward confident, specific answers, and annotators tend to resolve ambiguity rather than preserve it. Building an "I'm not sure" capability requires deliberate dataset design and evaluation metrics that reward calibrated uncertainty over confident assertions.

The three-stage approach to reducing hallucination reflects the tools available at each stage. SFT with high-quality, visually grounded data establishes a baseline of accurate description. Preference optimization (DPO or nSFT, discussed in "Preference Optimization for Visual Models" on page 334) then teaches the model to prefer grounded responses over hallucinated ones. Finally, inference-time techniques (beam search with visual grounding constraints, self-consistency checking across multiple samples, or auxiliary verification models) catch hallucinations that survive training. No single stage completely eliminates the problem, but each reduces it. Their combination brings hallucination rates to levels that enable practical deployment in domains where occasional errors are acceptable (product descriptions, accessibility captions).

Fine-Tuning VLMs for the Real World

Unlike fine-tuning for simple image-to-text inference, VLMs require multimodal annotations. These must reflect the task involved, such as image description or visual question answering (VQA), while at the same time being correct with respect to the image itself. This creates a joint complexity known as the *double burden* of VLMs.

The Double Burden of Multimodal Annotation

The data requirements for VLM fine-tuning compound the challenges familiar from text-only work with the additional complexity of multimodal coherence. Every image-text pair must satisfy not one but two constraints. The text must be appropriate for the task, and it must accurately reflect the visual content. A beautiful instruction-response pair is worthless if it incorrectly describes an image, and a perfectly accurate image description is worthless if it doesn't serve the task that the model is being trained for.

Annotation protocols for VLM datasets must therefore guide annotators to attend to visual details while constructing task-appropriate responses. This requires annotators with dual competencies—namely, visual perception sufficient to notice relevant details and linguistic facility to clearly articulate those details. Finding annotators with both skills proves harder than finding annotators with either, and supervising their work requires reviewers who can verify both dimensions. The practical consequence is that VLM annotation costs typically run two to three times higher than text-only annotation for comparable response lengths, and quality control requires more reviewer time per example.

Domain-specific VLM fine-tuning introduces additional dataset requirements. Medical imaging applications need annotators with radiological training, manufacturing inspection needs annotators familiar with defect taxonomies, and document understanding needs annotators who understand the structure of forms, invoices, and contracts. The intersection of domain expertise with annotation skill further shrinks the available workforce, making domain-specific VLM datasets scarce and expensive. Organizations with access to domain experts who can annotate effectively hold a significant advantage, while those without must either invest in training annotators or accept lower data quality. There are no shortcuts. The model can learn only what the data teaches, and poor annotation teaches poor visual reasoning. In line with the right annotation, information must also be collected in the right data format: Table 12-1 provides an overview of the main annotation types and when they are most appropriate.

Table 12-1: Annotation Types for Multimodal Datasets: Choosing the Right Approach

Annotation type	Best suited for	Example format	Typical cost
Bounding boxes	Object detection, localization, counting tasks	`[x, y, w, h, label]` for each object	Low–moderate
Instruction-response pairs	Visual QA, reasoning, open-ended generation	Image + question + expected response	Moderate–high
Dense captions	Detailed scene understanding, accessibility	Multi-sentence descriptions covering all visible elements	High
Region descriptions	Spatial reasoning, referring expressions	Region coordinates + natural language description	Moderate
Keypoint annotations	Pose estimation, fine-grained alignment	Named points with (x, y) coordinates	Low–moderate
Temporal segments	Video understanding, action recognition	Start/end timestamps + action labels	High (requires video review)
Multi-turn dialogues	Conversational VLMs, complex reasoning chains	Sequence of Q&A about single image	Very high

A particularly effective strategy for bootstrapping VLM datasets is to use a strong proprietary model (GPT-4o, Claude, Gemini) to generate draft annotations for a corpus of domain images, then have domain experts review and correct the outputs. This is, in essence, the same synthetic data pipeline described in Chapter 10, adapted for the multimodal setting. The proprietary model sees the image and a detailed system prompt describing the annotation task, and it produces a candidate annotation that a human refines. The economics are compelling: A radiologist who can annotate 10 images per hour from scratch might review and correct 40 model-generated annotations in the same time.

CHOOSING YOUR ANNOTATION STRATEGY

The annotation format shapes what the model can learn. Bounding boxes teach localization but not reasoning, instruction-response pairs teach reasoning but may not ground it spatially, and dense captions provide rich supervision but cost three to five times more per image.

Match annotation type to task requirements, not to what seems comprehensive. A manufacturing inspection system needs bounding boxes around defects with severity labels; dense captions describing the entire scene waste annotation budget on irrelevant detail. A medical imaging assistant needs instruction-response pairs that mirror clinical queries; bounding boxes alone cannot teach diagnostic reasoning. Start with the minimum annotation that could work and add richness only when simpler approaches demonstrably fail.

The risk is that model-generated annotations share systematic biases. If the proprietary model consistently misidentifies a particular pathology, the corrections will catch individual errors but may not reveal the systematic pattern. Mixing model-generated and human-originated annotations, and tracking error rates by source, helps manage this risk.

For organizations that cannot share images with external APIs because of privacy or regulatory constraints (a common situation in healthcare and defense), locally deployed, open source VLMs can serve the same bootstrapping role. The draft quality will be lower than from frontier proprietary models, but the review-and-correct workflow still outperforms annotation from scratch, and the data never leaves the organization's infrastructure.

> **VIBE CHECK: MULTIMODAL DATASET CURATION**
>
> Coding agents can dramatically accelerate multimodal dataset preparation. Given a corpus of images and annotation guidelines, an agent can generate draft annotations (bounding boxes, captions, instruction-response pairs) that human reviewers then correct rather than create from scratch. This review-and-correct workflow typically runs three to four times faster than annotation from a blank slate. The agent can also implement quality checks: flagging images that are too dark or blurry, identifying annotations that contradict each other, detecting near-duplicate images that inflate dataset size without adding information. For format conversion between annotation schemas (COCO to YOLO, VQA to instruction-tuning format), agents handle the tedious transformation while humans focus on content quality.

The Freezing Question

The decision of which components to train during VLM fine-tuning shapes everything that follows: data requirements, computational costs, adaptation depth, and forgetting risk. The vision encoder contains the model's fundamental visual vocabulary: its understanding of edges and textures, objects and spatial relationships. Freezing this component during fine-tuning preserves that vocabulary while limiting the model's ability to learn genuinely new visual concepts. For most enterprise applications, where the visual domain falls within the encoder's pre-training distribution, frozen encoders work well. For applications involving novel visual domains (such as specialized medical imaging modalities, unusual industrial inspection scenarios, or domain-specific document layouts), encoder training may be necessary, though it requires substantially more data.

The projection layer, mapping visual representations into the language model's embedding space, often represents the optimal target for efficient fine-tuning. Training only the projection layer requires modest compute, risks minimal forgetting, and can achieve substantial adaptation if the underlying visual and linguistic capabilities are already present. This approach asks the model not to learn new visual or linguistic concepts but to learn new mappings between existing concepts. When a manufacturing inspection VLM needs to learn that certain visual patterns indicate defects, projection-layer training may suffice if the vision encoder already represents those patterns and the language model already understands concepts of defect and quality.

Parameter-efficient methods extend naturally to VLMs, with LoRA adapters applicable to both vision encoder and language model components. A common pattern applies LoRA to the language model while keeping the vision encoder frozen and fully training the projection layer. This combination balances adaptation capability against computational cost, enabling meaningful fine-tuning on hardware that couldn't support full model training. The hyperparameters require some adjustment from text-only settings (learning rates for the projection layer may need to be higher than for LoRA adapters, and warm-up schedules may need lengthening to allow multimodal alignment to stabilize), but the basic machinery transfers directly. Table 12-2 lays out the spectrum of options available, as well as the data required, for fine-tuning VLMs.

Table 12-2: VLM Fine-Tuning Strategies: What to Train and When

Component	When to train	Data required	Risk
Projection layer only	Default for most tasks; task adaptation	1,000–10,000 examples	Low; minimal forgetting
LM + projection	Deeper adaptation needed	10,000–100,000 examples	Moderate; may lose general capability
Vision encoder + projection	Novel visual domain	100,000+ examples	High; may lose visual vocabulary
Full model	Maximum adaptation	Extensive; domain-specific	Highest; requires careful regularization
LoRA on LM + full projection	Balance of adaptation and efficiency	5,000–50,000 examples	Low to moderate

The Choice of a Base Model

The proliferation of open source VLMs has created an embarrassment of riches for practitioners planning a fine-tuning project. A year ago, the choice was essentially LLaVA or nothing, and now the landscape offers half a dozen production-quality options, each with distinct trade-offs. The decision matters because switching base models mid-project means rebuilding data pipelines, retuning hyperparameters, and rerunning evaluations—effort that a thoughtful initial choice can avoid.

Table 12-3 summarizes the leading options. The choice often comes down to three practical questions. First, what hardware is available? Qwen2.5-VL 7B and Gemma 3 4B can be fine-tuned on a single 24GB GPU with 4-bit quantization, while Llama 3.2 Vision 11B requires at least 40GB (or aggressive quantization). Second, what does the application need? Document understanding and OCR favor Qwen2.5-VL's dynamic resolution, which preserves fine text at native aspect ratios. General visual reasoning favors InternVL2.5 or Llama 3.2 Vision, which lead on reasoning benchmarks. Edge deployment favors MiniCPM-V 4.5 or Gemma 3 4B, which pack competitive capability into smaller parameter counts. Third, which fine-tuning framework will be used? Unsloth natively supports Qwen2.5-VL, Llama 3.2 Vision, Gemma 3, and Pixtral. LLaMA-Factory covers the broadest range, including InternVL and MiniCPM-V.[205] Hugging Face TRL provides first-class support for Qwen2.5-VL and Llama 3.2 Vision through its `SFTTrainer`.

Table 12-3: Open Source VLMs for Fine-Tuning: A Practitioner's Comparison

Model	Parameters	Vision encoder	License	Notable strength
Qwen2.5-VL	3B/7B/72B	ViT (dynamic)	Apache 2.0	Document OCR, any resolution
Llama 3.2 Vision	11B/90B	ViT + cross-attn	Llama 3.2	Reasoning, multilingual
Gemma 3	4B/12B/27B	SigLIP	Gemma	Multi-image, efficient
InternVL2.5	2B–78B	InternViT	MIT	Broad benchmarks
MiniCPM-V 4.5	8B	SigLIP2	Apache 2.0	Edge deployment
Pixtral	12B	Custom ViT	Apache 2.0	Long-context vision

When in doubt, Qwen2.5-VL 7B represents the safest default for most enterprise fine-tuning projects. It strikes a favorable balance between capability and cost, its Apache 2.0 license permits commercial deployment without restriction, and it enjoys the broadest framework support. Reserve larger models for tasks where the 7B variant demonstrably falls short, and use smaller models for latency-sensitive deployments where every millisecond of inference time matters.

The Practitioner's Toolkit

Three frameworks dominate VLM fine-tuning in practice, each occupying a different point on the spectrum between ease of use and configurability. Unsloth focuses on memory efficiency, reducing VRAM requirements by 40 to 70 percent through kernel optimizations and enabling 4-bit QLoRA fine-tuning of models that would otherwise require multi-GPU setups.[6] Its API emphasizes simplicity: Load a model, configure LoRA targets, provide data, and train. For teams with limited GPU access, Unsloth often determines whether a project is feasible at all. Axolotl, which is widely used for fast and configuration-driven fine-tuning of language models, is relatively feature-sparse when it comes to VLMs.

Unsloth's VLM support deserves particular attention because it makes fine-tuning accessible on hardware that many teams already have. A Qwen2.5-VL 7B model that requires 30GB+ of VRAM for full-precision training fits comfortably on a single 24GB GPU when loaded in 4-bit precision with Unsloth's optimized kernels. The framework provides granular control over which components to fine-tune through parameters like finetune_vision_layers, finetune_language_layers, and finetune_attention_modules, allowing practitioners to implement the staged training strategies discussed previously without writing custom training loops. Data preparation follows a conversation format; each example is a list of message dictionaries containing text and image references, with Unsloth's UnslothVisionDataCollator handling the conversion to model-specific tokens.

Hugging Face TRL provides the SFTTrainer with native vision support, integrating tightly with the broader Hugging Face ecosystem of datasets, model hub, and evaluation tools. TRL's advantage is ecosystem coherence: data loaded from Hugging Face Datasets, models saved to the Hub, experiments tracked with Weights & Biases, all through a consistent API. For teams already embedded in the Hugging Face ecosystem, TRL minimizes the friction of adding VLM fine-tuning to existing workflows.

LLaMA-Factory takes a configuration-driven approach, specifying training through YAML files rather than Python scripts.[205] It supports more than 100 models, including InternVL, MiniCPM-V, and GLM-4V variants that other frameworks may not cover. Its web UI provides a low-code interface for constructing training configurations, which can be valuable for teams exploring hyperparameter spaces or for domain experts who need to run fine-tuning without deep framework familiarity.

Listing 12-1 illustrates the core pattern for VLM fine-tuning with Unsloth. The recipe loads a model in 4-bit precision, configures LoRA targets across both vision and language components, prepares the conversational dataset, and trains. The entire workflow fits on a single GPU.

```
from unsloth import FastModel
from unsloth import UnslothVisionDataCollator
from datasets import load_dataset
from trl import SFTTrainer, SFTConfig

❶ model, tokenizer = FastModel.from_pretrained(
    "unsloth/Qwen2.5-VL-7B-Instruct",
    load_in_4bit=True,
)

❷ model = FastModel.get_peft_model(
    model,
    finetune_vision_layers=False,
    finetune_language_layers=True,
    finetune_attention_modules=True,
    finetune_mlp_modules=True,
    r=16, lora_alpha=16, lora_dropout=0,
)

❸ def format_example(sample):
    return {"messages": [
        {"role": "user",
         "content": [{"type": "image", "image": sample["image"]},
```

```
                    {"type": "text", "text": sample["question"]}]},
            {"role": "assistant",
             "content": [{"type": "text", "text": sample["answer"]}]}
        ]}

    dataset = load_dataset("unsloth/Radiology_mini")
    train_data = dataset["train"].map(format_example)
❹ eval_data = dataset["test"].select(range(50)).map(format_example)

❺ trainer = SFTTrainer(
        model=model, tokenizer=tokenizer,
        data_collator=UnslothVisionDataCollator(model, tokenizer),
        train_dataset=train_data,
        eval_dataset=eval_data,
        args=SFTConfig(
            output_dir="./Qwen2.5-VL-7B-radiology-ft",
            per_device_train_batch_size=2,
            gradient_accumulation_steps=4,
            learning_rate=2e-4,
            max_steps=500,
            max_seq_length=1024,
            bf16=True,
            warmup_steps=50,
            weight_decay=0.01,
            gradient_checkpointing=True,
            logging_steps=10,
            eval_strategy="steps",
            eval_steps=100,
            save_steps=500,
        ),
    )
    trainer.train()
    trainer.save_model("./Qwen2.5-VL-7B-radiology-ft/final")
```

Listing 12-1: VLM fine-tuning with Unsloth

The model loads in 4-bit precision ❶, reducing VRAM from more than 30GB to less than 16GB. We then attach our LoRA adapters to the language model ❷, while the vision encoder stays frozen (the default for most domain adaptation). The formatter ❸ turns each image and description pair into a chat snippet. A small evaluation subset ❹ is carved from the test split so that validation loss can be tracked during training. We then hand the training loop over to our trusted TRL `SFTTrainer` ❺, with the `UnslothVisionDataCollator` managing the conversion of images to vision tokens.

A common pitfall when saving fine-tuned vision models deserves mention. The standard `save_pretrained_merged` method may fail to correctly merge LoRA adapters for some vision architectures. If the saved model produces outputs identical to the base model, use `model.merge_and_unload` followed by a manual `save_pretrained` call instead. This work-around applies particularly to Qwen2-VL variants.

> **VIBE CHECK: AGENT-ASSISTED VLM DATA PREPARATION**
>
> Preparing multimodal training data is tedious. Images must be paired with conversation-format annotations, resized or validated, and converted to the specific format each framework expects. Coding agents handle this well. Given a folder of images and a CSV of captions, an agent can generate the conversation-format JSON that Unsloth, TRL, or LLaMA-Factory expects, flag images that are too small or corrupted, and split the dataset into train and validation partitions. The agent can also draft initial instruction-response pairs from image captions, creating a starting point that human annotators refine rather than build from scratch.

A Practical Example: Fine-Tuning for Radiology

To ground these techniques in practice, consider the task of fine-tuning a VLM to interpret chest X-rays. In this domain, the need is acute, the data exists, and the stakes are high enough to illustrate both the promise and the pitfalls of domain-specific VLM adaptation.

The starting point is a base model (Qwen2.5-VL 7B or Llama 3.2 Vision 11B) that understands images broadly but knows nothing about radiology. The vision encoder, pre-trained on natural images through CLIP or SigLIP, already represents edges, textures, and spatial relationships, but it has never learned to distinguish a pleural effusion from a normal costophrenic angle. The language model can follow instructions fluently, but its medical knowledge is shallow and unreliable. The goal of fine-tuning is not to teach the model radiology from scratch (that would require far more data and compute than most organizations can muster) but to connect the visual patterns it already represents to the clinical language that radiologists use.

The Radiology Objects in Context (ROCO) dataset provides a practical starting point: more than 80,000 radiology images with expert-written captions drawn from publications on PubMed Central. A curated subset available as *unsloth/Radiology_mini* on Hugging Face includes X-rays, CT scans, and ultrasounds paired with descriptive captions. For visual question answering, VQA-RAD provides clinical questions paired with radiology images. The training data is formatted as conversations: a user message containing the image and a clinical question ("Describe the findings in this chest X-ray"), and an assistant response containing the expert description.

The training recipe follows the staged approach. With 4-bit QLoRA through Unsloth, the vision encoder stays frozen, the projection layer trains fully, and LoRA adapters with rank 16 attach to the language model's attention layers. A learning rate of 2×10^{-4} with cosine decay, batch size of 2, and gradient accumulation over 4 steps keeps memory within a single 24GB GPU. Training for 500 to 1,000 steps on a few thousand examples produces measurable improvements in radiology-specific language generation. The model begins using terms like *cardiomegaly*, *consolidation*, and *mediastinal widening* appropriately, and it learns to structure findings in the format radiologists expect.

Listing 12-1 applies directly to this radiology scenario; the configuration shown already targets the *unsloth/Radiology_mini* dataset with the parameters described previously. To experiment with projection-only training (freezing the language model entirely), set `finetune_language_layers=False` in the `get_peft_model` call; this reduces trainable parameters by roughly half and serves as a useful baseline for measuring how much the language-model adaptation contributes.

Once training completes, inference mirrors the conversation format used for training data. Listing 12-2 shows the pipeline for generating a radiology description from the fine-tuned model.

```
from qwen_vl_utils import process_vision_info
from PIL import Image

❶ FastVisionModel.for_inference(model)

image = Image.open("chest_xray_pa.png")
messages = [{"role": "user", "content": [
    {"type": "image", "image": image},
    {"type": "text",
     "text": "Describe the findings in this chest X-ray."},
]}]

❷ text = tokenizer.apply_chat_template(
    messages, add_generation_prompt=True,
)
❸ image_inputs, _ = process_vision_info(messages)
inputs = tokenizer(
    text=text, images=image_inputs, return_tensors="pt",
).to("cuda")

❹ output = model.generate(
    **inputs, max_new_tokens=256, temperature=0.1,
)
prompt_len = inputs["input_ids"].shape[-1]
response = tokenizer.decode(
    output[0][prompt_len:], skip_special_tokens=True,
)
```

Listing 12-2: Generating a radiology description from a fine-tuned VLM

Unsloth's inference mode ❶ enables optimized generation, roughly doubling throughput compared to training mode. We once again convert the conversation into the model's preferred format ❷, inserting special vision tokens where the image will be encoded. Next, `process_vision_info` extracts the PIL image from the conversation structure and prepares it for the vision encoder ❸. In medical applications, temperature is generally set to a fairly low value (in this case, `0.1` ❹) to favor a deterministic, clinically conservative output.

Experimenting with different settings reveals what works and what does not. Projection-layer training alone would be sufficient to teach the model to associate visual patterns with radiological terms, but the descriptions would remain generic (for example, "opacity in the left lower lobe" without further characterization). Adding LoRA to the language model deepens the clinical language, enabling more specific descriptions. A critical finding from recent research is that combining domain-specific pre-training with instruction alignment can produce interference. Surface-level metrics like BLEU and ROUGE may drop even as diagnostic accuracy improves, because the model shifts from generating verbose, repetitive descriptions to producing concise, clinically focused ones. This interference effect means that automated metrics alone cannot guide training decisions. Radiologist evaluation is not optional but essential, and too much of a good thing, alas, can ruin the entire process.

WARNING *A VLM that achieves 90 percent accuracy on VQA-RAD benchmarks is not a diagnostic tool. Benchmark accuracy measures performance on standardized questions with unambiguous answers. Clinical radiology involves ambiguity, uncertainty, and the integration of imaging with patient history. Regulatory frameworks (FDA 510(k) in the United States, CE marking in the European Union) require clinical validation that goes far beyond benchmark performance. Organizations pursuing medical VLM deployment must budget for clinical trials, regulatory submissions, and ongoing monitoring–costs that dwarf the fine-tuning investment itself.*

Stanford's CheXagent illustrates the scale required for a production radiology VLM: It was trained on CheXinstruct, a dataset of 6.1 million instruction-answer pairs drawn from 1.1 million unique chest X-ray images across 28 publicly available datasets, and evaluated on CheXbench, a benchmark spanning eight clinically relevant tasks.[206] Microsoft's RAD-DINO demonstrates an alternative approach: Rather than language-supervised pre-training, the vision encoder is trained solely on radiology images via self-supervised learning (DINOv2), achieving competitive performance without requiring paired image-text data.[207] For practitioners without access to large paired medical datasets, RAD-DINO's approach of training the vision encoder on unlabeled domain images and then connecting it to a language model offers a path that circumvents the annotation bottleneck.

Preference Optimization for Visual Models

The preference optimization techniques from Chapter 5 extend naturally to VLMs, with particular value for the signature failure mode of visual models: hallucination. When a VLM describes objects that aren't present in an image, preference optimization provides a mechanism to teach the model not merely what to say, but what *not* to say—a distinction that SFT alone struggles to capture.

The data format mirrors text-only preference optimization. Each example consists of an image, a prompt, a preferred response (accurate, grounded in image content), and a rejected response (hallucinated, inaccurate, or poorly grounded). Constructing these pairs typically involves generating multiple responses per image from the fine-tuned model, then having annotators rank them for visual fidelity. The annotation cost is higher than for text-only preference data, because annotators must carefully compare each response against the actual image content rather than simply judging fluency or helpfulness.

The practical challenge is constructing these pairs at scale. The most effective approach generates rejected responses from the fine-tuned model itself: Sample three to five completions per image at elevated temperature, then have annotators identify which responses contain hallucinations. Hallucinated responses become the rejected examples, and either the best model response or a human-written ground truth serves as the preferred example. This approach has the advantage of targeting exactly the hallucination patterns the model produces rather than synthetic errors that may not match the model's failure distribution. The disadvantage is the cost of multiple inferences per training image, followed by careful human review. For a dataset of 5,000 images, expect to generate 15,000 to 25,000 candidate responses and spend 100 to 200 annotator hours constructing the preference pairs.

DPO applies without architectural modification, as the VLM produces text conditioned on image input, and DPO operates on the text-generation probabilities. Recent work on negative supervised fine-tuning (nSFT) offers an intriguing simplification: Rather than maintaining two or four copies of the model as DPO and PPO require, nSFT extracts the useful signal from rejected responses and integrates it into a standard SFT loss.[208] The approach achieved a 15-point improvement on hallucination benchmarks while requiring substantially less memory than full preference optimization—a meaningful advantage, given the already heavy memory demands of VLM training. For teams that have completed SFT and want to reduce hallucination without doubling their GPU budget, nSFT represents a practical middle ground.

Uni-Med, presented at NeurIPS 2024, illustrates a complementary approach to multimodal alignment through architecture rather than preference data.[209] Its Connector Mixture-of-Experts (MoE) module uses specialized expert projectors for various medical tasks (visual question answering, report generation, image classification), routing each example to the appropriate expert. This architectural specialization avoids the "tug-of-war" problem of training on one task degrading performance on another; this problem is particularly acute in multitask medical settings with a single model handling diverse imaging modalities and clinical queries. The insight is that sometimes the projection layer, the component connecting vision to language, benefits from task-specific specialization rather than one-size-fits-all training.

Why Benchmarks Mislead and Humans Remain Essential

Evaluation of VLMs must assess capabilities that neither pure vision benchmarks nor pure language benchmarks capture—namely, the integration of visual understanding with linguistic expression. Standard academic benchmarks (VQA with its short-answer format, grouped query attention [GQA] with its compositional questions, or visual reasoning tasks that test spatial and logical inference) provide useful signals but may mislead if taken as proxies for real-world performance. A model might excel at VQA's constrained format while failing to produce useful responses in open-ended enterprise scenarios, for example.

The solution lies in constructing evaluation sets that mirror deployment conditions. For a document-understanding application, this means using test documents representative of the documents the model will encounter, with questions and response formats matching actual usage. For manufacturing inspection, test images should include the full range of defect types at frequencies matching production reality, including challenging edge cases that distinguish capable from mediocre models. Creating such evaluation sets requires domain expertise and significant effort, but the alternative (deploying based on generic benchmark performance) invites surprises when the model encounters real data.

Human evaluation remains indispensable for VLM assessment, more so than for text-only models. Automated metrics can assess whether a generated caption mentions the correct objects but cannot assess whether the caption captures what matters about an image for a given purpose. Human judges can verify visual grounding (does the model's response correspond to image content?) in ways that automated metrics cannot. The practical protocol typically combines automated metrics for efficiency with human evaluation for validity. Screen candidate models via automated benchmarks, then assess the survivors with human evaluation before deployment decisions. This hybrid approach balances the cost of human evaluation against the risk of trusting metrics that don't capture what matters.

That said, the automated benchmark landscape has matured considerably, and knowing which benchmarks to use saves time in the screening phase. MMMU tests multidiscipline, multimodal understanding with questions drawn from college-level exams across 30 subjects, making it a reasonable proxy for general visual reasoning.[210] MMBench evaluates a broader set of 20 fine-grained abilities, from content recognition to spatial reasoning.[211] For domain-specific evaluation, CheXbench spans eight clinically relevant chest X-ray interpretation tasks and remains the gold standard for radiology VLM assessment. Table 12-4 summarizes the key options.

Table 12-4: Key VLM Evaluation Benchmarks

Benchmark	What it measures	Format	Best suited for
MMMU	Multidiscipline reasoning (30 subjects)	Multiple-choice, open ended	General capability screening
MMBench	20 fine-grained abilities	Multiple-choice	Detailed capability profiling
MME	Perception and cognition	Yes/no questions	Quick pass/fail assessment
VQA-v2	Visual question answering	Short answer	Baseline visual understanding
CheXbench	Clinical X-ray interpretation (8 tasks)	Task specific	Medical imaging evaluation
DocVQA	Document understanding	Extractive QA	OCR and document workflows

The critical point is that no single benchmark captures what matters for a specific application. Use MMMU and MMBench to screen candidates, DocVQA for document-heavy workflows, and CheXbench for medical applications. Always follow automated screening with domain-specific human evaluation.

> **WHY VLM EVALUATION NEEDS HUMANS**
>
> For text-only models, automated metrics such as BLEU, ROUGE, and perplexity often correlate well with human judgment. For VLMs, no such reliable proxies exist. An automated metric can check whether *dog* appears in a caption for a dog image but cannot assess whether the caption captures the dog's breed, size, activity, or expression, which are the details that might matter for the application. Until visual understanding metrics mature, human evaluation is not optional but essential.

Beyond Text: Speech and Sound

Speech carries far more than words: speaker identity, emotional state, emphasis, uncertainty. These, in turn, convey meaning, intent, and context that must form part of the model's understanding. Language models have come a long way but remain limited in their ability to reflect the domain scope of language use. This makes them prime candidates for adaptation.

When Standard Transcription Mangles Your Terminology

Speech-to-text models arrive from pre-training with broad capabilities across languages, accents, and acoustic conditions, yet they stumble on domain-specific terminology with predictable regularity. A model that transcribes everyday conversation with high accuracy will mangle medical terminology, legal jargon, financial terms, or product names that fall outside its training distribution. Early language models used in legal practice had an unhelpful tendency to transcribe *voir dire* as *war deer*, which, while a hilarious concept, was much less fun when it made its way into pleadings uncorrected. These failures matter, because a 95 percent accurate transcription system that mangles the 5 percent of words carrying the most meaning may be worse than useless. Hard negative training in fine-tuning for domain-specific content is indispensable.

Fine-tuning addresses these gaps by exposing the model to correctly transcribed domain audio. The data requirements, while substantial, are tractable for organizations with audio processing at scale. Tens of hours of carefully transcribed domain audio can dramatically improve recognition of domain vocabulary, and hundreds of hours can achieve near-human accuracy on domain-specific content. The transcriptions must be perfect (errors in training data become errors in the model), and the acoustic conditions should match deployment. A model fine-tuned on studio-quality medical dictation may still struggle with recordings from a busy clinic, and a model trained on conference room audio may fail with mobile phone recordings.

Beyond vocabulary, fine-tuning can adapt models to accent patterns, speaking styles, and format requirements. Regional accents that the base model handles poorly can be improved with representative training data. Particular speakers' idiosyncrasies can be learned if the application processes consistent voices. And output format requirements like punctuation style, capitalization conventions, or speaker diarization can be trained explicitly. The same techniques apply as for text-only fine-tuning. Construct a dataset of input-output pairs with audio features as input and correctly formatted transcription as output, then train to minimize the gap between model output and target. The technical simplicity belies the practical difficulty of constructing high-quality training sets, but for organizations processing significant audio volumes, the ROI is substantial.

Beyond Words: Emotion, Identity, and Paralinguistics

The acoustic signal carries far more than lexical content, including speaker identity, emotional state, emphasis patterns, uncertainty markers, and the subtle prosodic variations that distinguish confident statements from tentative ones. Speech models learn representations that capture these paralinguistic features alongside the words themselves, and fine-tuning can selectively preserve, extract, or transform these characteristics depending on application requirements.

Emotion-aware transcription represents one beneficial application. Models can be trained to annotate transcripts with emotional markers, distinguishing frustrated callers from satisfied ones, and anxious patients from calm ones. Customer service applications use such capabilities to appropriately route calls or flag conversations requiring supervisor attention. Healthcare applications might track patient affect over time, providing clinicians with longitudinal data that would otherwise require laborious manual review. The training requires audio labeled with emotional categories, a task that requires trained annotators but is tractable for organizations processing substantial call volumes.

Voice cloning occupies more ethically fraught territory. The same technology that enables personalized text-to-speech for individuals with vocal impairments can enable fraud, impersonation, and manipulation. Fine-tuning for voice cloning is technically similar to other speech model adaptation (learn a mapping between text and acoustic features for a specific voice), but the potential for misuse requires careful governance. Enterprises deploying voice-cloning capabilities must implement consent verification, use-case restrictions, and abuse monitoring. The technology itself is neutral, but responsible deployment requires active safeguards. Regulatory frameworks are emerging, though they lag the technology, and practitioners must make ethical judgments that anticipate rather than merely comply with regulation.

The Multilingual Challenge

Multilingual speech processing confronts challenges that text-only multilingual models avoid. Written text clearly delineates language boundaries through orthography, but spoken language flows continuously, and speakers routinely code switch, sometimes even shifting between languages mid-sentence or even mid-phrase. Growing up in a multilingual environment, I later had to get used to the fact that most people expect a sentence starting in one language to end in the same, and audio models have to tackle the reverse of this challenge. A speaker in Mumbai might begin a sentence in Hindi, switch to English for technical terms, and conclude in Hindi, all within a single conversational turn. A speaker in Brussels might intermingle French and Flemish. These patterns are natural for human speakers but challenge models trained to process monolingual utterances.

Fine-tuning for code switching requires training data that reflects actual multilingual usage patterns, a dataset type that is scarce and expensive to create. Annotation must segment language boundaries and correctly transcribe each segment in its respective orthography. The resulting models can handle natural multilingual speech, a capability increasingly valuable as global enterprises operate across linguistic boundaries. Call centers serving diverse populations, healthcare systems treating immigrant communities, and international organizations conducting multilingual meetings all benefit from models that gracefully handle code switching.

Enterprises rarely encounter a need to fine-tune for a new language as part of their workloads, except where stock language models fail to meet the needs of their audiences. This is particularly acute when either low-resource languages are involved or a particular terminology must be mastered. Some years ago, I was involved in fine-tuning the rudimentary audio models of the day to recognize some industry-specific terms in aerospace engineering; today, even lightweight stock models pick up these terms effortlessly. For low-resource languages, transfer learning offers partial solutions: For languages that share phonemic and prosodic properties, cross-lingual similarities are likely going to be beneficial for training. For instance, a model trained on Hungarian will adapt much easier to Csángó, a phonetically divergent dialect of Hungarian, than an English base model would. Strategic fine-tuning on limited data can leverage these cross-lingual similarities, achieving workable transcription quality with far less data than would be required from scratch. For enterprises operating in regions where low-resource languages predominate, this transfer learning approach may be the only practical path to speech-processing capability. The results won't match high-resource language performance, but they may still provide substantial value compared to having no speech processing at all. Perhaps more crucially, they also reflect the profound moral, ethical, and social commitment that lies behind honoring every individual's dignity and identity through respecting their chosen language.

The Frontier Beyond

While language models may capture most attention, academic and popular alike, the frontier of multimodality is ever expanding. Video, 3D point clouds from LiDAR, depth imaging, time series and many other new modalities have emerged over the last few years. Each requires specialized encoders, but the general architectural pattern established for VLMs echoes in their particular architectures.

Video: When Time Matters

Video presents the temporal dimension that static images lack. Events unfold, causes precede effects, and understanding often requires integrating information across sequences that may span thousands of frames. The challenge lies in efficiently processing this temporal structure while preserving the information that matters. A naive approach might process each frame independently, but this discards precisely the temporal relationships that make video distinct from a slideshow of images.

Current architectures navigate this tension through various strategies. Frame sampling selects keyframes at regular intervals, reducing computational cost at the expense of missing events that occur between samples. Temporal attention mechanisms allow models to attend across frames, capturing relationships between moments separated in time. Video-specific encoders like TimeSformer or ViViT process spatiotemporal patches directly, learning joint representations of space and time. Each approach trades off computational efficiency against temporal resolution, and the optimal choice depends on the application. Surveillance footage including brief events that matter requires higher temporal resolution than instructional videos with key steps spanning seconds.

Fine-tuning for video understanding remains less mature than image-language work, though the gap is closing rapidly. Qwen2.5-VL and Gemma 3 already process video natively by treating sampled frames as ordered image sequences within their existing architecture, eliminating the need for separate video-specific encoders. Grounded-VideoLLM introduces discrete temporal tokens enriched with timestamp knowledge, enabling fine-grained temporal grounding; the model can answer not just "what happens" but "when does it happen" and "what happens before and after." Molmo 2 extends this further with spatiotemporal grounding, tracking objects and pointing to specific moments in a video with spatial precision. These models use multistage training schemes that begin with simple video captioning and progressively introduce temporal grounding tasks of increasing complexity.

Training data must include temporal annotations, covering not just what happens in a video but when it happens and how events relate across time. The annotation burden increases substantially. A single image might require one caption, while a video might require dense annotations of actions, their durations, and their causal relationships. For enterprise applications like process monitoring, security analysis, or training-video indexing, the investment in temporal annotation can yield models that extract structure from video archives that would otherwise require exhaustive human review.

Video occupies a special position among modalities because it captures something no other data type does: the causal structure of the physical world. A static image shows that a glass is on a table, but a video shows the glass being placed, sliding, tipping, and shattering. This temporal causality makes video uniquely suited for training *world models*—systems that learn not merely to describe what they see, but to predict what will happen next and to simulate plausible futures.

Sora, Genie 2, and UniSim demonstrated that video-generation models trained on large corpora of unlabeled video implicitly learn physics: Objects fall, liquids flow, collisions produce consequences, and they do so in a physically plausible manner. The implications for post-training are profound. A model that has internalized physical dynamics through video pre-training can be fine-tuned for tasks that require physical reasoning (such as robotic planning, industrial process simulation, and surgical procedure prediction) in ways that a model trained only on images and text cannot.

We are still in the early stages of understanding how to harness these emergent physical representations, but the direction is clear: Video is not merely another modality to bolt onto a language model backbone, but a pathway toward models that understand how the world works rather than merely how it looks. For enterprise practitioners, this means that investment in video understanding today may yield capabilities that extend far beyond video captioning and search into physical reasoning, simulation, and planning.

Seeing in Three Dimensions

The physical world exists in three dimensions, and applications from robotics to augmented reality require models that reason about spatial structure rather than merely recognizing objects in two-dimensional (2D) projections. Point clouds captured by LiDAR sensors, depth maps from stereo cameras, and volumetric representations from medical imaging all provide 3D information that 2D image processing cannot capture. A robot navigating a warehouse must understand the spatial layout, not just recognize that shelves are present. An augmented reality system must understand where in 3D space virtual objects should be placed. A surgical planning system must reason about the spatial relationships between anatomical structures.

Models that integrate 3D perception with language are emerging but remain less mature than image-language systems. The architectural pattern resembles VLM approaches. A 3D encoder processes point clouds or volumetric data into continuous representations, a projection mechanism maps these representations into the language model's space, and the language model reasons over the combined inputs. Point cloud encoders like PointNet and its successors provide the 3D analog to vision transformers, learning to extract meaningful features from unordered sets of 3D coordinates.

Fine-tuning for 3D understanding faces a data bottleneck more severe than image-language work. Collecting point clouds requires specialized sensors, annotating spatial relationships requires annotators who can reason in 3D and articulate that reasoning linguistically, and the diversity of 3D data types (point clouds, meshes, voxels, depth maps) fragments the available training resources. Synthetic data generation offers partial relief. Simulation environments can generate unlimited 3D scenes with perfect annotations, and the gap between simulated and real data is often smaller for geometric structure than for visual appearance. Enterprises with 3D sensing infrastructure may find that their operational data, once annotated, provides fine-tuning material that is unavailable elsewhere.

The World of Sensor Data

Beyond images, video, and audio lies the vast space of sensor data, including temperature readings from industrial equipment, vibration patterns from machinery, electrical signals from medical monitors, motion data from wearables, and telemetry streams from IoT networks. This data often matters enormously (a subtle change in vibration pattern may presage equipment failure, and a shift in physiological signals may indicate deteriorating patient condition) yet it remains largely inaccessible to language models trained only on text.

The architectural template established for VLMs extends to sensor data. A specialized encoder converts time series or sensor streams into continuous representations, a projection layer maps these representations into the language model's embedding space, and the language model can then reason about sensor data in conjunction with textual context. The encoder architecture varies by data type, with convolutional networks for one-dimensional (1D) time series, recurrent architectures for sequences with long-range dependencies, and transformer variants for sensor data with complex temporal structure.

Most of the applications currently lie in the medical and industrial sector. Predictive maintenance systems, for example, can explain why a particular sensor pattern suggests impending failure, in natural language that maintenance personnel can act upon. Clinical monitoring systems can summarize hours of physiological data into actionable insights for clinicians, flagging anomalies and placing them in patient context. Process control systems can answer natural language queries about current conditions and historical trends. These applications have high value but limited existing training data, making them prime candidates for enterprise fine-tuning. The organization that operates the equipment, monitors the patients, or runs the processes has access to sensor data that is unavailable to model providers, creating opportunity for differentiation through domain-specific multimodal capability.

When Modalities Collide

A model processing both image and text must maintain consistency between what it sees and what it reads. This seems obvious but proves difficult, as models may accurately describe images in isolation yet contradict those descriptions when textual context misleads. Cross-modal coherence requires explicit training.

When Text and Images Disagree

Achieving cross-modal consistency requires examples where modalities must be integrated and contradictions must be resolved. The dataset should include textual descriptions that correctly match images, textual descriptions and images that conflict, and examples requiring the model to synthesize information across modalities to answer questions that neither modality could answer alone. The training objective should penalize responses that contradict available evidence in any modality while rewarding responses that demonstrate genuine integration. This is more easily stated than achieved, as defining *contradiction* in ways that training procedures can operationalize requires careful thought about what consistency means for various applications.

Evaluation for cross-modal consistency requires adversarial testing that probes for failures. Can the model be misled by textual context into making claims that contradict visible image content? Does the model recognize when textual and visual information conflict, or does it simply privilege one modality over the other? Constructing such evaluation sets requires creativity in generating plausible conflicts and care in judging whether model responses appropriately navigate them. For enterprise applications needing multiple information sources to be integrated (document understanding that combines scanned images with OCR text, for instance), cross-modal consistency is not a nice-to-have but a requirement for reliable operation.

Fine-tuning introduces its own consistency threat through a phenomenon researchers call *cross-modal feature drift*. As the language model's weights update during domain-specific training, the alignment between visual and textual feature spaces degrades, causing the model to "forget" how to connect what it sees with what it says. This is the multimodal analog of catastrophic forgetting (Chapter 8), but with an additional failure mode: The model may retain strong performance on both vision and language tasks individually while losing the ability to integrate them. Parameter-efficient methods like LoRA mitigate this by structurally isolating updates, preventing the destructive weight overwrites that cause drift in shared cross-attention layers. When fine-tuning for a new domain, monitoring cross-modal consistency on a held-out set of general image-text pairs—not just domain-specific accuracy—helps catch drift before it compounds.

New Modalities, New Attack Surfaces

The attack surface for multimodal systems extends beyond what text-only safety measures address. An image may encode harmful content that accompanying text describes innocuously, audio may carry emotional manipulation that transcripts fail to capture, and combinations of individually benign inputs may produce harmful outputs through their interaction. Each modality introduces vulnerability vectors that safety systems must address, and the interactions between modalities create additional vectors that neither modality would present alone.

Consider an adversary attempting to extract harmful information from a VLM. The textual request might be rejected by safety filters trained on text-only attacks, but embedding the same request in an image might bypass those filters if the model processes visual text differently from input text. Or an adversary might provide an image that appears benign but contains visual elements that, combined with seemingly innocent textual prompts, elicit harmful responses. These cross-modal attacks require safety systems that reason about the interaction between modalities, not just filter each modality independently.

Red teaming multimodal systems requires expertise that spans modalities and creativity in constructing attacks that exploit cross-modal vulnerabilities. The team needs members who understand image processing, audio manipulation, and textual adversarial attacks, and who can combine these capabilities to probe system defenses. The resulting red-team exercises take longer and require more diverse expertise than text-only evaluations, but they are essential for systems deployed in high-stakes contexts. For enterprise deployment, multimodal safety evaluation should be part of the predeployment checklist, not an afterthought discovered when the first adversarial user probes the system's boundaries.

Where Enterprise Meets Multimodal

The diversity of enterprise multimodal applications can obscure the commonalities that make transferable expertise possible. Document-understanding processes scan invoices, contracts, and forms whose text, tables, logos, and signatures must all be interpreted correctly. Manufacturing inspection examines products for defects that may be subtle variations in color, texture, or shape. Medical imaging supports diagnostic workflows as radiologists need AI assistance that understands both visual abnormalities and clinical context. Customer service systems must interpret the screenshots and product images that customers share when describing problems. Each application seems unique, yet all share fundamental requirements that this chapter's principles address.

The common thread is the need for domain-specific multimodal understanding that generic models lack. A VLM trained on internet images understands cats and cars but struggles with the subtle defects in precision-manufactured components. A model that can describe general documents may not understand the specific structure of insurance claim forms or engineering drawings. Post-training for these applications requires domain-specific data that captures the visual vocabulary of the domain (what defects look like, how documents are structured, and which features matter for diagnosis) paired with appropriate linguistic responses that serve the operational need.

Practitioners who master multimodal post-training will find their skills portable across this landscape. The technical mechanisms (vision encoders, projection layers, instruction tuning, and alignment) remain constant even as applications vary. The principles of dataset construction, evaluation design, and safety assurance transfer with modest adaptation. An engineer who has fine-tuned a VLM for document understanding will find the transition to manufacturing inspection less daunting than someone approaching multimodal AI for the first time. The applications are diverse, but the craft is one.

> **FROM THE TRENCHES: TRANSFERABLE SKILLS ACROSS APPLICATIONS**
>
> I've worked on VLM projects spanning document understanding, medical imaging, and industrial inspection. The applications look different, but the underlying work is remarkably similar. Dataset construction follows the same principles—namely, representative examples, clear instructions, and quality annotation. Evaluation requires the same hybrid of automated metrics and human judgment. Deployment involves the same trade-offs between capability and efficiency. You can master multimodal post-training once and apply it everywhere.

What Holds Across Modalities

Multimodal post-training extends the principles established for text-only models into richer perceptual territory. The architectural patterns, training techniques, and evaluation methods covered in this chapter apply whether the additional modality is images, audio, video, 3D data, or sensor streams. Specific encoders differ, but the projection-layer approach, the staged training strategies, and the need for domain-specific data remain constant.

The central challenge is annotation cost. Every multimodal example must satisfy constraints in both the perceptual and linguistic dimensions, requiring annotators who can perceive relevant details and clearly articulate them. This dual requirement typically doubles or triples annotation costs compared to text-only work, and domain-specific multimodal annotation (medical imaging, industrial inspection, specialized documents) requires expertise that further constrains the available workforce. Organizations with access to domain experts and operational data hold advantages that are difficult to replicate.

Synthetic data offers partial relief, but multimodal synthetic generation remains less mature than text generation. Generating realistic images, plausible audio, or coherent video that serves training purposes is harder than generating text, and the techniques from Chapter 10 require extension for multimodal settings. The cost pressure on multimodal annotation makes this an active area of development, and practitioners should expect rapid progress.

For visual data specifically, the most mature ecosystem is the NVIDIA Omniverse platform, whose Replicator framework illustrates how the economics of multimodal training data are shifting. Replicator renders photorealistic images from 3D scenes defined in Universal Scene Description (USD) format, applying physically based ray tracing alongside systematic domain randomization. Lighting conditions, surface textures, object poses, camera angles, and environmental parameters all vary programmatically across renders. The ground-truth annotations (bounding boxes, segmentation masks, depth maps, and surface normals) are produced automatically alongside each rendered frame, eliminating the manual labeling bottleneck. Once 3D assets and scene definitions exist, the marginal cost of each additional training image approaches zero, limited only by GPU compute cycles rather than annotator hours.

Defect detection models trained entirely on Replicator-generated data have achieved over 97 percent precision from a single CAD file, and robotics teams have used the companion Isaac Sim environment to produce tens of thousands of annotated training images without collecting a single real-world photograph. The NVIDIA Cosmos world foundation models extend the pipeline further, applying photorealistic style transfer to synthetic renders to bridge the remaining appearance gap between simulation and reality. For enterprises in manufacturing inspection, autonomous navigation, and warehouse robotics, the implication is concrete: Training data that would have required months of collection and thousands of annotator hours can now be generated in days at a fraction of the cost.

The tooling landscape has matured to the point where VLM fine-tuning is no longer the exclusive province of large research labs. Frameworks like Unsloth, TRL, and LLaMA-Factory have reduced the barrier to entry, making it possible to fine-tune a 7-billion-parameter VLM on a single consumer GPU. The radiology case study in this chapter illustrates what becomes feasible: a domain-specific visual assistant, trained on publicly available medical imaging data, that generates clinically relevant descriptions of chest X-rays. The gap between this capability and a production medical AI system remains large (regulatory validation, clinical trials, ongoing monitoring), but the gap between having no multimodal capability and having a working prototype has shrunk to days rather than months.

Preference optimization for VLMs addresses the hallucination problem that SFT alone cannot fully solve. Techniques like DPO and nSFT teach models what not to say, and they prove particularly valuable for visual models where confident descriptions of nonexistent objects pose a distinctive risk. The memory-efficient variants like nSFT make this stage practical even for teams operating under GPU constraints.

Safety in multimodal systems requires attention to cross-modal attack vectors that text-only safety measures miss. An adversary who cannot bypass safety filters through text alone may succeed by embedding requests in images or exploiting interactions between modalities. Red teaming must span all input modalities and their combinations, a more demanding exercise than text-only adversarial evaluation.

Summary

Multimodality is perhaps the most rapidly expanding frontier of new capabilities when it comes to enterprise post-training. The data quantities it requires have been hitherto prohibitive for most enterprise players, but the development of synthetic image generation in particular has revolutionized the economics of this domain, turning it from a backwater into a frontier. In the next and final chapter, we will examine what exactly lies on that frontier.

13

FUTURE DIRECTIONS: WHAT COMES NEXT

Frontier research is exploring methods that challenge assumptions we have treated as settled: test-time compute that trades inference cost for capability, mixture-of-experts (MoE) architectures that scale models without proportional cost increases, and context lengths measured in millions of tokens rather than thousands. Emerging techniques combine ideas from different paradigms: RL from execution feedback rather than human preference, curriculum learning that structures training by difficulty, and methods that blur the line between training and inference. These developments will reshape what is possible in post-training, though predicting which will prove transformative and which will fade remains uncertain.

This chapter surveys the frontier: the research directions that show promise, the emerging techniques that early adopters are testing, and the implications for enterprise AI strategy. We address what organizations should monitor, what experiments might be worth running, and how to prepare for a future where today's cutting-edge techniques, laid out in Table 13-1, become tomorrow's standard practice. The craft of post-training is not static, and practitioners who understand where the field is headed can position their organizations to adopt new capabilities as they mature. The book concludes with final thoughts on the practice of post-training as both technical discipline and organizational capability.

Table 13-1: Emerging Techniques: Readiness and Enterprise Applicability

Technique	Readiness	Best use case	Key requirement
Test-time compute	Production ready	Complex reasoning; high-stakes decisions	Budget for variable inference cost
Mixture of experts	Maturing	Efficiency at scale	Experience with sparse routing
Long context training	Production ready	Document processing; codebase QA	Long-context training data
RL from execution	Production ready	Code; mathematics; verifiable domains	Verification infrastructure
Automated curriculum	Research	Efficient training	Difficulty estimation capability
Continual learning	Research	Eliminating retraining cycles	Forgetting mitigation

The Shifting Frontier

What if compute spent per response became a variable rather than a constant? Test-time scaling inverts traditional economics. A simple question receives a fast, cheap answer, while a complex problem receives extended reasoning that may cost orders of magnitude more but achieves correspondingly better results.

Thinking Longer, Thinking Better

Test-time compute scaling makes computational effort per variable adjustable based on problem difficulty. A simple question receives a fast, cheap response, while a complex problem receives extended reasoning that may cost orders of magnitude more but achieves correspondingly better results. The technical mechanisms enabling this shift include beam search with verification (multiple candidate solutions are generated and evaluated before selection), iterative refinement (initial responses are critiqued and improved through multiple passes), and Monte Carlo tree search (the model explores a tree of possible reasoning paths, using learned value functions to guide exploration toward promising branches). Each mechanism trades inference compute for response quality, and the trade-off can be favorable. On difficult problems, a smaller model with substantial test-time compute may outperform a larger model generating single-pass responses.

The implications for post-training practitioners are significant. Training for effective test-time compute use requires different objectives than training for single-pass generation. Models must learn not just to generate good responses but to evaluate their own outputs, identify weaknesses, and improve iteratively. Reward models that assess intermediate steps (the PRMs covered in Chapter 10) become more important than those that only evaluate final answers. The training curriculum shifts toward harder problems where test-time reasoning provides advantage, rather than easier problems where quick answers suffice. Organizations that develop expertise in training for test-time compute will access a new dimension of capability improvement that pure model scaling cannot match.

> **THE NEW TRADE-OFF AXIS OF TEST-TIME COMPUTE**
>
> Test-time compute creates a new trade-off axis: response time versus response quality. A customer service application might use minimal test-time compute for fast responses, while a complex analysis might use extensive compute for accuracy. Training for this requires teaching models to effectively use additional compute, to improve with iteration rather than just generate more text. The capability is trainable, though the training differs from single-pass optimization.

Mixture of Experts: Not All Parameters All the Time

The MoE architecture challenges the assumption that all parameters must participate in every forward pass. Instead of a single monolithic network, MoE models contain multiple specialized "expert" subnetworks and a routing mechanism that selects which experts process each token. A model with 400 billion total parameters might activate only 50 billion for any given input, achieving the capability of a very large model at the inference cost of a much smaller one. This sparse computation fundamentally changes the economics, as the ratio of capability to inference cost improves dramatically.

Post-training MoE models introduces challenges absent from dense architectures. The routing mechanism must learn which experts are appropriate for which inputs, and fine-tuning can disrupt learned routing patterns. If training data skews toward certain domains, some experts may receive disproportionate training signal while others stagnate. This phenomenon, called *expert collapse*, degrades model capability. Load-balancing losses can encourage even expert utilization, but tuning these hyperparameters requires care. The optimal approach often involves freezing the router during initial fine-tuning, allowing experts to adapt before retraining routing to reflect new expert capabilities.

Domain adaptation for MoE models offers interesting possibilities. Different experts may develop specialization for different domains during pretraining, and fine-tuning can reinforce this specialization, producing experts that are genuinely expert in particular areas. A legal fine-tuning dataset might strengthen certain experts for legal reasoning while leaving others unchanged for general capability. This emergent specialization is not fully understood and cannot be directly controlled, but awareness of the possibility informs fine-tuning strategy. As MoE architectures become more prevalent (and the efficiency gains suggest they will), practitioners who develop intuition for their behavior during fine-tuning will hold valuable expertise.

Long Context Horizons

Context windows have expanded by orders of magnitude, from the few thousand tokens that seemed impressive in 2022 to millions of tokens that enable processing entire codebases or book-length documents. This expansion represents genuine progress, as truncation that once forced compromises in document processing is now often avoidable, and applications that require reasoning over extensive content become feasible. Yet raw context capacity does not automatically translate to effective context use. A model with a million-token window can see an entire codebase but may still fail to locate the function definition it needs. It can read an entire legal discovery document set but may miss the crucial email buried in the middle.

The gap between context capacity and effective utilization creates opportunity for post-training. Models can be trained to attend more reliably to information throughout their context, to answer questions that require integrating facts from distant locations, and to resist the recency bias that leads them to over-weight information near the end of their context. Training data for this purpose requires examples with long contexts where correct answers depend on information from various positions, not just the beginning or end. Creating such datasets is expensive but valuable, as organizations that develop expertise in training for effective long context use will extract more value from the same model capabilities.

Beyond extended context windows, research explores external memory mechanisms that persist across conversations and even across sessions. RAG represents one approach, querying external knowledge stores to supplement context, while learned memory systems that compress and store information for later retrieval represent another. These mechanisms aim to give models something like human long-term memory, retaining information from past interactions for use in future ones. The post-training implications are still emerging, but practitioners should monitor this research, because the ability to train models that remember and build upon past interactions would fundamentally change what AI assistants can accomplish.

What's Next

Human feedback is expensive, slow, and limited in scale. Execution feedback (Did the code pass its tests? Did the proof verify?) is cheap, fast, and unlimited. This asymmetry in feedback cost creates opportunity for training at scales that are impossible when every example requires human evaluation. The future of post-training focuses on ways of extracting value from such asymmetries.

Learning from Execution, Not Annotation

When a model generates code that either passes or fails its test suite, the test results provide a reward signal requiring no human annotation. When a model generates a mathematical proof that either verifies or does not in a proof assistant, the verification result provides ground-truth feedback at computational rather than human timescales. RL from execution feedback leverages this asymmetry to train models on verifiable tasks (coding, mathematics, and logical reasoning) with feedback loops that run autonomously. The model generates candidate solutions, execution or verification determines correctness, and the signal flows back to update the model.

Millions of iterations become feasible in situations where human-in-the-loop training could manage thousands. The resulting capability gains, particularly in mathematical reasoning and code generation, have been substantial. Models trained with execution feedback on competitive programming problems have achieved performance that would have seemed implausible just a few years ago.

The intriguing research question is whether capabilities developed on verifiable tasks transfer to domains where verification is impossible. If a model learns general reasoning skills through mathematical training, do those skills apply to problems that cannot be checked against ground truth? Early evidence suggests meaningful transfer, as models trained heavily on mathematics show improved performance on diverse reasoning tasks even when those tasks have no mathematical content. If this transfer proves robust, it suggests a path where automated feedback on verifiable domains develops capabilities that benefit unverifiable domains, reducing overall dependence on scarce human feedback.

Curriculum Learning: The Right Problem at the Right Time

Human education has long recognized that presenting material in an appropriate sequence facilitates learning. A mathematics curriculum begins with arithmetic before algebra, and algebra before calculus, not because later topics are arbitrarily "harder" but because earlier topics provide foundations that later topics require. The intuition that training order matters for ML is equally venerable, but implementing curriculum learning at scale has proven difficult.

Hand-designing curricula requires understanding both the task structure and the model's learning dynamics. Our way out of this, for the most part, has been to either use tests whose difficulty or complexity could be ascertained (for example, the USMLE) or use a sample of test-takers' results as a proxy. Automated approaches that adapt curricula to model performance offer a more scalable path.

The core idea of automated curriculum learning is to present examples at the edge of the model's current capability. Examples that are too easy provide little learning signal, since the model already handles them well. Examples that are too hard provide noisy signal, because the model cannot distinguish good from bad approaches when both fail. Examples at the edge (just beyond current capability but within reach) provide the richest learning opportunity. Automated systems can estimate example difficulty based on model performance, dynamically constructing curricula that evolve as the model improves. The result resembles a skilled tutor who adjusts challenge level in real time, always stretching but never breaking the student.

Implementation challenges are significant but not insurmountable. Difficulty estimation requires evaluating the model on candidate examples, adding computational overhead. Batch construction must balance curriculum considerations against hardware efficiency. Distribution shift during training can cause instability if not managed carefully. Yet early results suggest that the investment can pay off, as curriculum-trained models sometimes achieve higher final performance with less total training compute. For post-training practitioners, automated curriculum construction represents a frontier worth monitoring. The techniques are not yet standard practice, though they may become so as the field matures.

The Dream of Continual Learning

Current post-training practice treats model improvement as a discrete event with clear boundaries. A model is trained, evaluated, deployed, and then at some point (when performance degrades, new requirements emerge, or new data accumulates), the cycle repeats. This paradigm creates operational overhead, as retraining requires coordinating data pipelines, compute resources, and evaluation infrastructure. It also creates capability gaps, because the model deployed today reflects data available at training time and cannot incorporate lessons learned from production experience without the next retraining cycle.

Continual learning aims to eliminate this sharp boundary between training and deployment, enabling models that learn continuously from new data while preserving what they already know. The vision is compelling: a model that improves from every interaction, automatically incorporating new knowledge and adapting to shifting requirements without explicit retraining. The obstacle is catastrophic forgetting, the tendency of neural networks to lose previously learned capabilities when trained on new data. A model that learns a new domain may forget the old one, and a model that corrects a recent error may introduce errors elsewhere.

Research into mitigating catastrophic forgetting has produced promising techniques. Experience replay maintains a buffer of past examples, interleaving old data with new to prevent drift. Elastic weight consolidation identifies parameters important to prior capabilities and constrains their movement during new learning. Modular architectures add new capacity for new tasks rather than repurposing existing parameters. These techniques are not yet mature enough for production deployment in most contexts, but progress is steady. Practitioners should monitor this research while remaining realistic about current limitations; truly continual learning at scale remains a research goal rather than a deployable capability. Yet the economics are so favorable, as eliminating retraining cycles would dramatically reduce operational costs, that the techniques are likely to mature.

> **FORGETTING MITIGATION STRATEGIES**
>
> Three families of techniques address catastrophic forgetting:
>
> - Replay methods mix old examples with new during training.
> - Regularization methods penalize changes to parameters important for prior tasks.
> - Modular methods add new capacity rather than modifying existing weights.
>
> Each has trade-offs. Replay requires storing old data, regularization requires computing parameter importance, and modular approaches increase model size. None fully solves the problem, but combining approaches can preserve most prior capability while enabling meaningful adaptation.

Preparing for What Comes Next

The capabilities that require fine-tuning today may require only prompting tomorrow. This trajectory of advancing baselines has profound implications for enterprise AI strategy—namely, that organizations should invest in capabilities that will remain differentiating even as general progress commoditizes the rest.

What the Rising Tide Will Not Lift

Investments in building particular capabilities risk being overtaken by general progress in the field. The summarization model painstakingly fine-tuned in 2023 may have been surpassed by off-the-shelf capabilities in 2025, and the domain adaptation that seemed essential in 2024 may be achievable through zero-shot prompting in 2026. The strategic response is not to avoid investment but to focus it on capabilities that will remain differentiating even as baselines advance. This means avoiding generic capabilities (summarization, translation, and basic question answering) and focusing on domain-specific capabilities, which rely on data and expertise that providers cannot access. The organization's proprietary documents, internal processes, and accumulated domain expertise create fine-tuning opportunities that will remain valuable even as general capabilities improve.

The most durable advantages combine proprietary data with deep organizational integration. A model fine-tuned on an organization's historical decisions, embedded in its workflow systems, and continuously learning from its operational data cannot be replicated by a competitor using off-the-shelf APIs. The investment is substantial, but the result is defensible. Enterprises should evaluate potential AI investments through this lens: Will this capability remain differentiating as the field advances, or will general progress commoditize it? Investment should flow toward the former, while the latter may be better addressed through standard APIs that will improve automatically as providers advance their models.

Build vs. Buy in a Moving Landscape

The build-versus-buy calculus shifts continuously as provider offerings evolve. Fine-tuning through APIs, once limited to rudimentary parameter tweaking, now supports sophisticated customization workflows. Prompt caching reduces the cost of context that would otherwise require baking knowledge into weights. Prebuilt domain-specific models address common verticals. Each advance raises the bar for in-house post-training. Capabilities that justified custom development yesterday may be available off-the-shelf tomorrow, making the development investment look wasteful in retrospect.

This evolution does not eliminate the case for in-house capability but rather sharpens it. When provider offerings suffice, the wise enterprise uses them, avoiding unnecessary development cost and benefiting from continuous provider improvements. When provider offerings fall short, the case for in-house work becomes compelling precisely because the bar has risen. If an enterprise's requirements exceed what sophisticated provider offerings can deliver, those requirements likely reflect genuine differentiation that competitors cannot easily replicate.

Enterprises should regularly reassess their build-versus-buy decisions as the landscape evolves. A custom model built three years ago might now be replaceable with provider APIs that offer superior capability at lower cost. Conversely, requirements that seemed impractical to address through custom development may have become tractable as tooling improves. The decision is not a one-time choice but an ongoing evaluation. Organizations that cling to custom solutions when provider offerings have surpassed them waste resources on maintenance rather than innovation, while organizations that default to providers when their requirements justify custom work forfeit potential differentiation. Neither extreme serves well.

The Talent Bottleneck

The scarcest resource in post-training is not compute or data but talent: ML engineers who understand both the theory of training dynamics and the practice of debugging divergent runs, annotators who can provide feedback that improves model behavior rather than merely filling out templates, and technical leaders who can navigate technique selection and resource allocation with informed judgment. These specialists are in short supply and high demand. Organizations that wish to build serious post-training capability must grapple with talent acquisition and development as a first-order concern.

The talent market for post-training specialists is fierce and likely to remain so. Foundation labs compete aggressively for top researchers, well-funded startups offer equity packages that traditional enterprises struggle to match, and the academic pipeline produces graduates faster than ever but still cannot meet demand. For enterprises in the crucial middle, competing head-to-head with foundation labs for elite talent is often impractical.

Alternative strategies include developing internal talent through structured training programs, partnering with research institutions for access to emerging expertise, and building hybrid teams that combine a small core of specialists with broader engineering support.

Annotation workforce development deserves particular attention. High-quality human feedback requires annotators who understand both the task domain and the subtleties of what makes one response better than another. Building this capability takes time, as annotators must learn the domain, develop calibration through practice, and receive feedback that improves their judgment. Organizations that invest in annotation workforce development (rather than relying entirely on crowdsourced annotation or outsourced services) build a capability asset that compounds over time. The quality of fine-tuning data improves, and with it the quality of resulting models. The human capital investment, though less visible than compute spending, may ultimately prove more consequential.

Parting Thoughts

We began this book with a question: What separates organizations that extract remarkable value from AI systems from those that struggle to achieve production-grade results? The answer lies less in access to resources than in mastery of technique, and mastery of technique is what this book has aimed to provide.

What Remains When Techniques Change

Certain themes have recurred throughout our journey. Data quality matters more than data quantity, and a thousand carefully curated examples outweigh a million noisy ones. Evaluation must reflect deployment requirements, not merely benchmark performance, since a model that excels on academic tests may fail on operational realities. Every design decision involves trade-offs between competing goods: capability versus efficiency, adaptation versus preservation, and customization versus generality. There are no universally optimal choices, only choices appropriate to particular contexts. The practitioner's judgment lies in wisely navigating these trade-offs.

The techniques themselves will evolve. The specific algorithms that dominate today may give way to improved alternatives, the particular architectures may be superseded by novel designs, and the tools and frameworks will certainly change. Yet these underlying principles of careful data curation, rigorous evaluation, and thoughtful trade-off analysis will persist. A practitioner who has internalized these principles will adapt to new techniques more readily than one who has merely memorized current procedures.

The Path Forward

The reader who has engaged seriously with this material possesses the conceptual foundations for post-training work of genuine complexity. Concepts and foundations, however, are not the same as operational competence, and the gap between understanding a technique in principle and applying it successfully in practice is bridged only through doing. I encourage you to work through the accompanying notebooks, which provide hands-on experience with each major technique. Experiment with variations, change parameters and observe effects, and break things deliberately to understand why they broke.

Engage with the research community. The field moves fast. Techniques that seem cutting-edge today may be superseded within months, and staying current requires ongoing investment. Read papers, attend conferences (virtually or in person), and participate in forums where practitioners share experiences. Much valuable knowledge never makes it into formal publications but circulates through informal channels such as blog posts, X threads, and Discord servers. These are not distractions from serious work but legitimate sources of current practice that complement more formal learning.

> **VIBE CHECK: RESEARCH MONITORING ASSISTANCE**
>
> Coding agents can help manage the firehose of research output. Given a set of topics (such as *preference optimization*, *test-time compute*, or *multimodal alignment*), an agent can monitor arXiv daily, filter for relevant papers, and produce weekly digests summarizing key findings. The agent can maintain a reading list ranked by relevance to your current work, extract key claims and results from papers you flag as important, and track citation networks to identify emerging influential work.
>
> This does not replace reading papers yourself, but it dramatically reduces the time spent finding which papers to read. The alternative of manually checking arXiv, X, and conference proceedings consumes hours that could go toward implementation.

Build capability incrementally. Start with SFT (Chapter 3), which involves fewer moving parts and provides clearer feedback signals. Master single modalities before tackling multimodal challenges. Develop evaluation infrastructure before advancing to techniques that require sophisticated evaluation; each capability layer provides foundation for the next. The temptation to leap directly to advanced techniques is understandable (RL sounds more impressive than SFT), but skipping foundations leads to frustration and failure. The path from understanding to expertise is paved with practice, and there are no shortcuts.

Summary

Post-training is not merely a technical discipline but a bridge between the remarkable capabilities of foundation models and the specific requirements of real-world deployment. The techniques in this book enable that bridge, while the judgment to apply them wisely comes from experience and reflection. I have aimed to provide not just recipes but understanding—the *why* beneath the *how*—so that you can adapt to situations we have not anticipated and techniques that do not yet exist. The field will continue to evolve, but the principles of careful data curation, rigorous evaluation, and thoughtful trade-off analysis will not.

For enterprises in the crucial middle, post-training represents perhaps the most accessible path to meaningful AI differentiation. The foundation models are available, the techniques are documented, and the infrastructure is achievable. What remains is the commitment to develop capability systematically, the patience to do it right, and the wisdom to know when simpler approaches suffice. I hope this book has contributed to all three.

NOTES

1. Nick Bostrom. *Superintelligence: Paths, Dangers, Strategies*. Oxford University Press, 2014.
2. Lars Malmqvist. "Sycophancy in Large Language Models: Causes and Mitigations." arXiv. 2024. *https://arxiv.org/abs/2411.15287*.
3. Fabrizio Dell'Acqua et al. "Navigating the Jagged Technological Frontier: Field Experimental Evidence of the Effects of AI on Knowledge Worker Productivity and Quality." *Harvard Business School Technology and Operations Management Unit Working Paper* 24-013. 2023.
4. Tairan Fu et al. "Why Do Large Language Models (LLMs) Struggle to Count Letters?" arXiv. 2024. *https://arxiv.org/abs/2412.18626*.
5. Marianna Nezhurina et al. "Alice in Wonderland: Simple Tasks Showing Complete Reasoning Breakdown in State-Of-the-Art Large Language Models." arXiv. 2024. *https://arxiv.org/abs/2406.02061*.
6. Daniel Han, Michael Han, and the Unsloth team. Unsloth. 2023. *https://github.com/unslothai/unsloth*.
7. Axolotl maintainers and contributors. "Axolotl: Open Source LLM Post-Training." 2023. *https://github.com/axolotl-ai-cloud/axolotl*.
8. Guangming Sheng et al. "HybridFlow: A Flexible and Efficient RLHF Framework." arXiv. 2024. *https://arxiv.org/abs/2409.19256*.
9. Fali Wang et al. "A Comprehensive Survey of Small Language Models in the Era of Large Language Models: Techniques, Enhancements, Applications, Collaboration with LLMs, and Trustworthiness." arXiv. 2024. *https://arxiv.org/abs/2411.03350*.
10. OpenAI. "Sycophancy in GPT-4o: What Happened and What We're Doing About It." Apr. 29, 2025. *https://openai.com/index/sycophancy-in-gpt-4o/*.
11. Anthropic. "Disrupting the First Reported AI-Orchestrated Cyber Espionage Campaign." Nov. 13, 2025. *https://www.anthropic.com/news/disrupting-AI-espionage*.
12. OpenAI. "Our Updated Preparedness Framework." Apr. 15, 2025. *https://openai.com/index/updating-our-preparedness-framework/*.
13. Liwei Jiang et al. "Artificial Hivemind: The Open-Ended Homogeneity of Language Models (and Beyond)." arXiv. 2025. *https://arxiv.org/abs/2510.22954*.

14. Jay Barney. "Firm Resources and Sustained Competitive Advantage." *Journal of Management* 17.1. 1991, pp. 99–120. DOI: *10.1177/014920639101700108*.

15. Clifford Geertz. *The Interpretation of Cultures*. Basic Books, 1973.

16. Sewon Min et al. "Rethinking the Role of Demonstrations: What Makes In-Context Learning Work?" *Proceedings of the 2022 Conference on Empirical Methods in Natural Language Processing*. 2022, pp. 11048–11064. *https://arxiv.org/abs/2202.12837*.

17. Jiayi Yuan et al. "Give Me FP32 or Give Me Death? Challenges and Solutions for Reproducible Reasoning." arXiv. 2025. *https://arxiv.org/abs/2506.09501*.

18. National Institute of Standards and Technology. *Artificial Intelligence Risk Management Framework (AI RMF 1.0)*. Accessed Jan. 7, 2026. *https://nvlpubs.nist.gov/nistpubs/ai/NIST.AI.100-1.pdf*.

19. Board of Governors of the Federal Reserve System. *Supervisory Guidance on Model Risk Management (SR 11-7)*. Accessed Jan. 7, 2026. *https://www.federalreserve.gov/frrs/guidance/supervisory-guidance-on-model-risk-management.htm*.

20. Tony Z. Zhao et al. "Calibrate Before Use: Improving Few-Shot Performance of Language Models." arXiv. 2021. *https://arxiv.org/abs/2102.09690*.

21. Ari Holtzman et al. "The Curious Case of Neural Text Degeneration." arXiv. 2019. *https://arxiv.org/abs/1904.09751*.

22. Pengfei Liu et al. "Pre-train, Prompt, and Predict: A Systematic Survey of Prompting Methods in Natural Language Processing." arXiv. 2021. *https://arxiv.org/abs/2107.13586*.

23. Long Ouyang et al. "Training Language Models to Follow Instructions with Human Feedback." *Advances in Neural Information Processing Systems* 35. 2022, pp. 27730–27744.

24. Ziwei Ji et al. "Survey of Hallucination in Natural Language Generation." *ACM Computing Surveys* 55.12. 2023, pp. 1–38.

25. Matthew Dahl et al. "Large Legal Fictions: Profiling Legal Hallucinations in Large Language Models." *Journal of Legal Analysis* 16.1. 2024, pp. 64–93.

26. Karan Singhal et al. "Large Language Models Encode Clinical Knowledge." arXiv. 2022. *https://arxiv.org/abs/2212.13138*.

27. Patrick Lewis et al. "Retrieval-Augmented Generation for Knowledge-Intensive NLP Tasks." arXiv. 2020. *https://arxiv.org/abs/2005.11401*.

28. Llama Team, AI @ Meta. "The Llama 3 Herd of Models." arXiv. 2024. Describes Meta's iterative SFT + DPO post-training pipeline for Llama 3. *https://arxiv.org/abs/2407.21783*.

29. Nathan Lambert et al. "TÜLU 3: Pushing Frontiers in Open Language Model Post-Training." arXiv. 2024. *https://arxiv.org/abs/2411.15124*.

30. DeepSeek-AI. "DeepSeek-R1: Incentivizing Reasoning Capability in LLMs via Reinforcement Learning." arXiv. 2025. *https://arxiv.org/abs/2501.12948*.

31. Sara Hooker. "On the Slow Death of Scaling." *SSRN Electronic Journal*. 2025. *https://papers.ssrn.com/sol3/papers.cfm?abstract_id=5877662*.

32. Yuntao Bai et al. "Constitutional AI: Harmlessness from AI Feedback." arXiv. 2022. *https://arxiv.org/abs/2212.08073*.

33. Tianjun Zhang et al. "RAFT: Adapting Language Model to Domain Specific RAG." arXiv. 2024. *https://arxiv.org/abs/2403.10131*.

34. Trenton Bricken et al. "Towards Monosemanticity: Decomposing Language Models with Dictionary Learning." *Transformer Circuits Thread*. 2023. *https://transformer-circuits.pub/2023/monosemantic-features/index.html*.

35. Adly Templeton et al. "Scaling Monosemanticity: Extracting Interpretable Features from Claude 3 Sonnet." *Transformer Circuits Thread*. 2024. *https://transformer-circuits.pub/2024/scaling-monosemanticity/index.html*.

36. Eric Ho. "Feature Steering for Reliable and Expressive AI Engineering." Nov. 19, 2024. *https://www.goodfire.ai/blog/feature-steering-for-reliable-and-expressive-ai-engineering*. Nov. 19, 2024.

37. Maxime Labonne. "Uncensor Any LLM with Abliteration." June 13, 2024. *https://huggingface.co/blog/mlabonne/abliteration*.

38. Margaret Mitchell et al. "Model Cards for Model Reporting." *Proceedings of the Conference on Fairness, Accountability, and Transparency*. ACM. 2019, pp. 220–229.

39. Dylan Patel et al. "Scaling Laws, O1 Pro Architecture, Reasoning Training Infrastructure, Orion and Claude 3.5 Opus 'Failures.'" Dec. 10, 2024. *https://newsletter.semianalysis.com/p/scaling-laws-o1-pro-architecture-reasoning-training-infrastructure-orion-and-claude-3-5-opus-failures*.

40. Nathan Lambert. "Llama 2 Follow-up: Too Much RLHF, GPU Sizing, Technical Details." July 21, 2023. *https://www.interconnects.ai/p/llama-2-part-2*.

41. Ashish Vaswani et al. "Attention is All You Need." *Advances in Neural Information Processing Systems* 30. 2017.

42. Alec Radford et al. "Improving Language Understanding by Generative Pre-Training." OpenAI. 2018. *https://cdn.openai.com/research-covers/language-unsupervised/language_understanding_paper.pdf*.

43. Ian Tenney, Dipanjan Das, and Ellie Pavlick. "BERT Rediscovers the Classical NLP Pipeline." *Proceedings of the 57th Annual Meeting of the Association for Computational Linguistics*. 2019, pp. 4593–4601.

44. Gancsh Jawahar, Benoît Sagot, and Djamé Seddah. "What Does BERT Learn about the Structure of Language?" *Proceedings of the 57th Annual Meeting of the Association for Computational Linguistics*. 2019, pp. 3651–3657.

45. Nelson Elhage et al. "A Mathematical Framework for Transformer Circuits." *Transformer Circuits Thread*. 2021. *https://transformer-circuits.pub/2021/framework/index.html.*

46. Mor Geva et al. "Transformer Feed-Forward Layers Are Key-Value Memories." *Proceedings of the 2021 Conference on Empirical Methods in Natural Language Processing*. 2021, pp. 5484–5495.

47. Kevin Meng et al. "Locating and Editing Factual Associations in GPT." *Advances in Neural Information Processing Systems*. Vol. 35. 2022, 17359–17372.

48. Kevin Meng et al. "Mass-Editing Memory in a Transformer." *International Conference on Learning Representations*. 2023.

49. Philip Gage. "A New Algorithm for Data Compression." *C Users Journal* 12.2. 1994, pp. 23–38.

50. Rico Sennrich, Barry Haddow, and Alexandra Birch. "Neural Machine Translation of Rare Words with Subword Units." *Proceedings of the 54th Annual Meeting of the Association for Computational Linguistics*. 2016, pp. 1715–1725.

51. Jacob Devlin et al. "BERT: Pre-training of Deep Bidirectional Transformers for Language Understanding." *Proceedings of the 2019 Conference of the North American Chapter of the Association for Computational Linguistics: Human Language Technologies*. 2019, pp. 4171–4186.

52. Taku Kudo. "Subword Regularization: Improving Neural Network Translation Models with Multiple Subword Candidates." *Proceedings of the 56th Annual Meeting of the Association for Computational Linguistics*. 2018, pp. 66–75.

53. Taku Kudo and John Richardson. "SentencePiece: A Simple and Language Independent Subword Tokenizer and Detokenizer for Neural Text Processing." *Proceedings of the 2018 Conference on Empirical Methods in Natural Language Processing: System Demonstrations*. 2018, pp. 66–71.

54. Prathamesh Kalamkar et al. "The Tokenization Bottleneck: How Vocabulary Extension Improves Chemistry Representation Learning in Pretrained Language Models." arXiv. 2024. *https://arxiv.org/abs/2511.14365.*

55. Wen Tai et al. "exBERT: Extending Pre-Trained Models with Domain-Specific Vocabulary Under Constrained Training Resources." *Findings of the Association for Computational Linguistics: EMNLP 2020*. 2020, pp. 1433–1439.

56. Daixuan Cheng, Shaohan Huang, and Furu Wei. "Adapting Large Language Models to Domains via Reading Comprehension." arXiv. 2024. *https://arxiv.org/abs/2309.09530.*

57. Gautier Dagan, Gabriel Synnaeve, and Baptiste Rozière. "Getting the Most Out of Your Tokenizer for Pre-Training and Domain Adaptation." arXiv. 2024. *https://arxiv.org/abs/2402.01035.*

58. Shane Waxler et al. "Generative Medical Event Models Improve with Scale." arXiv. 2025. *https://arxiv.org/abs/2508.12104*.

59. Haotian Liu et al. "Visual Instruction Tuning." *Advances in Neural Information Processing Systems*. Vol. 36. 2023.

60. Hao Li et al. "Visualizing the Loss Landscape of Neural Nets." *Advances in Neural Information Processing Systems*. Vol. 31. 2018.

61. Huanran Chen et al. "Unveiling the Basin-Like Loss Landscape in Large Language Models." arXiv. 2025. *https://arxiv.org/abs/2505.17646*.

62. Jesse Dodge et al. "Fine-Tuning Pretrained Language Models: Weight Initializations, Data Orders, and Early Stopping." *Proceedings of the 58th Annual Meeting of the Association for Computational Linguistics*. 2020, pp. 2078–2089.

63. Almog Gueta et al. "Knowledge is a Region in Weight Space for Fine-Tuned Language Models." arXiv. 2023. *https://arxiv.org/abs/2302.04863*.

64. Anna Rogers, Olga Kovaleva, and Anna Rumshisky. "A Primer in BERTology: What We Know About How BERT Works." *Transactions of the Association for Computational Linguistics* 8. 2020, pp. 842–866.

65. Jeremy Howard and Sebastian Ruder. "Universal Language Model Fine-Tuning for Text Classification." *Proceedings of the 56th Annual Meeting of the Association for Computational Linguistics*. 2018, pp. 328–339.

66. Jaejun Lee, Raphael Tang, and Jimmy Lin. "What Would Elsa Do? Freezing Layers During Transformer Fine-Tuning." arXiv. 2019. *https://arxiv.org/abs/1911.03090*.

67. Yuhan Liu, Saurabh Agarwal, and Shivaram Venkataraman. "Auto-Freeze: Automatically Freezing Model Blocks to Accelerate Fine-tuning." *Proceedings of the 2nd Workshop on Machine Learning and Systems*. 2021, pp. 1–7.

68. Stephen Grossberg. "How Does a Brain Build a Cognitive Code?" *Psychological Review* 87.1. 1980, pp. 1–51.

69. Michael McCloskey and Neal J. Cohen. "Catastrophic Interference in Connectionist Networks: The Sequential Learning Problem." *Psychology of Learning and Motivation* 24. 1989, pp. 109–165.

70. Yun Luo et al. "An Empirical Study of Catastrophic Forgetting in Large Language Models During Continual Fine-tuning." arXiv. 2023. *https://arxiv.org/abs/2308.08747*.

71. James Kirkpatrick et al. "Overcoming Catastrophic Forgetting in Neural Networks." *Proceedings of the National Academy of Sciences* 114.13. 2017, pp. 3521–3526.

72. Ilya Loshchilov and Frank Hutter. "Decoupled Weight Decay Regularization." *International Conference on Learning Representations*. 2019.

73. Takuya Akiba et al. "Optuna: A Next-Generation Hyperparameter Optimization Framework." *Proceedings of the 25th ACM SIGKDD International Conference on Knowledge Discovery and Data Mining*. 2019, pp. 2623–2631.

74. Nitish Shirish Keskar et al. "On Large-Batch Training for Deep Learning: Generalization Gap and Sharp Minima." *International Conference on Learning Representations*. 2017.

75. Leandro von Werra et al. "TRL: Transformer Reinforcement Learning." 2020. *https://github.com/huggingface/trl*.

76. Loubna Ben Allal et al. "The Smol Training Playbook: The Secrets to Building World-Class LLMs." Oct. 30, 2025. *https://huggingface.co/spaces/HuggingFaceTB/smol-training-playbook*.

77. Andrei Z. Broder. "On the Resemblance and Containment of Documents." *Compression and Complexity of Sequences*. 1997, pp. 21–29.

78. Moses S. Charikar. "Similarity Estimation Techniques from Rounding Algorithms." *Proceedings of the 34th Annual ACM Symposium on Theory of Computing*. 2002, pp. 380–388.

79. Xian Li et al. "Self-Alignment with Instruction Backtranslation." arXiv. 2023. *https://arxiv.org/abs/2308.06259*.

80. Chunting Zhou et al. "LIMA: Less Is More for Alignment." *Advances in Neural Information Processing Systems*. Vol. 36. 2023.

81. Cheng-Yu Hsieh et al. "Distilling Step-by-Step! Outperforming Larger Language Models with Less Training Data and Smaller Model Sizes." *Findings of the Association for Computational Linguistics: ACL 2023*. 2023, pp. 8003–8017.

82. Ronen Eldan and Yuanzhi Li. "TinyStories: How Small Can Language Models Be and Still Speak Coherent English?" arXiv. 2023. *https://arxiv.org/abs/2305.07759*.

83. Suriya Gunasekar et al. "Textbooks Are All You Need." arXiv. 2023. *https://arxiv.org/abs/2306.11644*.

84. Timo Schick et al. "Toolformer: Language Models Can Teach Themselves to Use Tools." *Advances in Neural Information Processing Systems* 36. 2023.

85. Shishir G Patil et al. "Gorilla: Large Language Model Connected with Massive APIs." arXiv. 2023. *https://arxiv.org/abs/2305.15334*.

86. Yujia Qin et al. "ToolLLM: Facilitating Large Language Models to Master 16000+ Real-World APIs." arXiv. 2023. *https://arxiv.org/abs/2307.16789*.

87. Edward J. Hu et al. "LoRA: Low-Rank Adaptation of Large Language Models." *International Conference on Learning Representations*. 2022.

88. Thomas Wolf et al. "Transformers: State-of-the-Art Natural Language Processing." *Proceedings of the 2020 Conference on Empirical Methods in Natural Language Processing: System Demonstrations*. 2020, pp. 38–45.

89. Sylvain Gugger et al. "Accelerate: Training and Inference at Scale Made Simple, Efficient and Adaptable." 2022. *https://github.com/huggingface/accelerate*.

90. Omry Yadan. "Hydra: A Framework for Elegantly Configuring Complex Applications." 2019. *https://github.com/facebookresearch/hydra*.

91. Shen Li et al. "PyTorch Distributed: Experiences on Accelerating Data Parallel Training." *Proceedings of the VLDB Endowment*. Vol. 13. 12. 2020, pp. 3005–3018.

92. Samyam Rajbhandari et al. "ZeRO: Memory Optimizations Toward Training Trillion-Parameter Models." *International Conference for High Performance Computing, Networking, Storage and Analysis*. 2020, pp. 1–16.

93. Zongheng Yang et al. "SkyPilot: An Intercloud Broker for Sky Computing." *20th USENIX Symposium on Networked Systems Design and Implementation (NSDI 23)*. Boston, MA: USENIX Association, 2023, pp. 437–455.

94. Jared Kaplan et al. "Scaling Laws for Neural Language Models." arXiv. 2020. *https://arxiv.org/abs/2001.08361*.

95. Kohsei Matsutani et al. "RL Squeezes, SFT Expands: A Comparative Study of Reasoning LLMs." arXiv. 2025. *https://arxiv.org/abs/2509.21128*.

96. Paul F Christiano et al. "Deep Reinforcement Learning from Human Preferences." *Advances in Neural Information Processing Systems* 30. 2017.

97. J.J.C. Smart and Bernard Williams. *Utilitarianism: For & Against*. Cambridge University Press, 1973.

98. Ganqu Cui et al. "UltraFeedback: Boosting Language Models with Scaled AI Feedback." arXiv. 2023. *https://arxiv.org/abs/2310.01377*.

99. Yuntao Bai et al. "Training a Helpful and Harmless Assistant with Reinforcement Learning from Human Feedback." arXiv. 2022. *https://arxiv.org/abs/2204.05862*.

100. Josef Dai et al. "Safe RLHF: Safe Reinforcement Learning from Human Feedback." *Proceedings of the International Conference on Learning Representations (ICLR)*. 2024.

101. Deep Ganguli et al. "Red Teaming Language Models to Reduce Harms: Methods, Scaling Behaviors, and Lessons Learned." arXiv. 2022. *https://arxiv.org/abs/2209.07858*.

102. Ralph Allan Bradley and Milton E Terry. "Rank Analysis of Incomplete Block Designs: I. The Method of Paired Comparisons." *Biometrika* 39.3/4. 1952, pp. 324–345.

103. Jacob Eisenstein et al. "Helping or Herding? Reward Model Ensembles Mitigate but Do Not Eliminate Reward Hacking." *Proceedings of the Conference on Language Modeling (COLM)*. 2024.

104. Ronald J. Williams. "Simple Statistical Gradient-Following Algorithms for Connectionist Reinforcement Learning." *Machine Learning* 8.3–4. 1992, pp. 229–256. DOI: *10.1007/BF00992696*.

105. John Schulman et al. "Proximal Policy Optimization Algorithms." arXiv. 2017. *https://arxiv.org/abs/1707.06347.*

106. Marcin Andrychowicz et al. "What Matters In On-Policy Reinforcement Learning? A Large-Scale Empirical Study." arXiv. 2021. *https://arxiv.org/abs/2006.05990.*

107. Rui Zheng et al. "Secrets of RLHF in Large Language Models Part I: PPO." arXiv. 2023. *https://arxiv.org/abs/2307.04964.*

108. John Schulman et al. "High-Dimensional Continuous Control Using Generalized Advantage Estimation." arXiv. 2018. *https://arxiv.org/abs/1506.02438.*

109. Amanda Askell et al. "A General Language Assistant as a Laboratory for Alignment." arXiv. 2021. *https://arxiv.org/abs/2112.00861.*

110. Shangmin Guo et al. "Direct Language Model Alignment from Online AI Feedback." arXiv. 2024. *https://arxiv.org/abs/2402.04792.*

111. Devvrit Khatri et al. "The Art of Scaling Reinforcement Learning Compute for LLMs." arXiv. 2025. *https://arxiv.org/abs/2510.13786.*

112. Daniel Kahneman and Amos Tversky. "Prospect Theory: An Analysis of Decision under Risk." *Econometrica* 47.2. 1979, pp. 263–291.

113. Kawin Ethayarajh et al. "KTO: Model Alignment as Prospect Theoretic Optimization." arXiv. 2024. *https://arxiv.org/abs/2402.01306.*

114. Jixiao Zhang and Chunsheng Zuo. "GRPO-LEAD: A Difficulty-Aware Reinforcement Learning Approach for Concise Mathematical Reasoning in Language Models." *Proceedings of the 2025 Conference on Empirical Methods in Natural Language Processing*. 2025, pp. 5642–5665.

115. Mohammad Gheshlaghi Azar et al. "A General Theoretical Paradigm to Understand Learning from Human Preferences." arXiv. 2023. *https://arxiv.org/abs/2310.12036.*

116. Jiwoo Hong, Noah Lee, and James Thorne. "ORPO: Monolithic Preference Optimization Without Reference Model." arXiv. 2024. *https://arxiv.org/abs/2403.07691.*

117. Yu Meng, Mengzhou Xia, and Danqi Chen. "SimPO: Simple Preference Optimization with a Reference-Free Reward." arXiv. 2024. *https://arxiv.org/abs/2405.14734.*

118. Kishore Papineni et al. "BLEU: A Method for Automatic Evaluation of Machine Translation." *Proceedings of the 40th Annual Meeting of the Association for Computational Linguistics*. 2002, pp. 311–318.

119. Chin-Yew Lin. "ROUGE: A Package for Automatic Evaluation of Summaries." *Text Summarization Branches Out*. 2004, pp. 74–81.

120. Tianyi Zhang et al. "BERTScore: Evaluating Text Generation with BERT." *International Conference on Learning Representations*. 2020.

121. Mark Chen et al. "Evaluating Large Language Models Trained on Code." arXiv. 2021. *https://arxiv.org/abs/2107.03374.*

122. Jacob Austin et al. "Program Synthesis with Large Language Models." arXiv. 2021. *https://arxiv.org/abs/2108.07732*.

123. Zhaojian Yu et al. "HumanEval Pro and MBPP Pro: Evaluating Large Language Models on Self-Invoking Code Generation." arXiv. 2024. *https://arxiv.org/abs/2412.21199*.

124. Shahul Es et al. "RAGAS: Automated Evaluation of Retrieval Augmented Generation." arXiv. 2024. *https://arxiv.org/abs/2309.15217*.

125. Confident AI. "DeepEval: The LLM Evaluation Framework." Accessed Jan. 10, 2026. *https://github.com/confident-ai/deepeval*.

126. TruEra. "TruLens." Accessed Jan. 10, 2025. *https://github.com/truera/trulens*.

127. Jigsaw. *Perspective API*. Accessed Jan. 10, 2025. *https://perspectiveapi.com*.

128. Laura Hanu and Unitary team. "Detoxify." 2021. *https://github.com/unitaryai/detoxify*.

129. Samuel Gehman et al. "RealToxicityPrompts: Evaluating Neural Toxic Degeneration in Language Models." *Findings of the Association for Computational Linguistics: EMNLP 2020*. 2020, pp. 3356–3369.

130. Thomas Hartvigsen et al. "ToxiGen: A Large-Scale Machine-Generated Dataset for Adversarial and Implicit Hate Speech Detection." *Proceedings of the 60th Annual Meeting of the Association for Computational Linguistics*. 2022, pp. 3309–3326.

131. Boxin Wang et al. "DecodingTrust: A Comprehensive Assessment of Trustworthiness in GPT Models." *Advances in Neural Information Processing Systems* 36. 2024.

132. Hugging Face. "Evaluate: A Library for Easily Evaluating Machine Learning Models and Datasets." Accessed Jan. 10, 2026. *https://github.com/huggingface/evaluate*.

133. Lightning AI. "TorchMetrics: Machine Learning Metrics for Distributed, Scalable PyTorch Applications." Accessed Jan. 10, 2026. *https://github.com/Lightning-AI/torchmetrics*.

134. OpenAI. "OpenAI Evals." Accessed Jan. 10, 2026. *https://github.com/openai/evals*.

135. LangChain. "OpenEvals: Readymade Evaluators for Your LLM Apps." Accessed Jan. 10, 2026. *https://github.com/langchain-ai/openevals*.

136. Rachel K.E. Bellamy et al. "AI Fairness 360: An Extensible Toolkit for Detecting and Mitigating Algorithmic Bias." *IBM Journal of Research and Development* 63.4/5. 2019, 4:1–4:15.

137. Microsoft. *Fairlearn: Improve Fairness of AI Systems*. Accessed Jan. 10, 2026. *https://fairlearn.org*.

138. Alicia Parrish et al. "BBQ: A Hand-Built Bias Benchmark for Question Answering." *Findings of the Association for Computational Linguistics: ACL 2022*. 2022, pp. 2086–2105.

139. Nikita Nangia et al. "CrowS-Pairs: A Challenge Dataset for Measuring Social Biases in Masked Language Models." *Proceedings of the 2020 Conference on Empirical Methods in Natural Language Processing*. 2020, pp. 1953–1967.

140. Jieyu Zhao et al. "Gender Bias in Coreference Resolution: Evaluation and Debiasing Methods." *Proceedings of the 2018 Conference of the North American Chapter of the Association for Computational Linguistics: Human Language Technologies*. 2018, pp. 15–20.

141. Dan Hendrycks et al. "Measuring Massive Multitask Language Understanding." *International Conference on Learning Representations*. 2021.

142. Rowan Zellers et al. "HellaSwag: Can a Machine Really Finish Your Sentence?" arXiv. 2019. *https://arxiv.org/abs/1905.07830*.

143. Peter Clark et al. "Think You Have Solved Question Answering? Try ARC, the AI2 Reasoning Challenge." arXiv. 2018. *https://arxiv.org/abs/1803.05457*.

144. Lianmin Zheng et al. "Judging LLM-as-a-Judge with MT-Bench and Chatbot Arena." *Advances in Neural Information Processing Systems* 36. 2024.

145. Yann Dubois et al. "Length-Controlled AlpacaEval: A Simple Way to Debias Automatic Evaluators." arXiv. 2024. *https://arxiv.org/abs/2404.04475*.

146. Tianle Li et al. "From Crowdsourced Data to High-Quality Benchmarks: Arena-Hard and BenchBuilder Pipeline." arXiv. 2024. *https://arxiv.org/abs/2406.11939*.

147. Artificial Analysis. "Independent Analysis of AI." Accessed Jan. 10, 2026. *https://artificialanalysis.ai*.

148. Hongyu Wang et al. "BitNet: Scaling 1-bit Transformers for Large Language Models." arXiv. 2023. *https://arxiv.org/abs/2310.11453*.

149. Elias Frantar et al. "GPTQ: Accurate Post-Training Quantization for Generative Pre-Trained Transformers." *International Conference on Learning Representations*. 2023.

150. Ji Lin et al. "AWQ: Activation-Aware Weight Quantization for LLM Compression and Acceleration." *Machine Learning and Systems*. 2024.

151. Tim Dettmers et al. *LLM.int8(): 8-bit Matrix Multiplication for Transformers at Scale*. 2022.

152. Hicham Badri and Appu Shaji. *Half-Quadratic Quantization of Large Machine Learning Models*. Oct. 22, 2025. *https://dropbox.tech/machine-learning/halfquadratic-quantization-of-large-machine-learning-models*.

153. Tim Dettmers et al. "QLoRA: Efficient Fine-Tuning of Quantized LLMs." *Advances in Neural Information Processing Systems* 36. 2024.

154. Shih-Yang Liu et al. "DoRA: Weight-Decomposed Low-Rank Adaptation." arXiv. 2024. *https://arxiv.org/abs/2402.09353*.

155. Brian Lester, Rami Al-Rfou, and Noah Constant. "The Power of Scale for Parameter-Efficient Prompt Tuning." *Proceedings of the 2021 Conference on Empirical Methods in Natural Language Processing.* 2021, pp. 3045–3059.

156. Xiang Lisa Li and Percy Liang. "Prefix-Tuning: Optimizing Continuous Prompts for Generation." *Proceedings of the 59th Annual Meeting of the Association for Computational Linguistics.* 2021, pp. 4582–4597.

157. Xiao Liu et al. "GPT Understands, Too." arXiv. 2021. *https://arxiv.org/abs/2103.10385.*

158. Neil Houlsby et al. "Parameter-Efficient Transfer Learning for NLP." *International Conference on Machine Learning.* 2019, pp. 2790–2799.

159. Haokun Liu et al. "Few-Shot Parameter-Efficient Fine-Tuning Is Better and Cheaper Than In-Context Learning." *Advances in Neural Information Processing Systems* 35. 2022, pp. 1950–1965.

160. Qingru Zhang et al. "AdaLoRA: Adaptive Budget Allocation for Parameter-Efficient Fine-Tuning." *International Conference on Learning Representations.* 2023.

161. Nam Hyeon-Woo, Moon Ye-Bin, and Oh Tae-Hyun. "FedPara: Low-Rank Hadamard Product for Communication-Efficient Federated Learning." *International Conference on Learning Representations.* 2022.

162. Ali Edalati et al. "KronA: Parameter-Efficient Tuning with Kronecker Adapter." arXiv. 2022. *https://arxiv.org/abs/2212.10650.*

163. Shih-Ying Yeh et al. "Navigating Text-To-Image Customization: From LyCORIS Fine-Tuning to Model Evaluation." *International Conference on Learning Representations.* 2024.

164. Jonathan Frankle and Michael Carbin. "The Lottery Ticket Hypothesis: Finding Sparse, Trainable Neural Networks." *International Conference on Learning Representations.* 2019.

165. Tri Dao et al. "FlashAttention: Fast and Memory-Efficient Exact Attention with IO-Awareness." *Advances in Neural Information Processing Systems.* Vol. 35. 2022, pp. 16344–16359.

166. Tri Dao. "FlashAttention-2: Faster Attention with Better Parallelism and Work Partitioning." arXiv. 2023. *https://arxiv.org/abs/2307.08691.*

167. Jupinder Parmar et al. "Reuse, Don't Retrain: A Recipe for Continued Pretraining of Language Models." arXiv. 2024. *https://arxiv.org/abs/2407.07263.*

168. Shannon P. McPherron et al. "Evidence for Stone-Tool-Assisted Consumption of Animal Tissues before 3.39 Million Years Ago at Dikika, Ethiopia." *Nature* 466.7308. 2010, pp. 857–860. DOI: *10.1038/nature09248.*

169. Zuxin Liu et al. "APIGen: Automated Pipeline for Generating Verifiable and Diverse Function-Calling Datasets." arXiv. 2024. *https://arxiv.org/abs/2406.18518.*

170. Carlos E. Jimenez et al. "SWE-bench: Can Language Models Resolve Real-World GitHub Issues?" arXiv. 2024. *https://arxiv.org/abs/2310.06770*.

171. Shuyan Zhou et al. "WebArena: A Realistic Web Environment for Building Autonomous Agents." arXiv. 2024. *https://arxiv.org/abs/2307.13854*.

172. Grégoire Mialon et al. "GAIA: A Benchmark for General AI Assistants." arXiv. 2024. *https://arxiv.org/abs/2311.12983*.

173. Jason Wei et al. "Chain-of-Thought Prompting Elicits Reasoning in Large Language Models." *Advances in Neural Information Processing Systems* 35. 2022, pp. 24824–24837.

174. Karl Cobbe et al. "Training Verifiers to Solve Math Word Problems." arXiv. 2021. *https://arxiv.org/abs/2110.14168*.

175. Jonathan Uesato et al. "Solving Math Word Problems with Process- and Outcome-Based Feedback." arXiv. 2022. *https://arxiv.org/abs/2211.14275*.

176. Hunter Lightman et al. "Let's Verify Step by Step." arXiv. 2023. *https://arxiv.org/abs/2305.20050*.

177. Peiyi Wang et al. "Math-Shepherd: Verify and Reinforce LLMs Step-by-Step Without Human Annotations." arXiv. 2023. *https://arxiv.org/abs/2312.08935*.

178. Shunyu Yao et al. "Tree of Thoughts: Deliberate Problem Solving with Large Language Models." *Advances in Neural Information Processing Systems*. Vol. 36. 2024.

179. Thomas Hubert et al. "Olympiad-Level Formal Mathematical Reasoning with Reinforcement Learning." *Nature*. 2025.

180. Charlie Snell et al. "Scaling LLM Test-Time Compute Optimally Can Be More Effective Than Scaling Model Parameters." arXiv. 2024. *https://arxiv.org/abs/2408.03314*.

181. David Silver et al. "Mastering the Game of Go Without Human Knowledge." *Nature* 550.7676. 2017, pp. 354–359.

182. Benjamin Weiser. "Here's What Happens When Your Lawyer Uses ChatGPT." *The New York Times*. 2023.

183. Yizhong Wang et al. "Self-Instruct: Aligning Language Models with Self-Generated Instructions." *Annual Meeting of the Association for Computational Linguistics*. 2023.

184. Can Xu et al. "WizardLM: Empowering Large Pre-Trained Language Models to Follow Complex Instructions." arXiv. 2023. *https://arxiv.org/abs/2304.12244*.

185. Tao Ge et al. "Scaling Synthetic Data Creation with 1,000,000,000 Personas." arXiv. 2024. *https://arxiv.org/abs/2406.20094*.

186. Zhangchen Xu et al. "Magpie: Alignment Data Synthesis from Scratch by Prompting Aligned LLMs with Nothing." arXiv. 2024. *https://arxiv.org/abs/2406.08464*.

187. Loubna Ben Allal, Anton Lozhkov, and Daniel von Strien. "Cosmopedia: How to Create Large-Scale Synthetic Data for Pre-Training." Hugging Face blog. 2024. *https://huggingface.co/blog/cosmopedia*.

188. Pratyush Maini et al. "Rephrasing the Web: A Recipe for Compute and Data-Efficient Language Modeling." *Proceedings of the 62nd Annual Meeting of the Association for Computational Linguistics (ACL)*. 2024.

189. Harrison Lee et al. "RLAIF vs. RLHF: Scaling Reinforcement Learning from Human Feedback with AI Feedback." arXiv. 2024. *https://arxiv.org/abs/2309.00267*.

190. Zixiang Chen et al. "Self-Play Fine-Tuning Converts Weak Language Models to Strong Language Models." *Proceedings of the International Conference on Machine Learning (ICML)*. 2024.

191. Eric Zelikman et al. "STaR: Bootstrapping Reasoning With Reasoning." *Advances in Neural Information Processing Systems*. Vol. 35. 2022.

192. Eric Zelikman et al. "Quiet-STaR: Language Models Can Teach Themselves to Think Before Speaking." arXiv. 2024. *https://arxiv.org/abs/2403.09629*.

193. NVIDIA. "NeMo Curator: GPU-Accelerated Data Curation for Training AI Models." 2024. *https://github.com/NVIDIA-NeMo/Curator*.

194. Meta. "Synthetic Data Kit." Accessed Dec. 15, 2025. *https://github.com/meta-llama/synthetic-data-kit*.

195. The NeMo Data Designer Team, NVIDIA. "NeMo Data Designer: A Framework for Generating Synthetic Data from Scratch or Based On Your Own Seed Data." 2025. *https://github.com/NVIDIA-NeMo/DataDesigner*.

196. NVIDIA. "Nemotron-Personas." Accessed Dec. 15, 2025. *https://huggingface.co/collections/nvidia/nemotron-personas*.

197. Gretel.ai. "Symptom to Diagnosis Dataset." Accessed Dec. 15, 2025. *https://huggingface.co/datasets/gretelai/symptom_to_diagnosis*.

198. Yicheng Chen et al. "DataChef: Cooking Up Optimal Data Recipes for LLM Adaptation via Reinforcement Learning." arXiv. 2026. *https://arxiv.org/abs/2602.11089*.

199. Ilia Shumailov et al. "AI Models Collapse When Trained on Recursively Generated Data." *Nature* 631. 2024, pp. 755–759.

200. Lin Long et al. "On LLMs-Driven Synthetic Data Generation, Curation, and Evaluation: A Survey." *Findings of the Association for Computational Linguistics: ACL 2024*. 2024.

201. Alexey Dosovitskiy et al. "An Image Is Worth 16x16 Words: Transformers for Image Recognition at Scale." *International Conference on Learning Representations*. 2021.

202. Alec Radford et al. "Learning Transferable Visual Models From Natural Language Supervision." *International Conference on Machine Learning*. 2021, pp. 8748–8763.

203. Peng Wang et al. "Qwen2-VL: Enhancing Vision-Language Model's Perception of the World at Any Resolution." arXiv. 2024. *https://arxiv.org/abs/2409.12191*.

204. Haotian Liu et al. "Visual Instruction Tuning." *Advances in Neural Information Processing Systems* 36. 2024.

205. Yaowei Zheng et al. "LlamaFactory: Unified Efficient Fine-Tuning of 100+ Language Models." arXiv. 2024. *http://arxiv.org/abs/2403.13372*.

206. Zhihong Chen et al. "CheXagent: A Vision-Language Foundation Model to Enhance Efficiency of Chest X-Ray Interpretation." arXiv. 2024. *https://arxiv.org/abs/2401.12208*.

207. Fernando Pérez-García et al. "Exploring Scalable Medical Image Encoders Beyond Text Supervision." *Nature Machine Intelligence*. 2024.

208. Ke Zhu et al. "Continual SFT Matches Multimodal RLHF with Negative Supervision." *IEEE/CVF Conference on Computer Vision and Pattern Recognition*. 2025.

209. Xun Zhu et al. "Uni-Med: A Unified Medical Generalist Foundation Model for Multi-Task Learning via Connector-MoE." *Advances in Neural Information Processing Systems*. Vol. 37. 2024.

210. Xiang Yue et al. "MMMU: A Massive Multi-Discipline Multimodal Understanding and Reasoning Benchmark for Expert AGI." *IEEE/CVF Conference on Computer Vision and Pattern Recognition*. 2024.

211. Yuan Liu et al. "MMBench: Is Your Multi-Modal Model an All-Around Player?" arXiv. 2024. *https://arxiv.org/abs/2307.06281*.

INDEX

B

C

D

F

G

H

I

M

N

S

T

U

V

W

X

Y

Z

The fonts used in *The Craft of Post-Training* are New Baskerville, Futura, The Sans Mono Condensed, and Dogma. The book was typeset with LaTeX 2_ε package `nostarch` by Boris Veytsman with many additions by Alex Freed, Miles Bond, and other members of the No Starch Press team *(2023/07/19 v2.4 Typesetting books for No Starch Press).*

RESOURCES

Visit *https://nostarch.com/craft-of-post-training* for errata and more information.